# Aspects of Empire in Achaemenid Sardis

Elspeth R. M. Dusinberre proposes a new approach to understanding the Achaemenid empire based on her study of the regional capital, Sardis. This study uses archaeological, artistic, and textual sources to demonstrate that the two-hundred-year Persian presence in this city had a profound impact on local social structures, revealing the region's successful absorption, both ideological and physical, into the Persian empire. During this period, Sardis was a center of burgeoning creativity and vitality, where a polyethnic elite devised a new culture – inspired by Iranian, Greek, and local Lydian traditions – that drew on and legitimated imperial ideology. The non-elite absorbed and adapted multiple aspects of this new culture to create a wholly new profile of what it meant to be Sardian. As well as successfully bringing together the current information on the Achaemenids, this book is also an excellent contribution to empire studies.

ELSPETH R. M. DUSINBERRE is Assistant Professor in the Department of Classics of the University of Colorado, Boulder. She has published articles in *Ars Orientalis*, *Near Eastern Archaeology*, *the American Journal of Archaeology*, and *Anatolian Studies*, and she is currently working on her forthcoming study on Greeks and Persians in Achaemenid Lydia, and on the seals and sealings from Gordion, Turkey.

# Aspects of Empire
# in Achaemenid Sardis

ELSPETH R. M. DUSINBERRE

*University of Colorado, Boulder*

CAMBRIDGE
UNIVERSITY PRESS

PUBLISHED BY THE PRESS SYNDICATE OF THE UNIVERSITY OF CAMBRIDGE
The Pitt Building, Trumpington Street, Cambridge CB2 1RP, United Kingdom

CAMBRIDGE UNIVERSITY PRESS
The Edinburgh Building, Cambridge CB2 2RU, UK
40 West 20th Street, New York, NY 10011–4211, USA
477 Williamstown Road, Port Melbourne, VIC 3207, Australia
Ruiz de Alarcón 13, 28014 Madrid, Spain
Dock House, The Waterfront, Cape Town 8001, South Africa

http://www.cambridge.org

First published 2003

Printed in the United Kingdom at the University Press, Cambridge

*Typefaces* Swift 9.5/13 pt. and Frutiger      *System* LATEX 2$_\varepsilon$   [TB]

*A catalogue record for this book is available from the British Library*

*Library of Congress Cataloguing in Publication Data*

Dusinberre, Elspeth R. M.
Aspects of Empire in Achaemenid Sardis / Elspeth R. M. Dusinberre.
   p.   cm.
Revision of the author's thesis – University of Michigan at Ann Arbor, 1997.
Includes bibliographical references.
ISBN 0-521-81071-X
1. Sardis (Extinct city) – History.   2. Achaemenid dynasty, 559–330 B.C.   I. Title.

DS156.S3 D87   2002
939′.22 – dc21   2002073452

ISBN 0 521 81071 x hardback

*R. K. M. in memoriam*

# Contents

# Figures

All images of Sardis are copyright the Archaeological Exploration of Sardis/Harvard University.

# Preface

The Achaemenid empire has until recently been presented as stereotypically orientally despotic. There is perhaps now some danger of making the empire seem instead a benevolent paradise, in which everybody was delighted to live. Reality, of course, lies with neither image. The Achaemenids could be brutal, many people were certainly dispossessed, those in power no doubt abused it at times, and Persians did indeed wear that most barbaric of garments – trousers. But some people, and some parts of the empire, prospered under Achaemenid rule. In this book I argue that the ancient Lydian capital of Sardis was one of these places.

Studying Achaemenid Sardis has been an interesting challenge for me. How to lay aside a fundamental disapproval of imperialism and study its effects impartially? How to weight textual sources, all of them biased in different ways, and use them in tandem with often only partially satisfactory archaeological evidence? How to deal with past and present trends in scholarship in a way that foregrounds no one approach or category of evidence to the exclusion of others? The following study is my attempt to form a balanced picture of what happened in Sardis as a result of Achaemenid imperialist expansion.

This book has grown out of my dissertation, completed in 1997 at the University of Michigan at Ann Arbor. I would like to single out two scholars in particular for thanks. It is difficult for me to express my gratitude to Margaret Cool Root. Any ideas I have had concerning the Achaemenid empire are the result of and build on her pioneering work. Crawford H. Greenewalt, Jr., first introduced me in the summer of 1991 to Sardis and to the Lydians, to Turkey and to the joy that can come from archaeological excavation and discussion. I am thankful for his continued guidance and support, and for the opportunity in the summer of 1996 to focus entirely on research while at Sardis.

I am grateful to Amélie Kuhrt for reading and commenting on a draft of this book, as well as for other scholarly help. Daniel Potts offered helpful criticism and commentary on specific and general matters at crucial moments during the process of revision.

For the comments and advice of my dissertation committee – Crawford Greenewalt, Sharon Herbert, John Pedley, Margaret Root, and Carla Sinopoli – heartfelt thanks. For their assistance with ideas and illustrations, inspirational discussions, and general guidance, I thank İbrahim Akyar,

xiii

Cathy Alexander, Tomris Bakır, Linda Bregstein, Pierre Briant, Robert Bridges, Lucilla Burn, Nicholas Cahill, Don Cameron, Kim Codell, Dominique Collon, Gregory Crane, Toni Cross, Hasan Dedeoğlu, Keith DeVries, John Dillery, Yaşar Ersoy, Leslie Fitton, Kenneth Frazer, Laura Gadbery, Mark Garrison, Mariana Giovino, Elizabeth Gombosi, Ann Gunter, Gül Gürtekin, Sebastian Heath, Robert Henrickson, Charles Jones, Deniz Kaptan, Maggie Lynch, Hasan Malay, Marjorie McIntosh, Margaret Miller, David Mitten, Oscar Muscarella, İlknur Özgen, Daniel Pullen, Andrew Ramage, Christopher Ratté, Marcus Rautman, Richard Redding, Susan Rotroff, Kenneth Sams, Heleen Sancisi-Weerdenburg, Rüdiger Schmitt, Anthony Snodgrass, Phil Stinson, Matthew Stolper, David Stronach, Geoffrey Summers, Emily Vermeule, Mary Voigt, Bonna Wescoat, Henry Wright, Norm Yoffee, Marcia Yonemoto, Cuyler Young, the members of the Sardis Expedition and Office, the staff of the American Research Institute in Turkey in Philadelphia, Ankara, and Istanbul, and the Turkish Ministry of Culture, as well as the directors and staff of the Museum of Anatolian Civilizations, the Istanbul Archaeological Museums, the Ephesus Museum, the Manisa Museum, and the Izmir Museum. Special thanks to the Roots and Kenistons for their hospitality and patience. And thanks to Edward Dusinberre for support, humor, understanding, and inspirational music. All residual errors in this work are of course entirely my own.

The research presented here was made feasible by the financial generosity of the Jacob Javits Fellowship; the Mellon Goheen Prize; the John Williams White Fellowship at the American School of Classical Studies at Athens; the American Research Institute in Turkey/United States Information Agency predoctoral grants; and the Horace H. Rackham School of Graduate Studies travel grants and dissertation/thesis grants.

# Abbreviations

In the text and footnotes, classical sources are abbreviated according to the *Oxford Classical Dictionary* (3rd edn). The standard abbreviations of the *American Journal of Archaeology* are employed in the references.

| | |
|---|---|
| DB | Darius' trilingual inscription on the cliff face at Bisitun, on the left-hand side of the main caravan route from Bagdad to Hamadan. |
| DNa | a trilingual inscription on Darius' tomb at Naqsh-i Rustam, behind the sculpted figure of Darius at the top of the tomb. |
| DNb | a trilingual inscription on Darius' tomb at Naqsh-i Rustam, on either side of the door to the tomb. |
| DNc and DNd | labels identifying individuals, inscribed on Darius' tomb at Naqsh-i Rustam. |
| DPe | the trilingual inscription on the south terrace wall at Persepolis. |
| DPh | the Persepolis Foundation text, a trilingual inscription on gold and silver tablets buried in stone boxes under the two eastern corners of the Apadana at Persepolis. |
| DSf | the Susa Foundation text, a trilingual inscription on the building of the palace, with fragments of many copies on clay and marble tablets and on the glazed bricks of the great hall. |
| PFS | Persepolis Fortification seal. |
| PFT | Persepolis Fortification tablet. |
| XPh | the "Daiva inscription" on stone tablets excavated from the building on the southeast corner of the terrace at Persepolis (the garrison quarters?). |

# 1 Sardis in the Achaemenid empire

The Achaemenid Persian empire (*c.* 550–330 BC), founded by Cyrus II, centered on southwest Iran and lower Mesopotamia (fig. 1).[1] Under Darius I (521–486 BC) it reached its greatest extent, stretching from the Aegean sea to the Indus river, from Egypt to the modern central Asian Republics. Although there were subsequent fluctuations in territorial control, there were no major losses apart from Egypt (and that for less than sixty years). The empire encompassed within its boundaries people of many different backgrounds, speaking diverse languages, worshiping multiple deities, living in tremendously varied environments, and practicing widely differing social customs. The Achaemenid dynasty was to devise a method of hegemony that would allow these various peoples to function within the confines of the new imperial authority, to construct a system of empire flexible enough to provide for the needs of different peoples and ensure their ability to operate as part of the vast and complex system of the new Achaemenid empire.[2] This detailed study of Sardis, a regional capital in western Anatolia, within its imperial context helps us understand the ways in which the new Achaemenid administration worked with and within a pre-existing society to ensure the successful annexation of a region and its populace into the empire.[3]

Achaemenid administration was adapted to local needs and traditions, providing an effective system of government across the huge and varied empire.[4] The royal capitals at the geographical heart of the empire, newly founded at Persepolis and Pasargadae and with new palaces built at the ancient cities of Babylon and Susa, were reflected and extended by regional capitals in the various administrative provinces, or satrapies, of the

---

1 Throughout this work, I use "Persian" to signify only "ethnic" Persians. "Achaemenid" refers not so much to a discrete family line of Persians as to the ideological umbrella created by the imperial hegemony. See Root (1979).

2 This was clearly a matter of concern to the empire-builder Darius I: see Hdt. 3.38 for his interest in the differing attitudes of disparate peoples in the empire, and in Darius' own words, DB 1.17–20, 4.70, 4.88–92, DNa esp. 15–47, DNb (DB is Darius' text at Bisitun; DNa and DNb are inscriptions on his tomb at Naqsh-i Rustam near Persepolis). Texts and translations of these documents may be found in Kent (1953) and Lecoq (1997); Lecoq renumbers and reassigns some of the Old Persian inscriptions, updating Kent's edition. For examples of multilingualism practiced in official proclamations, see, e.g., Tuplin (1987b).

3 A recent study exploring similar issues in a central region of the empire is Potts (1999:ch. 9). See also Hansman (1972).

4 For a synthetic discussion of Achaemenid manifestations throughout the empire, with particular reference to work done in the past five years, see Briant (1997a).

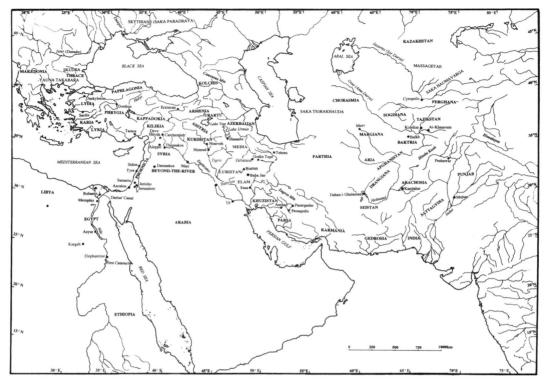

**Fig. 1** The Achaemenid Persian empire.

empire.[5] In many cases, the new rulers continued using old centers of control as administrative centers. These were generally strategically located for trade or warfare and already had in place administrative hierarchies or apparatuses appropriate for the area.[6] The satrapal capitals functioned very much like the royal centers: provincial taxes, paid in kind and in precious metals, were collected and stored there before being redistributed to local garrisons and to others working for the government, or before being sent to the central imperial treasuries.[7] The satraps, or governors, lived in elaborate residences, often in palaces taken over from previous rulers; when the great king traveled through his empire, he would be housed in satrapal palaces.[8] The satraps kept archives of official correspondence as well as

5 See Kuhrt (1995a:690–701 and bibliography). For another empire faced with incorporating disparate regions during an expansionist phase, see, e.g., Gruen (1984a, 1984b). For an example of a regional capital and the complexities of "center–periphery" models, see Invernizzi (1996).
6 One well-documented example is the satrapy of Egypt: see Dandamaev and Lukonin (1989:103–104 and references); for a particular example of Egyptian practices maintained in the Achaemenid period, see Verger (1964).
7 For taxes, see, e.g., Potts (1999:320 and references), Descat (1989), Koch (1989), Briant (1982).
8 Kuhrt (1995a:691).

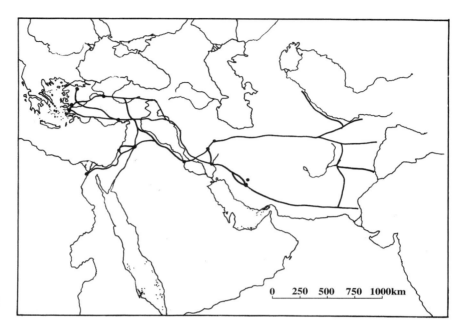

0   250   500   750   1000km

**Fig. 2** The Achaemenid road system.

records of regional bureaucracy (petitions to the satrap, satrapal decrees, food disbursements to local workers engaged in state work or people traveling on account, etc.).[9] The satrapal capitals were linked to the royal heartland in southwest Iran (Fars) and to each other by an extensive network of roads which supported rapid travel (fig. 2): way-stations were located at one-day intervals where messengers traveling on official business could obtain food, drink, and fresh horses.[10] Travel was monitored, and strategic points on the roads were guarded by armed soldiers.

Achaemenid rulers were sympathetic to and supportive of local religious and social customs, often finding syncretic connections between various religions rather than imposing their own cults on unwilling indigenous peoples.[11] This official approach led to striking diversity in the different regions of the empire: Achaemenid-period society and systems varied widely across the empire to accommodate already-existing local structures.

9 For satrapal archives, see Briant (1986:434–437); a copy of a royal decree kept in various capitals is described in Ezra 5.17–6.2. For evidence that the satrapal capitals had a bureaucracy similar to that of Persepolis, see Helms (1982). For the bullae that demonstrate the existence of a satrapal archive in Daskyleion, seat of Hellespontine Phrygia, see Balkan (1959), Kaptan (1990). For the administration of the eastern regions of the empire, see Briant (1984).

10 Hdt. 5.52–54; 8.98.

11 This was, of course, a feature of many empires, ancient and modern – a feature necessary to their longevity. For the ancient Mediterranean, see, e.g., Garnsey (1984). For specific examples in one region of the Achaemenid empire, see, e.g., Vogelsang (1987, 1992).

The duties of a satrap were very complex, and they depended to a certain extent on the region he or she was governing.[12]

> Royal power rests upon the army, and the army upon money, and money upon agriculture, and agriculture upon just administration, and just administration upon the integrity of government officials, and the integrity of government officials upon the reliability of the vizier, and the pinnacle of all of these is the vigilance of the king in resisting his own inclinations, and his capability so to guide them that he rules them and they do not rule him.

The tenth-century Arab scholar, al-Masudi,[13] here sums up a political-military viewpoint of the networks binding an empire and also points to some of the primary administrative obligations of the Achaemenid satrap.[14] A satrap had to juggle the needs of those in his region with the needs of the Great King. He had to maintain a well-equipped, well-trained, loyal army to protect the land; he had to exact taxes and might need the army to assist in tax collection. Although the army might give him the power to obtain taxes from those who might otherwise be unwilling, it could only be persuasive where the ability to pay existed.[15] The satrap therefore had to ensure the productivity of the land in order to be able to collect taxes: this required maintaining a sufficiently high level of satisfaction and capability among the people tending the land that they might husband it to good effect. Thus the satrap was chronically torn between needing to send the appropriate amount of tribute to the king now, and needing to ensure that the people under his hegemony would be capable of producing tribute again in the future.[16] In western Anatolia, this task was made the more challenging by the close presence of the Greeks, who trampled the land in marauding armies or occasionally sought to incite insurrection among those under the hegemony of the satrap. At times, "integrity" and "just administration" must have been rather tricky qualities for the satrap to judge: how might

---

12  Mania, a governor of Hellespontine Phrygia, is probably the best-known example of a female administrator (Xen., *Hell.* 3.1.10ff.). See Kuhrt (1995a:697–698). Women might hold vast tracts of land in the center of the empire, without being themselves satraps: Darius I's wife, Irtashduna (Artystone) is a good example. See Hallock (1969), Garrison and Root (2001, Introduction). For women in the Achaemenid empire, see Brosius (1996). For the sake of simplicity, and because as far as we know Sardis never had a female satrap, I will hereafter use the masculine gender in referring to satraps.

13  Al-Masudi ([1863] 1977:122).

14  See Petit (1990) for the administration of satrapies in the early Achaemenid period. For the late Achaemenid period, see Jacobs (1994). For Achaemenid systems of administration and taxation, see Tuplin (1987a). For non-satrapal financial transactions in the central regions of the empire, see, e.g., Stolper (1985, 1992), Cardascia (1951), Abraham (1995). Satraps no doubt also pursued their own personal ends which may or may not have benefited the king or the region.

15  Cf. the story of Themistokles and the Andrians, Hdt. 8.111.

16  Sancisi-Weerdenburg (1989) discusses the significance of the objects coming into the imperial treasuries.

he reconcile short-term and long-term goals, taking care at the same time to attend to his own safety?

## Ideology and imperialism

Even as Achaemenid bureaucracies were laid out and administrative networks put into effect, so too programs were established to support and promulgate the ideology of the empire. A legitimizing ideology is an important factor in uniting the inhabitants of a complex society, particularly at such a level as an empire.[17] Such ideologies may be manifested verbally. Darius I, for instance, wrote a text legitimating his accession to the throne and had it inscribed in three languages around the sculpted relief making the same claim carved in the cliff face at Bisitun, along the main road leading from Mesopotamia to Ekbatana (modern Hamadan) (fig. 3). Then he had the text translated into various languages and disseminated, along with copies of the image, to locations through the empire[18] – using the local languages was a strategy with profound symbolic as well as practical value.[19]

Ideology may also be manifested materially, through architecture, art, and luxury and everyday goods.[20] The composition of new imperial art forms and imperial texts in the Achaemenid empire often drew on pre-existing traditions: such references to time-honored and familiar patterns might provide ways to formulate a new ideology that legitimated the new regime in its position of power.[21] This couching of new ideology in familiar local forms was important in nullifying the seeming remoteness of foreign conquerors: in the multicultural milieux of the Achaemenid empire, ideology had to be translated into the cultural discourses of the various populations

17 See, e.g., Claessen and Skalnik (1978:628), Kurtz (1981:182).
18 The copy from Babylon is the most striking, with its pictorial representation and local linguistic version publicly set up. Only an Aramaic version has been found in Egypt, which may therefore have been intended for Achaemenid chancelry usage rather than public Demotic comprehension; its discovery among the Elephantine papyri shows the text was still being copied as late as the end of the fifth century. See Sayce (1906). A particularly interesting recent discussion of Darius' Bisitun text is Sancisi-Weerdenburg (1999). For local versions of the Bisitun monument, see Kuhrt (1995a:666–667). For the Babylonian version, see Seidl (1976), von Voigtlander (1978). For the Aramaic copy from Elephantine, see Greenfield and Porten (1982).
19 See Root (1991:4).    20 See, e.g., DeMarrais et al. (1996). See also Marcus (1995).
21 See Root (1979:309 ff.) for the impact of a new ideological program composed of various venerable traditions. Kuhrt (1990) has demonstrated ways in which Cyrus chose elements of the iconographic and textual traditions of Mesopotamia. The Seleucid kings took similar advantage of ancient Babylonian traditions to root their control in this important territory: see Kuhrt (1996). One difficulty, naturally, is to discern those objects with specific ideological messages, and to distinguish between "top–down" ideological significance and "bottom–up." See, e.g., Hays (1993). For a particularly thoughtful article exploring resistance to top–down ideology, see Brumfiel (1996).

**Fig. 3** Darius' relief at Bisitun: imperial rhetoric in images.

participating in the system.[22] And the expressions of ideology had to be flexible, adapting over time as well as place.

These ideological programs included the manipulation of artistic imagery to bear meaning within an imperial context, in ways sufficiently flexible to convey significance to local viewing audiences in widely disparate parts of the empire. Traditional local images were reworked to promote imperial ideologies in peripheral areas with different artistic customs than those of the Persian heartland. Official imperial iconography was translated into regional artistic syntaxes to make it intelligible to local viewing audiences. The adaptation of images had a self-reflexive function as well, for the appropriation and manipulation of local iconographies and styles signified the incorporation of these areas into the empire. By taking on and adapting traditional local imagery, the user might embed himself in an artistic framework that reinforced his own goals or sense of authority and power in those regions. Thus in the reworking of older imagery we see simultaneous streams of significance, spreading imperial ideology to distant parts of the empire, asserting power over those areas, and incorporating local imagery into official imperial art.

The impact of Achaemenid hegemony on local Anatolian practices may be seen in most aspects of the material record. Architectural influence generally seems to have concentrated on public buildings: administrative

22 Sancisi-Weerdenburg (1990:265).

buildings and palaces, temples and parks, were all the focus of attention in the Achaemenid period.[23] Mortuary customs in many areas changed under Iranian influence. This trend was perhaps connected with the sort of new social identities suggested by the changing styles of particular goods with profound semiotic significance: clothing and jewelry, parade weapons and harness, personal seals, and table vessels. Although these changes may have been initiated by the elite – a polyethnic group comprising indigenous and foreign peoples – they eventually permeated all strata of society, so that even the standard ceramic tablewares used by non-elite people also came to reflect Achaemenid presence. The blending of influences from east and west with local customs produced vibrant new styles in artifacts and modes of life throughout Achaemenid Anatolia.

## Achaemenid Anatolia

Anatolia in the Achaemenid period was divided into various satrapies, including at one time or another Armenia, Greater Phrygia (separated for administrative purposes into eastern and Hellespontine Phrygia), Lydia (called Sparda in Achaemenid texts),[24] Karia, Lykia, and Kilikia.[25] The borders of all the satrapies are rather unclear. The satrapy of Sparda, and its capital at the ancient city of Sardis, comprise the focus of this study.

The extent of Sparda is uncertain: before the Achaemenid empire, Lydia probably reached roughly from the Kaikos river in the north to the Maeander in the south, from just inland on the west (although certain Greek cities such as Ephesos and Miletos were under Lydian control or had treaties with the Lydians by the mid-sixth century BC) to somewhere around Güre in the east.[26] The Achaemenid province of Sparda saw some fluctuation in its

23 This concentration can only be called apparent, as it may be a reflection of excavated remains rather than actual practice in the Achaemenid period. The issue is complicated by at least two further elements: we might indeed not expect local non-palatial domestic architecture to change, to emulate Iranian structures of a different geographical and environmental context; additionally, as excavation of the Achaemenid period in Iran has itself focused on public buildings rather than non-elite domestic architecture, it is not yet clear that we would recognize an Iranian house (as distinct from a palace) even if it had been transported to Anatolia.

24 Imperial Achaemenid texts do not distinguish between Lydia and Sardis, calling the whole region by the name of its capital. Our word "Sardis" is a Hellenic transliteration of a Lydian word pronounced "Sfard-" or perhaps "Sward-." The Achaemenid region "Sparda" is simply another transliteration of the city's Lydian name. It was not common practice in the empire for an entire satrapy to be called by the name of its capital: Media and Ekbatana, for instance, are separately described in official texts. I do not understand the significance, if any, of the synecdoche used for the province of Sparda.

25 For the extent and nature of the Anatolian satrapies, see, e.g., Briant (1996:75–80 and references), Sekunda (1988, 1991), Petit (1990), Weiskopf (1982, 1989). I call the satrapies here by their Greek, rather than Persian, names; I will refer to the region of which Sardis was capital both as "Sparda" and as "Achaemenid Lydia."

26 See Greenewalt (1992:247–249). For imperialism and Sparda, see Balcer (1984).

territory, but its northern and southern borders probably remained roughly where they had been before Achaemenid hegemony, perhaps incorporating the Kaikos and Maeander river valleys.[27] Its territory included the Aegean seaboard and perhaps took in modern Afyon in its eastern boundaries. Its capital was Sardis; its satraps were at times close members of the royal family, but we do not know the parentage of all the men sent to administer this important province.

The region to the north of Sparda, Hellespontine Phrygia, included much of the modern Troad and extended to the east to include "coastal Phrygia" and the inland areas at least as far as modern Bursa and possibly farther east along the road to Gordion.[28] The new-founded city of Daskyleion formed the seat of Hellespontine Phrygia; its satraps were members of the royal family.[29] The border between Hellespontine Phrygia and Sparda is uncertain, although the Mysian mountains were part of Hellespontine Phrygia.[30] To the south, Sparda was bordered by Karia; to the east, by Phrygia and Kappadokia.

The archaeology of Achaemenid Anatolia has in many published accounts seemed rather elusive. The evidence has been portrayed as scanty, widely scattered, and fragmentary.[31] Authors have tended to downplay the importance of Achaemenid custom and culture by relegating it to a secondary position after mentioning the paucity of architectural remains that show Persian influence. Even those objects that were clearly affected by imperial artistic patterns are often by implication not Achaemenid creations, but simply off-shoots of earlier Near Eastern traditions. The Achaemenid Persians are thus by and large denied both artistic creativity and the ability to create an impact on local cultures in the empire. The very language used in describing that little impact authors have admitted often minimalizes its importance: a different rhetorical approach might bring out the profound impact of Achaemenid hegemony on public planning and urban design as well as on objects of personal semiotic significance such as jewelry, seal-stones, metal and glass tablewares, and textiles. A lack of Achaemenid effect on such aspects of material culture as the ceramic assemblage has generally been assumed – a proposition that until recently had scarcely been rigorously tested anywhere in the empire.[32]

27 See Sekunda (1991:91) for an alternative opinion about the Maeander valley.
28 Sekunda (1988:176).
29 Thuc. 8.6. For archaeological evidence concerning the satrapal seat at Daskyleion, see Kaptan (1997).
30 The tribes inhabiting these hills revolted frequently: see Xen, *Hell.* 3.1.13, *Anab.* 1.6.7, 1.9.14, 11.5.13, 3.2.23; see Sekunda (1988:176) for the border.
31 For the "politics of meagreness" surrounding modern portrayals of Achaemenid presence throughout the empire, see Root (1991). For a work that collects scattered evidence to make a strong case for intercultural mingling and imperial impact in another period in Anatolia, see Mitchell (1993).
32 Notable exceptions to this generalization include D. Stronach (1978), Summers (1993), Henrickson (1993, 1994, 1998).

For some, the apparent lack of Persian impact in the west may be explained as the result of official Achaemenid tolerance of, and accommodation to, local customs.[33] Although this view may reflect a sympathetic attitude to the Persians' rule, often it bears explicit or implicit negative assumptions about their culture. It implies the Achaemenid Persians were so devoid of traditions, of culture, of art forms of their own, that they essentially had nothing to impose and therefore made virtue of necessity through an official policy of assimilation and appropriation in far-flung regions of the empire.

There are indeed difficulties in understanding the archaeological evidence and reconstructing the history of Anatolia in the Achaemenid period. Many objects apparently dating to the Achaemenid period first appeared to contemporary scholars on the art market, rather than stemming from controlled excavations, and information on their sources must be regarded as suspect. The practice of dating art on the basis of purely stylistic criteria in places other than that for which a stylistic sequence was developed has also contributed to an unproblematized picture of the Achaemenid empire. And ceramic sequences for the Achaemenid period are still poorly understood in many parts of Anatolia, especially in its eastern regions.[34] Finally, Achaemenid impact on the material record of western Anatolia has often been overlooked or downplayed in published reports.

## Detecting the effects of empire

Studies of the Achaemenid empire have in the past fifteen years seen a shift in interest away from a narrow focus on the Great King and court life to encompass also the enormous population of the empire on whose daily efforts the governmental structure was based.[35] This shift has included a greater emphasis on archaeology, on Near Eastern textual resources, on Near Eastern art history. A concerted effort has been made to check and, when needed, correct the generalizations based on the Greek historiographic tradition that had previously determined the European outlook. How did the Achaemenid empire look when seen from the different perspectives of the various regions? How did the empire affect the existing traditions, the social and economic structures? Are there developments traceable in local situations which might be the result of interactions with the central state?[36]

---

33 See, e.g., Gray (1969).
34 They are not that well understood yet in Fars, either. The sort of careful excavation done by D. Stronach at Pasargadae will help to clarify issues of Achaemenid ceramic sequencing as more sites are excavated.
35 See, e.g., contributions to the *Achaemenid History* series. For a seminal discussion of some of the prejudices that have influenced the writing of Achaemenid history, see Said (1978). For a self-critical approach to writing history in the midst of such prejudice, see Prakash (1990).
36 See Kuhrt and Sancisi-Weerdenburg (1990).

In 1990, H. Sancisi-Weerdenburg outlined the difficulties that have been experienced in detecting Persian presence or impact, and proposed a new series of issues in developing a model of the Achaemenid empire. She pointed out that the search for the empire "has so far been mostly confined to phenomena that betray an Iranian influence, to artefacts of a typical or a hybrid Iranian provenience, to changes in the titulary and in the onomastica derived from the Iranian vocabulary.... Iranian 'traces' are, however, not the only kind of evidence which can lead us to detect the impact of the Persian empire."[37]

Several factors are important to keep in mind. Ethnic "Persian" people were spread throughout the empire both in small numbers and in larger concentrations: the existing Persian aristocracy must have grown in number, with implications for social stratification, but in much of the empire they cannot have been numerous.[38] One of the most important factors is related to this: in many cases in the empire, the means of control would have passed through native individuals and offices. This will have affected the manner in which such control was expressed, tending to state it in ways familiar to both the intermediaries and the intended audience. It will have been many places, and not Sardis alone, that saw the growth of a polyethnic elite in the Achaemenid period. Such factors may limit the appearance of specifically and recognizably "Iranian" material in the archaeological record.

Other features of the archaeological record may equally point to a strong Achaemenid presence or impact, however. Increased control may cause an intensification of social stratification, a phenomenon which often does leave an impact on the archaeological record.[39] External domination might also trigger change in the size of a given site or in commercial relations.[40] All of these things, while not recognizably "Iranian," may be due to the external control of the Achaemenid hegemony over an area.

In recent years, ongoing archaeological work and a fresh approach to the historical documents have begun to give us a better understanding of the extent and importance of Achaemenid influence in Anatolia from c. 550 to c. 330 BC. The cultural impact of Achaemenid presence in some areas lasted well into the Hellenistic period; this important observation demonstrates the degree to which local cultures adopted Iranian customs and blended them with local habits, rather than merely taking on the appearance of foreign traits to curry favor with barbarian despots.

---

37 Sancisi-Weerdenburg (1990:264).
38 Sancisi-Weerdenburg (1990:267–268), drawing on Briant (1982); Briant (1988a). For ethnic Persian satraps in the time of Cyrus and Kambyses, see, e.g., Briant (1996:93).
39 Brown (1986:113 and references in n. 19).
40 Sancisi-Weerdenburg (1990:272). See also the arguments in Bekker-Nielsen (1989) and Alcock (1993).

The city of Sardis in western Turkey, once capital of Lydia and satrapal capital for the region of the Achaemenid empire called Sparda, may serve as a case study for ways in which new discoveries combined with new approaches let us understand the manner in which Achaemenid presence affected local customs and social structures in one capital of the empire. Recent work at Sardis not only has made it possible to consider newly discovered material remains of the Achaemenid period in this city, but also may be used to inform the study of objects uncovered at the site earlier in the twentieth century. The picture is complex, with different sources of evidence illuminating different aspects of culture and society in Achaemenid-period Sardis.

## Sardis as an Achaemenid capital

In the mid-sixth century BC, Croesus, king of Lydia, worried about the overthrow of his old ally Astyages the Mede by the young Persian, Cyrus, sent to Delphi to ask if he should cross the Halys river, the boundary between Lydia and Media, to invade the realm of the upstart king.[41] "If Croesus crosses the river Halys, he will destroy a mighty empire," intoned the oracle at Delphi; and so Croesus set out from Sardis with joyous confidence, only to learn it was his own empire that would fall. When the Persians conquered Lydia, they were faced with the problem of incorporating this large and wealthy province into the empire so that it might function as an integral part of the larger whole. Such a transition affected culture as well as commerce, people as well as politics.

Sardis affords a unique opportunity to examine the workings of the Achaemenid empire in the western provinces. The Lydian capital retained its administrative importance during the Achaemenid period, becoming the seat of Persian satraps. Literary sources mention military and political activities at the city. Archaeological excavation at the site has unearthed aspects of the material culture of the Achaemenid-period city that allow a completely different kind of look into life at Sardis. The artifacts excavated include not only architectural and ceramic remains, but also representational objects such as sealstones and sculpture. Thus at Sardis one may combine literary, archaeological, and art historical approaches and perspectives. These various forms of evidence are complementary: each one leaves considerable holes

---

41 The date is uncertain; see Cargill (1977). It is *probable* that the Lydian conquest precedes that of Babylonia, and so should date somewhere in the 540s, but we do not know this, and probability is based to a considerable extent on chronological impressions we gain from Herodotos. The standard date, 547 BC, is nothing more than a guess. The Delphic response to Croesus' question is preserved in later sources: Aristotle, *Rhetorica* 3.1407a; Cicero, *Poetica Fragmenta* 90.

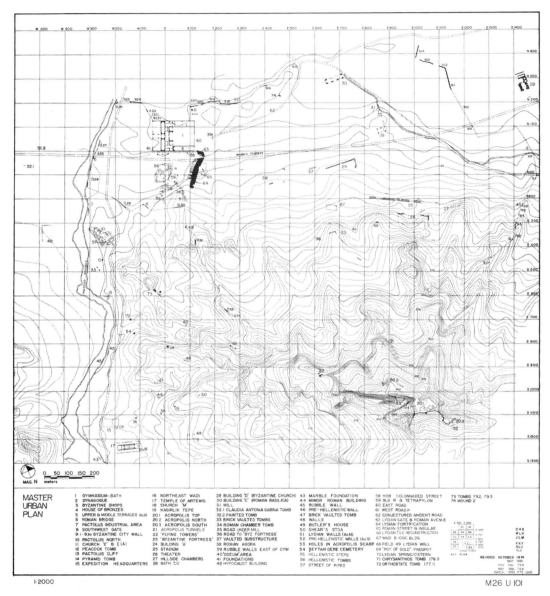

**Fig. 4** Sardis: master urban plan.

in the picture it provides, but the holes are often in different areas and do not overlap entirely. From the fragments of information available from each type of evidence, we may piece together a pattern that approximates the original, like reconstructing an old kilim from rags and tatters that have survived under countless other carpets in a mosque.

Comparatively little has been exposed of Achaemenid-period Sardis by excavation, a fact that has contributed to the paucity of previous studies of the topic.[42] The site of the Achaemenid city lay mostly to the east of the areas that have been excavated (fig. 4); and deposits next to the Paktolos river that flows by the site may have been washed away by floods. A problem of identification has also been raised by the apparent continuity of local ceramic traditions. Until recently, ceramic sequences were so poorly understood that it has been difficult, at times, to distinguish ceramics of the Achaemenid period from those of the later Hellenistic period or, indeed, of the earlier Lydian kingdom. These sequences are now beginning to be much clearer, however, and Achaemenid-period deposits may at last begin to be distinguished from those of earlier and later times.[43] But a caveat remains: Sardis is a large city, and only a fraction of it has been excavated. Of that fraction, only a few areas have produced remains clearly dating to the time of the Achaemenid empire. It is my hope that continued work at the site and elsewhere will expand on and change the picture of Achaemenid-period Sardis presented in this study.

## Approaching Sardis from the east

The approach to Sardis is usually described from the point of view of one coming from the west, from the Aegean sea. This is the way the ancient Greeks came to Sardis, from Smyrna or from Ephesos; it is the way many modern travelers also reach the site. Approached thus, the area around Sardis fits neatly into the inland Aegean climatic and geological systems. The broad fertile river valleys of Asia Minor, to be sure, contrast with the Greek mainland, but in general the climate and surroundings feel familiar, akin to the known world of those coming from the seacoast that lies to the west. This would not have been the case for those approaching from the east. The impact of the lush reaches of western Anatolia on a person who has just dropped down from the Anatolian plateau to the east must have been extraordinary. The following description of the approach to Sardis from the east seeks to embed Sardis within the Achaemenid empire.

Sardis is located some 2,400 km west of Susa and farther yet from Persepolis, a three-month journey for a person following the Royal Road by foot

---

42 Mierse (1983) summed up the evidence available in the 1970s; Greenewalt (1995b) compiled other evidence more recently.

43 Recent work by S.I. Rotroff on the Hellenistic pottery (forthcoming) has aided in solving this problem: I have benefited tremendously from discussions with her about Sardis' Hellenistic pottery. Discussion with C.H. Greenewalt, Jr., A. Ramage, and N.D. Cahill has helped me learn about pottery of the Lydian kingdom.

but quicker for one on horseback.[44] Along the way, the traveler would have passed 111 staging posts, perhaps akin to the Selçuk karavansarays, guarding a distance of 450 parasangs.[45] These way-stations made it possible for official travelers to move very quickly and for messages to be sent by a courier system that took messages rapidly across thousands of miles of plains and mountains. The road connected Sardis to Susa and thence to Persepolis and even India; it intersected with other roads that led to Palestine, to Egypt, to Media, to Baktria, and to Sogdiana. The road system and checkpoints it included thus provided an infrastructure that linked Sardis to the vast area of the Achaemenid empire so that it might remain in constant communication with even the most distant regions.

The road from Fars to Sparda first travels west through the foothills of the Zagros mountains and up the plains east of the Tigris, then through Kissia and Armenia, across the Euphrates, and finally through Kilikia and Kappadokia, turning west towards the Aegean to end at Sardis. Perhaps it branched at this point: most likely, one branch took a southern route, while another took a northerly path to cross the Halys river at a fortified point and pass into Phrygia.[46] The landscape through which it travels is highly varied and dramatic.

The traveler begins by skirting the Zagros mountains, moving northwest along the foothills. This part of Persia has beautiful and fertile areas where water is sufficient; modern Shiraz, near Persepolis, is famous for its wine and roses. The wind scuds across the plains, tossing the branches of pistachio and almond trees. As the traveler moves north, the silver heights of the Zagros ranges give way to the flat plains watered by the Diyala river, the Greater and Lesser Zab rivers and their tributaries; streams cascading from the mountains of Kurdistan water the plains so that they are carpeted with wildflowers in spring. Ferries are employed to take travelers across the rivers in their journey north.[47] They pass into Kissia and Armenia, where waves of grasses dance on the high plains.

---

44 The road between the capitals Persepolis and Susa is well documented. See discussion in Koch (1986, 1990). Most of our information on the routes linking the center of the empire with its western reaches comes from Herodotos' description of the imperial postal system, 5.52–53; 8.98. For a recent discussion of the Royal Road and its possible routes, see Graf (1994). For an alternative perspective that argues strongly for a southern route, see French (1998).

45 Hdt. 5.52–53. For the parasang, see Tuplin (1997:404–421). A Persian unit of measurement, the parasang was the equivalent of about thirty Greek stadia, according to Herodotos and Xenophon. Its exact length varied at different times and places; it was probably equivalent to three-and-a-half to four English miles.

46 This is the traditional view; against it, see French (1998) who argues (convincingly) that the road skirted the Halys, rather than crossing it, and that the bridges and channels Herodotos describes were merely displays of power on the part of the Achaemenids rather than necessary constructions.

47 See Graf (1994:179).

Here the ancient sources are ambivalent about the path of the road. Two major hypotheses exist for the route followed.[48] The "Southern Hypothesis" takes the traveler across the Euphrates at Zeugma, through the Kilikian gates, and across southern Kappadokia, skirting the mountains of Pisidia. The route then turns north through Laodikeia to end up at Sardis.[49] This was the route used by Cyrus the Younger in 401 BC, although it was at that time a remarkably difficult one to travel.[50] Moreover, Alexander of Makedon came through these same lands, possibly following the imperial road that transected them. A convincing argument has recently been made that the southern route was that of the official Royal Road in the Achaemenid empire.[51]

The "Northern Hypothesis" takes the traveler through Ankara. One of the three proposed northern routes takes the traveler north through Armenia to the mountains south of the Black Sea, and then west to Ankara via Erzincan and Sivas.[52] An alternative route[53] would cross the Euphrates in the hills near the Keban dam and take the traveler through Malatya and highland Kayseri, past Pteria, probably crossing the red torrents of the Halys river near the spot where the modern Ankara–Sivas highway runs. A third proposal suggests that the road crossed the Euphrates at Zeugma. Here the Euphrates flows broad and muddy; travelers must have either swum or paid to be ferried over except in the height of summer.[54] Crossing the jagged Taurus mountains through the high and narrow Kilikian gates, they would descend into the Kappadokian plain. There the road would turn to the north, perhaps passing to the west of Hasan Dağ and avoiding the Great Salt Lake and the silica heat of the Konya plain, past Kayseri and along the green limestone and volcanic heights of Kappadokia. All three of these routes have pre- and post-Achaemenid versions; it is possible that the Royal Road offered travelers a choice between routes, depending on weather conditions or reports of bandits.[55]

None of these hypotheses can be made to correspond directly to Herodotos' description. His account has inherent difficulties, as the summarized total of stages and parasangs he gives is greater than his itemized list.[56] This

48 Part of the problem is Herodotos' conflation of crossing the Halys river with passing the Kilikian gates. For the sources and ideas on which the various hypotheses are based, see Graf (1994:177–180). For possible predecessors to the road system of the Achaemenid period, see Birmingham (1961).
49 Ramsay (1920), Calder (1925).
50 For Cyrus' route, Xen., *Anab.* 1.2; for difficulties, *idem* 1.2; 1.5; 5.1; 5.2.     51 French (1998).
52 Winfield (1977). Dillemann (1962) argues that the Royal Road crossed the Euphrates near Malatya and identifies a number of the stations in Armenia, taking the traveler through the eastern Taurus mountains and over the Kappadokian plain past Pteria.
53 See, e.g., Magie (1950:788–789).     54 See French (1981).
55 Caravans traveled under armed escort in the Achaemenid empire; see, e.g., Wiesehöfer (1982), Briant (1991).
56 Itemized: 81 stages and 313 parasangs; summarized: 111 stages and 450 parasangs. For this discrepancy and its implications, see Graf (1994:178), Tuplin (1997).

obvious contradiction serves as a warning for the credulity with which we should regard his every statement concerning the Royal Road. Probably, the main branch of the road, that used by the royal armies and royal couriers moving between Susa and Sardis, took the southern route, while another branch passed through Armenia and Kappadokia, crossing the Halys and passing by Ankara. Our putative traveler elects this northern route. At the city mound of Gordion, the Sangarios river flows cold and green past the site, watering the fields of grain between white and red outcrops of rock.[57] Blue rollers dart from their nests to forage, and hoopoes hop along the ground.

West of Gordion, the traveler passes through a high volcanic area. Tufa and pumice ridges are covered in tattered rags of sagebrush and fields of golden grain. For many miles after the ragged pink volcanic teeth of Sivrihisar, the road runs across ground essentially flat and barren. At last it struggles up and over a ridge and down into the area around Afyonkarahisar. Afyon shines lush in the dusty heat, the "black fortress" itself an old volcano neck surrounded by fields of poppies rimmed with silver poplars. After Afyon, the road winds over another mountain ridge, and the climate and surroundings become progressively more Mediterranean as the traveler approaches the Aegean sea.

First the scrub oaks begin, then the wild olive, and then the fig trees; the air grows more humid and the soil turns from white to red with rich iron oxides. Rivers cut deep into wild soft volcanic terrain. Burial tumuli dot the landscape on prominent ridges. After passing through a fierce area of broken lava and black volcanic cones at modern Küle, which the ancient Greeks called *katakekaumene*, or "the burned lands,"[58] the road finally drops over another ridge into Sardis' valley, the valley of the Hermos river (modern Gediz), broad and flat and fertile.

Sardis is built to the north and up the flanks of an immense acropolis that dominates its landscape (fig. 5). This outcrop soars steep and red into the sky at the southern edge of the valley, just before the wooded hills that ascend the grey shoulders of the Tmolos mountains. To the west of the acropolis flows the Paktolos stream (modern Sart Çayı), which in ancient times ran rich with gold from the metal deposits in the hills. The watercourse divides the acropolis from the necropolis, another great red massif at the edge of the plain, its cliffs pockmarked with rock-cut tombs (fig. 6).

---

57 The accounts of Greek mercenaries, envoys, and other travelers suggest that Gordion was a station on at least one branch of the Royal Road. See, e.g., Xen., *Hell.* 1.4; Plutarch, *Them.* 30 and *Alk.* 37–39; *Hell. Oxy.* 11; Dio. Sic. 14.11. See also Graf (1994:177), Briant (1990). An east–west segment of paved road has been excavated running between Phrygian tumuli and was dated by the excavator to the late sixth century BC (Young 1963:348 and n. 6). This road surface probably dates to the Roman period (see Starr 1963:169, French 1980:704), but it might well follow the path of the earlier Royal Road.
58 Strabo 13.4.11/628.

**Fig. 5** Sardis: view of the acropolis, looking south.

**Fig. 6** Sardis: view of the necropolis, looking west.

The Hermos river valley is a rich agricultural plain, sown in modern times with grapes for sultana raisins, with such fruits as melons, peaches, cherries, and apples, and with market vegetables like eggplants, tomatoes, and peppers, as well as with tobacco; the hills flanking it are sown with wheat and

**Fig. 7** View of Bin Tepe – east-central and eastern part of Bin Tepe from Kır Mutaf Tepe with Karnıyarık Tepe on upper left.

barley, with olive trees scattered.[59] It makes a green and gold patchwork of fields, with poplars shining in the sun and dark green cypresses jutting into the sky like somber paintbrushes. Across the valley, often lost in the haze, is Bin Tepe (Turkish for "thousand hills"), a great ancient cemetery with scores of burial tumuli on low ridges next to the expanse of the Gygaean lake (fig. 7). Bin Tepe seems imposing and oddly magical, both when viewed from the city of Sardis and perhaps even more so when seen from amongst its own hills. In the spring, it is a carpet of wildflowers and green grain; by summer it is golden and parched brown under the blazing sun. Rimming Bin Tepe to the north, the Gygaean lake is in turn walled in on its north side by the silver hills that frame the valley.

Important for the development of Sardis was its location. Sardis lies inland, a three-day walk from Ephesos (fig. 8). The city is built near the junction of two important routes: the east–west route following the Hermos valley, and a north–south route that runs either through the Karabel pass towards Ephesos or over the saddle of Mount Tmolos towards Hypaipa to the south, and through a valley and pass via Akhisar towards Bursa to the north.[60] Sardis overlooks the east–west route and the Tmolos route; it may have been a base for people patrolling the Karabel route. The city may have

59 The crop percentages of the region in 1963–1964 were (excluding cotton, tobacco, and market fruits and vegetables): 45.5 percent wheat, 32.6 percent barley, 21 percent grapes, 0.9 percent olives. Ancient ratios may have included more olives. See Hanfmann (1983:5).
60 For the southern routes, see Greenewalt (1995b:125 n. 2).

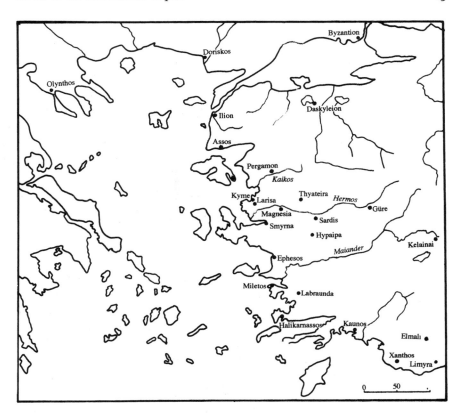

**Fig. 8**
Achaemenid
western Anatolia.

served simultaneously as sentinel, toll-gate, and market-place for traders following these paths. It may therefore have controlled a great deal of the
traffic moving between coast and inland, between the tremendous reaches
of the Achaemenid empire to north, south, and east and the important ports
of Ephesos and Miletos to the south as well as Smyrna and Phokaia to the
west.

To sum up: for the person approaching Sardis from the east, the rich fer-
tility of the valley would have been extraordinary after crossing the high
Anatolian plateau. If the person had come all the way from Fars, the lushness of Lydia would have contrasted with the windswept scrub of their home
even at the same time that the local flora might have recalled the sparer
but beautiful flowers and trees of Iran.[61] Sardis itself, heralded by burial

---

61 The beauty of the landscape is seen in recent accounts; so the archaeologist E.E. Herzfeld, traveling from Pasargadae to Persepolis in November of 1923, rhapsodizes (Herzfeld Archive, Freer
Gallery of Art and Arthur M. Sackler Gallery Archives, Smithsonian Institution, N-84, p. 11):
"The morning was splendid despite the frost: the area glittered like millions of stars, on everything lay a collar of long, light crystals. Even after the fabulous last sunset, the moonlight
on the grave of Cyrus was wonderful. The entire day marvelous: the narrow Pulvar valley,

tumuli along the road, rising massy and red-cliffed from the edge of the plain, surrounded by a system of immense fortifications and teeming with human activity, completely dominated the area around it. The rich agricultural wealth of the Hermos valley was added to by the gold washed down from the Tmolos mountain range by the Paktolos river. The cultural commingling that this study explores attests to the number of people coming from widely differing areas and cultural systems to meet at this Achaemenid capital, exchanging ideas and developing new cultural practices to accommodate or even foster the demands of the polyethnic society growing at Sardis.

## Geographical background

### Geology

The area around Sardis belongs to the "Aegean coastlands" part of the Alpine orogenic system, a series of east–west fractures producing a sequence of east–west mountain ranges with grabens between that have filled with nutrient-rich alluvial and colluvial deposits. These are the valleys of the Hermos (Gediz), Kaÿster (Küçük Menderes), and Maeander (Büyük Menderes) rivers. The area is still highly seismically active: over 350 earthquakes have been recorded since the eleventh century CE.[62] The Tmolos range, reaching an altitude of 2,159 m and forming the southern border of the Hermos valley, is part of the Maeander massif, one of Turkey's three oldest; on its northern side it comprises a series of marble limestones c. 1,000–2,000 m thick, with a front of biotite and non-dolomitic marble, while the southern side is mostly much older uplifted gneiss.[63] The northern foothills of the Tmolos range are sedimentary rocks of the Neogene: sandstone, limestone, and conglomerate, most of which are relatively poorly cemented and erode easily to sandy loams high in mineral nutrients. The acropolis massif of Sardis itself, c. 320 m high, is composed entirely of crumbling Tertiary conglomerate, of schist and gneiss pebbles loosely cemented with lime, that is highly

first a wild crevasse with cliffs of dolomitic limestone, broadens slowly, with the foliage becoming ever thicker. In the river meadows bulrushes, oleander, and almond trees. Even the cliffs slowly become grown over, like karst, and show that this area could indeed be forested and was perhaps much more thickly wooded in ancient times. The fall colors: the trees orange-yellow to carmine-red, the sky light turquoise, the mountains violet, blue, red, yellow. Splendid. I wished I could send something of the beauty of these days home."

I am indebted to the Smithsonian Institution for a postdoctoral fellowship in the spring of 2000, and to A.C. Gunter and C. Hennessey for their help during my tenure at the Freer and Sackler Galleries.

62 Ilhan (1971).

63 For the geology of the area around Sardis, see Brinkmann (1971:171), van der Kaaden (1971:201), Hanfmann (1983:3), Hanfmann and Waldbaum (1975:78), Kamilli (1978), Olson (1970, 1971, 1977).

susceptible to water erosion. The combination of Quaternary and Tertiary outcrops with Cretaceous lithologies, and the tremendous erosion caused by spring runoff, landslides, and earthquakes, makes the geomorphology of Sardis very complex.

## Climate

Sardis enjoys the climate of the Aegean coastlands of the Mediterranean, with mild winters (average temperatures in January *c.* 7–9 degrees Celsius) and hot summers (over 30 degrees Celsius in July and August).[64] Rainfall is quite heavy: 513 mm average annual precipitation puts Sardis in the "subhumid" zone. In addition, runoff from melting snow in the mountain ranges ensures the watering of the river plain as late as July or August; serious spring flooding was a normal part of each year until modern flood-control devices were built. This kind of flooding can result in subsequent drought in hot, dry climates; Strabo suggests the Lydians had dug the Gygaean lake "to contain the floods,"[65] and they may have used it as a reservoir. Wells and channels for water were certainly a part of the Sardian landscape. Elaborate waterworks and water-control systems were built in the Roman period for irrigation and also for public baths; the decay of these systems in later years contributed to the breakdown of regular irrigation and turned the plain into fragmented malarial marshes that isolated the villages.[66]

## Natural resources

In addition to its agricultural possibilities, Lydia possessed fine forests. Despite the severe deforestation caused in recent centuries by over-grazing and uncontrolled use of timber for building and fuel, even in modern times the area around Sardis is one of the major timber sources for Turkey. Trees include pine, juniper, cedar, oak, plane, beech, and poplar, as well as fruit trees. If Croesus seriously contemplated building a fleet to defeat the Ionians,[67] he probably had the timber to do so. The existence of royal forests in the Hellenistic period is demonstrated during the reconstruction of Sardis in 213 BC, when citizens were allowed to take wood from the royal forests at Tarantzoi.[68] Moreover, the existence not only of wood but of proficient carpenters during the reign of Darius I is suggested by the Susa foundation

---

64 The information in this paragraph is for the most part taken from Hanfmann (1983:4); some of it is based on personal observation.
65 Strabo 13.4.7. For textual sources on Sardis throughout its ancient history, see Pedley (1972).
66 Hanfmann (1983:4, 219 n. 41).    67 Hdt. 1.27; Dio. Sic. 9.25.1–2
68 In a letter of Antiochos III, Gauthier (1989:13–15). Quoted also by Sherwin-White and Kuhrt (1993:181) and Hanfmann (1983:7).

text (DSf):[69] "The men who wrought the wood, those were Sardians and Egyptians..."

The resources for which Lydia was best known to the Greeks, perhaps, were its metals. These included not only gold and silver but also copper and iron. As early as the time of Gyges, the Lydian kings were famous for riches in precious metals (so Archilochos 15: "I do not care for the things of Gyges, rich with gold"), and a gold refinery of the Lydian kingdom has been excavated on the banks of the Paktolos.[70] Both literary and archaeological evidence demonstrate active gold-mining at Sardis in the Achaemenid period.[71] Mining required considerable manpower: Plutarch has it that the legendarily wealthy Lydian, Pythios, coerced his fellow citizens to work digging gold in his personal mines, washing it (perhaps panning?), and carting it away, so that their own fieldwork could not be done and their normal agriculturally based subsistence was lost.[72] In the Achaemenid period, gold was probably sent to the Great King – Darius says in the Susa foundation text (DSf), "the gold was brought from Sardis and Baktria, which here was wrought."[73] Some of the gold and silver may have been sent to the king in the form of worked vessels and tableware, as the reliefs on the Apadana at Persepolis suggest; the presence of gold Croesids at Persepolis may also indicate the conveyance of some portion of taxes as coined metal.[74]

Textiles were one of the main products of Lydia: the Lydians were famous among the Greeks not only for their legendary gold, but also for their rich dyes.[75] The hues were due to the abundant mineral agents available in the vicinity: antimony, arsenic, cinnabar, yellow ochre, and sulphur are

69  Lecoq (1997:234–237), Kent (1953:142–144).
70  Ramage and Craddock (2000), Ramage et al. (1983), Ramage (1987).      71 Dominian (1912).
72  Plutarch, *Moralia, de mulierum virtutibus* 27 (262E–263).
73  That Sardis paid various sorts of tribute to the Great King is clear; see, e.g., DNa, DPe, XPh in which are listed lands that pay tribute. DNa is Darius' tomb inscription at Naqsh-i Rustam (Lecoq 1997:219–221, Kent 1953:137–138); DPe is the inscription on the south terrace wall at Persepolis (Lecoq 1997:228, Kent 1953:136); XPh is the "Daiva Inscription" on stone tablets found in the building on the southeast corner of the terrace (Lecoq 1997:256–258, Kent 1953:150–152). Good arguments have been made that the places named in the central Persian texts are to be taken as symbolic essential identifications with sites in the empire: thus "Sardis" means not necessarily that city itself but rather a spot at the far western reaches of the empire (see, e.g., Root 1979:7–9). For all we know, gold may also have been brought from Kush; but it is symbolically significant that Sardis is among the places chosen to be listed as a source for this most luminous of products.
74  The Apadana reliefs show Lydians bearing worked metal vessels as tribute (Delegation VI on the east and north facades, see Koch 1993). For the reliefs, see Schmidt (1953). For the vessels brought, their materials and places of origin, see Calmeyer (1993:152–153). For the Lydian coins at Persepolis, see Schmidt (1953), Root (1988), Stronach (1989a).
75  Because of its humid climate, we have no textiles preserved in Lydia as we have in Egypt and elsewhere. In contrast with Sardian cloth, Egyptian textiles were seldom dyed with bright colors: Harris (1993:57–65 and refs.). For the dyes of Lydia, see, e.g., *Iliad* IV, 142–145. Significantly, the Greek myth of Arachne makes her a Lydian: Arachne was such a skilled weaver that she even challenged the goddess Athena to a weaving contest. She incurred the wrath of the goddess not so much for her talent, in the end – her cloth was woven virtually as skillfully as that of the goddess – but for the scenes she chose to depict, mocking the loves

all attested to in ancient sources or have been found in modern investigations.[76] The proximity of the sea meant the availability of murex shells for
purple dyes as well. The resulting colors probably included white, black, hy-
acinthine (modern equivalent uncertain), the blue of woad, murex-purple,
the renowned phoinix – apparently a sort of blood-red, perhaps akin to deep
cochineal – madder-red, -pink, and -orange, and various yellows.[77] Fine wool
and mohair were available from the flocks of sheep and goats grazing the
Lydian hills. Flax was also perhaps grown in the area, for the Lydians wove
fabrics of linen as well as other elaborate, expensive, and difficult materials like cloth of gold.[78] Sardian carpets were exported to Persia, where they
were said to have been used exclusively by the king; their quality and bright
colors are implied by several ancient authors.[79] A fourth-century inscription
from the Heraion at Samos lists Sardian chitons with fringes; other authors
describe hats, embroidery, blankets and coverlets, couch covers, and cushions.[80] That the Lydians on the Apadana at Persepolis carry folded cloth as
part of their tribute suggests textiles may have been part of the taxes they
bore regularly to the king.

The natural resources of Sardis and its environs – agricultural wealth,
mineral and metal wealth, wealth in fibers that could be woven into textiles,
wealth in timber – made it a place particularly likely to thrive economically.
Its situation, on the intersection of both north–south and east–west trade
routes, let its inhabitants take full advantage of that likelihood. And its
position on the westernmost fringes of the Asian zone of the Achaemenid
empire, bordering on Greek lands and on the Aegean sea, lent it profound
political importance.[81]

## Overview

Achaemenid Sardis is a topic rich with information, but the information
is diverse and difficult to pull together without systematic and intensive

---

of the gods. Athena turned her into a spider as punishment for her hubris. A delightful and
learned article on Arachne is Weinberg and Weinberg (1956).

76 See Hanfmann (1983:7, 221 n. 1).

77 Greenewalt and Majewski (1980:136–137). For the importance of textiles as semiotic conveyors,
see Stronach (1994b).

78 Hanfmann (1983:11). The gold foil clothing appliqués discussed below may be at least partially responsible for the reputation of golden cloth; for a few gold threads from a Roman
sarcophagus at Sardis that may have been woven into cloth, see Greenewalt and Majewski
(1980:137 and fig. 4).

79 For royal use, see Herakleides Koumanos, *Persika* fr. 1 (*FGrHist* 3 C 689), ap. Athenaeus 12.514B-C.
For the quality and colors, see Clearchus Solensis, *Gergithius* fr. 25 (Müller, *FHG*), ap. Athenaeus
6.255E and Varro ap. Nonius Marcellus, *De Genere Vestimentorum* (*De Conpendiosa Doctrina* 20)
542, 13. Cited in Greenewalt and Majewski (1980:134–135).

80 Greenewalt and Majewski (1980:136), Hanfmann (1983:11).

81 Indeed, its wealth and assets made it a particularly desirable jewel in the crown for an
expansionist empire. See Gruen (1984b).

analysis. This work combines a study of textual sources with multiple object-oriented approaches in an effort to gain as comprehensive an understanding of Achaemenid Sardis as possible. It includes analyses of Near Eastern influences as well as Greek in an effort to embed Sardis in the western Achaemenid empire: Greek and Near Eastern texts, art historical material, and archaeological work have all contributed to the evidence examined. Thus, the architectural and artistic material uncovered by excavations at the heartland capitals of Persepolis and Pasargadae, and the Achaemenid imperial and administrative texts known from these excavations and from rock reliefs, play an informative role in the interpretation of materials excavated at Sardis. This attention to Iranian and other influences in the newly developing culture of Achaemenid Sardis is intended to balance the Greek material, providing a more judicious and accurate picture of the city than may be obtained by considering only the Greek historiographic and archaeological traditions.

Sardis in the Achaemenid period developed a culture of its own, a system of objects and actions that was particular to this city at this time. Enriched by the flow of people from other lands, the local population mingled with the newcomers to produce a cosmopolitan society in which national background apparently mattered less than status. A Persian satrap lived in Sardis, but it is interesting how little of the "satrapal" is evident in the archaeological record: the satrapal residence has not been discovered; satrapal archives have not yet been unearthed; precious tableware incised with satrapal names has not been found; tombs cannot be assigned to specific satrapal individuals. Nevertheless, satrapal presence, the development of Sardis as an Achaemenid capital, had profound effects on social organization at Sardis.

Chapter 2 of this book provides a historical overview of Sardis during the Achaemenid period. Written sources – Greek, local, and Near Eastern – provide the primary source of information for the political and military history of Achaemenid-period Sardis. Greek historical sources about Sardis in the Achaemenid period primarily deal with the diplomatic and military actions of the satraps as they affected Greeks. At Sardis, the satraps were supported by a polyethnic elite that included such wealthy Lydians as the famous Pythios, who was said by Herodotos to have offered Xerxes 2,000 silver talents and 3,993,000 gold darics before his invasion of Greece.[82] The satraps themselves were responsible to the Great King. The administrations they ran were designed to collect imperial taxes and keep their region of the empire under control. The safest and most effective way of keeping control over an area was to assimilate the local elite, thereby gaining a broad base of powerful support for the workings of the new administration. The satrap had

82 Hdt. 7.28.

to produce results favorable to those to whom he himself was responsible, both to the king and to the people living under his administration. Maintaining this delicate balance surely required good communication between satrap and king, between satrap and local population. The latter probably took place in part through the elite as intermediaries. The former certainly took place via correspondence, among other means of communication.

The Greek accounts examined here are enriched by Persian and other Near Eastern sources, including official imperial texts and such documents as the Persepolis Fortification tablets, records of food disbursements at the Persian capital of Persepolis. The official imperial texts present a twofold picture of the impression Sardis made on people in the center of the empire. On the one hand, the satrap at Sardis who rebelled on Darius' accession to the throne is not even mentioned in the Bisitun inscription, and would hence seem to have been of little importance to Darius in his efforts to consolidate power. On the other hand, Sardis was symbolically important to the Persians as a land so far away from the imperial centers at Persepolis and Susa, and so rich in natural resources, that it might count as one of the four corners of the empire in official texts. In purely practical terms, Sardians served as laborers in the Persian heartland, probably working on monumental constructions like those at Pasargadae and Susa, and certainly working as blacksmiths or iron forgers near Persepolis. Thus Sardians and their skills would have been known first-hand by those living in Persia. Links between Sardis and Persepolis are demonstrated by the accounts of the Persepolis Fortification tablets, which document travelers moving between the two capitals – one of whom bore a sealed document from the satrap Artaphernes to the king. The political/military history outlined in textual sources thus suggests a close connection between Sardis and Persia. The cultural history of Sardis as it appears through excavation problematizes this view, however, demonstrating a complex admixture of influences.

From the history of Sardis as learned from textual sources, this book moves to the physical, public appearance of the city. Chapter 3 examines the social implications of the city's layout and architecture. Achaemenid-period Sardis served as fortress, as populated urban environment, as center of worship, as elaborated landscape for official and ceremonial aspects of satrapal court life. Sardis was refortified in the Achaemenid period, indicating the sense of security the Achaemenid administration afforded the inhabitants of the city as well as demonstrating the profound strategic and symbolic importance of the city to its new Achaemenid leaders. Multiple lines of walls divided the city into zones with differential degrees of protection against invasion and may indicate social zoning as well. Non-elite domestic architecture seems to have continued the architectural traditions of the pre-Achaemenid period. The longevity of tradition in domestic architecture may attest to the continuity of the pre-Achaemenid Lydian population at Sardis. Satraps probably occupied the royal palace of the Lydian kings, demonstrating their willingness to work with pre-existing conditions and their savvy in co-opting existing locales of power. Certain architectural remains suggest new developments in the social patterns of the city, however: cultic monuments and perhaps rituals were elaborated to include multiple traditions, a development probably needed in a city whose inhabitants included people from thousands of miles away in various directions. The importation of specifically Persian ideologies and practices may be seen in the construction of formal gardens, or *paradeisoi*.

The sculpture discussed in chapter 4 belongs to this picture of Sardis' public appearance. Sculptures found at Sardis and dating to the Achaemenid period show a complex mixture of ideas and influences, resulting in a series of developments at Sardis that may not be classified simply as "derivative" but demonstrate creative processes, the result of interactions between patrons and artisans, that produced new art forms particular to the time and place. Many Sardian sculptures reflect eastern themes and ideas. The motif of banqueting, so common on funerary stelae, shows an association between funerary ritual and reclining banqueting seen also in the tomb structures discussed in chapter 4. Sculpted banquets, unlike couches actually introduced as tomb furnishings to support the corpse of the deceased, proclaimed the concept of eternal banquet to an external audience: they might be seen by passers-by, and seen for centuries. As the Lydian inscriptions mentioning Lydian names (discussed in chapter 5) suggest, stelae showing funerary banquets were not made only for Persians. Their use by local patrons demonstrates how deeply the idea of the ceremonial banquet, introduced from the east, had penetrated local consciousness. Some themes, on the other hand, seem not to show Persian influence, particularly the reliefs showing Kybele and Artemis. These sculptures demonstrate the ability of Sardian sculptors of the Achaemenid period to work with Phrygian and Greek as well as local traditions; they also demonstrate the desire of patrons for works evincing multiple influences. Free-standing statues of humans corroborate these ideas. The prevalence of lions among statues is marked and probably had ideological significance. They were the animals of Kybele and also of Ishtar/Anahita; they symbolized the power of the king in both Lydian and Persian traditions. The association of the eagle with the king as well as Zeus may explain its appearance also in the sculptural repertoire of Achaemenid-period Sardis. The sculptures of Achaemenid-period Sardis thus suggest a new pattern of social organization: at Sardis, local artists and patrons created and used a new series of themes and styles that reflected eastern, western, and local ideas, but that represented a new departure and a new artistic culture developed at Sardis in the Achaemenid period.

Chapter 5 moves on to the official and personal verbal statements of Sardians preserved in inscriptions. A small number of inscriptions dating to the Achaemenid period has been excavated at Sardis; this book offers up-to-date translations, taking into account the recent insights into the Lydian language offered by R. Gusmani and other scholars (who have generally not translated the inscriptions they study) and the new work of P. Briant, R. Descat, and others on the Greek-language inscriptions. The inscriptions from Sardis are mostly in the Lydian language and mostly adorn tombs, warning would-be looters away from the tombs and their contents. The use of Lydian throughout the Achaemenid period and the reign of Alexander, and the continuity of phraseology on these inscriptions and those of the Hellenistic period, demonstrate the degree to which local customs continued under Persian hegemony; the fact that at least two of these inscriptions are bilingual Lydian/Aramaic and two are Lydian/Greek shows the melding of people and probably of traditions in Sardis. Some of the inscriptions provide interesting onomastic evidence, reaffirming the sense of Sardis as a polyethnic cultural center. Others, like the famous Droaphernes Inscription, shed light on local religious practices. Two inscriptions detail the legacy left by a priest named Mitridastas to support the temple of Artemis. Importantly, a Greek inscription that was carved on to the walls of the Hellenistic temple of Artemis provides invaluable information about land-tenure systems in the Sardis region during the Achaemenid period. The inscriptions thus underline certain aspects of life in Achaemenid Sardis seen through other sources of evidence as well; they also illuminate new areas for which other information is not available.

Chapter 6 lays out the official and personal physical statements of Achaemenid-period Sardians that burial represents. Mortuary treatment at Sardis offers a different sort of insight into the complexity of society in the Achaemenid period than the avenues already explored. The introduction of funerary couches in the Achaemenid period may point to the appropriation of particular Iranian funerary rites and possibly also to the observation of the religious taboos of Mazdaism.[83] Funerary stelae and other embellishments of rock-cut tomb facades may have been intended to recall

---

83 The question of Zoroastrianism in the Achaemenid empire is tremendously troubled. For the time being, we can say with certainty only that the Achaemenid kings from Darius I onwards were worshipers of Ahuramazda: there were some cult developments in the 200 years or so of their control, but what precisely this entails remains unclear. The phrase "Mazdaism" that I have employed to signify Achaemenid royal religion sounds more precise than our understanding really is. The clearest statement of the problems is Kellens (1991a). A comprehensive account of research is Ahn (1992:93 ff.). For Zarathustra and the Avesta, see Kellens (1989, 1991b). For a judicious review of scholarship on the extent of Zoroastrianism in the empire, see Herrenschmidt (1980). See also Koch (1977). For a discussion of ancient Zoroastrian practices, see Boyce (1975, 1982). An architectural approach is taken by Boucharlat (1984).

the royal tombs of the Persian kings at Naqsh-i Rustam, near Persepolis in
Iran. Mortuary inclusions demonstrate that people of wealth did not necessarily bury their dead in the most energy-consumptive (and hence showy)
types of tombs, but rather chose between tumulus tombs, rock-cut tombs,
and cists. The reasons for the choices made are yet unclear. They may indicate a specific ethnic bias: ethnic Lydians may have buried their dead
in tumulus tombs as a conscious reference to the burial practices of the
Lydian kings, while embellished rock-cut tombs may have been commissioned by ethnic Persians of Sardis as a conscious reference to the burial
practices of the Persian kings. It may also be that the choices in tomb type
cut across ethnic lines, perhaps indicating conscious affiliation with Lydian
tradition or Persian royal precedent, but based on agendas other than individuals' ancestry. Interestingly, the mortuary inclusions from the various
tombs demonstrate the basic cohesion of the elite: despite the differences
in tomb structure, the elite seem to have worn similar jewelry and used
similar sealstones – even, perhaps, to have engaged in similar funerary rites
that probably included the idea of an eternal banquet.

Chapter 7 moves on to more individual, yet still in some sense official,
expressions, examining the sealstones used by Sardians in the Achaemenid
period. It begins with a closer look at the mortuary assemblage from one
sarcophagus in a rock-cut tomb, that provides an opportunity to consider in
its archaeological context a cylinder seal carved with central Achaemenid
Persian iconography, produced in a particular koine style of "Graeco-Persian"
type that is, by contrast, not represented at Persepolis but is common at
Sardis. Like Persepolis, Sardis seems to have had in operation at one time
a number of different glyptic workshops producing seals in different stylistic and iconographic visual languages. Thus, the choice by a patron of one
visual language over another may have had real significance. The visual system of the seals formed a unificatory artistic mode representing the new
polyethnic elite at Sardis and symbolizing the harmony and legitimacy of
the Achaemenid empire, as ruled through its elite. The unity of this stylistic
and iconographic system in mortuary inclusions at Sardis across distinctions
of mortuary structure is all the more interesting as it suggests a complex
expressive network of loyalties among members of the elite. Adherence to local traditions and to imported Achaemenid Persian traditions clearly might
exist side by side.

Chapter 8 shows Sardian society penetrated as a whole by altered dietary
practices: developments in the ceramic record during the Achaemenid period suggest the degree to which local culture changed. We lack stratified,
externally datable deposits for the period from the conquest of Sardis in the
mid-sixth century until *c.* 500 BC. The earliest securely datable deposits excavated so far, however, already include quantities of the ceramic drinking

vessel called the Achaemenid bowl, a shape apparently modeled on Achaemenid metal wares. These bowls outnumber skyphoi on a sherd count, showing the local Lydian vessel was supplanted by the imported form even in ceramic tablewares. One may imagine the same phenomenon might be observed also in vessels made of precious metals. Those missing five decades between the conquest and our earliest deposit were apparently enough to allow for the shape to be introduced, probably as a metal luxury ware, and to find its way into the common ceramic repertoire of the Sardian potters and drinkers.

The vessels form part of a large-scale shift in the ceramic assemblage at Sardis, away from plates and towards bowls. Of particular interest is the form of the bowls, which resemble vessels known from Iron Age Iran. In addition, the trays on which bread was probably baked are thinner and fired somewhat harder in the Achaemenid period than they had been earlier, as are cooking pots. This implies thinner bread and thinner stews, food that might be cooked at a hotter temperature and for shorter time than the thick porridges of the Lydian kingdom. Such a shift in the ceramic assemblage and dietary customs of the non-elite inhabitants of Sardis comes as something of a surprise. It seems counter-intuitive that the diet of an area should change very much when the sorts of foodstuffs that could be grown locally must have remained essentially the same (there is no evidence for large climatic shifts at Sardis in the Achaemenid period). The ceramic vessels being made and used at Sardis in this time demonstrate, however, that a shift in dining habits did take place. This shift apparently penetrated deeply into the customs and ideas of Sardians, too, for it did not change back again as soon as Alexander "liberated" the city. Rather, it continued well into the Hellenistic period.

In sum: the local social organization at Sardis changed markedly in the Achaemenid period, not simply taking on or rejecting Iranian culture, but combining aspects of local culture with external ideas to create a new system that might thrive independent of the areas of original influence. This development was a complex process of interaction, reaction, reception, adaptation, and creation. Thus at Sardis in the Achaemenid period, acculturation did not mean the simple taking on of external attributes by a pre-existing culture. Rather, it meant the development of a new culture, a new context in which new forms might develop. An intricate network of artistic and sociopolitical connections united the polyethnic elite of Achaemenid-period Sardis and reinforced Achaemenid ideology and hierarchy. Importantly, it was not only the elite that responded to Achaemenid presence: the ceramic assemblage demonstrates that the changes in material culture due to Achaemenid ideas and presence extended throughout the social hierarchy. Acculturation in Achaemenid-period Sardis, the complex process of interaction and creation in a new context, affected people from high to humble rank in society. It penetrated deep into consciousness and custom, continuing particular traits and forming the basis for further development long after the fall of the Achaemenid empire. At this Achaemenid capital, the effects of the Achaemenid regime on local culture were far-reaching and profound.

# 2  Textual sources and the effects of empire

The lushness of the Hermos valley is partly to thank for Sardis' legendary wealth in ancient times, but the metal deposits of the Tmolos mountain range added to the already rich resources of the area. The image the Greeks entertained of Mermnad Lydia as a land of unparalleled wealth ever after influenced their impressions of the Orient. This perception colored their writing about its history, a point that is important for the modern scholar trying to understand from contemporary Greek accounts events and underlying causes in the ancient Near East.[1] For history writing is more than telling or reconstructing events; it is also interpreting them through superimposed lenses of bias and perception. In discussing the history of the Achaemenid empire, for which much rich information may be gained from the Greek sources, we must keep in mind both the filters through which the Greeks perceived their eastern neighbors and those through which we perceive the writings of the Greeks.[2]

It is problematic that the overwhelming majority of texts concerning the history of Achaemenid-period Lydia are written by Greeks. Even the Lydian Xanthos wrote in Greek, for Greeks. No Lydian historical chronicles survive from pre-Achaemenid or Achaemenid times. There are some Lydian inscriptions from Sardis, discussed in chapter 5; they are mostly formulaic apotropaic texts associated with tombs, most of which date to the Achaemenid period. Additionally, some inscriptions in Greek from the Achaemenid and Hellenistic periods may shed light on the history of Achaemenid-period Sardis (see chapter 5). No administrative archive or evidence of such an archive has yet been found at Sardis – though surely there were extensive ones. In this regard, Sardis parallels another Achaemenid capital, Susa. Susa is usually thought of as the administrative hub of the central empire, but for various reasons it has not yielded many administrative tablets of the Achaemenid empire.[3] This silence of Sardian texts does

---

1 Important discussions of Greek perceptions of Persians and the way these have skewed our impressions include Briant (1989a), Root (1979:40–42), Starr (1975:40–42), Momigliano (1975:123–150), Orlin (1976). See also Hartog (1988) and Schmitt (1967). For artistic manifestations of this world view, see Gunter (1990).

2 For the kinds of problems involved and the ideologies that might motivate Greek tellings of Eastern history, see, e.g., Clifford and Marcus (1986); for Herodotos in particular, see Fehling (1989).

3 For one of those that has been recovered and the links it demonstrates between Susa and Persepolis, see Garrison (1996). For the organization of Achaemenid-period Susa, see Potts (1999:325–337 and refs.).

not mean, however, that we must rely entirely upon Greek literature for the history of the site in the Achaemenid period.

A few external sources do exist that may help us evaluate the bias of the Greek sources. So, for instance, Darius I describes his accession in his own words at Bisitun: his version differs in several key points from the account of Herodotos.[4] Darius I's text associated with the foundation of his palace at Susa and the inscription on his tomb at Naqsh-i Rustam describe gold and artisans brought from Sardis for use in the central regions of the empire.[5] Some contemporary Near Eastern texts mention Sardis itself and goings-on at (or goings-to and -from) the city, in a way that lets us consider the validity of the Greek accounts. The Nabonidus Chronicle, perhaps to be dated to *c.* 500 BC, mentions Cyrus' campaigns in the west before the conquest of Baby-lon.[6] In Persia, the texts of the Persepolis Fortification tablets (PFTs) record food disbursements made to people at Persepolis, transecting groups orga-nized by wealth or occupation and therefore providing valuable information about social structures in the Achaemenid empire. Some of the disburse-ments were made to people who had been traveling along the road to or from

---

4 The accounts of Herodotos (Hdt. 3.67–87) and Darius correspond in some aspects but not others. For instance, the names of five of the six men who conspired with Darius against "the false" Bardiya/Smerdis agree in both versions; entirely missing from the Bisitun text is the horse augury that plays such a role for Herodotos in the final selection of Darius as king. Some of the most interesting recent work on the Bisitun text has been done by Schmitt (1990a, 1990b). See also the commentary on DB in Kent (1953:159–160), Lecoq (1997:83–96). An early discus-sion of the monument is King and Campbell Thompson (1907); more recently, Hinz (1974) has explored the composition of the inscription. Luschey (1974) lays out the historiography of the monument before the 1970s. For a recent discussion of the Bisitun text, its ideology, and its relation to Herodotos, see Asheri (1996).

Herodotos' description of the deeds of Kambyses in Egypt, on the other hand, does not tally as closely with the local sources. Herodotos claims (3.1–38) that Kambyses defiled sanctuaries and slew the Apis Bull. Contemporary Egyptian sources do not agree: they demonstrate that Kambyses assumed the titles and the religious duties of Pharaoh, and that he also cut back the revenues of most of the cults. Perhaps Herodotos' Egyptian sources were disgruntled priests? For the Egyptian sources, see Posener (1936) and Burkard (1995).

Herodotos' credibility is discussed in Lloyd (1975:77–170) and Root (1979:39). See also Drews (1997), which contains some interesting comments on problems of reliability in using Herodotos to reconstruct lost remains of a city. Kuhrt (1995a:656–682) lays out the problems succinctly and clearly. Kuhrt (forthcoming) provides both Herodotos' account of history and culture and the impressions provided by Near Eastern sources, balancing them against each other and suggesting places where Herodotos had real knowledge of Near Eastern practices and where he augmented his accounts with the stuff of fable to set up a pleasing and satisfying contrast between Greek and "Other."

5 For the Susa foundation text (DSf), see Lecoq (1997:234–237). The imperial texts should not be taken as simple statement of fact, as Nylander (1974:317) has emphasized: DSf, for instance, "was a propagandistic demonstration of the vast resources in materials and manpower of the empire and a glorification of its ruler," rather than "a precise and truthful recording of the particulars of the construction process." It is thus important to remember that the Susa foundation charter should not be read to imply that the Sardians were responsible specifically for the carving of the columns. Rather, Sardis held symbolic value as one of the four corners of the empire; see, e.g., Root (1988, 1989) contra Richter (1946).

6 Lecoq (1997:181–185); trans. also in Grayson (1975).

Sardis (PFT 1321, 1404; Q 901, 1809).[7] Others were made to Sardians working near Persepolis (PFT 873, 1409).[8] The public royal texts of the kings clearly consider Sparda frontier land, one of the extreme regions of the empire.[9]

These Persian sources are not historical narratives dealing with Sardis. The Fortification tablets record food disbursements; the public imperial texts are not concerned with Sardis but rather with events in the Near East, and they mention Sardis only in passing as it pertains to the impetus of the text. The references to Sardis in the Fortification tablets therefore give an entirely different insight into ways the regional capital was embedded in the empire than might a literary text describing the city itself. The imperial texts, for their part, have significant symbolic subtexts that flesh out and narrativize Persian conceptualizations of the empire. Such conceptualizations might be very long-lived, as long-lived as particular administrative practices seem to have been.[10] The modern historian of Achaemenid-period Sardis may, therefore, balance Greek and Persian stereotypes of the city.

To the Greeks, Sardis and Lydia were of key importance. Lydia held a fascination and immediate significance for the Greeks that led them to write about events in the province, at least inasmuch as they affected Greeks. Due to the nature of Greek prose history as it developed in the fifth and fourth centuries, the texts foregrounded political and military events. Because of the wealth of Greek sources available and the nature of the evidence supplied in Near Eastern and Greek sources, we are forced to rely primarily on Greek sources for reconstructing the political and military history of Lydia in the Achaemenid period.

Most Greek sources focus on the doings of the satraps at Sardis. This is important precisely because the information available from textual records complements that available from the archaeological record. The historical summary presented here concentrates on the Sardian satraps in an effort to draw a fairly straightforward chronology of military and political events at Sardis.[11] What were the administrative functions and duties of the satraps,

7 Translations of the texts of 2,087 tablets were published in Hallock (1969) and another 33 in Hallock (1978). For the Persepolis Fortification seals, see Garrison and Root (2001).
8 For workers of different ethnicities and their actions in the Persepolis area, see Uchitel (1991). For human resource management in the area, see Uchitel (1988).
9 DB I, 12–17; DPh 3–10; DSf 35–55; XPh 13–28. Lecoq (1997:191–193, 219–219, 234–237, 256–258).
10 Indeed, sources that even postdate the Sasanian period may also be drawn on for Achaemenid narrative, for certain forms of government and life established in the Achaemenid period continued long past the end of the empire. For detailed justification of using much later sources for information on Achaemenid practices and concepts, see, e.g., Briant (1982:48 n. 3 et passim, 1990, 1994b). See also Kuhrt and Sherwin-White (1994), Wiesehöfer (1994).
11 This history of Sardis in the Achaemenid period does not attempt to explore nuances of the high tensions that exist in the current scholarly debate on what the Persian empire was "about" or how it functioned. There are, of course, major issues at stake among historians, illustrated by the difference of opinion and approach between two important and widely acknowledged Achaemenid experts: P. Briant and T. Petit. Briant (1994a) is a major and scathing

and how did these men affect activities in the area? The military/political scene developed even as social organization at Sardis was being reconfigured and as the shifting population of this Achaemenid capital constructed for itself cosmopolitan new cultural practices.

## Historical background: 550–330 BC

Literary sources for the history of Sardis begin in Greece with the first Greek literature: the *Iliad* mentions the beauty of the area and the skill of its inhabitants as early as the eighth or seventh century BC.[12] In the Near East, seventh-century Assyrian records mention Gyges as the king of Lydia, a land so far away that it had previously been unknown to the kings of the expanding Neo-Assyrian empire.[13] The records claim that Gyges first brought tribute to Assyria and then desisted; after the disastrous invasion of the Kimmerians, they continue, the son of Gyges (left unnamed) reinstated the tribute. Thus a close connection between Sardis and the Near East was established by the mid-seventh century BC: a connection which seems at least intermittently to have entailed the traveling to and fro of tribute-bearers, and which might therefore have provided an avenue for the dissemination of ideas already from the time of the first king of the Mermnad dynasty (the ruling family of the Lydian kingdom, from Gyges to Croesus, c. 680–547[?] BC).

The Mermnad dynasts and their capital city are mentioned sporadically by Greek lyric poets and by Near Eastern sources. For the most part, the Greeks are concerned with the expansionist desires of the Lydian rulers, who extended the borders of Lydia until it reached as far east as Güre and Sarayköy, where Croesus set up a boundary stone, 150–175 km inland from the coast.[14] For the Greeks of the seventh and sixth centuries BC, Sardis was wealthy, embraced by the gold-bearing Paktolos; it was the abode of tyrants and of priests of Kybele, of learned or skilled men, of warriors and charioteers, and of horses.[15] But beginning in the sixth century, we have a record of Greek literary testimonia which, pieced together with various archaeological materials, have made it possible for scholars to reconstruct

---

response to Petit (1993), incorporating archaeological and artistic material as well as an anthropological approach.

12  *Il.* 2.864–866; 5.43–44; 20.382–385, 389–392 locate the area and refer to its beauty or richness; *Il.* 4.141–145 describes one of its specialty crafts: staining ivory with purple to make cheekpieces for horses.

13  The Rassam Cylinder (644–636 BC), Cylinder B (648 BC), Cylinder E (640s BC), and a building tablet concerning the reconstruction of the temple of Sin at Harran (third quarter of seventh century BC) mention the Lydian king. The Rassam Cylinder, Cylinder B, and the Sin temple tablet are published in Luckenbill (1927:297–298, 323, 351–352). Cylinder B and Cylinder E are published in Piepkorn (1933:47, 17).

14  Hdt. 7.30. For the boundaries, see Greenewalt (1995a:1175).

15  Archilochos 15; Alkman 16; Sappho F 218, 219; Mimnermos F 13; Alkaios F 116; Hipponax F 42. See chapter 9.

the political and military history of the area in some detail. The following description of Sardis' history from the mid-sixth to the late fourth century BC draws primarily on Greek accounts, attempting wherever possible to supplement or correct them with Near Eastern texts.

King Croesus of Lydia, last of the Mermnad monarchs, was conquered by Cyrus the Great of Persia in the 540s BC, when Cyrus took Sardis and most of the terrain commanded from that city, extending from the Halys river in the east to the Aegean coast in the west.[16] Sardis itself became the administrative center of the new satrapy of Sparda, a logical choice for capital because of its commanding and defensible situation. The long history of governing from that city probably also meant that various parts of the apparatus for governing an imperial province – scribes, storehouses, barracks, accommodation for leaders – were already in place.[17] The Greek cities of the Ionian seaboard tried to negotiate with Cyrus after the fall of Sardis; when he rejected these overtures, they sent nervously to Sparta for help.[18] Sparta did nothing but send a rather feeble and meaningless warning to Cyrus, who set off again for Mesopotamia to conquer Babylon.[19]

The first satrap of Sardis, left behind by the victorious Cyrus, was a Persian man named Tabalos.[20] He directed an administration that apparently included many Lydians; the Lydian Paktyes was "in charge of the gold of Croesus and the other Lydians."[21] After a Lydian uprising led by Paktyes, however, Cyrus took reprisals against those who had aided him in his subsequent flight from the city and appointed another Persian named Oroites satrap at Sardis.[22] The story implies Cyrus' determination to extend his

16 Whereas Herodotos (1.86 ff.), Bacchylides (*Epinikia* 3.23–62), and Nikolaos of Damaskos (*FGrHist* 90 F 68) describe a miraculous divine rescue of Croesus from death, the Nabonidus Chronicle flatly states the king was put to death by Cyrus. For the Nabonidus Chronicle, see Lecoq (1997:181–183), Smith (1924:116). For the chronology of the event, see Cargill (1977). See also the Marmor Parium (*FGrHist* 239 F42), Hanfmann (1965), Segal (1971), Mallowan (1972), Erbse (1979), Balcer (1984:33), Greenewalt (1995a).
17 Cities that had previously been regional capitals often became satrapal headquarters in the Achaemenid empire. See Moorey (1980:128).
18 Hdt. 1.141–153.
19 Accounts of Cyrus' doings, based more or less entirely on European (Greek) sources, are given in, e.g., Olmstead (1948:35–45), Rogers (1929:35–70), Mallowan (1972:1–18), Dandamaev (1989:9–34), Cook (1982). Lewis (1977:32, 62, 123 n. 101) seeks to balance Greek sources with Near Eastern ones and consider the ways in which Greek biases might skew their perceptions and accounts of events. For Near Eastern accounts of Cyrus' activities, see, e.g., Potts (1999:309–314), Lecoq (1997:182–183), Beaulieu (1989). A consideration of archaeological evidence for Achaemenid dominance in the heartland and its effects on local customs is Sumner (1994). Briant (1996, for Cyrus see esp. 44–55, 75–80) is an example of how the various historical, epigraphical, and archaeological sources may be weighed against each other to provide a judicious and reflective historical narrative.
20 Hdt. 1.153.3. For the satraps and their ethnicities, see, e.g., Petit (1990).
21 Hdt. 1.153. For Paktyes' uprising, see Briant (1996:47–48).
22 Hdt. 1.154–157; 3.120.1. The word he uses is "hyparchos," his customary term for governor of a province; see Schmitt (1976), Tuplin (1987a). For the meanings of the various words for ruler, see Bivar (1961), Weiskopf (1982). For Oroites, see Briant (1996:134–135).

control to the Aegean (a settlement had already been reached with Miletos): his readiness to enforce this is signaled by his sending very high-ranking personnel when Paktyes absconded after his aborted revolt, to deal brutally (and successfully) with the western seaboard. Perhaps it was at this time that teams of skilled artisans – masons and carpenters, perhaps also sculptors? – were first taken from Sardis to Persia, to form part of the teams working on the palaces of Cyrus at Pasargadae and later on the monuments of Darius at Susa and probably at Persepolis.[23]

At Sardis, Oroites continued in his position as satrap through the reign of Kambyses. He was responsible for killing Polykrates, tyrant of Samos.[24] This satrap thus sought to expand his regional basis of power. "Around the time of Kambyses' illness," probably his final illness, Oroites rebelled against the boundaries laid down by the king and began moving against the Kappadokians to the east. He also had the Persian Mitrobates, satrap of Daskyleion, and his son Kranaspes killed. This kind of extension of power was a mistake, however, for it might all too easily appear to the king as imperial desire on the part of his satrap.

Darius came into power in 521 and, according to Herodotos, directly afterwards had Oroites removed from his position in reprisal for Oroites' murder of Darius' messenger to him – a clear act of rebellion.[25] Herodotos says a Persian named Bagaios was entrusted with this task: he had a series of orders to the Persian garrison stationed at Sardis drawn up on papyrus and sealed with the seal of Darius. At Sardis, he gave the documents one by one to the royal scribe to read aloud, thereby testing the loyalty of the soldiers to the new king. As he saw the army responding to the wishes of Darius, Bagaios had the order read, "King Darius commands the Persians in Sardis to kill Oroites."[26] Oroites' bodyguard, on hearing this, immediately drew their akinakes and killed the satrap. The story may have been rather more complex than the account given by Herodotos: after all, Oroites (despite Herodotos' hostile story) did add Samos to Achaemenid territory. It is conceivable that

---

23 See Nylander (1970, 1974). For individual sculptors' hands at Persepolis, see Roaf (1983).

24 See Hdt. 3.120–127 for the deeds of Oroites. Oroites effected the murder of Polykrates while he was at Magnesia on the Maeander – Herodotos' word is "hizomenos" which in this context should mean "having taken up quarters." I wonder if the Sardian satraps may have moved from one capital to another within their provinces, as the Great King did between his capitals? See Briant (1988b), and discussion of the movement of the king in Briant (1996) and Tuplin (1998).

25 It is Herodotos' narrative structuring which gives the impression that Darius I's first act on seizing the throne was the removal of Oroites. We have no real idea when this in fact occurred – sometime in the 510s? Before the Scythian campaign, whenever that was (see, e.g., Balcer 1972 and Borger 1982). The suggestion that Darius would move to cement his power in the area tallies well with the Bisitun text, which outlines a series of other actions Darius took in his first years of rule to put down or avert rebellion, to solidify and consolidate his power over the empire.

26 Hdt. 3.128.5.

Oroites was loyal to Cyrus' family and refused to accept Darius' claims to the throne (regicide and usurper that he was).[27]

Darius himself nowhere mentions Oroites in his account at Bisitun of the rebellions surrounding his accession. In addition to the quashed usurper Gaumata, Darius describes successfully quelled uprisings in Persia, Elam, Media, Armenia, Babylonia, Parthia, Margiana, Sattagydia, and Scythia.[28] Why does he not so much as mention Oroites at Sardis? The omission may conceivably reflect the relative significance of these lands in the mind of the king, or the perception of the relative threat posed by Oroites' treachery as compared with that of others: the usurpation of regional power at Sardis may have seemed important on a different order of magnitude to Darius than that of similar usurpation in Babylonia. Or the omission may be due to the symbolically charged rhetorical structuring of Darius' text.[29] Whatever the reason for imperial silence on Oroites' rebellion at Sardis, it is particularly interesting that Sardis does not merit a mention in this context at Bisitun, whereas in the foundation texts of Susa and the Apadana at Persepolis, it figures as a place of which the name and location would be recognizable to an audience, so recognizable that it might serve as one of the places representing the remotest edges of the empire.

Not until his return from the failed invasion of Scythia did Darius appoint his brother Artaphernes satrap at Sardis – perhaps in the 510s BC, although we do not really know when the Scythian campaign took place. Who had governed the district for the intervening few years is not known, but it may have been Bagaios.[30] Artaphernes defended the walled acropolis at Sardis, if not the lower town (also fortified), from the ravages of the Ionian revolt (499–494 BC) led by the Milesians. The lack of cooperation between the Ionians and the superior military power of the Achaemenid forces led after several years of fighting to the successful suppression of the revolt, although not before it involved Karia and Kypros as well as Ionia.[31] The Persepolis Fortification tablets document the journey from

27 For Darius' illicit usurpation of the throne, see Kuhrt (1995a:665). The importance of the incident involving Oroites' bodyguard should not be underemphasized: see Gilliam (1965).

28 DB II, § 21.2.5–8. Kent (1953:123), Lecoq (1997:187–216). See also Schmitt (1991a) for a recent edition of the Old Persian Bisitun text. Darius also mentions Egypt in passing. For a recent overview of the monument and the scholarship surrounding it, see Potts (1999:314–320).

29 Darius lists the key usurpers Gaumata, Açina of Elam, and Nidintu Bel of Babylon; the remaining rebels (not counting the later addition, Skunkha the Scythian) were, he says, those who rebelled "while I was in Babylon." The way the list is arranged, there are nine major areas of rebellion. He also says there were nine kings of Persia, counting himself. Thus the nine legitimate kings of Persia parallel the nine usurpers. Could this be a reflection of the Egyptian symbolism in the Nine Bows, making the number nine a goal in and of itself? For connections between Bisitun and Egyptian prototypes, see Root (1979:218–222).

30 Hdt. 5.25. For a description of Artaphernes' initial actions as satrap, see Hdt. 6.42.

31 Hdt. books 5 and 6, Thuc. 3.65, 82. Wardman (1961), Hegyi (1966), Chapman (1972), Tozzi (1978), Lateiner (1982), Balcer (1984:227 ff., 1997).

Sardis to Persepolis of one Datiya in 494 BC; this was probably Datis the Mede, who later commanded the Persian expedition at Marathon, perhaps bringing to the king at Persepolis an account of the successfully quelled rebellion.[32]

Other tablets document the movement at this time (509–494 BC) of other people traveling from Sardis to Persepolis, or of Sardian men working or traveling in the center of the empire.[33] They demonstrate close links between these capitals; they also show that Sardian men continued to live and work in the center of the empire through the troubled times around the revolt.[34] Of the two tablets recording food disbursements to Sardians in Persia (rather than travel rations for those moving along the road linking Sardis to the center of the empire), one (PFT 873) records the ordinary monthly rations paid to nine Sardian blacksmiths (lit. "smiters of iron") living at Kurra, not too far from Persepolis.[35] The other tablet (PFT 1409) records rations given to specialty craftsmen, two men from Sardis who make *halapzi*, an unusual good the precise identification of which is uncertain. These men receive 1.5 QA of flour, or roughly one and a half quarts, normal rations for skilled laborers, given to them directly by an elite guide (perhaps overseeing the transport of their work?). Thus the Fortification tablets document the existence in central Achaemenid lands of skilled artisans from Sardis, artisans other than the carpenters and masons recognized for so long from the Susa foundation texts and the remains at Pasargadae. These craftsmen continued their work even in the heat of a revolt that was rocking their native city.

Both Darius and Xerxes seem to have used Sardis as a base and mustering-point for their forces before and during the wars with Greece in 490 and 480 BC.[36] Xerxes spent the winter of 479 at Sardis.[37] Sardis must therefore have had at the time both adequate fortifications to allow the safe mustering of troops and a dwelling for the king (see chapter 3), and, in 479, sufficient surplus resources to support the king and his entire entourage through the winter months.

A second Ionian revolt was led in 479/8 BC by the Samians. This revolt was successful in achieving for that island independence from Achaemenid (but not Athenian) tribute, probably in part because of Xerxes' decision to focus his attention on Egypt, Baktria, and Babylonia rather than the Greek islands.

---

32 PFT Q 1809, discussed in Lewis (1980).      33 PFTs 873, 1321, 1401, 1409. See Hallock (1969).

34 Moving subject populations is, of course, a common feature of consolidating empires. For the role of colonization in moving people, see, e.g., Cohen (1983). For foreign populations at work in the Achaemenid empire, see, e.g., Dandamaev (1963, 1975). More recently, see Uchitel (1991). Lydian stonemasons were apparently brought to the Achaemenid heartland as soon as Lydia was brought into the empire: see Nylander (1970, 1974).

35 For the siting of places named on the Fortification tablets, see Koch (1990).

36 Hdt. books 6 and 7.      37 Hdt. 8.116; 9.108–109.

It may be significant that Miletos was not a member of this uprising, for this was an important port city. The very fact that the Lydians did not join the Ionians in either revolt bespeaks more strongly than perhaps anything else the degree to which they had been assimilated into, or had at any rate accepted, Achaemenid hegemony.

Artaphernes' measures in governing and in assessing taxes and military obligations in 493 BC, involving a careful and elaborate survey of land, were thought unusually fair and just.[38] They stayed in effect through the fifth century and may also have been the basis for the tribute exacted by the Athenians from those Ionian city-states that joined the Delian League.[39] That the military obligations were honored even under extreme circumstances may be seen in the lists of peoples in the Achaemenid army that invaded Greece.[40] The son of the satrap, another Artaphernes, was general with Datis at Marathon,[41] an honor which shows the esteem and trust of the king rather than any specific connection with Sardis, but the same man led the Lydian contingent in Xerxes' invasion of Greece and was therefore probably known to or at least involved with the affairs of the Sardians. He may have been himself their satrap at the time, as he seems to have been later.[42]

Following Artaphernes II, sometime after 450 BC, the satrap at Sardis was another member of the royal family: Pissouthnes, grandson of Darius I and son of Hystaspes II.[43] This man formed a collaboration with the Samians when they revolted from Athens in 440 BC. He was replaced during the turbulent years of Darius II, perhaps after a revolt mentioned only by Ktesias,[44] by one Tissaphernes: a member of another Persian family but perhaps not of the direct royal line.[45] Tissaphernes is portrayed by Thucydides as a cheater, a liar, one who cannot be trusted.[46] If viewed from his own side, however, he may be seen as a brilliant diplomat who kept the Greeks at each others' throats and eventually in 412/411 BC led them to sign a treaty that granted back to the king all the land in Asia Minor that had been his – effectively undoing the depradations of the Ionian revolts and all the uncertainties in the years preceding and following those uprisings. Tissaphernes, who as satrap at Sardis would have been responsible for providing the western cities' tribute to the king, must have heaved a real sigh of relief at the

---

38 For Artaphernes and his actions, see Hdt. 6.42–43. Briant (1987) makes the point that a crucial element was defining the boundaries between the poleis in order to quash endless frontier squabbling between cities: establishing the Persian satrap in Sardis as the judicial-arbitrating authority, court of last instance, etc., was an essential part of Artaphernes' actions.

39 Agricola (1900), Murray (1966), Balcer (1984:204–205).     40 Hdt. 7.60 ff.     41 Hdt. 6.94.2.

42 Hdt. 7.74; Balcer (1984:168).     43 Thuc. 1.115–117. See also Balcer (1984:168, 176).

44 Ktesias §§ 50–53.

45 None of the Greek or Near Eastern sources mentions Tissaphernes' father or ancestors. Although it is possible he was a member of the royal family, there is at this point no evidence to suggest his parentage.

46 See Schmitt (1983).

signing of the King's Treaty and the close of the Peloponnesian war. But now began the task of exacting tribute, made perhaps more complicated by growing tensions between the satraps of western Anatolia. And Athenian reconquests in the area between 411 and 407 rendered the treaty partially vain.

In 407 BC, Darius II appointed his younger son, Cyrus, to be satrap of Sparda, Greater Phrygia, and Kappadokia – most of Anatolia's richer provinces – and put Tissaphernes in charge of Karia and Ionia.[47] This move may have been intended to circumvent uprising in the area in protest against Tissaphernes' politics.[48] The nomination of Cyrus to this position coincided with the arrival in Sardis of a particularly active and charismatic Spartan nauarch, Lysander. The two became allies, and Lysander was able in 406 to reinforce his navy with ships and men, thanks to the resources Cyrus made available to him. Cyrus must indeed have felt his fortunes on the rise, when in the year of his father's death (between September 405 and April 404) his ally won a decisive victory over the Athenians at Aigospotamoi (April–May 404). It was in this year that he began amassing troops, nominally to lead against an uprising in Pisidia (so, at least, he claimed to the Greek mercenary troops in his service[49]). In 401, he led the same troops to Babylonia instead in an effort to overthrow his brother, Artaxerxes II, king since 404.[50]

Chief among Cyrus' Greek mercenary troops were some 8,100 men from the Peloponnesos, rounded out by 1,500 men with their general Memnon from Thessaly, and by those who came along with the generals Klearchos the Spartan (2,000), Sosis the Syracusan (300), and Agias the Arkadian (1,000).[51] The force was later augmented by 700 more Spartans. In addition, Cyrus may have had as many as 100,000 non-Greek troops. These armies were divided into two separate groups: non-Greeks had their own admiral, generals, and equipage. The two divisions of the army seem to have fought two virtually separate battles at North Babylonian Cunaxa in 401; it was this feature of the battle as much as anything, perhaps, which led to the eventual breaking of the battle line and the defeat of Cyrus.

---

47 See Briant (1996:608–629) for the information in the following paragraph; also Lewis (1977).
48 Briant (1996:611–612).
49 Xen., *Anab.* 1.1–2. Perhaps the Greeks would have thought it foolhardy to lead a mission against the king – rightly, as it turned out. See also Plutarch, *Artaxerxes*. For a different chronology of events, probably drawn from Ephorus, see Dio. Sic. 14.11, Nepos, *Alcibiades* 9, and Plutarch, *Alcibiades* 37–39. See Briant (1996:635 ff.).
50 Plutarch, *Artaxerxes* 2, says quite clearly that Darius II appointed Artaxerxes his successor (difficult to do after his death!). The obsession of the Greek sources solely with the revolt of Cyrus against Artaxerxes II has tended to lead to the suppression of a simultaneous revolt of Egypt against the king; see Briant (1996:633–637). For the date of Artaxerxes' succession, see Stolper (1983).
51 Xen., *Anab.* 1.2.

It is not clear to what extent Cyrus' rebellion was supported by other Persians in Anatolia. Greek sources by and large claim the satraps of Anatolia and the Persian elite in general were loyal to Cyrus and in direct or implied opposition to Artaxerxes II.[52] But some of the satraps along the way blocked the passage of the army, and many other members of the elite clearly did not support his endeavor.[53] The members of the elite were rewarded or punished by the king each according to his deserts: so Tissaphernes, who had traveled in person to warn the king of the approaching army of Cyrus, was rewarded with all of the provinces that had been Cyrus', in addition to his own.[54] He was therefore back in command at Sardis and responsible for the re-establishment of order in much of Anatolia.

Tissaphernes' first acts at the beginning of the fourth century BC make it clear he had decided to whip his satrapy into shape, if need be by making an example of some: when the Ionian cities refused to pay the newly reinstated tribute, he ravaged the territory of Kyme and besieged the city.[55] This action emphasized his assertion of Achaemenid hegemony over lands previously owing allegiance to Sparta. The spring of 399 saw the first Spartan troops set sail in response to pleas from the Ionians, and the renewal of larger-scale hostilities between Greeks and the Achaemenid empire in western Anatolia.[56] The warmth that had bound Cyrus and the Spartans and resulted in their active collaboration in his efforts was thought by the Greeks to have sparked in Artaxerxes II a particular hatred for them.[57] His appointed satrap Tissaphernes took this hatred on to the battlefield.

The Greeks first described the ensuing war as a war simply against Tissaphernes,[58] and the Spartan general Thibron moved against the satrap's main military bases at Magnesia and Tralles.[59] His successor in 398, Derkyllidas, however, made a truce with Tissaphernes in order that the Spartans might wage war against Pharnabazos; he freed various Ionian city-states from Achaemenid hegemony (under which they had probably not been very long) and put down some Chian exiles who had been launching raids against the Ionians.[60] Meanwhile, Artaxerxes II made Pharnabazos subordinate to Tissaphernes, to whom he granted full military power in the

---

52 So, e.g., Dio. Sic. 14.19, 24; 2.5; Xen., *Anab.* 1.8, 9; 2.1; 3.2; *Oikon.* 4; Plutarch, *Artaxerxes* 11; Ktesias § 58; Arrian 2. These constitute some of the few references outside Herodotos where individual Persians are given names in Greek sources; see Briant (1996:642).
53 Briant (1996:643–644). For satraps blocking passage, see, e.g., Xen., *Anab.* 1.4; Dio. Sic. 14.20.
54 Xen., *Hell.* 3.1; see also Briant (1996:649 ff.). Artaxerxes II practiced clemency toward many; with the exception of Tamos, the leader of Cyrus' fleet, who fled to Egypt, the other principals in the rebellion paid homage to Artaxerxes as king and were granted royal pardon. See Dio. Sic. 14.35, 80; Polyaenus 7.11; *Hell. Oxy.* 14; Xen., *Hell.* 14.1.
55 Dio. Sic. 14.27, 35; Xen., *Hell.* 3.1. Tissaphernes seems at no point to have had control over the Greek coastal cities.
56 See Lewis (1977:137).      57 Deinon, *FGrHist* 690 F 19; Plutarch, *Art.* 22.1.
58 Xen., *Anab.* 7.6, 7.      59 Dio. Sic. 14.36.      60 Xen., *Hell.* 3.1, 2. See also Lewis (1977:140).

west.[61] Tissaphernes overcame the Spartan army thanks to his large cavalry. The Spartans refused to sign a truce that banned both Spartans and their army from Anatolia, but withdrew for the time being. The summer of 397 saw major rearmament on the part of Artaxerxes, who began rebuilding a formidable navy. This rearmament eventually led to a decisive Achaemenid victory at Knidos in 394, re-establishing Achaemenid power in Ionia, and the establishment of a navy that could be used against the province of Egypt, which had revolted successfully in *c.* 400.[62] Before this, however, clashes with the Spartan king Agesilaos ended in a battle outside Sardis itself in 395. The resulting Achaemenid loss angered the king and caused him to send a new satrap, Tithraustes, to Sardis to replace and execute Tissaphernes.[63] Tithraustes was to end (by winning) the combat that the king saw as essentially Tissaphernes' personal war.[64]

The terms Tithraustes quoted in 395 were that the Spartans should return home, and that the Greek cities in Anatolia should be autonomous but pay tribute to the Achaemenid empire.[65] Agesilaos, himself a great diplomat, made a truce with Tithraustes with an agreement that the Spartans would move against Pharnabazos. With Pharnabazos he shortly thereafter established a truce as well.[66] But this success was short-lived; a year and a half later, Agesilaos and his army had been called home, while Pharnabazos with the new Achaemenid navy had destroyed the Spartan fleet and was ravaging the Lakonian coast.[67] Having completed his mission successfully, Tithraustes was recalled by the king and replaced with an old friend and advisor, Tiribazos, who was granted the satrapy and some form of overarching military command.[68] It was with this man that the Spartan Antalkidas finally agreed to the terms of the peace treaty: that the Spartans would withdraw from the mainland, and that all the Greek cities of the Anatolian mainland would pay tribute to the Achaemenid empire, leaving the islands and the Greek mainland autonomous and free of tribute obligations.[69] Although the terms of this treaty were at first turned down by the king, three years later, in 386, he agreed to it.

Tiribazos was confirmed in his command at Sardis, while Pharnabazos was married to one of the king's own daughters.[70] The satrapies of western Anatolia were thus linked firmly to the king in Persia. At Sardis, Tiribazos

61 Xen., *Hell.* 3.2.
62 Xen., *Hell.* 3.4; Philochorus 328 F 144–145; Isoc. 4.142; *Hell. Oxy.* 19; Dio. Sic. 14.35, 79.
63 Dio. Sic. 14.80.
64 Xen., *Hell.* 3.4; Dio. Sic. 14.80 and Plutarch, *Art.* 23 suggest the royal mother, Parysatis, may have instigated punishment of Tissaphernes as her own revenge for her son Cyrus.
65 Xen., *Hell.* 3.4; Dio. Sic. 14.80. *Hell. Oxy.* 21 suggests the treaty related only to Lydia.
66 Xen., *Hell.* 3.4; 4.1.      67 Xen., *Hell.* 4.8.
68 Xen., *Hell.* 4.8; *Anab.* 4.4; Dio. Sic. 14.85; Plutarch, *Art.* 7.
69 See Lewis (1977:145) for a discussion of this treaty.      70 Xen., *Hell.* 5.1.

summoned the Greeks, displayed to them the king's seal, and read to them the king's edict:[71]

> Artaxerxes the King thinks it just that the cities of Asia shall be his and of the islands Klazomenai and Kypros, and that the other cities, small and great, shall be autonomous except Lemnos, Imbros, and Skyros; these shall be Athenian as before. Whichever side does not accept this peace, I shall make war on them along with whoever wishes, by land and by sea, with ships and with wealth.

This edict was reaffirmed twice, on the initiative of the king: once in 375 and again in 371. In 371 the Spartans were decisively defeated by the Thebans at Leuktra, destroying their power in Greece and relieving the king of further worry about their influence in Anatolia.[72]

The satrapy of Sparda had but short respite from war, however: the "satraps' revolt" broke out in 361, and it had surely been brewing for several years before its eruption.[73] Epigraphic evidence from Anatolia and Egypt demonstrates that the so-called satraps' revolt probably consisted of a series of local revolts rather than a concerted and unified effort on the part of the Achaemenid elite in various regions of the empire. The revolts were all put down, the local satraps replaced. Autophradates, installed as satrap at Sardis perhaps in 362, was one of those who rose up in revolt. No evidence suggests how many of the elite (Persian or otherwise) at Sardis may have supported Autophradates in the uprising.

In 359 Artaxerxes III succeeded to the throne. His accession was accompanied in the next decade by revolts in Persia, in Egypt, in Phoinikia and Kypros.[74] Sardis and the area around it seems, however, to have remained quiet, although the area to the north was in unrest.[75] Around this time, Artabazos went to the court of Philip II in Makedon. No surviving records detail happenings at Sardis in the next two decades. In 338 Darius III became the last of the Achaemenid kings before Alexander.

Of happenings at Sardis in the short reign of Darius III we know little. At the time Alexander arrived, in 335, the city was still fortified: Alexander was reportedly impressed by the triple wall on the acropolis.[76] But the satrap, Mithrenes, opened the gates without struggle and made over the treasury to Alexander's usage.[77] Surrender, and the option to continue living much as they had been, apparently appealed more to the Sardians and their satrap than fighting and earning certain reprisals. Archaeological evidence demonstrates that material culture at Sardis remains virtually

---

71 Xen., *Hell.* 5.1.    72 Xen., *Hell.* 6.4; Dio. Sic. 15.50. See Briant (1996:675).

73 Diodorus Siculus 15.90 ff. See Briant (1996:675–694) for a synthesis of events and a cogent discussion of the historiographical problems associated with them. Briant has based much of his account on Weiskopf (1989).

74 Briant (1996:699–706).    75 Dio. Sic. 16.52; Ktesias § 52.    76 Arrian, *Anab.* 1.17.

77 Arrian, *Anab.* 1.16, 17; Dio. Sic. 17.21.

unchanged into the Hellenistic period. Thus the political history of Achaemenid Sardis, torn with wars and conflict, ends with a decision to surrender that enabled its inhabitants to continue living much along the lines they had developed through more than two centuries of Achaemenid hegemony.[78]

## Conclusion

Literary sources make it clear that satraps were ultimately responsible to the Great King by whose favor they held their positions.[79] They ran civil administrations designed to collect the satrapal levies that were then sent to the king; to be effective, these administrations needed to take into account the interests and needs of the local populations. A satrap could not push the local population too far in exacting tribute or taxes, lest he incur local rebellion. Such uprisings were doubly expensive, as they not only cut off tribute but meant costly military repression of rebels. And in order to wage retaliatory war against one part of a satrapy, the satrap needed to be able to count on the loyalty of the other parts. The safest and most effective way of keeping control over an area was probably to assimilate the local elite, thereby gaining a broad base of powerful support for the workings of the new administration. This administration was made up of Persian and local elite, filling offices or governing the subdivisions of the satrapy, and with some command over the army. The actions of the satrap may have been under random and perhaps sometimes secret surveillance by one or more representatives of the king, the "King's Eye."[80] And the satrap's power was curtailed by the king, whose assent was required for such major steps as Artaphernes' invasion of the Kyklades (Hdt. 5.31). A satrap thus filled a role with complex obligations, being responsible for instigating certain actions and decisions designed to produce results favorable to those to whom he himself was responsible. He probably often took the brunt of displeasure from both sides.

While the sorts of historical perspectives and information that may be gleaned from the historical sources concentrate on military exploits and the activities of named individuals, these are not the only form of information available. Archaeological remains afford entirely different insights

---

78 For an excellent discussion of Sardis' civic institutions at the time of Alexander, see Briant (1993).
79 See Weiskopf (1982).
80 The question of the "King's Eye" is a vexed one: was there really such an institution? Who were the Eyes and what did they do, what were their duties and how carried out? See, e.g., Balcer (1977).

into the social history of the city. The cultural history of Sardis demonstrates a remarkably complex mixture of influences: as we shall see in the following chapters, the local social organization at Sardis changed markedly in the Achaemenid period, combining aspects of local tradition with ideas from other cultures – including Iranian – to create an eclectic and fluid new system that might thrive independently of the areas of original influence.

# 3

# The urban structure of Achaemenid Sardis: monuments and meaning

With a sense of the city's military and political background providing a framework of reference, we turn now to consider what forms the social institutions of Sardis took in the Achaemenid period. This chapter examines Sardis' architecture, exploring the social implications of the city's form and monuments, the way in which Sardians inhabited their city and exploited its space.[1] As we shall see, Sardian architecture suggests a complex picture of social interactions at the satrapal capital: while some aspects of building and spatial organization reflect Lydian tradition, others seem to take as their impetus the cultures of Iran, Greece, and elsewhere.[2] The resultant mix is uniquely Sardian, and helps us understand how this city functioned during the Achaemenid empire. We do not see the simple taking on of particular cultural traits from other societies, but rather the full-scale incorporation into Sardian society of certain material aspects and, apparently, the cultural traits they reflect. The result was a new culture that grew out of a number of past traditions but fully resembled none.

Because detailed surface survey has not been done at the site, this chapter focuses on non-funerary architecture in and near the city, integrating literary, representational, and archaeological evidence in the analysis.[3] Although many of the monuments have been discussed elsewhere, the architectural remains of Achaemenid-period Sardis have never been analyzed together. Some of the structures discussed here have only recently come to light and have not previously been examined for their social implications.

As mentioned in chapter 1, the city center of Sardis during the Achaemenid period lay farther to the east than the areas that have been the main focus of excavation. This makes the presence of Achaemenid-period remains in the areas excavated somewhat surprising and particularly significant, as they demonstrate the large area over which architectural traces of Achaemenid presence may be found. During the Achaemenid period these

---

1 The symbolic importance of the landscape in understanding local social structures is well explored in an early study by Cosgrove (1984); see also the contributions to Cosgrove and Daniels (1988).

2 For imperial impact on city-planning, see, e.g., Eck (1991).

3 For funerary architecture, see chapter 6. The lack of systematic exploration of Sardis' hinterland is due to high erosion in the Hermos river valley, which may blanket ancient remains by 7 meters or more of soil (as excavation shows). This makes it difficult to assess the relationship of Sardis with its immediate environs. Interactions between urban and rural environments may of course be considered without the benefit of archaeological survey, but such study generally relies on ample epigraphic evidence (missing at Sardis).

outlying areas, inasmuch as they have been exposed by excavation, were built up or modified, used in different ways or in the same ways they had been pre-conquest, or sometimes abandoned. Thus we gain a sense of Sardis' use and development in the Achaemenid period.

Perhaps the royal capital of Persepolis, as we are now coming to understand it, would be a good model for what we might expect to find at Sardis under ideal conditions and with a great deal more of the city explored through excavation and survey.[4] If the urban arrangement of Sardis reflected that of Persepolis, an acropolis with ceremonial palaces and garrisons would be surrounded by an inner fortification with offices built directly into or just within the walls, where storerooms were filled with the archives of administrative bureaucracy. Just below this plane would be found residential palaces, surrounded by another wall. Below this would come another walled zone, filled with houses, shops, workshops, and all the other apparatus of city life. At Persepolis, of course, the areas excavated are mostly the opposite of those exposed at Sardis: great ceremonial and administrative formal remains and garrisons, but little yet uncovered in the way of lifestyle or burial systems of non-elites.

This chapter begins with the fortification wall at Sardis and the small domestic or other structures directly next to it, exploring the ideas of defensibility, safety, and domesticity. It then moves to consider the sacred structures of the city in the Achaemenid period, looking in particular at two altars. From this probably public, shared, space, we move to consider areas that may or may not have had public access: the area next to the Paktolos river and a fountain-house there form the basis for a discussion of formal gardens, or *paradeisoi*. Such gardens, laid out and maintained by the satraps, were probably not public space. A last few structures, known from textual sources but not yet from excavation, complete the corpus available to date and fill out our picture of the city.

## Fortification wall

Sardis was a walled city. An enormous fortification wall or series of walls surrounded it, so impressive that Greek authors commented on the circuit surrounding the acropolis, from almost the first chroniclers to discuss the city to those of the Roman period. The descriptions in the literary accounts combine with the archaeological evidence – the physical remains of the

---

4 For Persepolis, see Schmidt (1953, 1957, 1970), Sami (1955). See also Herzfeld (1933, 1941), Krefter (1971). For an early discussion of the layout of the Achaemenid capital at Susa, see Dieulafoy (1893); more recently, see Ghirshman (1963a, 1963b), Perrot (1981), Boucharlat (1990a, 1997). Most recently, see Potts (1999:320–337).

city wall, excavated over the course of the past twenty years – to provide a coherent idea of the city's fortifications in the Achaemenid period.

Greek literary sources include information about the city's fortification wall at various times of its history. On both occasions when the city was sacked, by Cyrus in the mid-sixth century BC and by Antiochos in 213 BC, this was achieved by scaling the wall at a point that had seemed impregnable: in the case of the Persians, up the face of the acropolis on the side facing Tmolos, and in that of Antiochos, along a steep and jagged ridge extending down from the acropolis (Polybios 7.15.6–8). Herodotos (1.91) suggests the walls were impregnable wherever they were guarded when Cyrus sacked Sardis; only a spectacular feat of mountaineering, scaling the almost vertical and extremely crumbly face of the acropolis, finally breached them. Croesus' advice to Cyrus about collecting booty demonstrates there were multiple gates at the beginning of the Achaemenid period: "Put guards from among the spearbearers at all of the gates."[5]

Part of the city extended beyond the fortification walls during the Achaemenid period and was therefore open to destruction by such marauders as King Agesilaos.[6] People lived outside the city walls in the Lydian period as well:[7] the fortifications thus divided the city into zones with differing degrees of protection, separating the city into a hierarchy of safety.[8] Indeed, the Sardians built multiple rings of walls for added protection of particular areas in the city. Herodotos' description of the revolt of Paktyes, who besieged the governor Tabalos on the acropolis of the city, demonstrates that the acropolis was separately fortified already at the beginning of the Achaemenid period.[9] The inner defense wall was apparently maintained, for Artaphernes successfully held the acropolis against the Ionians in 499 BC even though the lower city was destroyed.[10] This type of city fortification, with multiple rings of defense walls, is known also from roughly contemporary Near Eastern cities, in particular, Median ones. The Median city of Harhar, shown on the reliefs of Sargon at Khorsabad,[11] has concentric fortifications. And the Median capital of Ekbatana was known to Herodotos for its multiple walls, each of a different color.[12] The Achaemenid capital,

---

5 Hdt. 1.89. Might the "spearbearers" be the Immortals, the royal bodyguard who bore spears with ends shaped like apples? These men may have been deemed particularly trustworthy and suitable for such a job as this.

6 Xen., *Agesilaos* 1.33.

7 The entire excavation area of HoB, and probably that of PN, is outside the fortification wall.

8 See chapter 9 for implications of zoning.        9 Hdt. 1.152 ff.        10 Hdt. 5.100–101.

11 See Gunter (1982, esp. pls. II, III, IV). The Median cities of Shurgadia (?), Bit Bagaya, Kisheshim, Kindau, Kisheslu, and Harhar, the Mannaean city of Pazashi, and the Elamite city of Hamanu, all seem to have multiple walls: if the apparent interior wall is merely a result of Assyrian perspective, the Median cities Harhar and Kisheshim at any rate still have multiple rings of walls. Harhar is illustrated also in Roaf (1995:61, fig. 26).

12 Hdt. 1.98. Glazed bricks may have been a means by which something approximating Herodotos' description of colored walls could have been achieved (for glazed bricks at Susa,

Persepolis, also had multiple walls: the fortification around the takht was the innermost wall, but there seem to have been at least two others.[13] This concept of degrees of protection apparently was shared by Sardis in the Achaemenid period.

The fortification walls of Sardis also caused comment in later Greek authors. Alexander was impressed by the fortifications on the Sardian acropolis:[14] "He climbed the acropolis where the Persian troops were garrisoned: and the place seemed secure to him, for it was very high and precipitous on all sides, and was guarded by a triple wall." Multiple walls may also be implied by Aristotle:[15] "The Athenians sailed with twenty ships to help the Ionians. And they marched to Sardis and took the entire area around Sardis outside the walls of the royal palace."

The frequent mention of Sardis' fortifications by Greeks was amply deserved by the sheer magnitude of the walls, unlike anything known in the contemporary Greek world. An enormous fortification wall, built of apparently unbaked mudbrick on a stone socle, has been exposed at Sardis by recent excavations.[16] At the time Cyrus sacked Sardis, this wall measured fully 20 m across at its base and may have stood as much as 35 m tall (fig. 9). A batter of 10 percent and the probable existence of ledges brought it to a narrower breadth at its top, perhaps as little as 5 m across (still enough for two chariots to pass one another); the top rampart seems to have been further protected by wooden shutters, perhaps indicating the existence of battlements. In places, the wall had a low stone socle faced with squared stones, with mudbrick on top (fig. 10); in other places, the stones extended higher and might be either squared or roughly shaped, a kind of cross between close polygonal joins and "Cyclopean" masonry (fig. 11). Its base was filled with rubble; the mudbrick superstructure was filled with pisé or with laid mudbrick courses, while reed mats or layers of slender saplings were placed at intervals (in places, every eleven courses). Interior compartment walls of mudbrick or stone lent the fortification added stability. The

see Muscarella 1992). The Iranian excavations at Hamadan/Ekbatana have revealed part of one massive wall already; see Sarraf (1997:40–41); see also Abdi (forthcoming), Brown (1997). Boucharlat (1998) has a useful discussion of the recent excavations at Ekbatana, including an interesting discussion about brick size and shape. A close Urartian parallel exists for the large storage facility uncovered at Ekbatana; see Forbes (1983). Urartians were famous for walls and masonry, but their fortifications do not really resemble those of Sardis. Not all Median sites had multiple walls, of course: Kerkenes Dağ (Median?) and Godin Tepe each have only one terrific wall.

13 Mousavi (1999) with references to other work at Persepolis. At Susa, the walls that appear in some plans are, for the Achaemenid period, a fiction of early archaeologists. Surely there were walls – a gate has been uncovered – but we do not yet know what the Achaemenid-period fortifications looked like.

14 Arrian, 1.17.     15 *Analytica Posteriora* 94a.

16 The name "Colossal Lydian Structure" was applied to the structure by its early excavators because of initial uncertainty that it was a fortification wall. The following description is cast only in the most general of terms; for more detailed descriptions, see progress reports in the *AJA*, *BASOR* and *AASOR* and forthcoming publication by C.H. Greenewalt, Jr.

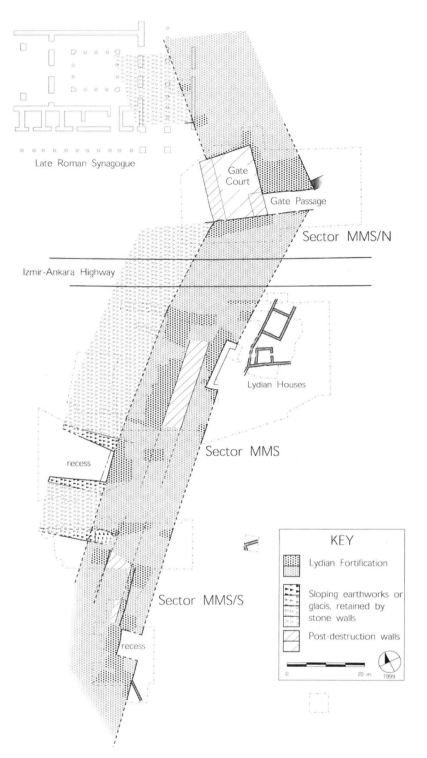

Late Roman Synagogue

Gate
Court

Gate Passage

Sector MMS/N

Izmir-Ankara Highway

Lydian Houses

Sector MMS

recess

Sector MMS/S

recess

KEY

Lydian Fortification

Sloping earthworks or
glacis, retained by
stone walls

Post-destruction walls

0                    20 m.          1999

**Fig. 9** Sardis:
Sectors MMS,
MMS/N, MMS/S:
archaic
fortifications and
domestic
structures,
schematic plan.

**Fig. 10** Sardis:
MMS-I, colossal
Lydian structure,
sloped east face
of coursed
mudbrick with
stone socle.
80.042:13.

mudbrick faces of the wall were built of exceptionally high-quality, dense, unfired bricks. An elaborate system of earthworks – eleven sloping layers of gravel and clay – to the west of the excavated segment of the wall functioned as a glacis (fig. 12). Fortifications built on this scale were unknown in the contemporary Greek world, although immense fortifications had a long history in Anatolia, Mesopotamia, and central Asia.[17]

17 In Anatolia, the walls of Troy, Hattusas, and Gordion are of course particularly well known. For Troy, see Blegen et al. (1950–1958). For Hattusas, see the synthesis in Bittel (1970). Phrygian Gordion's walls were 9 m thick, with a polychrome monumental gateway; as at Sardis, internal walls divided the city's interior. See Young (1955, 1956, 1957, 1958, 1960). Many Mesopotamian cities had enormous fortifications; a particularly well-known example is Babylon, for which see, e.g., Koldewey (1918) and Wetzel (1930). For central Asian fortifications, see, e.g., Francfort (1979, 1985).

**Fig. 11** Sardis: MMS/S, east face of archaic fortification wall, with (at left) north salient corner of recess in east face. 95.026:09.

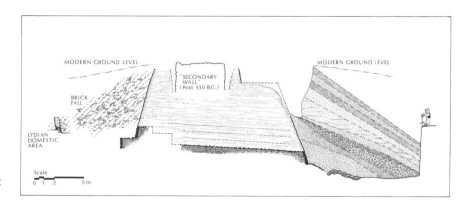

**Fig. 12** Sardis: MMS scarp section at highway, looking south.

This wall was demolished in the mid-sixth century BC.[18] The mudbrick was pushed from the upper parts of the wall, creating a spectacular destruction debris of multicolored bricks, some partly fired as if in open air and some burned so badly as to vitrify, which covered and preserved the burned houses of the Lydian kingdom built snugly up against the wall itself.[19] This debris was apparently not shoved mindlessly over the edge of the wall but rather dumped into the various recesses of the structure on both the east and the west sides, making a smooth and uninterrupted line which was used as the basis for rebuilding. For the city was refortified in the Achaemenid period (fig. 13). This point is significant: it demonstrates the confidence of the new rulers that they could keep control of the city. Thus Sardis served as a fortified satrapal capital at the western edges of the empire, a safe base for launching military operations, a citadel that might be held against insurrectionists.

After the sack of the city by Cyrus, the Lydian city gate excavated in sector MMS/N was thoroughly blocked by two cross-walls ("Lydian West Wall" and "Lydian Wall Z") that continued the line of the Colossal Lydian Structure (CLS) in an unbroken defense (fig. 14). The space between these walls was filled with a gravelly deposit. The superstructure of this part of the wall is unclear: it may have operated as a raised gate or road of some sort, or the area may have been built up to the full height of the wall. Any addition, however, was removed along with other material at the time of the late Roman remodeling of the area.[20]

The city wall was rebuilt to the south of this area. A second wall (the "secondary wall") was constructed atop the remains of the earlier one, extending the height of the wall and presenting a smooth impenetrable face to potential attackers. This addition had a rubble-packed stone socle faced with fieldstones and reused cut stones, probably topped with mudbrick to bring the overall height of the wall to at least 20 m. It is not clear how much of the fortification wall was refurbished in this manner, but the entire extent so far excavated includes remains of this secondary wall. Might it have been constructed after the Ionian revolt, when it would have been painfully apparent how necessary better defenses were for the lower city, but before Xerxes spent the winter of 479 at Sardis? Such a measure would

---

18 Ramage (1986).
19 The battle and conflagration also left their mark in the form of partial skeletons within the destruction debris and buried underneath it, as well as an iron helmet and sword, and a large quantity of arrowheads near the city gate.
20 Could the blocked gate have been replaced by another nearby? Polybios (7.15.6–7) mentions a Persian gate to the city, on the opposite side of the city from the ridge known as the "saw", which is probably to be identified with a particularly nasty-looking ridge on the east side of the city. The "Persian gate" thus probably faced west, away from Persia – perhaps it was called "Persian" because it had been constructed by Persians.

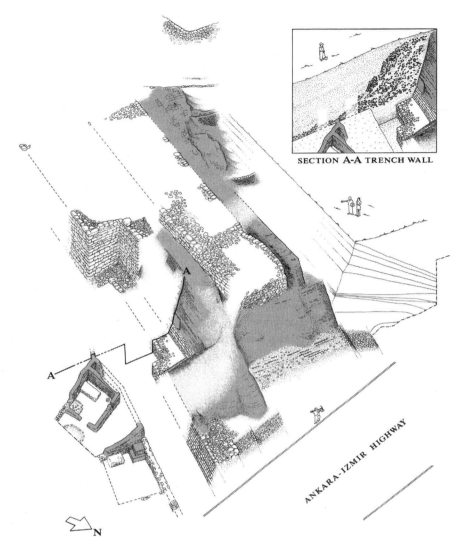

SECTION A-A TRENCH WALL

**Fig. 13** Sardis: MMS perspective view, northeast to southwest, with stone Achaemenid-period "secondary wall" atop mudbrick archaic fortification.

in any case have been a precaution mandated by simple good sense after the events of 499.

The Lydian fortification's mudbrick was used to fill in the recesses of the wall, while steeply sloping earthworks made partly of destruction debris and decomposed mudbrick were constructed on both sides of the fortification to protect the wall from sapping attempts from east or west. In some cases the destruction debris was transported a considerable distance to shape the landscape to its desired form. A new glacis was built to the west of the wall, the full extent of which is yet to be explored (fig. 15).

**Fig. 14** Sardis: MMS/N: Lydian features plan, with Achaemenid-period walls blocking the archaic gate.

The fortification walls of Sardis were enormous, the result of huge amounts of labor organized into transporting raw materials, hewing and fitting stone, weaving rush mats to place between courses of mudbrick within the wall, cutting saplings and laying them, digging clay and making bricks of varying qualities, and finally constructing the edifice. The result was a city divided into "inside" and "outside," "protected" and "unprotected." The curtain wall(s) within the fortified circuit elaborated these zones, layering safety: at all times, inhabitants of Achaemenid Sardis must have been aware of these levels, the arenas of human activity represented by their houses, sanctuaries, palaces, and administrative buildings protected differentially against invasion. Thus Sardis saw space divided not only in such ways as private/public, sacred/secular, higher up the acropolis/deeper into the lower town, but also in nesting layers of defensibility and safety against external threat.

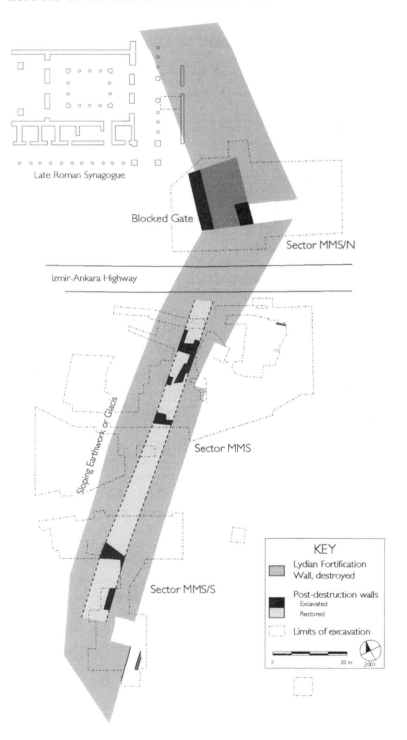

**Fig. 15** Sardis:
Achaemenid-
period
architecture,
MMS/N, MMS,
MMS/S.

## Residences and rebuilding

Domestic space remains something of an unknown for Achaemenid Sardis.[21] The area directly next to the fortification wall was apparently not occupied in the Achaemenid period, due to the enormous amount of mud-brick piled up to make the defensive earthworks. The area seems mostly to have been abandoned until extensive re-landscaping efforts, perhaps in the third century BC, leveled the slope to the east of the wall and allowed for reoccupation.

Lack of occupation did not mean lack of use, however. Although for the most part the destruction debris overlying the destroyed Lydian houses directly beside the fortification wall was left undisturbed after the sack, some people survived the catastrophe who knew what had been where before the arrival of the foreigners. Thus, somebody found it worthwhile to dig through the debris, apparently to retrieve from a workshop the cullets of opaque red glass that had been manufactured there or perhaps the tools used to make it.

This disturbance of the destruction debris blanketing the area directly next to the fortification wall is of great significance. Opaque red glass was particularly difficult to make and was an expensive item.[22] Presumably, if someone bothered to move that much dirt to get at the cullets, the market for red glass still existed after the sack of the city. This suggests either that the glass may have been made for export from Sardis and such markets were considered by the inhabitants to be still operative, or that the glass cullets were made for local use (at Sardis itself?), and the inhabitants presumed they would still be desired even under new patronage. Perhaps more importantly, the digging in the area demonstrates someone knew this spot would repay effort. This strongly implies the existence of Lydian survivors of the sack – it is interesting to have archaeological evidence to back up the suggestion that Lydians survived, that the population in the Achaemenid capital was polyethnic, and that someone had sufficient initiative to quarry the glass workshop for its treasures.

The strip of land exposed by modern excavation next to the fortification wall continued to be used sporadically through the Achaemenid period, although apparently not for occupation (see fig. 15). The area by the glass workshop in sector MMS saw two refuse pits dug that were filled with detritus dating to *c.* 500 BC and *c.* 300 BC. And two walls were constructed in the Achaemenid period (MMS-I 93.1 Walls Lots 8 and 9). No occupation or use

21 This is due partly to preservation and partly to the areas excavated. No Achaemenid-period houses have been excavated. For the sort of social analysis that may eventually be possible, see, e.g., Haselgrove (1995); see also the issues and approaches in Parker Pearson and Richards (1994).
22 Brill and Cahill (1988). Opaque red glass was also found at Persepolis, and there was a small workshop at Achaemenid-period Nimrud; see discussion and references in Kuhrt (1995b).

surfaces were discovered in connection with these walls. Their construction demonstrates continuity of population in the area: they are similar to Lydian walls of the pre-Achaemenid period, being made of unworked fieldstones, ranging from fist-sized to head-sized, set in mud mortar. This makes sense, as these are the materials locally available for wall construction; indeed, the inhabitants of the modern village continued to make walls very similar to these until the invention of cinderblocks. The stone portion of these walls extends rather higher than their Lydian counterparts in the same area, and no trace was discovered in excavation of a mudbrick superstructure. This may suggest the walls were of stone for their entire height. In the absence of occupation surfaces we must keep in mind the possibility that these Achaemenid-period structures were outdoor walls, perhaps of compounds or animal pens.

One of the few other parts of the city to the east of the fortification wall excavated down to Lydian levels, approximately 100 m south of these structures (sector MMS/S), possibly also includes Achaemenid-period architecture. A wall that may be Achaemenid in date (MMS/S 94.1 Wall Lot 18) is of an apparently domestic structure, made of fist-sized stones laid in mud mortar, preserving a very rough herringbone pattern on the west face and laid in a careful vertical line of somewhat larger stones at the corner. The wall is sunk approximately 40 cm into the mid-sixth-century mudbrick destruction debris and runs parallel to the fortification wall. It has been insufficiently exposed to determine its use, although larger stones at the southwest corner may suggest the wall turns to the east here and encloses an unexcavated area to the east.

The wall's construction date remains uncertain, as it lies at the edge of the trench and its internal use surfaces are unexcavated. External surfaces would fit with a possible Achaemenid date. To the west, a fourth-century (?) and a third-century (?) surface both ran up to the wall. Its western face is uneven and poorly consolidated enough to suggest it backed into soil. If so, it may be the lower part of the wall of a pit house built into the slope of destruction debris.

Pit houses at Sardis were probably not new: a domestic structure found near the Lydian gold refinery by the Paktolos that dates to the pre-Achaemenid period seems to have been a pit house.[23] But pit houses at Gordion probably date to the Achaemenid period.[24] The ceramic record at Gordion demonstrates an increase of Lydian imports into Gordion in the Achaemenid period; evidence at Uşak of commingled Phrygian, Lydian, and Achaemenid Persian influences and tastes attests to a similar cosmopolitan atmosphere in western Anatolia. Our wall at Sardis may therefore fit into

23 Ramage (1978); and personal communication, summer 1994.
24 M.M. Voigt, personal communication, summer 1994.

this sort of eclectic koine in the Achaemenid west. It is also possible, however, that the Sardian wall simply functioned as a terrace wall. If this is the case, it may date to the Achaemenid period or may rather be part of the intensive landscaping of the area that seems to have gone on in the third (?) century.

To summarize: although no Achaemenid-period domestic architecture at Sardis has yet been excavated, we have gained a rough idea of how houses may have looked. A contemporary Greek description of houses in the Achaemenid period essentially conforms to the archaeological evidence: built of mudbrick, with reed-thatched roofs.[25] Individual walls of buildings show a continuity of tradition from Lydian times into the Achaemenid period, with walls constructed of locally available materials: stones and mud. This is perhaps to be expected, as the materials available locally had not changed; the marked similarity of construction may be an indicator of Lydian survivors of Cyrus' sack. The small fieldstones and riverstones used in construction were carefully laid in more or less level courses in mud mortar, sometimes with attention paid to the pattern of the stones and usually with attention paid to such critical structural considerations as the strength and stability of walls at their corners. The few excavated remains of houses thus combine a continuity of building traditions from the pre-Achaemenid Lydian city with practices current elsewhere in this part of the empire.

## Sacred space

Religious customs and their archaeologically discernible effects may vary greatly depending on cultural and temporal context. Sacred spaces reflect, reify, and even spur on social developments, serving as active participants in human interactions with other humans and with the divine. Thus an examination of the cultic areas that have been excavated at Sardis may provide us with insight not only into the changing nature of worship or ceremony, but also into ways these sacred spaces dovetail with social changes.[26] How did religious ceremonies develop in the Achaemenid period? Was there a change from Lydian times – and if so, how does this change inform our understanding of the developing culture of the Achaemenid-period city? How does the sacred space of the Achaemenid period affect our understanding of the city?

25 Hdt. 5.101. Herodotos claims that at the time of the Ionian revolt, in 499, "Most of the houses in Sardis were of reeds, and even those that were of brick had roofs of reed." Examples only of the latter houses have been excavated.
26 A tremendous amount of scholarship has been devoted to the study of sacred landscapes in the archaeological record. For connections between cult practice and social systems, see, e.g., Blagg (1985, 1986). For other kinds of insights that may be drawn from sacred space, see, e.g., Farrington (1992), Alcock (1991), Price (1984), Bradley (1984, 1990), Hall (1976), Marcus (1973).

It is unfortunately impossible to gain a comprehensive sense of the sacred landscape of Achaemenid Sardis, or to understand in detail how it may have differed from that of the Lydian kingdom. Two altars have been excavated, however, that provide key insight into the changes of the Achaemenid period and the role of the sacred in the lives of Sardians at the time: an altar to Artemis, constructed in the Achaemenid period, and an altar originally dedicated to Kybele by the Lydians that was probably converted to a fire altar in Achaemenid times. The two altars lie on the east bank of the current course of the Paktolos, outside the line protected by the fortification wall (see fig. 4). The altar to Artemis is located to the southwest of the city, between the acropolis and the necropolis, west of the Hellenistic temple of Artemis (which faces west, towards the altar and the necropolis). The converted altar to Kybele is farther north, still west of the fortification wall, about half a kilometer downstream from the altar to Artemis. Owing to our lack of knowledge about Sardis' interior, it is impossible to know at this time if the location of these altars is significant.

## The altar to Artemis and syncretism

Literary sources provide a particular kind of information about cult places dedicated to Artemis that has been used extensively in trying to understand the sanctuaries of Sardis. Pausanias, describing events of *c.* 323–322 BC, mentions one Adrastos, who evidently died in the Lamian war (7.6.6): "The Lydians erected a bronze statue of Adrastos himself in front of the sanctuary of Persian Artemis, and wrote an epigram saying that Adrastos met his end fighting against Leonnatos on behalf of the Greeks." That an altar to Artemis at Sardis was held in great respect by the Persians is demonstrated in Xenophon's account of Cyrus the Younger quizzing one Orontas who was engaged in treachery against him (*Anabasis* 1.6.7): "Is it not the case," said Cyrus, "when again you learned your real [lack of] power, that you went to the altar of Artemis and said that you repented, and did you not persuade me, giving me tokens of faith again and receiving them from me?" Where was the sanctuary, and who was Persian Artemis?[27]

An altar has been excavated at the west end of the Hellenistic temple of Artemis in the sanctuary of Artemis on the east bank of the Paktolos. It was discovered by the first expedition to Sardis, led by H.C. Butler between 1910 and 1914, and was re-excavated by the Harvard/Cornell expedition in 1969 and 1970.[28] The altar is built of "calcareous tufa" blocks; as preserved, it consists of three steps on top of a single-course euthynteria, or leveling course

27 For a discussion of Artemis-Anahita, perhaps to be identified with "Persian Artemis," see Brosius (1998).
28 Published by Frazer and Hanfmann (1975) and analyzed by Ratté (1989b:216–217). This discussion draws on these reports. For definitive publication, see Ratté (forthcoming).

**Fig. 16** Sardis: view of the Artemis altars LA 1 and LA 2, looking south.

(fig. 16), measuring 8.14 m by 8.82 m. The altar is a solid masonry structure, stepping in evenly on its north, west, and south sides to a height of 1.18 m. The third step is the only one preserved on all four sides, with a dimension of 6.10 m by 6.80 m; setting marks show that there was originally at least one more step above this. The blocks are individually cut to fit their neighbors; many of those around the edges are tied to adjacent blocks with iron staple clamps set in lead poured into I-shaped cuttings (fig. 17). The excavators in 1969 and 1970 believed the altar was faced in marble and reconstructed it to resemble the oblong altar of Poseidon at Cape Monodendri.[29]

The dating of this monument seems secure. The specific masonry techniques of the building are not helpful for dating, as they are without parallel at Sardis.[30] Significantly, the only other stepped monuments at Sardis are two Achaemenid-period tombs, the Pyramid Tomb and Tomb 813. This alone might indicate an Achaemenid-period date for the altar. And the finds from within the altar demonstrate a secure Achaemenid-period date: a fragment of a skyphos, a fragment of a stemmed dish, three fragments of a cup, and – most importantly – a fragment of a lamp nozzle and a sherd of an Achaemenid bowl.[31]

29 Ratté (1989b:217–218).
30 Ratté comments (1989b:91): "This structure stands apart from the other monuments in the catalogue in several respects, including the building material, technical details such as the plain staple clamps, and the building type."
31 The lamp is L69.10/8036; the Achaemenid bowl was uninventoried. For Achaemenid bowls, see ch. 8 below.

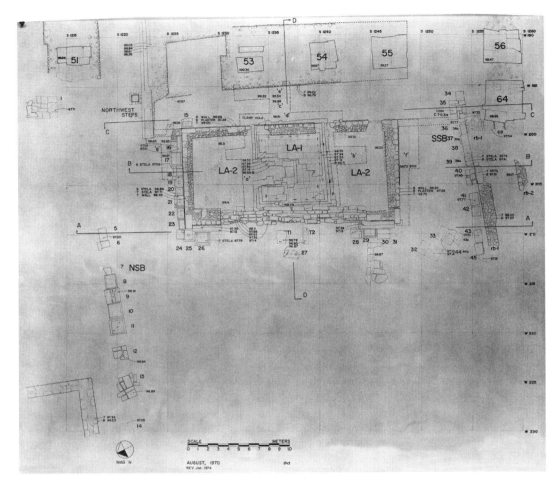

**Fig. 17** Sardis: structure LA and adjacent monuments: condition in 1970.

The altar is at the site of the Hellenistic temple to Artemis. The likelihood of continuity of cult suggests the Achaemenid-period altar was sacred to Artemis; its form is a traditional local one. This suggests a possible continuation of earlier religious practices at Sardis in the Achaemenid period and the worship of a local deity under Achaemenid hegemony. It has been suggested the cult was an offshoot of that of Ephesian Artemis.[32] The identification of the deity worshiped at the Sardian altar as a local version of Artemis is borne out in addition by the local inscriptions that mention Artemis of Sardis. Artemis of Sardis was an important goddess of western Anatolia and figures in many of the Lydian-language Achaemenid-period inscriptions

32  See Hanfmann (1987).

from Sardis itself (see chapter 5); it seems reasonable to suppose this altar was sacred to Artemis in the Achaemenid period.[33]

The importance of such a monument in helping us consider the social situation at Sardis in the Achaemenid period is great. This large and elaborate altar, perhaps faced in marble, was built in the Achaemenid period to a local goddess. The altar is not an Achaemenid Persian shape, but rather reflects the religious architectural traditions of the Ionian Greek cities. The addition of steps is a key point, however: steps of this nature are an important feature of Persian fire altars, as they are illustrated in the reliefs adorning the royal tombs at Naqsh-i Rustam and on seals impressed on the Persepolis Fortification tablets.[34] N.D. Cahill has argued convincingly that the Achaemenid-period tomb at nearby Taş Kule, between Sardis and Phokaia, has cuttings, including steps, that would have served as a fire altar in front of its eastern face.[35] The structure of the Artemis altar is thus a remarkable and important hybrid of the East Greek form with the Persian fire altar form.[36]

The freedom to worship particular gods, or to worship in a particular way, is indicated also by the presence at Sardis of a sealstone showing a Neo-Babylonian worship scene, carved in a Neo-Babylonian style (see fig. 95).[37] This seal, of course, does not prove that its owner worshiped in the Neo-Babylonian manner, but it may suggest that. The large number of Neo-Babylonian worship seals impressed on the Persepolis Fortification tablets, some of which must be new productions rather than heirloom curiosities, demonstrate that many of the seals were serving a particular clientele who specifically wanted that imagery.[38] There are also significant references to Babylonians at Persepolis in the Persepolis Fortification texts: these facts strongly suggest that Babylonians continued their religious traditions under the Achaemenids. They may, perhaps, even have continued them when they moved to other areas of the empire such as Sardis.

We do not know what form worship may have taken at the altar to Artemis. One seal from Persepolis shows how complicated Achaemenid worship might be, even in the Persian heartland. PFS 75 (fig. 18), retrieved from multiple impressions on the Fortification tablets, shows one figure pouring a libation (?) on to a fire altar, while another brings a horned quadruped

33 The connection between the goddess worshiped at this altar and "Persian Artemis" is not clear.
34 For fire altars, see Stronach (1985), Schippmann (1971), Erdmann (1941).
35 Cahill (1988).
36 The importance of assuming architectural features from another culture is explored in Dodge (1990).
37 See chapter 7 for a more complete discussion of this seal, IAM 5133.
38 Root (1998).

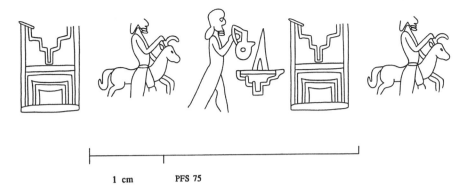

**Fig. 18**
Persepolis
Fortification seal
75, composite
drawing of
impression.

1 cm          PFS 75

to, presumably, a sacrifice – all in front of the facade or door of a temple or palace, or, perhaps, another fire altar.[39] Although we cannot assume this is a literal representation of actual ritual, the combination of figures demonstrates how complex rituals at altars may have been in the Achaemenid period, and how little we understand them. Another Achaemenid seal even shows an animal sticking down into a fire on an altar![40] The new and elaborate, hybrid-style, altar to Artemis and the altar to Kybele discussed below may perhaps have seen use as fire altars and also as sacrificial altars where animals and other offerings were burned in the flames – for worship, as well as religious structures, might take on hybrid forms in Achaemenid Sardis.[41]

Great effort and much money were expended in the Achaemenid period to build this large and glorious altar to a local deity in a newly contrived hybrid style. We do not know if private individuals or public officials spearheaded such an initiative, but the financial capability to build the altar existed and so did the freedom to build. This demonstrates the openness of the Achaemenid administration to the continuation of earlier religious practices in an ostentatious and very public manner, even in the city that was the satrapal capital.

## The altar to Kybele and conversion

A different approach is perhaps to be seen at another part of the site. On the eastern bank of the Paktolos river, about half a kilometer to the north of the Artemis altar, a gold refinery prospered in Lydian times (fig. 19).[42]

39 Garrison (2000:142). See also Garrison and Root (1996/1998:95), Garrison and Root (forthcoming).
40 Moorey (1979).
41 For a study exploring the role of religion and acculturation, the role of imperial power in the cults of the empire, see Millett (1995).
42 Ramage and Craddock (2000), Ramage (1987:10–12).

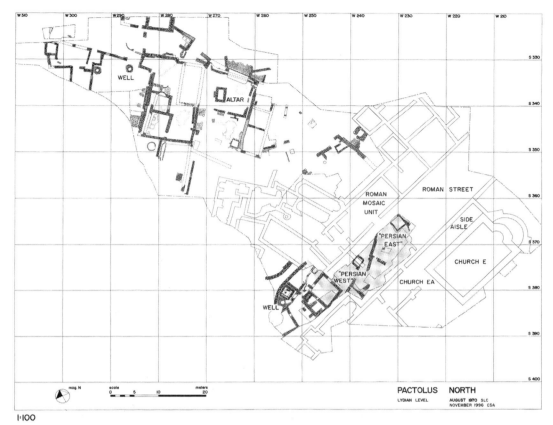

1:100

**Fig. 19** Sardis: Paktolos north Lydian level (plan).

It consisted of small ovens and cupels for smelting, loosely grouped about an open space. In its middle was a small free-standing rectangular altar with a lion at each corner, apparently sacred to the goddess Kybele.[43] At the southeastern edge of the refinery area was a fountain-house. There is no evidence that the gold refinery continued in use after the Persian conquest of the city;[44] the altar in its center was rebuilt, probably in the Achaemenid period (fig. 20), as was the fountain-house (see below).

The altar was 1.75 m high, 3.10 m long and 2.05 m deep, built of roughly dressed gneiss laid in a mud mortar.[45] Both the interior and exterior faces

43 Ramage and Craddock (2000:72–81).
44 Ramage and Craddock (2000:78–80), Hanfmann (1983:37). This seems surprising, given the evidence that gold-mining, -refining, and -working continued to be important at Sardis in the Achaemenid period, and that coins were minted at the Achaemenid city. The refinery may have been moved farther from the city, so that the noxious fumes associated with smelting lead alloys were less offensive and dangerous to city-dwellers.
45 Information from excavators' notebook (PN V:93–105), Hanfmann (1983:36–37), and Ramage and Craddock (2000).

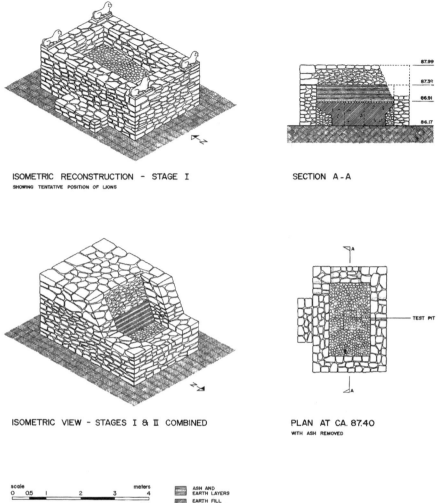

**Fig. 20** Sardis: Paktolos North: altar of Kybele (plan, isometrics, and section).

of the walls were squared; the interior was filled with packed rubble and disintegrated mudbrick, with a cobbled surface covered with at least eleven layers of alternating clay and ash, with a few small fragments of bone and horn in the ash, and with occasional very fine layers of white burned bone. The altar had a coping of *c.* 0.5 m, and on each of the four corners was a crouching lion, carved of limestone, probably facing west.[46] The altar underwent major reconstruction, apparently in the Achaemenid period: the

46  Ratté (1989a); for the orientation, Ramage and Craddock (2000:72–74).

lions were removed from the corners and carefully placed in the interior of
the altar, which was built up higher out of larger, coarser layers of gneiss
on the exterior and schist and limestone on the interior.[47] The top showed
clear traces of burning. Thus we see the reconstruction of a pre-Achaemenid
Lydian altar to Kybele, incorporating the lions into the newly heightened superstructure, with burning on its top.

It has been suggested that this represents the conversion of the structure
to a fire altar.[48] A fire altar might conform to the practices of Mazdaism;[49]
although there is no mention in the excavators' reports of bone in the up-
permost layer of burning, the seals mentioned before show burnt sacrifice
might be associated with fire altars in the Achaemenid period. The fire altar
at Taş Kule mentioned above demonstrates the presence of Mazdaism in the
near vicinity and underscores the possibility that such practices may have
been introduced also at Sardis. This converted altar would form a telling
contrast to the continuation of local practices seen in the altar to Artemis
discussed above.

Ample literary evidence exists of a sanctuary to Kybele at Sardis (Hdt.
5.102): "Sardis was set alight and also the temple of the goddess Kybebe,
the epichoric goddess. The Persians were thinking of this when they later
burned the temples in Greece." The marble temple model discovered built
into the late antique synagogue (see chapter 4, fig. 45) may replicate a contemporary temple of Kybele.[50] Literary evidence for fire altars at Sardis is
rather less prevalent, however. Pausanias, himself perhaps from Lydia, describes worship at a fire altar nearby in Lydia (5.27.5 ff.):

> For the Lydians who are called Persians have sanctuaries in the city called
> Hierokaisareia and at Hypaipa. In each of the sanctuaries there is a building
> and in the building are ashes on an altar. But the color of the ashes is other
> than normal. When the magus has gone into the building and piled dry wood
> on the altar, first he sets a tiara on his head, and then he invokes some one
> of the gods, speaking foreign gibberish that no Greek understands. He speaks
> reading aloud from a book. Indeed, it is required that the wood be kindled
> without any fire, and that the bright flames radiate light from the wood.

The converted altar at Sardis may perhaps have been used for such rituals.

If this is the case, the altar in the gold refinery area shows an important
difference to the altar to Artemis. The gold refinery seems to have gone out
of use in the Achaemenid period, and the altar to Kybele with its marble
lions was rebuilt to hide the lions and provide an area for repeated burning,
perhaps as a fire altar. Rather than continuity of religion, here we see the

---

47 Ramage and Craddock (2000:74), Hanfmann (1983:37), and excavators' notebooks.
48 Ramage and Craddock (2000:74).      49 See Herrenschmidt (1980).
50 See Mitten (1964), Hanfmann and Waldbaum (1969:268–269).

co-option and conversion of a sacred monument. The cult of Kybele was apparently discontinued at this structure, which was used instead as a center for a newly imported cult. And yet literary sources indicate the presence of a thriving cult of Kybele in Achaemenid-period Sardis.[51] Taken together with the altar to Artemis, the altar to Kybele shows a complex picture of religious dynamism at Sardis. Some local religious practices were fostered and allowed or even encouraged to continue under the new regime, perhaps as part of the syncretism of religions and deities apparent in the melding of such names as Artemis-Anahita. At the same time, in some areas new religious practices took the place of the old. Although the cult of Kybele continued alive and well elsewhere in Achaemenid Sardis, the altar in the gold refinery was rebuilt and converted to new use, perhaps as a fire altar.

## Temples

A few sculptural representations provide all of the evidence available so far for Achaemenid-period temples at Sardis: none has been excavated, and there are no literary references or epigraphic sources beyond Herodotos' mention of a temple to Kybebe. This silence parallels that of the Lydian period, for which we also have as yet no information on temple architecture – a gap in our knowledge that is made all the more obvious because of the vast temple of Artemis at Ephesos, for which Croesus dedicated columns inscribed with his name. Construction on the Artemision at Ephesos continued into the Achaemenid period, and we may perhaps take the example of the Artemis altar at Sardis to imagine that temple construction to local gods also continued at Sardis under Achaemenid hegemony.

    Two halves of a marble pediment decorated in relief and dating to the Achaemenid period have been found at Sardis, apparently forming part of a temple-shaped mausoleum (see chapter 4, fig. 35). The pediment may attest indirectly to the existence of pedimental temples at Sardis. Such temples are familiar from the contemporary Greek world, generally with columns at fore and sometimes aft and around the sides. Precisely such a structure is shown in the marble model of a temple (see fig. 45), dating to *c.* 540–530 BC.[52] The model may show a temple type that could have been found at Sardis, if we combine it with the form suggested by the sculpted pediment (see chapter 4 for an alternative interpretation). The temple model is probably of the Ionic order (the tops of the columns are broken off), with a detached or semi-attached peripteros. The walls of the cella are decorated with figural decoration consisting of discrete groups of figures in bands like those on

---

51 Rein (1993).
52 S 63.51:5677; the columns may be intended to be semi-attached. See ch. 4 and Appendix 1.

the Ishtar Gate at Babylon, apparently mythological figures in separate but related action groups like the metopes of Temple E at Selinus.[53]

The marble temple model has been identified as a temple of Kybele,[54] and it may suggest an equivalently grand edifice was to be found in contemporary Sardis for the worship of this goddess. But Kybele may not have been the most important goddess of Achaemenid-period Sardis: the common references in Achaemenid-period inscriptions to Artemis of Sardis and the importance of the cult suggest her temple may equally have been so monumentally graced. Although as yet there are no traces of any temple in the Achaemenid-period architecture uncovered at Sardis, the statuary suggests that monumental temples did indeed exist. If the temple model may be taken as a fair indication of the temple types to be found at Sardis in the Achaemenid period, they may have been built in a style or styles that drew heavily on Greek ideas and also on Near Eastern schemes of decoration.

## Water in an urban environment

Constructed waterworks were important to the Persians, even in well-watered Sardis. Achaemenid rulers paid great attention to the use of water throughout the empire. In Persia proper, of course, and in Egypt, the concerted deployment of the qanat technique – probably as a centralized mechanism – took advantage of local conditions to control the water resources advantageously. In Baktria, it seems that the Achaemenids took over the local highly developed techniques of irrigation. In Babylonia, the Murashu archive makes it clear that under the Achaemenids, canal systems and the bureaucracies to support them were maintained and involved high-status enterprise.[55]

Major waterworks had been constructed at Sardis along the Paktolos river, possibly in association with the Lydian gold refinery, with an apsidal fountain-house and channels to carry the water brought up from wells (fig. 21).[56] The water may have played a role in the refining process. The fountain-house was built of rubble set in mud; in the Achaemenid period, its walls were built higher than in the Lydian period and may have

---

53 For a recent discussion of the metopes of Temple E, see Marconi (1994), reviewed in Pedley (1996).

54 See ch. 4. For the Kybele cult, see Rein (1993).

55 Egyptian qanats include those at the el-Kharga oasis: see Briant (1996:491) for Darius at el-Kharga; for Baktria, see Briant (1984), Gardin and Gentelle (1976), Gentelle (1978); for the Murashu family, see Stolper (1985, 1992), Cardascia (1951).

56 Most of the deposits at PN, near the gold refinery, that were called "Persian" at the time of excavation are actually Hellenistic, as reconsideration of the pottery demonstrates. The analysis here is based on discussion with A. Ramage as well as rereading the excavation reports and fieldbooks. See also Ramage and Craddock (2000), Schaeffer et al. (1997), Hanfmann (1983:37).

**Fig. 21** Sardis: PN apsidal structure and Hellenistic wall, looking east.

been reinforced or thickened. This fountain seems to have remained in use throughout the Achaemenid period, finally being abandoned in the third century when the wells were blocked up. The function of the fountain-house must have been different in the Achaemenid period than it had been in the Lydian period, as the refinery was no longer being used for metalworking.

Public waterworks were an investment of time and labor as well as money. They suffered not only from the dilapidations of normal wear and tear, but also from willful misuse.[57] The operation of this fountain-house through the Achaemenid period, therefore, reflects a need for clean available water that made worthwhile the maintenance costs. This may suggest use of water in some civic capacity, or perhaps for irrigating elaborate formal gardens. Such gardens would have required extensive irrigation, even in the generous climate of Sardis. It is therefore possible that the apsidal fountain-house may have served to water formal gardens in the Achaemenid period as well as provide water for thirsty citizens.

## Blatant Persianisms: *paradeisoi*

*Paradeisoi* indicate a different type of Persian presence at Sardis: they were overt Persian imports to Sardis and would have been visible reminders of

---

57 Plutarch, in *Themistokles* 31, describes a statue Themistokles had made and dedicated from the fines he extracted when he caught people stealing and siphoning off water from public water sources in Athens.

the power and tastes of the new Achaemenid elite.[58] Royal gardens planted with exotic flora and populated by exotic fauna were part of the earlier Near Eastern backdrop of imperial expression (e.g., the Assyrians). But there is no evidence, textual or archaeological, suggesting pre-Achaemenid *paradeisoi* at Sardis. There is at present a total gap between the emphatic testimony of ancient authors that *paradeisoi* existed at Sardis in the Achaemenid period and any excavated traces of the same, but from Greek sources it seems clear that more than one satrap laid out formal *paradeisoi* at Sardis, just as the satraps of Hellespontine Phrygia established them at Daskyleion.[59] Some seem to have served as hunting parks; others apparently included imported trees. The order and formality of the gardens was of utmost importance and had ideological ramifications.[60] As part of a widely spread manifestation of specifically Achaemenid Persian tastes and preferences, they may additionally have had the more homely function of providing familiar surroundings and ease of mind to expatriate Persians.

Although some formal gardens may have been laid out within the city's confines, that of Tissaphernes certainly lay outside the city walls. In the time of Tiribazos' satrapy, Agesilaos ravaged the *paradeisos* (Dio. Sic. 14.80.2): "Coming into the country as far as Sardis, he destroyed the garden and the *paradeisos* of Tissaphernes, which had been carefully and expensively laid out with plants and all other things that contribute to luxury and the peaceful appreciation of good things." Cyrus the Younger also planned gardens at Sardis and worked on them in person, as well as showing around them such distinguished guests as the Spartan Lysander.[61] Apparently each of these satraps, viewed at least by the Greeks as particularly powerful Persians, went to the trouble and expense of laying out and planting formal gardens.

The appearance of such gardens has been recently suggested by excavations at Pasargadae.[62] Pavilions with many columns form an integral part of a series of formal rectilinear gardens, each with trees and shrubs laid out in straight lines. Like moving past a modern vineyard planted in regiments of individual vines, walking or riding along the paths of such a garden would create a constant sense of linear rearrangement as new vistas opened down

---

58 For *paradeisoi*, see, e.g., D. Stronach (1978), Dandamaev (1984). For one at Sardis, see Descat (1992). For the Mesopotamian tradition of royal parks, see Oppenheim (1965).

59 The lack of excavated *paradeisoi* at Sardis may be in part due to erosion: literary testimonia suggest they were laid out in the river valley, where erosion and soil deposition have made their discovery through excavation most unlikely. For Daskyleion, see Bakır (1991, 1995, 1997), Ateşlier (1997). For early work, see Akurgal (1956). *Paradeisoi* were also said to have been laid out at Sidon; see Clermont-Ganneau (1921).

60 See Briant's discussion of gardens (1996:98–99, 245–251, 456–459); and Stronach (1989b, 1990). See also Tuplin (1996:80–131).

61 Xen., *Oikonomikos* 4.20–22; cf. also Cicero, *de senectute* 59.

62 Stronach (1994a).

the rows of plants or along diagonals. The gardens were irrigated by means of finely dressed stone watercourses. The placement of buildings and – in the case of Pasargadae – thrones was carefully aligned to the garden beds.

The ideology of power behind the strict alignment of the *paradeisos* at Pasargadae was profound; the excavator comments:[63]

> [T]he manner in which the central axis of the principal garden of Cyrus was made to fall directly in line with the permanent throne in the main portico of one of the two major palatial buildings at Pasargadae, Palace P, provides an unequivocal demonstration of the way in which, from the second half of the sixth century BC onward, a recognizable symbol of power at the apex of a garden design could be used to imbue a visual, axial avenue with potent indications of authority.

The rectilinear nature of the garden may also be a geometrical articulation of the ideology inherent in the title "king of the four quarters." The unguarded, open *paradeisoi* may indeed have been intended as microcosms of the Achaemenid empire, ideally "a well-ordered, productive estate, free from external and internal disruption."[64] Thus the construction of *paradeisoi* at Sardis was of profound ideological importance, and the role they play in Greek narratives demonstrates the impact they made on the mind of the foreign beholder. *Paradeisoi* were a recognizably Persian import to Sardis, an import of a specifically Persian notion of civilization and of empire.

## Public space

Archaeological exploration at Sardis has investigated few public spaces or monuments from the Achaemenid period other than the cult centers discussed already. Some monuments are known to us, however, through mention in the literary sources, usually Greek. The *paradeisoi* discussed above fall into this category, as do several other important public monuments. As might be expected, the literary sources mention public buildings rather than private ones, with an emphasis on the military and on the political.

### Exedra

A reconnaissance platform of white stone, probably marble or limestone, was said by Strabo to have been built by the Persians on the summit of Mt. Tmolos, affording a view of the surrounding area and particularly the

---

63 Stronach (1994a:3).
64 Stronach (1994a:9), after Weiskopf (1989:14); see also Briant (1996:98–99, 245–251, 456–459).

Kaÿster river valley to the south of Sardis. He says (13.4.5): "Tmolus lies above Sardis, a blessed mountain, having at its summit a lookout post, an *exedra* of white stone, a Persian work, from which are visible the plains all around, and especially the plain of the Cayster." Such reconnaissance platforms were probably a common feature of ancient societies, although few have been specifically identified as such – but without satellite technology to assist in military operations, lookout posts located high in the hills would have been essential for advance warning of others' movements.

The platform mentioned by Strabo is perhaps to be identified with the area recently discovered on Mt. Keldağ, apparently an archaic sanctuary, which does indeed afford such a view.[65] The area was of prime military importance, commanding the long fertile river valleys to north and south, and protecting the pass over the Tmolos range that leads directly into Sardis' own backyard. The use of white stone may have been due simply to expediency, to the availability of white stone from the immediate area. Alternatively, it may have been intended to have a deterrent effect, a sort of ever-visible lookout to warn potential intruders of troops deployed and scouts on guard against attack, to deflect their approach before it was even attempted.

## Residential palace

The residential palace, used by Croesus and probably also by the Persian satraps, is currently known to us only through literary references. Palaces were of crucial importance to the makeup of Achaemenid cities, as they were used for public audiences with the satrap – or the king, if he was in residence.[66] Greek sources tell us that Sardis' palace was built by Croesus and had remarkable continuity in various official functions. It was constructed of mudbrick and was apparently well fortified;[67] it still stood after the conquest of Cyrus, through the entire Achaemenid period, through the arrival of Alexander, and long into the Roman period. It was converted into a meeting-house for elders, perhaps in the Hellenistic period. Before this, it probably served as the residential palace for the Persian governors of the city: although there is no evidence for this at Sardis, in other capitals of the empire such as Susa and Babylon, the Achaemenids occupied earlier palaces as well as (eventually) building public audience halls of typical Achaemenid type.[68] Thus the palace served as the governmental headquarters for the

---

65 See publications by Uğur and Rose-Lou Bengisu, forthcoming.
66 For audiences, see Kaptan (1996), Borchhardt (1980). For the Achaemenid palace at Susa and the associated audience hall, see, e.g., Pillet (1914), Amiet (1974, 1994), Boucharlat (1990a, 1997).
67 See Bacchylides (*Epinikia* 3.32) and Herodotos (1.9; 1.34).
68 For Susa, see Boucharlat (1990a, 1997).

**Fig. 22** Sardis: Lydian defensive walls on the north side of the acropolis.

Lydian kingdom and as the point of convergence for the council of elders in the Roman period, and it may have been the seat of the Achaemenid satraps as well.[69]

Archaeological explorations on the ridge at Sardis called ByzFort did not produce clear traces of a building that was necessarily a palace, but the monumental ashlar Lydian terrace walls containing this spur of the acropolis and other parts of its north slope formed just the sort of location that would have been likely for a palatial situation (fig. 22). Specifically satrapal palaces have not yet been uncovered in other satrapies of the empire, although excavations at Daskyleion are targeting areas that may

69  Pliny, *Naturalis Historia* 35.172; Plutarch, *An seni respublica gerenda sit* 4 (785E); idem, *De Herodoti malignitate* 24. See esp. Vitruvius 2.8.9–10: "Itaque nonnullis civitatibus et publica opera et privatas domos etiam regias a latere structas licet videre...Croesi domus, quam Sardiani civibus ad requiescendum aetatis otio seniorum collegio gerusiam dedicaverunt."

elucidate our understandings of satrapal palaces. The discovery of distinctively Achaemenid architectural elements such as animal protome capitals here and there in the empire, however, suggests the existence of grand official structures built in the Persian manner in far-flung regions of the empire (including the western periphery).[70] So far, no remnants of such items have been discovered at Sardis, but future excavation may turn up these or similar elements of imperial public architecture. Moreover, numerous representations in sculpture found in Achaemenid-period Anatolian contexts echo Persian rites of holding audience (see chapter 4). These representations suggest a range of performative aspects of satrapal authority that must have had a physical backdrop of palatial architecture: such architecture probably reflected heartland modes.

## Conclusion

Although our only way of understanding the urban composition of Sardis at the moment is through its monuments, the architectural remains of Achaemenid-period Sardis do indeed shed light on the concerns and practices of people from all walks of society living in the city. The private practices of non-elite individuals left their archaeologically discernible marks in the form of refuse pits and terrace walls, house walls and the dirt thrown up from perhaps illicit looting after the sack of the city. Through literary sources and excavation, we may describe the appearance of domestic structures of Sardis in the Achaemenid period: small stones laid in mud mortar formed the socles of walls that were finished in mudbrick and probably thatched. This follows the patterns of pre-Achaemenid times, as is to be expected. One wall sunk into the slope of the hill may be part of a pit house or may function as a retaining wall for the slope behind: such landscaping efforts probably also conform to earlier practices. The private architecture of the non-elite therefore attests to the strong continuity of pre-Achaemenid tradition and probably of a part of the population of Sardis. But this is only part of the societal picture at Sardis.

Whereas private structures are lacking so far from excavated Achaemenid Sardis, public monuments are better represented. These public monuments fall into several main categories: administrative, religious, and utilitarian. The palace of Croesus was of course in some ways a private structure, in that it seems to have served as home for Croesus and his family; but it certainly had a public function as well as being the seat of the government. Its highly

---

70 In the west, animal protome capitals have been found at, e.g., Sidon and on Kypros; Roman versions from Ephesos may hearken back to local Achaemenid predecessors.

public function in the Roman period, along with the common phenomenon of functional continuity, suggests it served as residence and administrative headquarters for the Achaemenid satraps at Sardis as well.

Achaemenid Sardis' sacred ideologies and practice are suggested by religious structures: the altar to Artemis and the converted altar to Kybele have been explored archaeologically and show the dynamically different ways Achaemenid presence affected the city's ceremonies. Sculptural evidence suggests there may additionally have been at least one pedimental columned temple, a structure that links Sardis to Greek cultic practices. The architectural remains of Achaemenid-period Sardis therefore demonstrate the syncretism of cult attested to in inscriptions and literary sources as well, and show Sardis to have been a locus for the development of new eclectic practices that combined the influence of east and west as well as indigenous traditions. Other monuments with profound ideological importance – *paradeisoi* – are spoken of by Greek authors in a manner that attests to the efficacy of the projected impact of these specifically Persian imports on a Greek audience.

Public structures of a more utilitarian function include the fountain-house by the Paktolos stream, an edifice possibly built during the Lydian kingdom to aid in refining gold and kept up in Achaemenid times. As it apparently had no wall in the Achaemenid period, it seems likely it was open to public use and provided water to the various inhabitants of the city as well, perhaps, as to new phenomena like the *paradeisoi*. Also of great practical public use were the military structures of the Achaemenid period: the exedra/lookout on Mt. Tmolos, and the refortifying of the city defense walls at Sardis itself. The importance of being able to fortify Sardis would have been clear after the Ionian revolt even if not before, and the reconstruction of the fortification wall in the Achaemenid period demonstrates the time, effort, and money the Achaemenid administration was willing to invest in securing this important city.

Achaemenid-period Sardis was complex, thriving, and cosmopolitan. Private homes seem to have been built along much the same lines as before. This may attest to the continuity of the pre-Achaemenid Lydian population at Sardis, a continuity attested to also by the use of the Lydian language in inscriptions into the Roman period. But life at Sardis did not remain entirely unchanged by the arrival of Achaemenid presence in the city; just as the ceramic assemblage demonstrates a shift in emphasis (see chapter 8), so too the architectural remains show new developments in the social patterns of the city. Cults became more eclectic, more syncretic, more encompassing of multiple traditions under one rubric. Certain Persian ideologies and delights were manifested in the imported concept and matter of the *paradeisoi*. The administration may have continued to occupy the earlier governmental palace, symbolizing their willingness to work with pre-existing conditions and traditions so clearly shown in religious architecture. And the city was refortified, indicating the confidence of the Achaemenid administration in the inhabitants of the city and demonstrating in the most obvious way possible the profound importance of the city to its new Achaemenid leaders.

# The urban structure of Achaemenid Sardis: sculpture and society

## Adorning Achaemenid cities: sculpture in the empire

Built monuments are but one aspect of Sardis' civic appearance. Sculptures, another important part of the city's public aspect, allow us to explore Sardis' urban appearance and cultural makeup, and to connect it to the rest of the empire. Remnants of large-scale sculpture from elite contexts around the Achaemenid empire demonstrate a broad range of themes and formats. The iconography of the imperial centers was reproduced and adapted through-out the empire, often rendered in regional styles. Two additional issues flesh out the system of interactions: items might be made in one place but trans-ported to another part of the empire; and items might be made according to the stylistic specifications of a particular patron, reflecting heartland or other regional styles. In this way, sculptures repeat and reinforce the sense of artistic production in different locales of the empire suggested by seals (see chapter 7).

If we were to postulate that satrapal capitals would exhibit sculptural relationships of formats, themes, and styles similar to the nexus found in seal carving, what kinds of sculptures might we expect to find at Sardis in the Achaemenid period? A brief survey of sculptures from around the empire may help to illuminate the question.

Persepolis offers evidence of great diversity in its sculptural remains and conveys some idea of what we would expect to see at a royal, heartland, capital. The palaces of Darius and Xerxes are embellished with relief sculp-tures, resonant with imperial overtones.[1] The reliefs adorning the Apadana staircases are complemented by the sculptures decorating the doorjambs in the imperial palaces. The Apadana reliefs show the peoples of the realm bringing gifts to the king, who sits enthroned as his subjects are about to be ushered before him (fig. 23). The reliefs on the doorjambs in the palaces show a variety of themes, including the king enthroned (and held aloft by rejoicing subjects) and the Persian hero figure conquering various animals and monsters (fig. 24). These sculptures were carved in a newly designed style that drew on elements of sculptural tradition from throughout the empire to create a fresh syncretic style that was uniquely Achaemenid.[2] But the royal capitals include free-standing imports as well as the reliefs on

1 See Root (1979) and Schmidt (1953); also Amiet (1974).
2 For the style of these sculptures, see Root (1979), Roaf (1983).

**Fig. 23**
Persepolis:
audience scene
from the
Treasury, *c.*
522–486 BC.

the palaces: a Greek marble statue of the "Penelope" type was brought to Persepolis, presumably from Greek lands over 2,400 km away (fig. 25).[3] Similarly, at Susa was excavated a statue of Darius made in Egyptian Heliopolis of Egyptian granite and with hieroglyphic renditions of the peoples of the lands on its base – this now headless statue was only one of several such.[4] Also excavated at Susa were fragments of a colossal statue of Darius that probably showed him as a royal hero, rather than as crowned king (he wears strapped non-royal shoes).[5]

As seen already, Darius had a monumental relief carved into the cliff face at Bisitun, showing himself receiving divine favor from Ahuramazda as he overcame rebellions to secure his power as Great King (see fig. 3).[6] He and succeeding kings embellished their rock-cut tombs at Naqsh-i Rustam near Persepolis with reliefs bearing powerful messages of piety, power, and divine sanction (fig. 26).[7] Thus, relief sculptures in highly visible places – above key roads, at tombs, on palaces – might be exploited to reaffirm the importance of kingship and the power, rectitude, piety, and accomplishments of the king. They embedded his reign in the most ancient Mesopotamian traditions and symbolically equated the king with a god, by placing him in positions previously reserved only for deities.[8]

These relief sculptures represent other historical individuals as well, a matter of importance in thinking about satrapal capitals, where the visual

3 Schmidt (1953).
4 For the Egyptian statue found at Susa, see Kervran et al. (1972, 1974) as well as discussion of the hieroglyphs on the statue's base in Yoyotte (1974), Perrot (1974).
5 For the hero statue from Susa, see Scheil (1929:57–58), de Mecquenem (1947:47), Schmidt (1953:29–33). Parrot (1967) has a good view of the head fragment. See also Boucharlat (1990b).
6 For the identification of Ahuramazda, see Root (1979:210–213).
7 Schmidt (1970).    8 Dusinberre (2002).

**Fig. 24**
Persepolis: Palace
of Darius, hall,
west side, south
doorjamb relief,
from northeast.
The hero
conquers a
monster.

emphasis might be expected to emphasize people other than the king. At
Bisitun, for instance, Darius is followed by two weapon bearers, identified by some modern scholars as Gobryas and Intaphernes.[9] He steps on
the prostrate and kicking rebel Gaumata; other rebel leaders proceed in
bonds towards Darius. They are differentiated by dress and hairstyle, and
are named with labels.[10] These latter figures, therefore, are carved in a way

9 Schmidt (1970:86). For the identification of the figures, see Luschey (1968).
10 In addition to the label naming Gaumata the Magian, the labels read (in order from left to
   right): "This is Açina, who claimed 'I am king in Elam,'" "This is Nidintu-Bel, who claimed
   '. . . I am king in Babylon,'" "This is Phraortes, who claimed '. . . I am king in Media,'" "This is
   Martiya, who claimed 'I am Imani, king in Elam,'" "This is Ciçantakhma, who claimed 'I am
   king in Asagartia . . . ,'" "This is Vahyazdata, who claimed '. . . I am king,'" "This is Arkha, who
   claimed '. . . I am king in Babylon,'" "This is Frada, who claimed 'I am king in Margiana,'"
   and "This is Skunkha the Scythian." See Kent (1953:134–135), Lecoq (1997:215–217).

**Fig. 25**
Persepolis:
marble statue of
a Greek woman.

**Fig. 26** Naqsh-i
Rustam: Darius
I's tomb. Upper
main panel: king,
god, fire altar,
thronebearers.
Dignitaries, and
mourners. View
from SE.

that represents a *people*, but their names clearly indicate their *individual* personae as well. In a rather different way, at Naqsh-i Rustam, the tomb of Darius shows him borne aloft by the peoples of the realm, differentially carved and labeled with their ethnicity to make the point particularly clear. But he is also followed by specific Persians, again labeled to demonstrate their individuality.[11] The importance of the reliefs' visual rhetoric could be increased by copying it: at least two other royal capitals, Babylon and Susa, displayed copies of the Bisitun relief.[12] The labeled figures carved on the base of the Egyptian statue found at Susa replicate the system of Naqsh-i Rustam.

Large-scale sculptures at the royal capitals were not confined to portrayals of humans. Renderings of the figure in the winged disk (Ahuramazda?) have been found at Persepolis, Bisitun, and Susa (fig. 27). In addition to human figures, various reliefs at Persepolis and glazed bricks at Susa display heraldic sphinxes, parading lions, and lions overcoming bulls (figs. 28 and 29). These animals were all charged with meaning in an Achaemenid context and reinforce a sense of cosmic order and kingly might. The sculptural decorations at Persepolis also include free-standing stone figures of animals, especially couchant lions, standing bulls and ibexes, and séjant dogs (fig. 30). There are a wide variety of vast animal protome capitals as well (fig. 31). All of these sculptures might be found at satrapal capitals; the animal protome capitals are a specifically Achaemenid invention and might therefore be seen as a particularly strong statement of imperial control if found at outlying centers.

It would be surprising to have preserved many free-standing stone statues of royal or noble people, given the preponderance of precious metals described in literature. These textual references give us a sense of the sculptural repertoire of the empire at its center. Thus we hear of a statue made of solid gold of Darius' favorite wife, Irtashduna (Artystone)[13] – a woman whose personal seal is preserved on the Persepolis Fortification tablets. Gold was also set aside for statues of the king and his mother.[14] Another golden statue, of the goddess Anahita, was said to have been set up by Artaxerxes II, as well as statues made of unspecified materials set up in the capital cities of Babylon, Susa, Ekbatana, Persepolis, Baktra, Damaskos, and Sardis.[15] In addition to the statue of Artystone, other royal statues include a (stone?) statue of Xerxes that was overturned by Alexander's soldiers at

11 DNc and DNd: "Gobryas, a Patischorian, spear-bearer of Darius the King," and "Aspathines, bowbearer, holds the battle-axe of Darius the King." See Lecoq (1997:224–225), Kent (1953:140); also Schmidt (1970).

12 For Babylon, see Seidl (1976). For the possibility that another version exists in glazed brick fragments from Susa, see Muscarella (1992). For the version of the Apadana reliefs found at Meydancikkale in Anatolia, see below.

13 Hdt. 7.69. See also commentary in Brosius (1996:84–85). For refined gold, see Ramage and Craddock (2000).

14 Brosius (1996:85 n. 2).

15 Discussed, with bibliography, in Olmstead (1948:471 n. 50). Most recently, see Brosius (1998).

**Fig. 27**
Persepolis:
Ahuramazda
symbol on north
jamb of east door
of the Tripylon.

Persepolis.[16] Greek sources refer to a golden vine and a golden plane tree
that stood by the king's bed at Susa;[17] we can only assume there were other
statues of similar unique sorts.

16 Plutarch, *Alexander* 37.3.
17 Pythios the Lydian gave the plane tree and vine to Darius; see Hdt. 7.27. Although the Greeks
  claim Theodoros of Samos made the plane tree, it would fit well as a sculptural type with
  long-standing Near Eastern traditions, and may in fact have been a Near Eastern production.
  One need only think of the royal tombs of Ur, with gold-and-lapis rams in golden thickets,
  or the floral headdresses of Queen Pu-Abi and her attendants, to see the history such golden
  trees had in the Near East – a history continued in the Assyrian queens' tombs at Nineveh. For
  Ur, see Zettler and Horne (1998), Woolley (1934); for the Assyrian tombs, see Damerji (1999,
  esp. pls. 42–45).

**Fig. 28**
Persepolis:
Darius' palace,
south stairway,
balustrade,
center. Sphinx
panel close-up.
Now in the
Tehran museum.

**Fig. 29**
Persepolis:
Apadana, east
stairs, outer part,
east face, south
side. Lion and
bull.

There does not seem to be a strong tradition of free-standing sculptures of private individuals (as opposed to kings) in Achaemenid culture. But some statues of non-kingly Achaemenid nobles do seem to have existed. Diodorus Siculus (17.17.6) mentions a statue of Ariobarzanes, satrap of Phrygia, set up in an Athena temple in the Troad. Letters of Arsham, satrap of Egypt,

**Fig. 30**
Persepolis:
mastiff entrance
statue.

**Fig. 31**
Persepolis:
bull-protome
column capitals
and lion-griffin-
protome column
capitals.

record equestrian statues of himself.[18] He employed a western Asiatic sculptor to create the images: the fact that the sculptor was neither Persian nor Egyptian, and yet was working between Egypt and Susa for Arsham, is significant in thinking of the sculpture adorning satrapal capitals through the empire, and the potential versatility and mobility of sculptors. The statue of the Egyptian Udjahorresnet, a high officer and naval commander under the Egyptian kings and priest under Kambyses, shows that sculpted renditions

18 Driver (1957:32, 71–74), Root (1979:23, 129). Root points out (personal communication, 1999) that her characterization of Arsham's sculptor as Egyptian is wrong.

of individuals might be found.[19] Importantly, Udjahorresnet wears a Persian robe and jewelry – here is sculptural evidence for the same kind of sartorial koine as that found at Sardis (see chapter 6). At least one statue may also have existed that showed Darius in a transitional state between noble and king: Herodotos refers to a stone sculpture of a man on horseback, with the inscription, "Darius, son of Hystaspes, by the virtue of his horse and of his groom, Oibares, won the kingdom of Persia."[20] Although only a fraction of the sculptures that must once have adorned the empire survives, still they give an idea of the richly varied themes and formats exploited by artists and patrons.

Elsewhere in the empire, central Achaemenid iconography and ideas were reworked in local styles and sometimes placed in new contexts on local structures. Even a quick overview – by no means intended to be exhaustive – can give us a sense of the broad range of themes and contexts. Thus, in Egypt are a temple built and decorated in the reign of Darius at el-Kharga oasis, showing Darius in typical Egyptian style worshiping and being nourished by the Egyptian gods; tombs with reliefs of individuals in the service of the court; and four fragmentary stelae set up in the name of Darius at the canal joining the Nile and the Red Sea.[21] The statue of Darius found at Susa was originally set up at Heliopolis: unlike the el-Kharga reliefs, it is carved in central Achaemenid style, with a trilingual inscription in Old Persian, Elamite, and Akkadian on the garment as well as a longer hieroglyphic inscription on the base that proclaimed Darius was "both a pious Egyptian warrior-monarch *and* a foreign conqueror."[22] Other Achaemenid sculptures in ancient cultural centers include the copy of Darius' Bisitun inscription set up at the palace at Babylon.[23]

In Anatolia, the amount of sculpture reflecting Achaemenid themes and iconography is great. Again, the following overview attempts merely to give an idea of the sorts of things that might be found. Most of these sculptures are apparently from mortuary contexts. Relief sculptures found all along the western part of Anatolia from Daskyleion to Sardis include stelae with Achaemenid iconography showing the local themes of funerary processions and funerary banquets, rendered in a variety of local styles that tend to be lumped together as "Graeco-Persian:"[24] a marble kline from İkiztepe at Güre with legs that rest on couchant animals that serve as pedestals;[25] reliefs at

19 Vatican 196. Bresciani (1985), Posener (1936:1–26), Lichtheim (1980:36–41), Lloyd (1982), Bares (1996).
20 Hdt. 3.88.
21 For el-Kharga, see, most recently, Gousquet (1996), Grimal (1995), Mathiesen et al. (1995). For Suez, see Posener (1936:46–87), Hinz (1975), Tuplin (1991).
22 See discussion in Kuhrt (1995a:668–669), Kervran et al. (1972), Yoyotte (1974).
23 For the palace at Babylon more generally, see Haerinck (1973).
24 For Daskyleion, see Nollé (1992).     25 Özgen and Öztürk (1996).

**Fig. 32** Xanthos: relief from Building G, BM 313. Horses with Persian conformation and trappings.

Limyra and from Building G at Xanthos showing horses with the conformation and knotted tails and forelocks of Persian horses (fig. 32); the garrison site of Meydancikkale in Kilikia, with its relief that closely parallels the Ionian tribute bearers from the Apadana at Persepolis: bearded figures move to the left, wearing chiton and himation and with their hair in curls at the nape of the neck, bearing cups and other vessels in their upraised hands.[26] The Lykian sarcophagi, mostly from Xanthos, show more examples of imagery influenced by Achaemenid types, including the "satrap sarcophagus" with its funerary banquet.[27] The Nereid Monument at Xanthos boasts reliefs carved in a Greek style that project motifs of the heartland Achaemenid repertoire: a seated authority with a parasol, being presented with tribute or gifts (fig. 33).[28] At Halikarnassos, the Maussolleion was built and elaborated with sculpture during the Achaemenid period; beneath it were discovered a number of alabaster jars, one inscribed in Old Persian cuneiform and Egyptian hieroglyphs: "Xerxes, the Great King."[29] The Maussolleion also included representations of specific individuals, Maussollos and Artemisia.

26 Davesnes et al. (1987), Laroche and Davesnes (1981); also Hermary (1984).
27 Kleemann (1958). For Persian sartorial impact on Lykian monuments, see, e.g., Bernard (1964). For connections between Lykia and Persia, see, e.g., Childs (1981, 1983:229). See also Jacobs (1987), des Courtils (1995). For a recent discussion of Persian-Lykian interactions, see Briant (1997b).
28 For the Nereid Monument, see, e.g., British Museum (1900); Jacobs (1987) examines the sculptures with an eye to ethnic influence. For the parasol, see Miller (1992).
29 For the Maussolleion and its sculptures, see, e.g., Jeppesen (1990), Danish Archaeological Expedition (1981–1997). For the alabastra, see Newton (1862–1863).

**Fig. 33** Xanthos: "satrap" from the Nereid Monument.

Three non-mortuary contexts in western Anatolia that have produced sculpture dating to the Achaemenid period are Labraunda, Assos, and Ephesos. The bearded marble sphinx from the large andron at Labraunda reflects central Achaemenid iconography and ideas but is rendered in a local style (fig. 34).[30] The temple of Athena at Assos, usually dated *c.* 540–530, includes various Achaemenid themes, including two pairs of confronting sphinxes and banqueters hefting Achaemenid bowls.[31] Ephesos, a city with strong Greek and Lydian presence before the Achaemenid period and with an apparently strong Persian presence during the time of Achaemenid hegemony, provides an interesting example of the sorts of hybrids that formed: thus the temple of Artemis, with its Ionic frieze along the parapet sima and the famous *columnae caelatae* probably begun by Croesus and finished in the Achaemenid period, was also adorned with bulls modeled in high relief either on its antae or a propylon before the temple, much like Assyrian and Achaemenid guardian colossi.[32] Ephesos also provides an example of the longevity of Achaemenid iconography that extends far beyond the tomb

30  Gunter (1989).
31  The dating of this temple is a knotty question. My own feeling is that it was most likely built somewhat later than 540–530 and is carved in an archaizing manner. For a similar view, see Gunter and Root (1998). If the temple really dates to 540, the inclusion of the Achaemenid bowls indicates a surprising awareness of Iranian material culture. For the significance of Achaemenid bowls, see chapter 8, and Nylander (1999).
32  The bulls are in the British Museum. Lethaby (1908:12–13) suggests that the heads were attached to the antae. See Bookidis (1967:276, 281) for sima and columns. For the *columnae caelatae*, see, e.g., Muss (1983), Rugler (1988:24–26).

**Fig. 34**
Labraunda:
sphinx.

at Belevi with its lion-griffins: the Roman bouleuterion had columns with double-bull protomes on it.

This overview of Achaemenid-period sculpture lets us hazard a guess as to what we might expect to find at Sardis, if we excavated in the right contexts. It is possible we would unearth funerary monuments of various kinds that employed Achaemenid iconography. Some sort of temple elaboration might reflect imperial themes. We would perhaps come across free-standing statues, perhaps of animals, perhaps of individuals. We might find animal protome capitals. The sculpture would thus include private and public monuments. All of these themes might be more or less explicitly "Persian," with courtiers or specifically Persian garb or embellishment. Many of them would presumably be rendered in a hybrid local style; others would probably be imports, monuments coming into Sardis as gifts or trophies that had nothing to do with Achaemenid imperial stylistic hybrids but much to do with the imperial situation. And some monuments produced at Sardis might have been made in a central Achaemenid court style.

## Decorating the city: sculpture at Sardis

The Achaemenid period sees a complex mix of stylistic and thematic ideas in Sardian statuary (see Appendix 1).[33] As well as Greek, artisans at Sardis adapted Iranian and Mesopotamian sculptural ideas. The sculptors working in the polyethnic environment of the satrapal capital took advantage of multiple influences, establishing new artistic forms and experimenting with the manifestation of new ideas. Sardis was a creative center, combining and recreating multiple pre-existing traditions to establish a wholly new identity.[34]

The types of Achaemenid-period deposits that have been excavated at Sardis affect the information available in the analysis of sculptural remains. As already emphasized, comparatively little has been exposed of Achaemenid-period Sardis. Those sculptures that have been found are almost without exception retrieved from a secondary use context as building blocks in late Roman and Byzantine structures: we do not know how they might originally have been displayed, nor where. Despite the various limiting factors, however, the sculptures of Achaemenid-period Sardis demonstrate significant patterns that tie in to those suggested by other forms of evidence explored in chapters 3, 6, and 7.[35]

While themes and formats may show the influence of imperial Achaemenid iconography, the styles of these sculptures demonstrate the development at Sardis of local, hybrid styles that combine eastern, western, and local traditions. The sculpture of the later sixth century shows stylistic influence from Greece; experts suggest either Ionia or Athens as primary locales for inspiration.[36] In the fifth century, two main Greek styles seem to have influenced local artisans at Sardis: the Ionian "soft style" and the

---

33 I regret I am unable to illustrate certain sculptures now in Manisa and Istanbul.

34 For the importance of public art, public monuments, and private objects in signifying identity, see Hodder (1989).

35 The following characterization of sculpture includes some pieces to which an Achaemenid-period date can only be tentatively assigned. In all cases, the dates given here reflect the opinion of the publishers. Here, I wish only to discuss the plausibly Achaemenid-period sculptures as indicators of trends in cultural life at the satrapal capital.

36 Hanfmann and Ramage (1978:19). See Ridgway (1977:9–10) for the variable influence of geography on style and the need for flexibility of approach.

Cycladic-Thessalian-Boeotian circle.[37] These Greek influences were suggestive rather than determinative: artisans working in Sardis in the Achaemenid period do not seem to have strived to imitate Greek styles but rather to have worked in a milieu in which the ideas inspiring Greek statuary were part of their own concepts of sculpture. Moreover, a patron's choice may have been as much involved in the style of a composition as the artisan's range of associations.[38] Sculptures like free-standing human figures were often sculpted in a Greek style, but with details such as jewelry that firmly located them in cosmopolitan Achaemenid Sardis (cf. chapters 6 and 7).[39] The sculptors also portrayed themes that had originated in the east, like animal friezes and funerary banquets, but that by the mid-sixth century had been completely assimilated into the local repertoire. The sculptures are almost exclusively carved of local marble.

Significantly, many funerary monuments were adorned with Achaemenid iconography. Temples and public buildings of the Achaemenid period have not yet been excavated at Sardis, as discussed in chapter 3, and no significant fragment of their sculptural embellishment has yet turned up from later contexts: we can thus not yet speak of the presence or absence of columns with animal protomes as capitals, nor developments in temple sculptures.[40] Free-standing statues of humans are suggested by the Droaphernes inscription discussed in chapter 5, as well as by several extant examples of stone statues found at Sardis. Many free-standing statues of lions may be dated to the Achaemenid period: lion statues were also known in Lydian Sardis, but their prevalence in the Achaemenid period may suggest influence from Persia. In addition to these monuments, a number of stelae showing the local goddesses Kybele and Artemis have been found, and a few other sculptures that add to our sense of the rich sculptural environment of Achaemenid Sardis, however dimly glimpsed at this distance.

37 Hanfmann and Ramage (1978:19–20).
38 That competent artists could work in multiple different styles, overriding their personal or cultural tastes or practices to produce art in the style of a different milieu, is amply demonstrated by the Petosiris tomb in Egypt. Here a painted relief dating to the end of the fourth century BC shows specifically Egyptian artists manufacturing vessels that are specifically Achaemenid Persian in style. See Lefebure (1924), Root (1979:14), Muscarella (1976). A mishap in learning to produce vessels of this style is published in Frankfort (1950).
39 E.g., Manisa 325, discussed below. Examples of humans carved in a local style but with Achaemenid-style jewelry are known from elsewhere in the empire, as well. See, e.g., the statue of Udjahorresnet, discussed in Cooney (1953). Free-standing statues of humans were of course known not only in Greek lands, but also in, e.g., Egypt, Syria, Mesopotamia, and Iran. The disturbed contexts of the Sardian sculpted human figures make their precise social function(s) difficult to compare with such figure types in other locales.
40 There are a few architectural reliefs which I shall not discuss in this chapter: NoEx 64.5, S69.12, S68.26. See Hanfmann and Ramage (1978:nos. 50, 51, 52).

## Embellishing the dead

### Funerary sculptures

With few exceptions, most of the Sardian funerary sculptures are stelae showing banqueting scenes. Funerary inscriptions are in the Lydian language and usually follow a standard form, naming the person and his father, and invoking the wrath of the gods upon anyone who violates the mortuary arrangements of the dead man.[41] The uniformity of theme in these funerary monuments is striking, especially in contrast to the diversity in burial context.

The earliest of the sepulchral stelae, probably almost a century older than the next oldest monument yet known, does not conform to the type of the later sculptures. It is an inscribed stele with a proposed date of *c.* 520–500 BC,[42] showing a man seated at a table, holding writing implements (Manisa 1).[43] The inscription names the owner of the stele as one Atrastas, son of Sakardas. The portrayal of a seated man is unique at Sardis. Although it was a not uncommon theme in Greek and Etruscan reliefs of the late sixth century, the motif of a seated figure also has a particularly long history in Egyptian funerary reliefs, including those showing scribes.[44] The inscription makes no mention of the occupation of the dead man, but it may perhaps be assumed that the relief portrays him, and that the relief and inscription thus operate as separate and complementary sources of information about the dead man. The inscription mentions Artemis of Ephesos rather than Artemis of Sardis; might Atrastas have been a priest or perhaps an accountant for the holdings of the cult of Artemis at Sardis sent out from Ephesos?

In contrast to the early Atrastas stele, most of the other sepulchral sculptures depict banqueting men, with women and usually also servants attending them. As will be discussed in chapter 6, mortuary ritual in Achaemenid-period Sardis seems to have included the idea of banqueting, with an apparent emphasis on providing the dead with the needed paraphernalia for an eternal banquet. The banquet stelae probably form part of this same picture; the figures they portray represent individuals in a symbolic, rather than veristic, sense, showing a type of individual engaged

---

41 See chapter 5. Use of the masculine gender is here a generalization.
42 Hanfmann and Ramage (1978:55–56).
43 See Hanfmann and Ramage (1978) for sculptures in Manisa and Istanbul.
44 For Greek and Etruscan reliefs, cf. *ibid.* Egyptian funerary reliefs with seated figures begin in the First Dynasty (*c.* 3200–2980 BC). See, e.g., the stele of Merka from Saqqara, in Emery (1958:pl. 39). Funerary reliefs showing scribes are common; the tomb of Horemheb at Saqqara is probably one of the most famous examples. See Stevenson Smith (1990:339–344 with citations).

**Fig. 35** Sardis: S69.14:8047, NoEx 78.1. Pediment.

in a specific activity of significance. But those stelae that include inscriptions naming the individual clearly link the motif of banqueting with the person buried: the depiction becomes a representation not only of the symbolic essentials of the person but also a representation by extension of the person, if not of the person's facial features.

The earliest sculpture portraying a funeral banquet is a pediment for which a date of *c.* 430–420 BC has been proposed based primarily on stylistic considerations, that may have come from a temple-shaped mausoleum (see also chapter 3) (fig. 35). The relief sculpture shows a reclining bearded male at center, with three seated females at the left. A servant at the right brings a vessel to the reclining figure, while another, smaller, servant at the right stands by a laden table.[45] The two later funerary sculptures are both stelae showing banqueters and inscribed with names, presumably those of the dead men. NoEx 77.15 (fig. 36), dating to the fourth century, shows a man reclining on a kline, with a woman seated on its end and a servant standing at its foot. The "Atrastas Stele" in Istanbul, IAM 4030 (not to be confused with Manisa 1, described above), shows a man wearing Iranian clothing reclining on a kline and a woman seated at its foot. Its inscription dates it precisely to 330–329 BC. These are years at the transitional point, in political terms, from the Achaemenid empire to that of Alexander. The stele's Lydian inscription and theme as well as the garb of the man connect

45 Hanfmann (1974a:299), Hanfmann and Erhart (1981).

**Fig. 36**  Sardis:
NoEx 77.15,
IN77.008. Lydian
funerary relief.

it to the themes and ideas of the Achaemenid period. The formula of
the inscription is particularly interesting, as it names the date according
to the Achaemenid formula of regnal year – but the king in question
is Alexander. This stele thus affords an example of the melding of new
impetus with accepted traditions at the end of the Achaemenid period,
just as the Kybele shrine S63.51 (see fig. 45), discussed in part already in
chapter 3, shows a similar mingling at the beginning of the Achaemenid
period.

Two other stelae from Lydia (but not Sardis), now in the Manisa Museum,
are uninscribed but are certainly further examples of Achaemenid-period
funerary stelae. Manisa 172, from Bagis, shows a male figure reclining on a
kline, with a servant holding a fly-whisk standing behind him and a hound
under the kline. Manisa 6225, from Alaşehir, shows a figure reclining on a
kline, with a woman seated at the foot of the couch and a servant behind

her. These stelae are further examples of the multiple traditions underlying the production of funerary monuments in Lydia.

The idea of funerary banquets probably was current in Lydia before the conquest by Cyrus: the preponderance of drinking vessels included in grave assemblages of the Lydian kingdom suggests as much.[46] But the association of *reclining* banqueting with mortuary treatment is apparently a phenomenon of the Achaemenid period. And it is only in the Achaemenid period that people begin to represent banquets in funerary art at Sardis. The motif itself was apparently Mesopotamian – the image from Nineveh of Assurbanipal reclining to banquet with his enthroned wife is well known and has been suggested as a specific prototype for banqueting scenes in western Anatolia (it is of course not funerary).[47] Although no royal Persian reliefs have yet been discovered with scenes of reclining people banqueting, reliefs at Persepolis and Susa show *provisions* for banquets being brought into certain palaces.[48] The image of reclining is widely spread through western Anatolia in the Achaemenid period, being found at Karaburun near Elmalı in Lykia,[49] on funerary stelae from Daskyleion and Ödemiş, and at Altıntaş and Çavuşköy to the east, as well as to the south on the "satrap sarcophagus" from Sidon.[50]

Inclusions in tombs at Sardis suggest that funerary banquets were associated with the elite (see chapter 6); the sculpted funerary stelae add another piece of evidence to this conclusion. The majority of those who had their tombs embellished with sculpture chose scenes of banqueting. Interestingly, those figural stelae that are inscribed not only are inscribed in the Lydian language but also give Lydian names to the dead. Neither of these features need point to the Lydian "ethnicity" of the person entombed; but they do attest that the Lydian language was alive and well, and that elite parents frequently gave their children Lydian names. Thematically influenced from the east and stylistically from the west, the funerary sculptures of Sardis include local characteristics to create a compelling new form.

---

46  See chapter 8.
47  British Museum WA 124920, published in Barnett (1976); see also Reade (1983:figs. 102, 103). For the sculpture as a prototype for western Anatolian scenes of banqueting, see Dentzer (1971, 1982). For the development of banqueting as an iconographic trope in Near Eastern art on which Assurbanipal might draw, see Selz (1983). Ridgway (1977:139–40, brief bibliography 146) disagrees with a Near Eastern origin for the motif of the reclining figure; she apparently thinks it originates in Samos. Others have made a rather good case for the Levant or Kypros as the origin of the prone banquet. For a recent discussion, see Reade (1995).
48  Sancisi-Weerdenburg (1989, 1998). Banquet scenes are thus a motif known from Assyrian palaces and from Achaemenid-period western Anatolia, without representations extant from Achaemenid Persia – this is true also of city reliefs; see Childs (1978:107–108).
49  For this tomb, Mellink et al. (1998), Mellink (1974).
50  For Daskyleion, see notes 24 and 82. For other sites in Anatolia, see Dentzer (1969). For the satrap sarcophagus, see Winter (1894), Kleemann (1958).

**Fig. 37** Sardis:
NoEx 73.1.
Anthemion of a
Lydian grave
stele.

## Funerary stelae without relief sculpture

Stelae from the Achaemenid period, dated on the basis of inscriptions or the
style of their decorative anthemia, have been found at Sardis only in association with rock-cut chamber tombs.[51] The anthemia consist of volutes and
palmettes; the inscriptions are formulaic curses against those who violate
the tombs. Two chamber tombs were found with stelae still *in situ* at their
front: Tomb 813, which had an undecorated limestone stele three meters
tall at its entrance (see chapters 6 and 7), and a fifth-century tomb with a
small inscribed stele "beside and at the end of a long dromos" leading to a
chamber.[52] Other tombs apparently had stelae within the chamber proper;[53]

---

51 This section is based on Hanfmann and Ramage (1978:23–28, 73–76), Ratté (1994a).
52 Buckler (1924:13–14).
53 Butler (1922:83); "these had been preserved but the color designs had disappeared."

it is not clear if they were *in situ* or had been disturbed by robbers in antiquity.

The stelae were tall slender pillars of limestone or marble, crowned with anthemia composed of two Ionic volutes and a palmette, apparently conceived as one unit and arranged in an oval or triangular pattern (fig. 37). The volute-and-palmette anthemia of Samos, by contrast, are more strongly geometrical, and their separate components are more rigidly distinguished one from the other.[54] Although the sculptors of anthemia at Sardis probably knew the work of East Greek anthemion sculptors, the soft organic nature of the Sardian anthemia and the Sardian preference (into the fourth century) for broad floral ornament give the examples from Sardis a different feel from the sharp, crisply carved forms of the Greek stelae. Those stelae carved with relief sculpture were not found with anthemia, but their counterparts at Daskyleion had them, and it is not unlikely that the Sardian versions also finished in a floral crown.

## Human sculpture in the round

Humans sculpted in the round at Achaemenid Sardis are represented by four pieces, all dated solely on the basis of style. The earliest of these, the "Mantle-Wearer" (Manisa 325), dating to *c.* 530–520, is of uncertain sex. Long-haired, bejewelled, and cloaked, it walks forward with arms at its sides. A torso, probably of a kore, S67.37 (fig. 38), was carved around 500; this figure holds a bird or animal in a manner similar to East Greek korai. S59.10 (fig. 39), the upper torso of an Amazon or Artemis, was carved *c.* 510–460. And from the fifth century comes NoEx 63.12 (fig. 40), the upper part of an under-lifesize female torso. With no clue as to the original position of these statues, it is risky to conjecture about their function; but one might envisage them set up in temple precincts, as seems to have been the case at Samos and Ephesos.

Most or all of these statues represent females. This is interesting, as marble sculptures are a particularly elaborate and often expensive artistic medium. Female imagery is often used to express concepts of "the Other" – it is important, and unsurprising, for instance, that Greek sources equate the East with the feminine and dwell on the sexual license and social power of eastern women as opposed to Greek (men and women alike).[55] Thus, Herodotos says in the same breath that the prostitutes contributed the greatest share to the construction of the tumulus of Alyattes at Sardis, and that all Lydian

---

54 Buschor (1933).

55 For women as "Other," see, e.g., Warner (1985). For the power of Lydian women in Greek myth, consider Herakles and Omphale, as well as the (unnamed) wife of Kandaules – in the latter case, the king seems to have been king because he was married to the woman who held power. For women's roles and responsibilities in Persia, see Brosius (1996).

**Fig. 38** Sardis:
S67.037:7593.
Kore torso.

women prostituted themselves to earn their dowries: his use of the theme
"prostitution to earn dowry" as a trope to describe the Other practices of
eastern women should lead us to suspect his veracity.[56] Herodotos goes on to
say Lydian women chose their husbands, rather than being chosen – another
example of "Lydian as Other," in contrast to Greek customs.[57]

The marble sculptures of women in Achaemenid-period Sardis by no
means point to the economic prosperity or social clout of women, but may
even indicate the opposite. I do not propose to examine gender relations at
Sardis in any detail here – especially on the basis of but four statues! – but
a few points are worth reiterating.[58] First, gender construction is a function
of society. Second, although it seems male supremacy was a given in ancient
Greece and probably in Lydia, the position of women in Lydian society was
undoubtedly very complex. Third, female bodies and female minds sparked
ambivalent reactions in men. Finally, art reflects ideology.

We simply do not know enough about gender relations in Sardian society
to enable the sorts of productive gender studies recently blossoming in the
study of Greek art. Does the superficial resemblance between Sardian and
Greek sculptures let us say for Sardis, on the basis of very few sculptures,

56 For the tomb of Alyattes, see Hdt. 1.93. Kuhrt (forthcoming) debunks the notion that Babylonian women prostituted themselves to earn a dowry.
57 For Greek portrayals of "free Greek male citizen" as normal and female/animal/barbarian as
  Other, see, e.g., duBois (1982), Stewart (1997).
58 These are adapted from Stewart (1997:8).

**Fig. 39** Sardis: S59.010:1419. Amazon or Artemis upper torso.

**Fig. 40** Sardis: NoEx 63.012. Upper part of under-lifesize female torso.

that which has been said of Greece, on the basis of many? Probably not: the culture of Achaemenid-period Sardis was not like that of contemporary Greece. As in Greece, the statues of Sardis surely do not literally reflect daily life – but why the preponderance of draped female figures among free-standing statues? Possibly they suggest the domestication of women: women clothed, as culturally conceived beings (not "natural," naked ones), conforming to the (male-dominated) societal regulations that defined them. Thus the high percentage of females may be a reinforcement of gender roles. Their images can be called into being at the whim of a patron and/or sculptor.

This statue type is not a simple Greek element of the Sardian repertoire. In her seminal work, Ridgway emphasized the kore's debt to Anatolian, particularly Phrygian, prototypes.[59] At Sardis, we see a situation in which the idea system behind the sculpture type may well go back to a long-standing indigenous tradition of freestanding cult statuary of female figures, here carved in a style that is heavily influenced by Greek tradition.

An additional free-standing human statue is implied by the Droaphernes inscription, which describes a statue of a man dedicated to Zeus.[60] It is of course impossible to know the statue's material or appearance, but the inscription demonstrates that human statues might be dedicated to the gods at Sardis. The phenomenon of a person with a Persian name dedicating a statue to the Greek god Zeus at a Lydian site demonstrates the cultural amalgamation and mingling that made Sardis the creative locale it was in the Achaemenid period.

## Rendering animals: lions, sphinxes, and eagles

Ten sculptures from Achaemenid-period Sardis represent lions: a very large number, given the limitations of sculpture retrieval.[61] These animals were associated with the goddess Kybele, who seems to have been considered the protectress of Sardis. Their preponderance on Sardian seals suggests they may have been thought to have apotropaic force or to be symbolic of particular traits such as courage or physical power.[62] In sculpture, they might be rendered in relief (fig. 41) or in the round. Sardian lions combine stylistic features of Neo-Assyrian, Neo-Hittite, and Greek models, with eastern stylistic influence being greater in the period of the Lydian kingdom, and Greek influence predominating in later years. Although there may have been lions

---

59 Ridgway (1977:110–112, 113–114).     60 See Briant (1998) and chapter 5.
61 For Lydian lions, see Ratté (1989a).
62 For apotropaic powers, see, e.g., Herodotos' story of King Meles, who carried a lion around
    the city's circumference to protect it: 1.83. For the seals, see chapter 7 and Curtis (1925).

**Fig. 41** Sardis: S63.035:5356. Part of frame with walking lion.

**Fig. 42** Sardis: S62.031:4548 and S63.037:5394. One of two pairs of addorsed lions séjant.

in western Anatolia during the Achaemenid period – perhaps even imported to paradeisoi for royal hunts – artists working at Sardis portrayed the animals in a manner that suggests emulation of nature was not their primary goal. Some details are rendered correctly on some individuals (such as the dew claws on S62.31 and S63.37) (fig. 42), but by and large the sculptors seem to have worked from an idea of "lion," rather than with an actual beast as model. This idea included manes, snarling mouths, rounded heads and ears, large bolsters at the eyes, and stylized rendering of clawed feet

**Fig. 43** Sardis:
NoEx 63.001.
Lion's paw.

**Fig. 44** Sardis:
S70.007:8108.
Lion's right foot
on plinth.

(figs. 43 and 44). Certain lions have dog-like characteristics such as teats all down the belly; in general the lions of Achaemenid Sardis take on an increasingly dog-like appearance, gaining the lithe slender bodies of hunting hounds and the thin high knees and hocks of dogs rather than the lower-slung heavier legs of cats. In this trend they follow the pattern of Greek lions.[63] Some lions may have been associated with shrines to Kybele or, perhaps, Artemis. Some may have flanked a figure or served as table supports. Some were throne supports.

63 Hanfmann and Ramage (1978:22).

Whereas Greek sculptures of lions often had funerary implications, Sardian lions have yet to be discovered in a funerary context. Given the large number of Achaemenid-period graves excavated at Sardis (especially compared with anything else from the Achaemenid period), it is particularly interesting that *none* of the free-standing sculpted lions has yet been found in the funerary context typical of the Greek sphere. In this regard, they perhaps parallel more closely Near Eastern prototypes and represent a continuation of their Lydian connotations.

Achaemenid-period lion sculpture could work at multiple levels. The association of lions with royalty in Lydia may be suggested by the early electrum coins showing a lion's head. And lions were a motif with a kingly aura in Persia. Free-standing sculptures of lions have been found at Persepolis, as well as in Egypt and at Neo-Hittite sites in western Asia such as 'Ain Dara and Göllü Dağ. Lions or parts of lions were an important element in Achaemenid Persian iconography of architectural and royal furniture support (addorsed capitals, platforms supporting the king on royal tomb facades, feet and legs of thrones and footstools, etc.). In addition to the relief sculptures of Persepolis and Naqsh-i Rustam, the free-standing bronze support from the Treasury at Persepolis in the form of three walking lions is well known.[64] Couchant lion sculptures were excavated at the palatial compound of Persepolis, serving as entrance statues.[65] And of course the ubiquitous use of walking lions on representations of textiles – the royal baldachin at Persepolis, hems of garments on the Persepolitan reliefs prepared to receive added paint – is a further indication of the importance of the lion at the Persian court.[66] Lions had a long local history in Persia as well as Lydia: their connections to kingship and to Kybele, to apotropaic forces and to connotations of power, make it small wonder they should have such preponderance in the sculpture of Achaemenid-period Sardis.

Of the five remaining Achaemenid-period animal sculptures so far found at Sardis, three are sphinxes. The two seated sphinxes are perhaps both throne supports. Like the lions, the sphinxes resemble Greek rather than eastern models in the late period. The remaining two sculptures are birds: perhaps both eagles, or one may be the lower half of a siren. The care taken with the realistic rendering of the feathers is striking on both.

The limited number of animal types is remarkable. Like the lion, the eagle may have had associations with power, courage, and protection. In Greek mythology, the eagle is the bird of Zeus; it is tempting to wonder if the same held true at Sardis. Moreover, and importantly for our understanding of multiculturalism at Achaemenid Sardis, the eagle was associated

64 Schmidt (1970:pl. 33).    65 Schmidt (1957:36).    66 Schmidt (1953), Tilia (1978).

with the Persian king and was portrayed on the standard he bore into battle.[67]

## Kybele and Artemis

The earliest of the Achaemenid-period sculptures showing a goddess (*c.* 540–530) is a marble block mentioned in chapter 3, carved to look like a colonnaded temple with a draped female figure, who is identified as Kybele because of the snakes she appears to hold, standing at one of its narrow ends (S63.51, Manisa 4029) (fig. 45). It has been described stylistically as belonging to a "late Croesan" phase of sculpture at Sardis, a continuation of local Lydian style that lasted as late as *c.* 525 – the same style as that in which some of the figures on the *columnae caelatae* of the Artemision at Ephesos are presumably carved (also *c.* 540 BC).[68]

This early sculpture in a local style demonstrates the willingness of local artisans to experiment with eastern ideas. The walls of the temple between the columns are carved in low relief panels so that figural representations moving towards the front of the temple extend over the full height of the wall. The most likely source of influence for such representation is the east. One possible origin might be the Ishtar Gate at Babylon, constructed at the beginning of the sixth century BC, with animal friezes marching along its walls towards the gate.[69] In Babylon, the figures of the friezes – bulls, lions, and dragons of Marduk – are not arranged in vertical registers like those on the Sardis temple; the columns on the Sardian model, however, divide the walls into vertical panels. Indeed, "The Sardis design looks like a bold attempt to combine the Mesopotamian figurative tradition with colonnaded Greek temple architecture."[70] Perhaps more than it resembles the Ishtar Gate, however, the sculpture from Sardis resembles the tombs of the Achaemenid kings at Naqsh-i Rustam:[71] a main tableau incorporated into an architectural setting, with the central focal section of the representation flanked by three registers of small-scale figures.

It has been suggested that the model is a literal representation of a temple at Sardis dating to *c.* 570–560 BC, about thirty years before the proposed date of the model's sculpting.[72] If this is the case, it bespeaks the openness of the Lydians to eastern ideas and traditions even before the arrival of the

---

67 Nylander (1983). I am grateful to C.H. Greenewalt, Jr., for drawing my attention to the tile facsimile of the mosaic in Chatsworth that shows a bird that looks like a rooster, and the tile facsimile in Potsdam with a griffin.
68 Hanfmann and Ramage (1978:18). See also Rein (1993).
69 Koldewey (1918), Amiet (1980:323, 526), Roaf (1991:192).
70 Hanfmann and Ramage (1978:45).     71 Schmidt (1970).
72 Hanfmann and Ramage (1978).

**Fig. 45** Sardis:
S63.51:5677.
Kybele shrine.

Persians in the area, an openness that should not be surprising given the
close family connections between the Mermnads and royal Medians.[73] But
this model may simply represent a temple type: with no physical remains of
either Lydian- or Achaemenid-period temples yet found at Sardis, we cannot
be certain the model reproduces a specific temple, nor in what period such
a temple (if it existed) might have been built. Certainly the model blends
Mesopotamian traditions (figured friezes decorating the entire height of the
walls) with western Anatolian or Greek (Ionic columns, colonnaded temple),

73 Hdt. 1.73, now perhaps supported by archaeological evidence from Kerkenes Dağ in Kappadokia. See Dusinberre (in press).

**Fig. 46** Sardis: S68.6:7678. Stele with Artemis, Kybele, and two worshipers.

construing them in a local style (doughy bodies, rope-like folds of cloth), with local flavor (mythological and other scenes represented on the walls), and to fit local needs (Kybele).

A stele that may date to over a century later, *c.* 430–420 BC, shows two goddesses holding animals, approached by small worshipers (S68.6, Manisa 3937) (fig. 46). As one of the goddesses holds a deer and the other a lion, with a tympanon hanging behind her, they have been identified as Artemis and Kybele, respectively. Kybele is slightly smaller than Artemis. The stele originally had a triangular pediment with acroteria, supported by two Ionic pilasters; all four figures stand on a platform. The structure of the stele is therefore highly architectural and may have been intended to represent a

**Fig. 47** Sardis: NoEx 58.27. Relief of Kybele with lion in her lap and at her feet.

contemporary structure: the figures of the goddesses may represent over-lifesized cult statues.

This is important for understanding cult at Sardis in the later fifth century. It suggests that Kybele and Artemis were worshiped as two separate goddesses,[74] although their connection may have been perceived as so great that they shared a temple. Or it may be, as some scholars have suggested,[75] that they shared a temple only while the temple of Kybele was being rebuilt after it was burned in the Ionian revolt of 499.[76] The Artemis portrayed recalls the Ephesian type with her hinds, although Artemis of Ephesos is generally flanked by a deer on either side, whereas this Artemis cradles hers in her arms. This relief may represent the cult of the goddess at Sardis that had stemmed from Ephesos.[77] Might the figures of the man and woman portrayed on the stele represent those who erected it to the two most important goddesses in their city, Artemis of Sardis and Kybele?[78]

Kybele is represented in a different form by the next century, perhaps in response to the immensely popular and influential image by Agorakritos (?) in Pheidian style showing the goddess with a tympanon and two lions at her sides. The relief from Sardis, NoEx 58.27 (fig. 47), combines this form

74 For a discussion of the implications of this point, see Hanfmann and Waldbaum (1969).
75 Hanfmann and Ramage (1978:60).     76 Hdt. 5.102.
77 As described in the "Sacrilege Inscription." See chapter 5; also Hanfmann and Waldbaum (1969:265), Hanfmann (1987).
78 Hanfmann and Waldbaum (1969:265–266).

with a very widespread late archaic form showing the goddess seated with a lion in her lap. The relief, which has clamp cuttings that indicate it was fastened into a wall, is rectangular but cut to indicate a shallow naiskos with a pitched roof and three acroteria, supported by pilasters on the sides. Kybele sits on a square throne, with a lion lying in her lap and another seated at her side. She holds a tympanon and a small round bowl, which she extends out over the head of the seated lion. This relief demonstrates the continued ability of sculptors in the fourth century to meld influences from disparate areas: the archaic image is known in dozens of reliefs, and certainly also circulated at Sardis. But the sculptor of this image incorporated the additional lion that brought his relief into line with contemporary notions on the Greek mainland. Sardis thus continued its tradition as a place where ideas from disparate locations might be combined and reworked into local expressions.

## Other reliefs of female figures

Kybele and Artemis were not the only female figures represented: two other stelae show females, perhaps goddesses. Both may have been votive dedications. NoEx 60.13 (fig. 48), dating to *c.* 520–500 BC, is a free-standing stele that shows a standing draped frontal female figure wearing elaborate jewelry. She lacks the attributes of either Artemis or Kybele and may be mortal. Similar frontal figures in an unelaborated frame are interpreted at Miletos as votive offerings,[79] and this is a possible interpretation of this relief's function. The other relief is S69.11 (fig. 49), a free-standing stele with a veiled frontal female figure dating to the fifth century BC. Not enough is preserved of this piece to determine if the figure is human or a goddess. The finished back suggests a votive function rather than a funerary one.[80] Thus, these reliefs were probably both set up as votaries. This practice would parallel Greek customs of the period and may point to systems of worship closely related to Greek ones. It is interesting to note that as yet no votive relief sculptures that portray male figures have been found at Sardis.

## Conclusion: fleshing out the civic environment

We can assume a rich sculptural environment at Sardis in the Croesan and Achaemenid phases – but as indicated already, almost all the remnants presented here have been found reused as architectural blocks in buildings of the Roman period and later. Thus, we are dealing with a very

79 Richter (1968:no. 70), Hanfmann and Ramage (1978:53).
80 Hanfmann and Ramage (1978:58).

**Fig. 48** Sardis: NoEx 60.13. Relief of frontal standing draped female figure.

restricted sample of the original sculptural imagery that once adorned the city of Sardis. Again, Ephesos may furnish a useful comparison: the archaic Artemision was lavishly decorated with sculpture, but the remains themselves are sadly fragmentary, small in number, and mostly found built into late Roman or Byzantine contexts with some other pieces found scattered about the site. Under the circumstances, it is not always possible or even appropriate to attempt to determine absolutely whether certain works belong to the phase before Cyrus' conquest in the mid-sixth century or after it: at Ephesos, the *columnae caelatae* were conceived in the reign of Croesus, but the actual carving of these columns seems to have continued long after the conquest by Cyrus – perhaps extending deep into the fifth century.[81]

The sculptures of Sardis in the Achaemenid period show a fusion of multiple influences to create an eclectic new manner of expression in Achaemenid

81 Bookidis (1967:279, 471), Boardman (1959).

**Fig. 49** Sardis: S69.11:8032. Stele with veiled frontal female.

Lydia. This is important, for it suggests some of the same phenomena of social organization at Sardis in the Achaemenid period that we will see from various other sources of evidence (chapters 5, 6, 7, 8). Unlike the stelae from Daskyleion,[82] Sardian sculpted style does not reflect eastern traits but is rather a local style strongly influenced by Greek models. This powerful Hellenic stylistic influence, giving visual expression to themes decidedly international, remains pronounced throughout the Achaemenid period. It reflects the relative proximity of the major sculptural schools in Ionia,

82 For Daskyleion, see Akurgal (1966), Dolunay (1967), Möbius (1971), Pfühl and Möbius (1977), Altheim-Stiehl et al. (1983).

the Kyklades, and Athens, with their master carvers who are known to
have accepted commissions over a wide geographical area.[83] Such a proximity would have created long-term, deep-seated cultural affinities over
the centuries, beginning from a time well before the conquest by Cyrus
in the mid-sixth century and demonstrated by the involvement of Lydian
kings with Greek sanctuaries. Additionally, accessibility to sea trade would
have enhanced the direction of a certain amount of cultural focus in a
broad sense. This is not to imply there was no impetus from the east,
however.

The mobility of artists (and their ideas) apparently contributed greatly to
the development of the sculptural repertoire at Sardis. Internationalism already informed architectural and sculptural programs in the Mediterranean
and Near East before the time of Cyrus. More broadly speaking, the tradition of bringing artisans from far and wide (as prisoners of war or as enticed
"guests" – or in some capacity in between those two poles) for major projects
is well attested in the ancient Near East and Egypt as well as Greece. The
Babylonian paylists demonstrate a direct link between Lydian craft traditions
and the Mesopotamian sphere, and thence by association with artisans from
Iran and Egypt.[84] But there is also the evidence of the sites themselves. At
Ephesos, for instance, the bulls carved on the antae of the temple of Artemis
or on a propylon are a clear reference to Mesopotamian traditions – the
same traditions Xerxes drew upon in his Gate of All Lands at Persepolis.[85]
The Egyptian notion of the column drums carved with relief figures in cult
procession is part of the same international picture.[86] The international
exchanges pertaining in the artistic creations of Asia Minor were highly
complex. Some influence may have occurred via the conscious mandates of
political leaders and other patrons. Some influence also will have occurred
via the natural and inevitable sharing of ideas and techniques among people working side by side in an alley of workshops in a bazaar or in a palace
system, or at the site of a quarry or building.

We have no epigraphic or literary evidence suggesting names of individual sculptors at Sardis, or suggesting that known artists made sculptures
at Sardis. Equally, there is no evidence suggesting the ethnicities of the

83  E.g., Endoios, who (whether Ionian or Athenian by birth) worked in Asia Minor, perhaps even
    on the *columnae caelatae* of Ephesos, as well as at Athens. See Ridgway (1977:138, 284–290),
    Viviers (1992), Pedley (1994). While some places actually supported workshops, others took
    advantage of sculptors' willingness to travel and work on demand. See Bookidis (1967:507–510)
    for an important discussion of complexities in relations between local masons at building
    sites and imported artists and/or artworks.
84  Root (1979:32).      85  Bookidis (1967:278–280, 280).
86  *Ibid.* For the figured columns of the temples in, e.g., Luxor, see Strudwick (1999), Saleh (1998),
    Gayet (1894). For an interesting recent analysis of the temple's artistic program, see Schüller-
    Gotzburg (1990).

sculptors working there. The lack of context for the Achaemenid-period sculptures at Sardis makes a detailed study of workshops difficult.[87] There is simply not enough adequately preserved material from any one phase of Achaemenid-period Sardis to deploy a methodology of analyzing style to identify links with artists' hands or regional workshops. But if there were (and someday there may be), this would be an important next level in attempting to understand how the processes of creation of (elite-serving) elements of Sardian material culture worked.

The sculptures that flesh out our picture of Sardis certainly were affected by an exchange of ideas between artisans from different stylistic and iconographic traditions. Masonry techniques suggest Lydian stoneworkers were in Iran as early as *c.* 540, to assist in the construction of the palaces at Pasargadae.[88] Conversely, the sculptures of Sardis show, even as early as *c.* 540–530, the effects of new ideas from the east: the reliefs of the Kybele shrine indicate immediate familiarity with the adornment of monumental architecture in Mesopotamia and Persia and a translation of these ideas into a western Anatolian context. The twenty-seven sculptures from the Achaemenid period included in the appendix here give us new insight into what that context may have been. It is not a homogeneous picture: the quality of the pieces ranges widely, and the stylistic schools they recall vary. Many of the subjects reflect eastern themes and ideas. That at least some of them, like the banquet stelae, were made for local patrons demonstrates once again how deeply these ideas had penetrated local elite consciousness. Some themes seem peculiarly Sardian: the reliefs showing Kybele and Artemis, and the many lions. The sculptures of Achaemenid-period Sardis, like the architecture, show it was a place where eastern and western influences met and merged with local concepts to produce a fusion of ideas, themes, and styles.

87 See Ridgway (1977:283–302) for sculptors and workshops. See Pedley (1976) for an analysis of workshops across a wider geographical area.
88 Nylander (1970).

# 5 Inscriptions: Sardians in their own words

Sardis' architecture and sculpture suggest a thriving society that drew on multiple ethnic traditions for forms of expression. How is this picture altered or enhanced by Sardians' own words, preserved in the form of inscriptions in stone, set up in places where they would be seen? Inscriptions are both official and personal verbal statements, and belong to our understanding of Sardis' public environment.

A small but important selection of inscriptions dating to the Achaemenid period has been excavated at Sardis. This discussion offers new translations of all the datable Lydian inscriptions, from the period of the Lydian kingdom to the death of Alexander (Appendix 2). It includes also the few Greek inscriptions from Sardis that concern the Achaemenid period as well as the famous Sacrilege Inscription from Ephesos that mentions Sardians. Most of the datable inscriptions from Sardis before the Hellenistic period use the Lydian language and alphabet; a few bilingual Lydian/Aramaic and Lydian/Greek inscriptions provide the key for translating Lydian. They also show the multilingualism that prevailed at Sardis in the Achaemenid period, even though Lydian probably remained the language most commonly used.[1] In the Hellenistic period, by contrast, Greek was the most common language. A relatively large number of the inscriptions are indecipherable or include words the meanings of which we still do not understand. The texts fall into several broad categories by subject: those that warn would-be looters away from graves, those that claim possession of an object, those that describe dedications, those that deal with religious matters, and those that outline legal contracts.

## A brief overview of the Lydian language

Lydian is known to us from roughly a hundred inscriptions, most of which are very short but some of which are more than twenty lines long. Because many of these inscriptions are formulaic, the language has been particularly difficult to decipher: relatively few words account for the substance

---

1 For multilingualism in Achaemenid Anatolia, see Lemaire and Lozachmeur (1996); for Achaemenid Karia, see, e.g., Mayrhofer (1979), Metzger et al. (1974); for Aramaic bilinguals in Egypt, see Kornfeld (1973), Lipinski (1975). For Aramaic in formal and formulaic texts in the Persian heartland, see, e.g., Bowman (1970).

of many of the longer inscriptions, while the shorter inscriptions are often only a few words long and therefore provide little contextual help in understanding meaning. The initial key to translating Lydian came in the form of a relatively long bilingual inscription in Lydian and Aramaic, that provided scholars with a kind of limited Rosetta Stone (Appendix 2: No. 9).[2] At this time, only the four Lydian bilinguals already mentioned are known, two Lydian/Aramaic and two Lydian/Greek, which help to solidify our understanding of aspects of Lydian, including pronunciation as well as grammar and vocabulary.

Lydian is an Indo-European language that uses an alphabet similar to the East Greek.[3] The linguistic stem of the language has been the subject of much discussion, as Lydian includes unusual features such as infixes and has an agglutinative quality that distinguishes it from modern Indo-European languages. In the 1910s, E. Littmann and W.H. Buckler recognized certain indications that Lydian was Indo-European, such as the use of *nid* as a negator, the pronouns *qis, qid* (or *pis, pid*), and the grammatical construction of conditionals; shortly after the initial publication of Lydian, F. Hrozny demonstrated connections between Lydian and Hittite, another recently deciphered ancient Indo-European language.[4] Although there seems to have been a latent desire to claim its own language group for Lydian, the consensus is that Lydian is indeed Indo-European and related to other Anatolian languages, perhaps particularly Hittite.[5]

The majority of the extant inscriptions are written from right to left, with spaces between words and no punctuation. The oldest inscriptions apparently date to the second half of the seventh century BC (a graffito and the early Lydian coins);[6] Lydian certainly continued to be written through the reign of Alexander the Great, until around 323/322 BC.[7] Most of the inscriptions have been found at Sardis itself; of the remainder, most are from the Hermos valley between Maionia and Magnesia ad Sipylum, with a few from the Kaÿster valley, from Ephesos, and from Pergamon. The geographical extent suggested by the findspots may roughly indicate the area within which Lydian was spoken in antiquity.

---

2 For the importance of the bilingual in deciphering Lydian, see Littmann (1916), Buckler (1924), Sayce (1925). For translations and discussions of the bilingual itself, see Cook (1917), Cowley (1921), Cuny (1920, 1921), Elderkin (1925), Kahle and Sommer (1927). Torrey (1917–1918) deals almost exclusively with the Aramaic. Without doubt the most extensive, detailed, and helpful discussion of the Lydian language is Gusmani (1964, 1986). I follow Gusmani's transcription of the Lydian alphabet.

3 For the alphabet, see Gusmani (1964:20–21); for a summary of the Indo-European nature of Lydian, see Littmann (1916), Gusmani (1964:25–27), Friedrich (1932).

4 Hrozny (1917:191–193).          5 Heubeck (1960).

6 Gusmani (1964:17). The date of the *walwei* coins is disputed; I follow Gusmani.

7 The twelfth year of Alexander, if the conquest of Anatolia in 334/333 was the first year.

## Inscriptions associated with graves

The majority of decipherable Lydian inscriptions are associated with the dead: they are generally carved on the stone doors to rock-cut tombs or on stelae that were originally set up before a tomb's entrance (all found out of context) to warn evil-doers away from the tomb and its contents. They are all associated with the rock-cut tombs dug into the cliffs of the necropolis and the hills around and to the south of the Hellenistic Artemis temple at Sardis, rather than with the built tumuli across the valley at Bin Tepe. They take the form of curses against those who damage the grave, its owner, or his possessions, and generally follow the same formula: "This is the [grave chamber, stele, etc.] of X, son of Y. If anybody damages [it, them], may [one or more gods] punish/destroy him." Different parts of the grave are often, but by no means always, singled out for specific mention. The meanings of the words describing the parts of tombs have been derived in part from their funereal context: thus, *mrud* apparently means a stele (the stele that has been inscribed), while *vănas* probably means grave chamber (one of the few terms that appear in all the tomb inscriptions). Some words, like *asina-*, seem to indicate a part of a grave, but their precise meaning cannot as yet be determined. I have followed convention here in translating all names as masculine, but this may be false: Lydian does not have a separate feminine gender, so it is very difficult to identify the sex of people named. It has been suggested that a list of three names may be son, father, grandfather; a list of four may include the great-grandfather, or may combine patronymic and matronymic, or perhaps indicate a profession.[8]

The gods who appear in these inscriptions are presumably those responsible for justice: Artemis of Ephesos, Artemis of Koloe, and Artemis of Sardis (not included in the inscriptions translated here, as the Lydian inscription naming Artemis of Sardis is not datable); a god named Qλdāns who has been associated with Apollo on the basis of his pairing with Artemis; and occasionally Levs, who has been associated with Zeus. Qλdāns is only mentioned together with Artemis, in the hope they will together punish those who damage the property of the inscriber. Levs is invoked with the wish that he be kindly to those who behave well and destroy those who misbehave, and thus seems to be a god who can bend fate a little to his own liking. Artemis appears most frequently, often without mention of another god but frequently paired with herself in multiple aspects: thus, "Artemis of Ephesos and Artemis of Koloe" is a common phrase on the grave inscriptions. Koloe is generally associated with the Gygaean lake, across the Hermos valley from the city of Sardis; Artemis of Ephesos is probably to be associated

8 Gusmani (1985), Benveniste (1965). See also Hanfmann (1987:4).

with the cult of Ephesian Artemis established at Sardis. It is not clear to what aspect of the goddess the Achaemenid-period altar to Artemis excavated at Sardis (see chapter 3) was dedicated. It is possible that "Artemis of Ephesos," "Artemis of Sardis," and the explicitly Persianizing form known from Pausanias, "Artemis-Anahita,"[9] may have been conflated and worshiped together, or they may have been worshiped in separate sites through the city and elsewhere. In any case, the inscriptions demonstrate that "Artemis of Ephesos" was one of the primary deities of the city and suggest her power as a law-enforcer. They thus expand on and refine the understanding of Sardis' sacred practices we have gained already from an analysis of monuments.

The tomb inscriptions use the same formula for all three centuries they span. This demonstrates a striking continuity of tradition from the time of the Lydian kingdom through the Achaemenid period and the reign of Alexander. It is perhaps doubly striking to find a Lydian/Aramaic bilingual inscription, with the Lydian formula translated into Aramaic: does the use of the Achaemenid *lingua franca* suggest the person buried in the tomb spoke Aramaic, or was he a Lydian-speaker particularly eager to warn off Aramaic-reading looters from the tomb? The names indicated on the bilingual seem to be ethnically Lydian, as is the case of all names in the Lydian grave inscriptions. Do we see here a purely Lydian tradition that continues through the Achaemenid period, with an occasional nod to the likelihood that Aramaic-readers might rob tombs as well as readers of Lydian? Or the inclusion of Aramaic may suggest that written curses were not thought to be magically operative once carved in stone, but rather functioned as explicit warnings aimed at the literate. But this literal reading of the written message may be naive. Might the Aramaic not point to a more profound absorption of the Achaemenid chancelry language as a "powerfact"? Thus the inscriber may be invoking not only the power of the gods to keep his tomb inviolate, but also that of the Achaemenid authorities (backed by the Achaemenid army). By writing his tomb inscription in Aramaic as well as Lydian, the inscriber might thus have brought to his aid the forces of justice on earth as well as in heaven.

As is unfortunately the case with all of the grave inscriptions, we cannot firmly identify the tomb from which the bilingual doorstone came, so there are no associated finds that might aid us in finding an answer to the linguistic or cultural background or leanings of its author. The fact that we cannot determine his ethnicity is particularly interesting, since mortuary

---

9 In 5.27.5, Pausanias describes the "Lydians who call themselves Persians" and worship Artemis-Anahita at nearby Hypaipa. For a recent discussion of Artemis-Anahita, see Brosius (1998).

inclusions also give us no clue of ethnic background (see chapter 6). Like the objects included with the burials, this bilingual inscription from a tomb offers us an idea of the polyethnic culture of Achaemenid-period Sardis, where people of different backgrounds lived together and took on the ideas and practices of multiple traditions to create a new culture.

## Claiming possession

In some fundamental way, the tomb inscriptions proclaim the ownership by the dead of the tombs' contents, including various structural aspects of the tombs. Violation of property rights will result in bad things happening to the impious, they aver. But graves and grave goods were not the only items inscribed with claims of ownership in Achaemenid-period Sardis. A certain number of seals are inscribed in Lydian, all with brief inscriptions probably naming the owner of the seal.[10] The two inscribed seals known from Sardis (Appendix 2: Nos. 17 and 18) are inscribed with a linear symbol surrounded by writing, claiming possession of the seal and the items it was used to mark. A similar concern with ownership is manifested in the graffiti on vases excavated from Sardis (e.g., Appendix 2: Nos. 3, 4, 7, 26, 31, 37, 42). Most of these inscriptions, scratched into the exterior walls of drinking vessels after they have been fired, claim "this is the vessel of X" or claim the contents of the vessel. It is not clear why the Sardians felt such possessiveness over pots – particularly pots used for drinking.

There is an important difference between the ownership signified by the inscriptions on seals and that suggested by messages scratched into ceramic vessels. The seals served as public signs of individuals (see chapter 7), many of whom may have been serving in an official (if perhaps not state) capacity. Some seals may have been the mark of offices rather than of a specific person. The seals were probably used to stamp varied items, perhaps including correspondence and receipts as well as goods. The vessels, by contrast, were probably not intended for wide distribution. They show, rather, the desire of individuals to mark objects as their own for use, perhaps as exclusively their own; this might apply either to vessels or to their contents. The messages claiming possession, therefore, were inscribed both on artifacts designed for a wide public audience and on those aimed at a more private, personal audience.

10  See Boardman (1970b, esp. nos. 1–8). Only three of these seals have a known provenance: 1 and 2 are from Sardis, and 5 is from Kertch. Boardman's recent supplement (1998) includes no further seals inscribed in Lydian, but does expand on his list of linear devices used to mark stamp seals. As most of the seals Boardman discusses are not from controlled excavations, they do not play a major role in the present discussion.

## The sacred and the inscribed: dedications

Dedications to the gods are a powerful indicator of Sardians' religious practices. The dedications mostly take the form of votive tablets (e.g., Appendix 2: Nos. 12, 37?, 50, 53) – that is, the inscription itself serves as a votive offering – but at least one dedication is of a clay vessel (No. 27). The most notable dedication is probably to be found in the first half of the so-called Droaphernes Inscription (No. 40). The Droaphernes Inscription was found in 1974, where erosion had brought it to light in the bed of the Paktolos.[11] It is a Roman recarving, probably dating to the second century, of two different edicts separated with a small carved leaf.[12] While the second half of the inscription deals with cults at Sardis and is of debatable date, the first half certainly dates to the Achaemenid period. It describes a dedication, in which Droaphernes son of Barakes, hyparch of Lydia, dedicates a statue of a human (probably a male – *andrias*) to a cult of Zeus first established by Baradatas (perhaps a relative of Droaphernes?) in the thirty-ninth year of the reign of Artaxerxes. The date of the original inscription is uncertain: the Artaxerxes in question could be either Artaxerxes I or II.

Both Droaphernes and Barakes are plausible Iranian names,[13] if not yet attested in Persian sources; the word "hyparch" demonstrates Droaphernes' high position in the administrative echelon.[14] Although the inscription need not show a state action taken by a public official, it does demonstrate the degree of acculturation at Sardis, in a situation where multiple cultures were mingling: Baradates, a person with a name that may be Iranian but in any case seems not to be Greek, apparently founded a cult of Zeus – a Greek god – in Sardis, a city of Lydia. Droaphernes, an Iranian, dedicates a statue of a human, perhaps made of bronze, to the god.[15] All of these actions took place in the Achaemenid period. The development of this cult at Sardis shows the impetus of many different cultural traditions combined to create something fully new and idiosyncratic to Sardis itself. The Droaphernes Inscription thus supports the notion of Sardian sacred practices suggested by the hybrid nature of the altar to Artemis (see chapter 3).

---

11 For the history of its discovery, see Greenewalt (1978c).
12 I agree with Briant (1998) in his interpretation of the stone, presented here. For the date of the recarving and an earlier interpretation, see Robert (1975).
13 R. Schmitt, personal communication 16 August 2000. See also Briant (1998:206–207), Robert (1975:311–312), Mayrhofer (1973, 1974).
14 If not, perhaps, "satrap": see Weiskopf (1982), Sekunda (1985) for levels of rank in Lydia.
15 Recarving the inscription implies the marble block was standing alone at the point of reinscription, which may suggest the statue was of bronze and had been melted down.

## Matters of religion and law

### The Mitridastas Inscriptions

In Achaemenid Sardis religion encompassed also the law, which was underwritten by divine justice and punishment. Although there was very likely a secular arm to sacred justice,[16] the Lydian inscriptions deal only with the divine. But religion and law were inextricably connected in the Sardian epigraphic record. The divine as source of justice is, of course, a widespread belief and need not imply that priests were in charge of legal matters (after all, in the Christian west people are still asked to swear on the Bible in court), but priests and legality, divinity and justice, were closely intertwined in Achaemenid Sardis.

Two decrees set up by one Mitridastas near the site of the Hellenistic temple to Artemis at Sardis (Appendix 2: Nos. 13 and 14) date either to the Achaemenid period or to the subsequent Hellenistic period. Although their position near the Hellenistic temple may indicate a date in the Hellenistic period, the presence of the Achaemenid-period altar to Artemis demonstrates the site was a sanctuary before the construction of the monumental Hellenistic temple as well. The identification on the inscriptions of the gods Qλdãns and Artemis of Ephesos by their Lydian names, as opposed to the Greek language and terminology more common in the Hellenistic period, has led me to include the two decrees with the Achaemenid-period inscriptions here, but this assignation is by no means certain.

The first, No. 13, apparently deals with the dedication of a temple to Qλdãns and Artemis (by Mitridastas?), and the establishment of a trust fund entailing all of Mitridastas' belongings, to be held by the association of the temple (apparently a council of priests) for the maintenance of the temple. The second, No. 14, which is missing its final lines, is also a legal document recording the handing over of Mitridastas' possessions to the association of the temple. In the first inscription Artemis of Ephesos herself and Qλdãns the mighty are held to be responsible for the good conduct of the overseers and for ensuring proper use of the trust: if anyone were to damage Mitridastas' property or interfere with its overseeing, the gods were to destroy him and his property. Artemis was additionally to destroy those who tampered with Mitridastas' decree. Similarly, in the second inscription Artemis was to destroy those who damaged the property that Mitridastas handed over to the association of the temple. Such an overt

---

16 Certainly the Sacrilege Inscription, discussed below, demonstrates that the secular arm packed a mighty wallop by the Hellenistic period!

inclusion of the gods is interesting. It seems that Artemis herself was the highest punitive body in Sardis at the time the decrees were set up, that justice was accredited to the gods, perhaps without recourse to human correctional institutions as intermediaries. These inscriptions also suggest that the curse formulas of the grave inscriptions are couched in legal language, that the formula "if anyone damages anything, may the gods destroy him" should be considered binding and a necessary and sufficient deterrent to wrong-doers.

The two decrees of Mitridastas demonstrate once again the degree of cultural mingling at Sardis, and the importance of wealth rather than ethnicity as a determinant of status. Mitridastas is an Iranian name, but here at Sardis we see him as a priest presumably of Artemis and/or Qλdāns. He perhaps dedicated a temple at Sardis to the local god Qλdāns and the imported cult of Artemis of Ephesos; certainly he donates all his apparently substantial wealth and property for the upkeep of the temple. And he sets up inscriptions in Lydian. Thus we see again Iranian, Lydian, and Greek (?) influences combined to form what is an essentially Sardian composition.

## The Droaphernes Inscription part II

The second half of the Droaphernes Inscription (No. 40) deals with cults at Sardis. It has been reconstructed by some to refer to Droaphernes and to Zeus of Baradata;[17] more recently, it has been suggested that this regulation of cultic ritual stems from the sanctuary of Zeus (not Droaphernes) in the Hellenistic or Roman periods.[18] The discrepancy between the private dedication described in the first half and the public ruling outlined in the second, as well as the particularly Greek words used to describe positions and concerns in the latter half, raises doubts about the continuity of the inscription. It is also highly unlikely that a ranking Persian official would involve himself to this degree in regulating a local cult or manifesting such an official degree of attachment to a local divinity.[19] The second half of the Droaphernes Inscription, therefore, is probably best dated to a later period: the mystery cult of Sabazios, the cults of Angidistis and Ma, cannot be said to have arrived at Sardis during the Achaemenid period. It thus does not figure in the current discussion.

## The Sacrilege Inscription

The well-known Sacrilege Inscription (Appendix 2: No. 54) is a Greek-language inscription from Ephesos. It has been much discussed; here I seek

17 E.g., Robert (1975).     18 Briant (1998:220).     19 Briant (1998:221).

only to offer a few additional thoughts for consideration. It was found by the Austrian excavators of Ephesos in 1961, reused as a wall block in a room west of the Prytaneion; it deals with religious matters and provides much information on the social makeup of Sardis at the end of the Achaemenid period.[20] Fifty-seven lines long, the inscription probably dates to *c.* 334–281 BC and prescribes the death penalty for forty-five Sardians who had been found guilty of interfering with the rites of Ephesian Artemis at Sardis.[21] The messengers sent by Ephesos to Sardis had been taking sacred objects to the Sanctuary of Artemis of Ephesos at Sardis, but they were beset by a group of people who profaned the sacred things and assaulted the messengers; the inscription records the assaulters' names and often those of their fathers and even grandfathers. The accused were probably all young, as none of them is described as having a profession.[22]

The inscription includes names of Lydian, Greek, and Iranian origin, as well as some names the origins of which are uncertain.[23] It is clear from this inscription that parents in the late fourth century BC named their children according to different criteria than simply the ethnicity of the father: thus "Paktyes (L) the son of Karous (L) the son of Herakleidos (G)," "Mithridates (P) the son of Tuios (L) the son of Manes (L), the slave of Attis (L?)," and "Pythes (L) the son of Strombos (G) the son of Kadodos (P) the son of Babados (P)." Do these naming practices suggest intermarriage, acculturation, or simply personal taste for particular names? Although the inscription cannot illuminate these questions, it does underscore the potential difficulty of relying on onomastic evidence for such specific cultural phenomena as colonization. The procedures for naming individuals (x son of y, x son of y son of z, x son of y son of z son of q) do not conform to standard Greek practice. This feature of the Sacrilege Inscription and the empty spaces left on the stele may point to Ephesian confusion at recording a system of naming and family relationships that was unfamiliar to them. Apparently the inscription affords a glimpse into Sardian ideas of kinship and identification in the late fourth century.

A number of professions are listed on the inscription, all associated with relatives of the accused. The professions include: oil-seller (*elatopoleus*), bathman (*balaneus*), shoe-seller (*pelmatopoleus*), sandal-seller (*hypodematopoleus*), goldsmith (or gold-refiner?) (*chrysochoos*), sacred herald (*hierokeryx*), and *boukopos* – perhaps a profession, bull slayer or sacrificial attendant, rather

---

20 First published by Knibbe (1961–1963). I draw greatly on Hanfmann (1987).
21 Robert (1967) connected the Sacrilege Inscription with another at Ephesos to show that a Sardian citizen conducted the investigation of the culprits, then apprehended them and extradited them to Ephesos. I am not convinced that Hanfmann (1987:1–2) is correct in asserting that a Sardian citizen at this time would necessarily be ethnically Lydian.
22 Hanfmann (1987:3–4).
23 See commentary in Hanfmann (1987:2–3, 6–7).

than a personal name. What kind of oil the oil-seller was selling, or for what purpose it was used, we cannot know – it may have been used in a culinary, cosmetic, ritual, mortuary, or other capacity. The mention of the bathman is interesting, as it demonstrates that Sardis had provisions for cleanliness other than the oil-and-strigil method of the Greeks; if it is correct that there was no ritual bath associated with Artemis at Sardis,[24] it implies the existence of other, perhaps civic, baths. The shoe- and sandal-sellers may have been peddlers rather than cobblers, selling rather than making their wares. It is impossible to know whether their shops or booths were associated with the temple in any way, or whether they were set up elsewhere in the city. We see also a sacred herald, perhaps two priests (bull slayers), and a "slave of Attis" who may be a *hierodoulos*, or sacred slave, of the god.

It is likely, although not certain, that the great majority of the forty-five individuals convicted were Sardians: the mingling of ethnicities implied by their names corresponds closely to the mingling of artistic and other traditions we see at Sardis in the Achaemenid period. Two people are clearly indicated as coming from other places: Karous son of Manes son of Atas from Ibis Kome, and Sisines son of Eumanes from Hiera Kome. The site of the village Ibis Kome is unknown, and it is not clear if only grandfather Atas was from the village or if his son and grandson also considered it home. Hiera Kome, by contrast, is the later Hierokaisereia, site of a cult of the Iranian goddess Anahita who was assimilated to Artemis.[25] Hanfmann, following R. Schmitt, suggests Eumanes is an Iranian name.[26]

This connection of Iranian names with a site known to be the center of a cult to an Iranian goddess has led some to suspect a conspiracy: L. Robert even suggested "that the resistance to the Ephesian Artemis may have had something to do with the presence of this representative of Anaitis."[27] To suggest that a person with an Iranian name from Hiera Kome was necessarily a "representative of Anaitis" seems far-fetched, however, without any supporting evidence and in the teeth of the recognition that there are twice as many men with Lydian names and twice as many Greek names on the inscription as there are Iranian. More likely, we are to see the sacrilege against the sacred messengers of Ephesian Artemis not as a nationalistic plot inspired and conducted by conniving Iranians defending their version of Artemis against another, but rather as an uprising on the part of a large number of Sardian youth, where by "Sardian" I mean the entire cultural spectrum that made up the city's populace at the end of the Achaemenid period.

24 Hanfmann (1987:5).    25 Brosius (1998).    26 Hanfmann (1987:7).
26 Quoted in Hanfmann (1987:3).

## The Mnesimachos Inscription and Achaemenid land-tenure systems

The so-called Mnesimachos Inscription (Appendix 2: No. 55) was discovered in July 1910, carved in two columns on a white marble block that formed part of the south face of the north anta to the temple of Artemis.[28] The top few lines of both columns are missing, where the top of the block was chiseled away at the time this part of the temple was converted to a reservoir, probably in the seventh century CE.[29] The inscription represents the middle and final clauses detailing a mortgaged property: it describes the handing over of Mnesimachos' lands and their appurtenances to pay back the loan of 1,325 gold staters he had borrowed from the temple of Artemis but was unable to repay in specie. The lands paid annual dues to the king's officers; they had been given directly to Mnesimachos by one Antigonos.

The date of the inscription has been the focus of much discussion. The text could not have been engraved before the Artemis temple was constructed in 281–222 BC. It is generally thought on the basis of letter forms to represent a reinscribing in the latter part of the third century of an original decree dating to the end of the fourth century (306 BC is the date given for Antigonos' adoption of the royal title and hence probably represents a *terminus post quem* for this inscription).[30] The institutional vocabulary – in particular, the mention of the *chiliarchy* – and the onomastic evidence, with more Greek names than in the Sacrilege Inscription, have been held to reinforce this position.[31]

The lost beginning of Column I probably gave the date and the names of the parties as well as particulars of the loan made to Mnesimachos by the temple-wardens (presumably the same body described by Mitridastas in Lydian as *serlis srmlis*, the association of the temple). The opening lines of the column as preserved include the last few words explaining how he acquired the estate (*oikos*) from Antigonos. The rest of the column details the specific lands conveyed to the temple and lists certain properties exempt from conveyance.

---

28 Buckler and Robinson (1912, 1932:1–7). They suggest the wall formed part of a treasury or opisthodomos, apparently not recognizing that the temple faces west rather than east. This error was noted by Atkinson (1972:45); Gruben (1961) suggests the wall was part of the pronaos until the Roman period.

29 Buckler and Robinson (1932:1).

30 For the date of the inscription, see Debord (1972, 1982); for its reinscription on the temple wall, see Hanfmann (1983:119, 125). For the letter forms, see Descat (1985:98).

31 Descat (1985:98–99). For a letter of Antiochos III to Sardis, in which a certain Zeuxis controls western Asia Minor, see Robert (1964:I.1.8).

The lost beginning of Column II probably began with the granting clause, providing for reconveyance of the lands to Mnesimachos or his descendants if they paid off the loan within a fixed period; after that time neither they nor anyone else should have the right to redeem any of the lands, which would pass into the ownership of the temple of Artemis. The column begins with these words and continues with a guarantee: if anything happens to the lands to deprive the treasury of Artemis of their proceeds, the treasury will receive double the amount of the initial loan (namely, 2,650 gold staters), and Mnesimachos and his descendants will indemnify the treasury for loss of income and for any improvements it may have made on the land. If the king confiscates the land, Mnesimachos and his descendants will repay the treasury of Artemis the initial loan value; if Mnesimachos and his descendants default on payment, they will need to repay the treasury double the loan value. Lastly, Mnesimachos and his descendants are to be held liable for the full amount due until it is repaid *in toto*.

The conveyance includes lands from three different places: the plain of Sardis, the Water of Morstas, and Attoudda. We cannot ascertain the location of these places with any security. In the Sardian plain, the villages (*komai*) of Tobalmoura, Tandou, and Kombdilipia paid annual dues of 50 gold staters, while the allotment (*kleros*) of Kinaroa near Tobalmoura paid 3 staters; in the Water of Morstas, the village of Periasasostra paid 57 staters, while an allotment at Nagrioa paid 3 staters 4 obols; in Attoudda, the village of Ilos paid 3 staters 3 obols annually. A few specific estates, belonging to Pytheos and Adrastos, are exempted from the mortgage description: one *aule* and two *paradeisoi* from Tobalmoura, and from Periasasostra various farmsteads, as well as various houses (*oikiai*) of people (*laoi*) and slaves, and specific slaves mentioned by name. The total annual dues that were thus conveyed to the treasury of Artemis comprised 116 gold staters and 7 gold obols.

R. Descat has demonstrated that the lands described in the Mnesimachos Inscription, awarded to Mnesimachos as a *dorea*, or gift of the king, after the Macedonian conquest of the area, were divided and assessed according to Achaemenid land-tenure systems.[32] Comparing the lands and dues outlined in the inscription with the discussion in Herodotos 3.90–95, Descat reconstructed an Achaemenid fiscal system, showing the division of lands, their gift by the king to loyal subjects, and the taxes collected from them payable to the king. He demonstrates that the villages of Tobalmoura, Tandos, and Kombdilipia paid 50 darics revenue; the *kleros* at Kinaroa paid 3 darics; the village of Periasasostra paid 57 darics; the *kleros* at Nagrioa paid 3 1/3 darics; and the village of Ilos paid 3 1/3 darics.[33] Descat suggests that the parasang was the official unit of measurement: like the Greek system, he suggests,

32 Descat (1985).    33 Descat (1985:101).

the Achaemenid system would have defined a one-parasang unit of land as a rough rectangle, one parasang in circumference. He shows that a land parcel roughly one square kilometer would be worth 40 darics and yield taxes of 3 1/3 darics.[34] Thus the 116 2/3 darics payable yearly to Mnesimachos (or the treasury of Artemis) would correspond to land holdings of roughly 3,500 ha, a holding that bears some resemblance to Turkish land allotments around Sardis in the nineteenth century.[35]

The dues payable yearly represent roughly one-twelfth of the estimated value of the land.[36] They are assessed on three distinct categories: land (*komai, kleroi, oikopeda*) and men (*laoi*); dues rendered in silver and labor; and products (wine, produce and fruits).[37] This suggests a certain flexibility in assessment, or in the possibility of shuffling funds, that is perhaps a key to why the Achaemenid tribute system remained in effect into the Hellenistic period. Another fluid aspect of the tributary system is implied in Column II of the Mnesimachos Inscription: lands might change hands. Here, Mnesimachos promises to pay double the loaned amount if someone else should claim any of the lands in question, but to pay only the amount itself in full if the king should recall the lands and assign them to someone else. The implication is that the lands would continue to be taxed, perhaps at the same rate, but to be payable to somebody else. By this means, the king might show disapproval to those he no longer trusted or needed and grant benefits to those in his favor.

The Mnesimachos Inscription provides key insights into Achaemenid land-tenure systems at Sardis. Lands were apparently in the gift of the king. They were measured by the parasang. The yearly tax rates were one-twelfth of the overall value of the area given, drawn from an assessment of the land and the people living on it, the productivity of the land and its particular products, and dues payable in silver and labor. What proportion of the dues was drawn from each of these categories was presumably left to the discretion of the person to whom the land had been given. The lands and their dues were considered the property of that person, to do with as he wished, until the king decided to reclaim them and give them to another: thus the king retained his absolute suzerainty over the land. This system, with its flexibility and the absolute authority of the king over the specific authority of the favored person, was so effective that it remained in place from the assessment of Artaphernes in 494 into the Hellenistic period some two centuries later.

---

34 His complex reasoning is clearly laid out in Descat (1985:102–106).
35 Descat (1985:106–107).
36 For the discrepancy between this number and that given by Ps.-Arist., *Oikon.* II 1.4, who names one-tenth of the value as that payable in the Achaemenid empire, see Descat (1985:108).
37 See also Briant (1973, 1985a).

## Conclusion

Some of the information available from the inscriptions is also ascertainable from other sources of evidence. Thus, the mingling of Lydian, Iranian, and Greek names at Sardis might have been guessed from the literary sources with their clear indication of multiple ethnic presences at the city. The continuity of wording on the grave inscriptions might also have been surmised, based on the continuity of their form through the Achaemenid period: even the addition of Persianizing features like the Lydian/Aramaic bilinguals might have been postulated after seeing the introduction of couches into the tombs during the Achaemenid period (see chapter 6). But the inscriptions comprise our only source of information for various other aspects of life at Sardis in the Achaemenid period.

From the Mitridastas Inscriptions and the Mnesimachos Inscription, we gain a sense of the importance of the cult of Artemis at Sardis as a financial and legal institution. The temple treasury clearly functioned as a kind of bank, offering loans and serving as the executor of trusts – perhaps in much the same way that the cult of Artemis at Ephesos seems to have done, when the Athenian Xenophon entrusted his funds to Megabyzos, its high priest, in 401 BC. We recognize the expense of temple and cult upkeep, suggested by the properties being given by Mitridastas to support these costs. The savvy of the council of priests is suggested by the formal language of the Mnesimachos Inscription and its terms, which seem by no means unfavorable to the goddess. The temple association was apparently a powerful and wealthy body that wielded great juridical might backed up with the persuasive measure of the divine curse.

We also gain some insight into the manner in which land may have been distributed in the Achaemenid period by gift of the king. Its value was apparently assessed based on its productivity and on the worth of its real estate and human tenants, slave and other. Yearly dues were payable based on this assessment. The land's dues could be transferred to another by the person to whom the king had given it: thus Mnesimachos could convey the yearly dues to the treasury of Artemis, and the inscription clearly implies the land and its structures would be maintained or improved by the treasury. In effect, he could transfer usership and benefit of the land to the treasury of Artemis. But real ownership remained with the king – if the king chose to take his gift back from Mnesimachos and give it to another, neither Mnesimachos nor the treasury of Artemis would be able to stand in the way of his decision. Instead, Mnesimachos would need to find other sources for repaying the treasury's loan.

Thus, the inscriptions from Achaemenid-period Sardis provide additional evidence for some of the patterns seen in other material. The use of Lydian as a language into the Hellenistic period, the prevalence of Lydian names, and the continuity of the grave inscriptions demonstrate the ability of the Achaemenid regime to prosper while allowing local customs to continue. The corpus of inscriptions also shows the importance of the cult of Artemis in financial and legal terms. It demonstrates the existence of a council of priests that seems to have been a particularly powerful body. It shows that Iranian administrators like Droaphernes were involved with local cults and adopted local practices of dedication that were foreign to Mazdaism. It gives us an idea of the workings of land tenure in the Achaemenid period. The dynamic flexibility of Achaemenid administration is thus highlighted, and our understanding of it filled out, by the Sardian inscriptions.

# Mortuary evidence: dead and living societies

Mortuary material problematizes the picture of a unified elite gained so far from other sources of evidence. As a whole, the city's elite embraced the newly developed local culture, but individuals adhered at times to separate traditions that had pertained before the Achaemenid period. Mortuary practices show that elites signaled their status in similar ways, drawing on a newly developed iconographic and stylistic system that indicated wealth but *not* ethnicity and showed inclusion in the empire-wide elite, incorporating multiple aspects of imperial ideology. At the same time, however, the Sardian elite might choose to bury their dead in different tomb types based on differing traditions, probably to claim particular aspects of "Lydianness" or "Persianness" (or even "Egyptianness") as their own.

## Approaching mortuary evidence

Through remains of funerary rituals we can learn not only about attitudes towards death and an afterlife, but also about living societies, their organization and attitudes towards matters of the living.[1] Funerary rituals may be suggested by material remains included with the dead or by traces of activities surrounding the disposal of the dead. The attempt here to reconstruct ancient social organization by analyzing mortuary remains is based on the following principles and assumptions.

The archaeological record is, of course, a product of social action, in which social identities may be materially manifested; the mortuary record is particularly informative among archaeological corpora in that it is at least in part the direct result of conscious actions and selections of symbolically invested objects.[2] The assumption underlying most analyses of mortuary remains is that an individual's treatment after death bears a traceable relation to his or her state in life and to the organization of the society to which he or she belonged. Thus, when archaeologists excavate mortuary remains they are

---

1 For a recent synthetic work, see Parker Pearson (2000).
2 Parker Pearson (2000:21–32) summarizes the scholarship on mortuary ritual. For specific stages along the scholarly journey, see, e.g., Saxe (1970:4); processualists Binford (1971) and Brown (1971); energy-consumption modelers Peebles and Kus (1977) and Tainter (1978); "New Archaeologist" O'Shea (1984); the collected post-processualist essays in Chapman et al. (1981); classicist Morris (1988); and critic of New Archaeology Parker Pearson (2000:31–32), who points out problems inherent in sweeping generalizations and in a processualist approach that focuses on "*what* people did rather than *why* they did it."

excavating not just individuals, but coherent social personalities who had relationships with other social personalities according to rules and structures dictated by the larger social system. Therefore the discussion below of funerary couches, for instance, seeks to embed them within their cultural context, exploring their symbolic meaning as mortuary embellishments and considering what this may imply about the living society.

Conscious social identity need not be reflected in the mortuary record; but when social differentiation is obvious in mortuary remains, this probably does reflect the social organization of the living society.[3] Yet how helpful mortuary evidence really is to modern scholars may vary greatly. Archaeological formation processes and post-depositional processes will select for the survival of particular kinds of evidence over others – inorganic substances over organic, adult bones over infant, burials over exposures in tree-tops – skewing the information available to the archaeologist. The same will be the case where grave robbing has taken place: robbers, be they human or other animal, will select for particular items from a grave in preference over others (jewelry or magical emblems, tasty thighbones). Multiple interments in the same grave, a common phenomenon at Sardis, may confuse discrete deposits by adding or taking away material from earlier burials.

The degree of conscious choice associated with different funerary objects or actions also will affect their significance. Inclusions in a grave may have been deposited with varying degrees of intention: they may be intentional, coincidental, or accidental. Intentional deposition might include constructing a mortuary site, treatment of the body, or placement of objects in a grave; it may reflect the ideas of the survivors or specific requests on the part of the deceased. Coincidental deposition is non-purposive, or not the focus of attention: it might include buttons on the clothes a person was wearing. Accidental inclusions may be the result of post-depositional site formation processes, or of trauma – an arrowhead lodged in bone or a piece of shrapnel embedded in flesh. These complicating factors would all be present, even if one were dealing with the careful excavation of a complete site in which no graves were missed and all evidence were properly recorded!

It is also important to remember that it is not the dead who dispose of themselves, but the living. And the living may alter the material

---

3 "Social organization" encompasses politically/ideologically and religiously mandated protocols. For the role of material culture in symbolizing social identity, see, e.g., Appadurai (1986); also Turner (1967:50–51, 292), Ortner (1978:5), Pollock (1983:12 ff.). An object or symbol may have one meaning in an individual context and another in a societal context. For the importance of symbol *use* in conferring and propagating meaning, see, e.g., Pollock (1983:10–11), Kus (1982:47–62), Douglas and Isherwood (1978), Bourdieu (1977:25). The physical manifestation of social identities may be idiosyncratic and based on personal experience, or it may be more generalized, shared by many people and passed on from one generation to the next. See Turner (1974:13 ff.).

surroundings of the dead to suit their own needs, or may select for particular items they feel represent the personality of the dead person. Clothing may serve as an example of this phenomenon. As one scholar notes:[4]

> As with other forms of material culture, it is easy to lie – to misrepresent ourselves – with clothes, to take on a personality and status which is other than our normal self. Clothes and ornamentation are strategic representations through which we project our personalities and values. But at a funeral, choosing what to wear for the big event is not a matter decided by the deceased. Even the decision to leave the corpse in the clothes the dead person wore in life is one taken by the living. The dressing of the dead is always carried out by the living and consequently the costume of the dead constitutes the mourners' reading or representation of the dead person's former self-representation through dress.

This matters because archaeologists try to reconstruct ancient meaning and social identities on the basis of symbolic objects, often objects with multiple symbolisms whose meanings will vary depending on their context and the way in which they are used.

Thus the interpretation of the mortuary record is complicated: there is no simple congruence between a living society and mortuary treatment. This is at least in part because personal preference – personal identity – plays a role in the treatment of the dead, as does social identity, producing a great degree of potential variability in mortuary ritual and remains. Personal choice (of deceased or survivors) played an important role in mortuary treatment at Achaemenid Sardis: for instance, personal ornaments or seals in a particular style might signal an individual's elite status, but not all elite individuals chose to have ornaments or seals made in this style. Even with all the uncertainties surrounding the interpretation of mortuary remains, however, Achaemenid-period burials at Sardis provide us with a great deal of information about the living inhabitants of the city.

## Understanding mortuary treatment at Sardis in the Achaemenid period

At least three different modes of mortuary disposal were prevalent in Achaemenid Sardis:[5] built chamber tombs, usually covered with a tumulus; rock-cut tombs dug into the cliff faces of the necropolis hill across from the acropolis and in the gullies at the south of the acropolis; and inhumations in cist graves. The latter two sometimes but not always included

---

4 Parker Pearson (2000:9).
5 A complete analysis of all Sardian tombs from all periods is forthcoming by C.H. Greenewalt, Jr.; my comments here are provisional. I am grateful to him for letting me make use of his manuscript in writing this chapter. The appendix included here is adapted from Dusinberre (1997b). See also Ratté (1989b, forthcoming), McLauchlin (1985).

sarcophagi of wood, terracotta, or marble. The Pyramid Tomb, described below, is another, anomalous, tomb form that may be dated to the Achaemenid
period. The coexistence of three very different common forms of mortuary
treatment is interesting, although what we can say about them is somewhat circumscribed. Certain features of the Sardian context complicate the
analysis of Achaemenid-period mortuary remains.

Circumstances of observation have affected the potential for study in particular ways. The very great majority of those graves explored are rock-cut
tombs excavated by the Butler expedition between 1910 and 1914, and again
in 1922: at least 1,154 graves were opened in these years.[6] Some 160 of these
tombs still contained objects, generally in disturbed contexts. These artifacts
were described on object cards kept by the expedition, arranged according
to tomb number. Few tombs were drawn or even described, and much of the
information about their structure is the result only of notes on the cards
stipulating the findspot of the objects: "rear bed," for instance, implies the
existence of at least two rock-cut benches or couches, one of which was
along the rear wall of the tomb; "dromos" implies the existence of a narrow passageway leading into a larger chamber. It has proved in most cases
impossible to check these descriptions against modern observations, as no
plan or map exists which locates the graves explored in these years. Thus,
connecting objects to the tombs from which they came has been fraught
with difficulty. None the less, some information is available about certain
tombs excavated by Butler and all of the graves explored by the modern
expedition.

Chronology is another real issue in the study of Achaemenid-period tombs
at Sardis. The date at which Cyrus may have conquered Sardis, 547 BC, is
a precise and finicky date – how can one be certain if a grave was made
before or after that year? And what if it was constructed in April, rather
than December? The matter is particularly knotty as our understanding of
the local ceramic sequence for the latter half of the sixth century BC is still
shaky: no deposits that may be securely dated to this period have yet been
excavated at Sardis (see chapter 8). As well as ceramic evidence, however,
jewelry and other ornamentation are helpful indicators of the general date
of those tombs which contained objects.[7] It seems, moreover, that those

---

6 Greenewalt (1972:115 n. 5). Most of the information about the form of these graves comes from
   brief descriptions of artifact findspots on the object cards written by G.H. Chase in 1914 and
   T.L. Shear in 1922.
      For the funerary inscriptions, mostly in Lydian, all from the Achaemenid period, see
   chapter 5. Many of the Lydian inscriptions were on tomb entrance plugs carved in the shape of
   doors; for similar doors, see, e.g., Tritsch (1943), Waelkens (1986), Özgen and Öztürk (1996:50).
7 It remains to be seen if linear chronological stylistic development is an appropriate concept
   in Achaemenid-period Sardian art. I have not assigned specific dates to any of the artifacts
   discussed here, rather categorizing them as "Achaemenid period."

tombs which include couches or benches and which may be securely dated on the basis of masonry techniques or associated finds were all constructed in the Achaemenid period. Couches in tombs may therefore perhaps be taken to indicate an Achaemenid-period date.[8] Stone and ceramic alabastra are common inclusions in Achaemenid-period burials both at Sardis and elsewhere, but are perhaps not necessarily indicative of a burial date in the Achaemenid period.[9] Those stone and terracotta sarcophagi at Sardis that may be securely dated apparently stem from the Achaemenid period and later, but it would probably be dangerous to make too much of such negative evidence in a case where the sample is so small and retrieval so arbitrary. Of the approximately 150 burial tumuli at the great Lydian cemetery at Bin Tepe, those smaller tumuli that have been excavated may be dated on the basis of masonry techniques and other evidence to the Achaemenid period and later.

Surprisingly few tombs have been excavated at Sardis that may be convincingly dated to the pre-Achaemenid period of the Lydian kingdom. The three largest tumuli at Bin Tepe, however, seem to predate Achaemenid conquest. These are ascribed on the basis of literary testimonia, architectural technique, and ceramic evidence to the Lydian king Alyattes and, perhaps, two other members of the ruling family. Tumuli seem thus to be securely identifiable as a specifically Lydian tradition for at least several decades before the Achaemenid conquest. Several rock-cut tombs, without couches but with ceramic inclusions that apparently all date to the pre-conquest period, demonstrate the existence of this parallel tradition at Sardis during the time of the Lydian kingdom. And it seems very likely that cist graves were part of the pre-Achaemenid Lydian tradition.

This last underscores another problem with mortuary analysis at Sardis: retrieval of tombs. Tumuli are for the most part highly visible, often made more so by their situation on promontories or outcrops.[10] This feature means we have a fairly good idea of the location and number of tumuli in the Sardis region, and the interiors of a number of tumuli have been explored

8  See also McLauchlin (1985:152). The Sardians may have been using couches in other contexts before the Achaemenid conquest: such is certainly implied by Hdt. 1.50, in which Croesus makes a grand sacrifice that includes "couches covered with gold and silver," as part of a great feast offered to the gods. This raises questions about the beginning of reclining banqueting – thought by many to be another Achaemenid import. See Dentzer (1982). It is possible Herodotos added to Croesus' sacrifice luxurious items that seemed to him stereotypically eastern, without much care for or perhaps knowledge of chronological realities. For the development of couches over time in Near Eastern and Greek contexts, see Kyrieleis (1969).

9  These vessels clearly had great importance in Achaemenid-period burials of western Anatolia, however: beneath the Maussolleion at Halikarnassos Newton discovered a number of alabaster jars (in fragments), one with the cuneiform and hieroglyphic inscription: "Xerxes, the Great King" (Moorey 1980) (see chapter 4). For alabaster alabastra included in a (bronze) sarcophagus burial at Susa, see Tallon (1992).

10 Ramage and Ramage (1971).

by the Sardis Expedition and the Manisa Museum.[11] Rock-cut tombs were vigorously sought by the Butler expedition, and several tombs were opened or re-examined by the modern expedition.[12] But the discovery of simple cist graves or buried sarcophagi has been and must remain largely a matter of chance. The sampling of graves at Sardis therefore is greatly skewed toward the rock-cut tomb and the built chamber tomb covered with a tumulus. This discussion thus cannot present a comprehensive picture but seeks only to raise some questions of interpretation posed by the remains currently available.[13]

## Mortuary structures and status

Some have argued that the amount of energy expended in mortuary treatment, combined with the expectation of pyramid-like rank membership, might lead to an impression of the status of the individual buried: for instance, simple inhumation requires less energy than a disarticulation of the skeleton, which is in turn less energy-consumptive than a built tomb, so we might say that those who were simply inhumed were of lesser rank than those whose corpses were enclosed in a tomb.[14] But energy expenditure on mortuary treatment is only a one-way street: expensive tombs surely indicate wealth, but inexpensive tombs do not necessarily indicate a lack of wealth.[15] An individual who *could* potentially expend the energy on tomb construction might choose not to.[16] Thus tombs that are expensive to build *must* have been made by those with the resources to build them and may reflect conscious rank indication or other differentiation within a living society, whereas those which are inexpensive to build could have belonged either to people with fewer available resources or to those who simply chose not to expend their resources.

At Sardis, wealth was not the determining factor for mortuary structure: wealthy people chose various methods of disposal and chose them for

---

11  Thirteen built chamber tombs with tumuli over them that date or probably date to the Achaemenid period have been excavated: BT62.4, BT63.2, BT66.1, BT66.2, BT66.3 (?), BT66.4 (?), BT66.6 (?), BK71.1, Tomb 77.1 (?), Tomb 82.1 (?), Tomb BC/T 2 (?), Tomb BC/T 5 (?), and Tomb 1976–1. I use the numbering system of the Sardis Expedition where possible and follow McLauchlin (1985) otherwise.

12  Hanfmann (1960a:10–12), Greenewalt et al. (1987).

13  Why are there so few grave stelae from Sardis, and so many from Daskyleion, the satrapal capital of Hellespontine Phrygia? Perhaps this is a result of a strong local tradition at Sardis and an openness to eastern as well as western cultural attributes (see chapter 8), whereas Daskyleion seems (based on the large amount of imported Attic pottery) primarily to have been looking westward for cultural stimulus. For "Graeco-Persian" grave stelae, see, e.g., Akurgal (1966), Altheim-Stiehl (1983), Nollé (1992:55 ff.), Cremer (1984:89–90), Radt (1983), Dolunay (1967), Borchhardt (1968), Polat (1994).

14  Ucko (1969), Tainter (1977).      15  See also Parker Pearson (2000:32–44).

16  See, e.g., burial practices in nineteenth-century Cambridgeshire: Cannon (1989, 1991).

various reasons, perhaps ideological. Although the grave inclusions found with some of the tumulus tombs confirm their use by people of wealth and, apparently, status, they are equalled by the inclusions in some of the rock-cut tombs (see below). Xenophon also suggests high-ranking rock-cut burials in *Kyropaideia* 7.3.4–5, describing the tomb of the Persian noble Abradatas dug into a ridge by his servants and eunuchs. Indeed, the tombs of the Achaemenid kings at Naqsh-i Rustam were cut into cliff faces.[17] Clearly other factors beyond conspicuous expenditure of energy might play into choice of tomb type. And of the two cist graves opened by the modern expedition, one included a gold melon-shaped bead of a sort usually dated to the Achaemenid period and a barrel-shaped banded agate bead on a gold wire suspension. The person buried in this grave therefore was possessed of some personal wealth.[18] A similar phenomenon may be seen at Susa, where exceptionally valuable inclusions were found in an Achaemenid-period sarcophagus in a cist.[19] The type of tomb chosen at Sardis thus need not indicate the status or wealth of the person buried.[20]

## Different mortuary structures and funerary ceremonies

This discussion of funerary ceremonies considers mortuary inclusions as well as structure. Ceramic objects included in tombs of all types of the Achaemenid period are for the most part associated with drinking parties or symposia. The overwhelming majority of pots are drinking vessels – cups (skyphoi, Achaemenid bowls), storage vessels (amphorai, hydriai), mixing vessels (kraters), and pouring vessels (oinochoai) – and such unguentaria as lekythoi, alabastra, and lydions.[21] Of the more than 250 vessels recovered from tombs at Sardis, at least 100 are drinking vessels and another 100 or so are unguent vessels. Funerary rites may therefore have included some idea of an eternal symposium after death, as suggested also by sepulchral sculptures, with an emphasis on drinking rather than eating. Providing the

---

17 Schmidt (1970).
18 Of course, the presence of gold jewelry in this cist does not imply possessing the resources necessary to build a tumulus.
19 See Tallon (1992).
20 The fact that there are only three major kinds of tombs suggests there may have been particular kinds of culturally defined restrictions within which individuals and their families were choosing. It is possible there was some logic here that cannot yet be identified.
21 For the lydion, see Greenewalt (1972:132–133); for its contents, see Greenewalt (1972), Rumpf (1920:165 ff.), Roebuck (1959:56). The association of scented oils with banqueting in the Greek world seems clear, and it is likely they were associated in Persia also. Alabastron-type vessels are shown carried by several figures in interior doorways of, e.g., the palace of Darius at Persepolis, where supplies for banqueting are shown carried on the stair up to the level of the building. See Schmidt (1953). Only forty vessels from Sardian tombs had to do with eating (McLauchlin 1985:153–154).

dead with the means for proper drinking, including such paraphernalia as scented oils, was clearly of importance to survivors. The addition of couches in the Achaemenid period is perhaps a continuation of an idea stemming from the time of the Lydian kingdom, kitting the dead out with such symposiastic furnishings as were now appropriate, given the change in banqueting trends.[22]

Tumuli have perhaps been the most carefully explored of the tomb types at Sardis and have yielded information about funerary activities. Charcoal layers have been recovered from above the limestone ceiling beams of several built chamber tombs/tumuli, including at least one tumulus of the Lydian kingdom (the Tomb of Alyattes) as well as smaller tumuli dating to the Achaemenid period (including BK 71.1).[23] These fires need not indicate incineration of bodies – indeed, probably do not[24] – but rather most likely represent some type of ceremony involving fire, conducted at the tomb site.[25] Pyres are attested in the ceremonies surrounding the use of tumulus tombs in both the pre-Achaemenid period and the Achaemenid period, and one may hypothesize the continuity of a Lydian funerary tradition into the Achaemenid period. The addition of funerary couches to tumulus tombs does suggest some alteration in the ceremony as a whole, however (again, BK 71.1 is a good example).

It is possible that the couches found in rock-cut tombs and built chamber tombs had some symbolic significance in addition to that of banquet ceremonies. Some form of Mazdaism was practiced by the Achaemenid kings and probably some other Persians at least from the time of Darius I. It is absolutely contrary to (later) Zoroastrian beliefs to bury the dead rather than exposing them to the air. The fact that the Achaemenid kings were entombed in built or rock-cut tombs that elevated their bodies above the earth may point to similar taboos; certainly many inhabitants of Achaemenid-period Sardis also avoided covering corpses with earth. Perhaps the couches served a religious purpose for some of the inhabitants of the city in Achaemenid times, lifting corpses off the ground and symbolically surrounding them with air, "exposing" them even within the confines of tombs otherwise built according to local traditions.

Various permutations of disposal of the dead in the Achaemenid empire are described by Greek authors, including Herodotos' famous description of

---

22 See Dentzer (1969, 1971), Collon (1992).
23 For the Tomb of Alyattes, see Greenewalt (1972:128 n. 12), von Olfers (1858:547), Hanfmann (1963:55), McLauchlin (1985:171–174), Ratté (1989b:157–162). For BK 71.1, see Ramage (1972: 11–15), McLauchlin (1985:197–200), Ratté (1989b:189–195).
24 McLauchlin (1985:156–158).
25 Another example of ash above the chamber of a tumulus tomb is at İkiztepe, near Güre, on the border between Lydia and Phrygia (Özgen and Öztürk 1996). Fires might also be associated with completely different tomb types near Sardis: see Cahill (1988).

the Magi (1.140).[26] Is it possible that his assertion that the "Persians" bury their dead, taken in connection with Xenophon's mention of the rock-cut tomb constructed for Abradatas (*Kyropaideia* 7.3.4–5) and the couches prevalent in Achaemenid-period tombs at Sardis, might provide some explanation for this? I do not mean to suggest that all Persians were practicers of Mazdaism and therefore established new funerary customs at Sardis: the picture is far more complex. The burial in a sarcophagus sunk into the ground of the man who wore the cylinder seal IAM 4581, discussed in chapter 7, conforms to the sarcophagus found at Susa and is an example of the eclectic nature of developing funerary practices at Sardis.

It may have been that Mazdaism banned the burning of corpses in the sacred fire. Herodotos reports the burning of Amasis' mummy by Kambyses, an order which was considered sacrilegious by both Egyptians and Persians.[27] There is no evidence for the use of funerary couches as supports for cinerary urns or other receptacles for the ashes left by cremation; indeed, they would provide uneasy rest for a body in a flexed position and probably supported corpses that were laid flat. The Sardian couches do not necessarily indicate that those laid upon them were practicers of Mazdaism. Yet these couches are not only concordant with imperial Achaemenid mortuary treatment but indeed may represent a modification to local tomb structures and burial practices that bring earlier local traditions into accordance with imperial Mazdaism.

Whether couches are a reflection of Achaemenid belief or a modification of a tradition that provided the dead with the accoutrements for drinking parties reflecting a different social imperative, they represent a change in local mortuary practices at Sardis in the Achaemenid period. Such a change in treatment of the dead most likely reflects a change in the symbols of the living: the importation into Sardis of particular symbolic furniture that had significance among the living in the context of banqueting and among the dead perhaps additionally in a new religious belief system.[28]

This idea is convincingly borne out by investigations in Iran. The Tomb of Cyrus consists of a thick-walled, gable-roofed chamber closed with a small double door, standing on a stepped pedestal (fig. 50).[29] The interior of the

26 It is clear Herodotos misunderstood certain aspects of the foreign religion and translated others into a more Greek context that made sense to him or his listeners. See Young (1988:99–103).

27 Hdt. 3.16. This story naturally runs counter to the order by Cyrus (as reported by Herodotos) that Croesus be burned on the pyre (Hdt. 1.86–92); but the folktale aspects of this story in this version and in versions by Bacchylides (*Epinikia* 3.23–62) and Nikolaos of Damaskos (*FGrHist* 90 F68) have been noted by many scholars. See, e.g., Kirk (1974). For Herodotos' account of Darius' behavior at Nitokris' tomb and its relation to Achaemenid beliefs, see Dillery (1992). For Achaemenid approaches to fire, see Boyce (1975).

28 For a recent discussion of the symbolic significance of the reclining banquet in Assyria, see Nylander (1999).

29 The Tomb of Cyrus stands alone south of the palaces at Pasargadae: its base is 5.5 m high, and its cella 6.4 m by 5.35 m across and 5.5 m high. The burial chamber is approx. 3 m by 2 m.

**Fig. 50**
Pasargadae: the
tomb of King
Cyrus.

chamber is now empty, but this was not the case in the Achaemenid period. When Alexander the Great passed Pasargadae, his chronicler Aristoboulos entered the tomb. Arrian,[30] following Aristoboulos' account, describes a couch with a golden coffin on it, and a table; Strabo[31] says Aristoboulos claimed to have seen a golden couch and coffin, and a table with drinking cups. It is possible that a Greek of the fourth century BC, by now accustomed to an association of banqueting with treatment of the dead in the Achaemenid empire, might have invented the drinking vessels on the table. The common inclusion of drinking vessels in other tombs of the Achaemenid period, however, suggests it may be an accurate description.[32] Thus we see in the Tomb of Cyrus a couch and the necessary equipment for banqueting, just as we see in the tombs of Achaemenid-period Sardis.[33]

The roof is double-sloping, with a molded, Ionic-style cornice; the front gable is decorated with a rosette. See Stronach (1978:24–43, 1963, 1964, 1965), Nylander (1970), Sami (1956).

30 *Anabasis* 6.29.      31 *Geog.* 15.3.7.

32 Even the sarcophagus burial from Susa includes three vessels: a silver phiale and two alabaster alabastra. See Tallon (1992).

33 These Greek accounts comprise the evidence available for reclining banqueting in a funerary context. As yet, evidence of reclining banqueting in a living context is lacking for the center of the Achaemenid empire. This is not to say that the Persians never reclined, but none of the extant evidence indicates that reclining was the usual way to participate in banquets. The numerous representations on seals and seal impressions, for instance, portray people seated to dine. On the other hand, I am unaware of any Near Eastern seals showing reclining banqueters, including seals dating to the Assyrian period when the sculptures from Nineveh show Assurbanipal reclining.

Importantly, there may have been a connection between the practice of banqueting in life and considerations of death. Herodotos claims that wealthy Persians gave banquets (called *tykta*, which he correlates to the Greek word *teleios*) on their birthdays.[34] A birthday celebration is of course associated with longevity and continued life; it is also an acknowledgment of mortality and possible death, escaped for now. If indeed *tykta* corresponds to *teleios,* it may reinforce the connection between banqueting, birthdays, and death. The Greek word *teleios* means complete, having reached its end, or perfect. It is closely connected to *telos,* which may mean goal or end but also signifies completion of a full cycle, in the sense of German *Vollendung*. It is thus significant that it was on his birthday, when his mortality was most predictably at the front of his mind, that the king should have anointed his head and provided a tremendous banquet with gifts for the Persians. The importance of banqueting in a living context among high-status Persians is also suggested by Achaemenid imperial art, in repeated "banquet" provision motifs.[35]

Thus the presence of couches in Achaemenid-period tombs at Sardis is particularly significant. The association of banqueting with death may have been traditional for the Lydians, as their grave inclusions suggest. It was apparently also an idea that mattered to the Persians. The couches of the Achaemenid-period tombs at Sardis may articulate an association of the banquet couché with banquets for the dead in a manner that corresponded to the practices of Mazdaism as well as Lydian funeral customs.

## Mortuary structure and ethnicity

It is impossible to tell from tomb structure whether the person buried within a tomb at Sardis was ethnically "Lydian," "Persian," "Greek," or anything else.[36] It is also impossible to tell the ethnic background of a person after

---

Diodorus Siculus (19.22,1–3) describes a post-Alexandrian feast at Persepolis at which participants reclined in concentric rings according to their status. The problem with using this anecdote to reconstruct Achaemenid banquets is that we cannot demonstrate that this feast emulates an Achaemenid custom. For Hellenistic royal banquets in a reclining position, see Murray (1996).

34 Hdt. 1.133; 9.110.    35 See also Briant (1989b), Lewis (1987).

36 Research in the field of ethnicity has its roots in colonialism, and particularly in economic studies: its pioneer is Furnivall, who published (1944) a study of the plural, or ethnically divided, economy of Netherlands India. "Ethnicity" was first formulated in theoretical terms by the Norwegian anthropologist Barth (1969). It has subsequently been abandoned by social anthropologists as an unmeaningful construct: the variables are not only too many to understand but shift constantly depending on context. See, e.g., Lockwood (1984). For some problems of definition, see Moerman (1965, 1968). An interesting attempt to explore ethnicity through ancient texts is Goudriaan (1988). A recent work exploring self-identity and nationalism is Anderson (1991).

examining the objects included in the grave. Ethnic background is not explicitly signaled in mortuary treatment at Sardis in the Achaemenid period, at least not in a way that a modern scholar can detect. This is a crucial point, as it suggests it was not a difference that was important to the living society to make clear in mortuary treatment. Rather, grave inclusions suggest the presence of a cosmopolitan, polyethnic elite at Sardis: an elite that was devising a new symbolic language of personal ornamentation and funerary inclusion to symbolize membership in and adherence to the new standards and ways of the wealthy and those of high status in Achaemenid-period Lydia. Thus the goods included in tombs (discussed below). Tomb *structures*, however, show that the picture may have been more complex than this harmonious description might suggest.

Traditions of people coming from diverse lands contributed to the culture of Achaemenid-period Sardis. Some of the individuals buried at Sardis at this time were buried in ways that strongly recall these external influences. This may indicate the blood "ethnicity" or nationality of the person buried. Conceivably, however, it represents rather the conscious appropriation of signifiers of one ethnic group by a member of a different group, or by a person of multiple-ethnic heritage.[37] The Pyramid Tomb, for instance, may have been intended to demonstrate some sort of specific adherence to Achaemenid practice (fig. 51).[38] This tomb, with a stepped base on which was a built chamber, has been convincingly reconstructed to bear a close resemblance to the Tomb of Cyrus at Pasargadae.[39] Even if the chamber was enclosed within a stepped pyramid that continued all the way up to a pointed apex,[40] the masonry techniques used in the construction of Cyrus' tomb and the Pyramid Tomb remain strikingly similar.[41] Masonry techniques without recognizable formal similarities may reflect the techniques of a cosmopolitan labor force that had by this time worked in Lydia, Babylon, and Pasargadae, its members flowing with the locus of activity.[42]

As cultural historians whose inquiry is rooted in a specific historical environment, however, scholars of Achaemenid studies have been very concerned with trying to understand the nature and complexity of administration in a polyethnic situation. Prosopographic approaches to disentangling ethnic background in Achaemenid Anatolia include Sekunda (1985, 1988, 1991), Bryce (1986). For recent work on cultural cross-fertilization and issues of identifying ethnicity via art, see, e.g., Root (1998, 1999).

37 Intermarriage between people of different ethnicities must, of course, have taken place throughout the empire. This topic is one that needs further study in western Anatolia. For prosopographic studies of western Anatolia, see, e.g., Sekunda (1985, 1988, 1991). A nuanced study of names and ethnicity is Schmitt (1991b).

38 For another apparently unique Achaemenid-period tomb in the region, see Cahill (1988).

39 I follow Ratté (1992), who proposes a reconstruction of the Pyramid Tomb as a gable-roofed chamber atop a stepped platform, on the grounds that the weight of a pyramid-shaped tomb would be too much for the ceiling beams to bear.

40 See Ratté (1989b:212–214), Kaspar (1984, 1988).

41 Stronach (1978:17), Nylander (1970).    42 Nylander (1970), Root (1979).

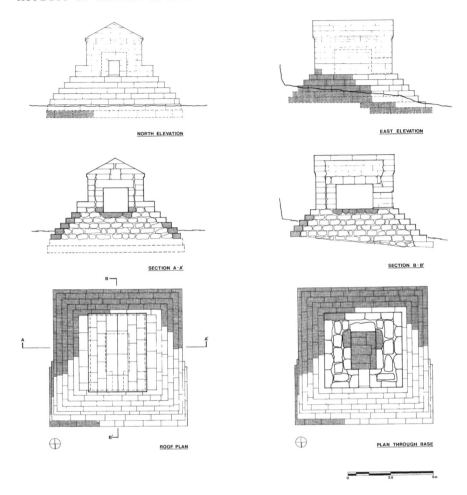

NORTH ELEVATION

EAST ELEVATION

SECTION A-A'

SECTION B-B'

B

A

A'

B'

ROOF PLAN

PLAN THROUGH BASE

0        2.5        5m

**Fig. 51** Sardis: Pyramid Tomb: conjectural reconstruction.

The question of relative date is a curious one, however. It has long been assumed that the Pyramid Tomb postdates the Tomb of Cyrus, largely on the grounds that it is reconstructed to look like Cyrus' tomb.[43] The recent discovery and publication of Achaemenid bowl sherds found in the rubble fabric of the Pyramid Tomb clearly demonstrate that the tomb postdates Persian arrival in Sardis (see chapter 8). On the basis of masonry techniques, the tomb was built between the mid-sixth and early fifth centuries BC.[44] It would seem there are simply no precedents for the Tomb of Cyrus, in

43 For the Pyramid Tomb postdating Cyrus', Butler (1922:166 ff.). For the contrary suggestion, Stronach (1978:41). The date of Cyrus' tomb is not entirely clear but has in general been put between 546 and 530, as no claw-chisel marks are visible on the tomb. See Nylander (1970), Stronach (1978:24–43).

44 Ratté (1992:152–154).

Iran or elsewhere.[45] Two similar, later, structures have been found in Persia, however: the Gur-i Dukhtar and the Takht-i Gohar.[46] Thus there are parallel examples from Persia of tombs that copy that of Cyrus. This makes a tomb of similar structure, built at Sardis on the far edges of the empire probably within fifty years of the construction of Cyrus' tomb, all the more interesting.

Was the tomb constructed by someone who was her or himself an "ethnic Persian" and wished to make that clear, or was it built by an "ethnic Lydian" or somebody else who wished to make a statement of adherence to the policies or ideologies of the polyethnic Achaemenid elite? For that matter, if the tomb was actually a stepped pyramid that enclosed a chamber within, could it have been commissioned by an "ethnic Egyptian" or perhaps by someone (a Lydian?) who had been to Egypt and was so impressed by what he or she saw there that its recreation at home seemed a good idea? In a city probably swelled with people from all corners of the world, who lived together with (or as) the Achaemenid elite and constructed new cosmopolitan cultures and social organizations, what did "ethnicity" signify? A consideration of the tumulus tombs at Sardis problematizes the issue yet further.

As mentioned above, three enormous tumuli were constructed at Bin Tepe before the Achaemenid conquest of Lydia: the Tomb of Alyattes, Karnıyarık Tepe, and Kır Mustafa Tepe, all thought to be tombs of the ruling Mermnad family.[47] In the Achaemenid period and probably in the Hellenistic period use of the cemetery increased dramatically: of the approximately 150 tombs at Bin Tepe, *only* the three largest are fairly securely datable to the Lydian kingdom. Those smaller tumuli that have been excavated may be dated on the basis of masonry techniques and other evidence to the Achaemenid period and later. The grave goods indicate the embracing of Persian luxury accoutrements: they include dozens of gold foil clothing appliqués and other jewelry that conform to Achaemenid-period iconography in Lydia, including such features as stamped appliqués showing winged human-headed bulls and earrings that end in lion's-head terminals (see fig. 56).[48] And at least one of the tumuli had a chariot burial – complete with horse(s) – in its dromos.[49] But inclusion of these materials does not in itself demonstrate the ethnicity of the people buried in the tombs. What, then, is the significance of the burgeoning activity at Bin Tepe in the Achaemenid period? Two alternative interpretations suggest themselves to me in lieu of more concrete evidence in the form of grave goods found *in situ*.

At Achaemenid-period Bin Tepe, many people began emulating the socially symbolic burial practices that had previously apparently been limited

---

45 Stronach (1978:39–43).     46 Stronach (1978:300–304).
47 See Ratté (1994b) for Karnıyarık Tepe.
48 Manisa Museum 6277 and 5225, respectively.     49 Kökten (1997).

to the Lydian kings. It is possible this is the result of increased social mobility in Achaemenid-period Sardis, where suddenly the ranks of the elite were opened to many more people who wanted to make the most direct statement they could about their new status. What better way to symbolize membership in the ranks of the privileged than to bury your dead in a manner previously the prerogative only of the ruling family? According to interpretation one, then, the large numbers of tumuli at Bin Tepe that date to the Achaemenid period reflect increased social mobility in Achaemenid Sardis, and a relaxing of the lines that had previously kept royalty demarcated from those of lesser social status.

Interpretation two suggests burial at Bin Tepe was a specific statement of social identity as "Lydian." The tumuli of the Lydian kings stood for all to see, according to Herodotos (1.93) the greatest work of human hands in all the world outside Egypt and Babylon. Perhaps these tumuli were seen as specifically Lydian, something to adhere to and be proud of, in a way rock-cut tombs were not. Perhaps it was Lydian Sardians who buried their dead in tumuli at Bin Tepe, specifically to emphasize their Lydian ethnicity and to differentiate themselves from the Achaemenid conquerors. Or conversely, perhaps ethnic Persians chose to bury their dead in Lydian-style tumuli, thereby co-opting the local cultural tradition. These built chamber tombs none the less frequently include funeral couches. Thus even in a potentially self-conscious "ethnic" statement of adherence to pre-Achaemenid Lydia, the paraphernalia associated with funerary banqueting reflect this change found also in the rock-cut tombs. It is not incongruent that a person should have wished to equate himself with the old epichoric traditions of the region in selected aspects of funerary treatment, yet have taken on funerary banqueting patterns that conformed to certain customs of the conquerors.[50]

If interpretation two is correct, it shows a fascinating mix of culture and sentiment at Sardis: an assumption of Achaemenid adornment and funerary banqueting customs combined with a purposive adherence to a Lydian social identity. Mortuary *inclusions* suggest that ethnic self-identification was not a matter of paramount importance to the elite: most people are buried with a similar range of styles and objects that seem to display allegiance to the Achaemenid hegemony. Mortuary *structures*, by contrast, suggest it was important at least to some people to signal allegiance to a personal (Lydian) ethnic heritage through tomb architecture. Perhaps the very visible association with local tradition that tumuli represent might even give families or

---

50 See Cosgrove and Daniels (1988) for the symbolic importance of epichoric traditions. For a recent study exploring the superposition of external cultural paraphernalia and the simultaneous emphasis on local tradition, see Arcelin (1992).

individuals at Sardis a secure base from which they might collaborate (or cooperate) all the more effectively with the new Persian overlords.

The flexibility of Achaemenid governing practices perhaps even encouraged mixed reactions to Achaemenid hegemony. Indeed, mixed reactions must have been common, encompassed by official and personal practice. At the center of the empire, the royal stance (personal and official) to the issue of personal "ethnicity" versus the hegemonic ideology of a world of various peoples brought together as one expresses the two aspects simultaneously in a dynamic equilibrium. A concern with personal "ethnicity" is made explicit in Darius' imperial inscriptions, where he not only mentions the specific nationalities of those with whom he deals, but repeatedly emphasizes his own Persian nationality.[51] Such sculptures as the king being borne aloft by the peoples of the realm (e.g., relief sculptures at Naqsh-i Rustam and Persepolis [fig. 52]; the Egyptian sculpture of Darius found at Susa), on the other hand, emphasize the holistic nature of the empire and the unifying of the various peoples of the world into one empire.[52] Perhaps the Sardian tumulus tombs are a local elite reflection of this royally expressed concept of "ethnicity," with simultaneous adherence to a personal ethnicity and to an acceptance of unifying hegemony.

Other factors may have helped in determining the treatment of the dead at Sardis in the Achaemenid period. Grave stelae and "phallic markers" were used as funerary markers to emphasize or embellish tombs.[53] The "phallic markers," stone pillars with a swollen rounded top that slightly resemble mushrooms, have been found only in connection with tumuli. Funerary stelae, on the other hand, seem to be particularly associated with rock-cut tombs. The stelae were sometimes inscribed in the Lydian language, a few were sculpted in relief, and others have apparently plain shafts (perhaps painted in antiquity) crowned with floral anthemia (see chapter 4). Those stelae which have been dated on the basis of stylistic or other criteria all date to the Achaemenid period or later. This is a particularly interesting point when considered in connection with the rock-cut tombs of the Persian kings at Naqsh-i Rustam, embellished with sculpted reliefs and, in the case of Darius, with multilingual inscriptions.[54] The rock of the necropolis and acropolis hills at Sardis is too soft and crumbly to take sculpting. Is it

---

51 E.g., DNa, DPe. Kent (1953:136–138), Lecoq (1997:219–221, 228).
52 Root (1990) lays out imperial texts that characterize the diversity of the empire.
53 As mentioned in chapter 4, lions and sphinxes, common grave guardians in the Greek world, have not been found in funerary contexts at Sardis. The "phallic markers," or *ouroi*, may have been used not to distinguish the grave but to commemorate the efforts of those who contributed to the construction of the tumulus. See McLauchlin (1985:115–116).
54 Schmidt (1970).

**Fig. 52**
Persepolis: south
face to the east
door of the
Hundred-Column
Hall. The king on
high.

possible that the funerary stelae found in association with Achaemenid-
period rock-cut tombs at Sardis recalled the royal tombs at Naqsh-i Rustam,
a practical way to facilitate emulation of features of tomb display associated
with the cachet of the Achaemenid royal family?[55]

55 This would naturally have been true only in a generalized sense; actual representations on the
   royal tombs are different and very specific. Given the lack of any burials of Persian aristocrats

A last tomb type at Sardis is suggested by the pedimental reliefs that show a bearded figure banqueting, discussed above in chapters 3 and 4.[56] The pediment has been reconstructed as coming from a temple-shaped mausoleum.[57] It is uncertain what the form of the mausoleum may have been: was its platform stepped or podium; did it have Ionic columns or caryatids supporting the pediment, or was it supported only by two antae? Reconstructions are varied but in general follow types known from Karia and Lykia.[58] This pediment, however, probably dating to *c.* 430–420 BC, predates the Ionic temple-tombs that have been used in proposing its reconstruction: no east Greek predecessors have yet been found.[59]

It is not inconceivable that expression of the type should have originated in such a place as Achaemenid Sardis.[60] An elevated chamber tomb would raise the body above the ground in a manner that was visibly impressive and that kept the body exposed to the air (like the Tomb of Cyrus). The pediment, sculpted with a banquet scene, probably formed part of an ornate architectural facade that again might recall the sculpted facades at Naqsh-i Rustam – it is possible, indeed, that the pediment is from an elaborate facade decorating a rock-cut tomb, rather than being part of a free-standing chamber tomb.[61] In any case, ideas that may have originated in Persia were here translated into a temple milieu familiar to those living at Sardis. Although the expression of the temple-mausoleum became associated with Eastern Greek ideas and reached its apogee in the Maussolleion at Halikarnassos, it may well have had an eastern underpinning that could in such a place as Achaemenid-period Sardis have reached a new expression which was then translated into a Greek context by others.[62]

## Mortuary inclusions: signalling elite status in a polyethnic clime

A study of mortuary inclusions at Sardis must deal only with partial assemblages, with what was left behind by plunderers and by differential

in the center of the empire, we cannot assess how mortuary treatment at Sardis may parallel or diverge from responses in Persia to royal paradigms.

56 NoEx 69.14 and NoEx 78.1.　　57 Hanfmann and Erhart (1981:89).

58 Hanfmann and Erhart (1981:86, 89).　　59 Hanfmann and Erhart (1981:89).

60 The concept of a temple-tomb had a long history in the Near East, of course. Hatshepsut's mausoleum-temple at Deir el-Bahri, built during the early Eighteenth Dynasty (*c.* 1570–1450 BC), is a famous example. For an overview of this building, see Stevenson Smith (1990:225–226, 231–245). For the discovery of Hatshepsut's temple-tomb, see Nauille and Carter (1906); for more recent analyses of the monument, see, e.g., Polish State Enterprise (1972, 1973, 1979).

61 The tombs of Myra present examples of this concept carved into the hard rock of the cliff face.

62 For Maussollos, satrap of Karia, his personality and politics, see Hornblower (1982). For the Maussolleion, see Jeppesen (1990).

preservation problems. Furthermore, in many cases the tombs were used for reinterment in ancient times, so that tombs do not necessarily represent closed deposits of only one use. The original occupants of the tombs were generally missing at the time of twentieth-century excavation. The original arrangement of inclusions can in most cases not be reconstructed, either because the inclusions were disturbed before excavation or because of the cursory nature of the records kept by early excavators. Any interpretation of the symbolic or actual use of these objects must therefore proceed with great caution. Despite all these difficulties, however, the inclusions available for study are rich in information to the modern scholar.[63]

The grave inclusions from those wealthy Achaemenid-period tombs at Sardis that still retained all or part of their original assemblage are remarkably consistent from one grave to the next. They demonstrate the emergence of a new eclectic artistic style that signaled membership in the elite.[64] This style has no precursor, but instead was newly formed and is immediately recognizable; it is local to western Anatolia in the time of the Achaemenid empire. Importantly, most of the objects would have been highly visible in use and were personal in choice and arrangement.

By far the greatest part of the artifacts made in this distinctive newly constructed style consisted of jewelry, personal seals, stamped gold foil ornaments, and banqueting paraphernalia.[65] The ornaments are made by stamping gold foil with a cut stone or metal stamp bearing an image in intaglio (figs. 53 and 54).[66] They share the same technique as personal sealstones and share some of the repertoire of compositional formats; the same artisans may well have been responsible for cutting both sealstones and the stamps that would make the clothing ornaments. They were apparently sewn to cloth or possibly leather, as the perforations or small loops for attachment to clothing indicate. Some of the ornaments were also found with bodies in patterns that suggest they were sewn on to garments around hem lines or along seams. The artifacts designed in the new style of the Sardian Achaemenid elite were therefore all objects in use in sight of the public eye, to be associated with a particular individual. They were designed to make a clear public statement about the social identity and status of that individual.

The gold clothing appliqués from Sardis are all made in this eclectic syncretic style and also share iconographic traits, with strongly Achaemenid

---

63 This discussion is prefatory: complete analysis awaits Greenewalt's publication of the tombs.
64 For the use of style in signaling identity, see, e.g., Pasztory (1989).
65 Illustrated in Curtis (1925). See chapter 7 for the sealstones.
66 See Özgen and Öztürk (1996) for examples of such stamps.

**Fig. 53** From Sardis: IAM 4608. Kite-shaped appliqué.

overtones (fig. 55).[67] Crenelations, bearded sphinxes, winged man-bulls, and winged figures resembling the Ahuramazda figure of, e.g., the Bisitun sculpture, all form part of this symbolically significant iconographic repertoire. Importantly, seals carved in similar styles demonstrate the polyethnic nature of the users: a seal from Kertch, now in St. Petersburg, with two bearded crowned sphinxes is inscribed in Lydian "Manelim," or "of Manes."[68] At Persepolis, the sealings on the Persepolis Fortification tablets demonstrate vividly that seal owners of a particular ethnicity (or at least ethnic name) do not necessarily use seals that conform to our notions of ethnic divisions along lines of artistic style. So, too, the tombs at Sardis suggest that artistic style and iconography are not ethnic indicators but rather status indicators, signaling membership in the polyethnic elite of Achaemenid western Anatolia.

67 For the rosette-and-lotus motif, see Dusinberre (1997a).
68 Boardman (1970b:39 pl. 5).

**Fig. 54** From Sardis: IAM 4653. Sphinx appliqué.

The gold foil clothing appliqués would have been highly visible while worn during life: they would have been immediately discernible conveyors of information, and their style and iconography are therefore of great importance. The artistic style and iconography of these appliqués are the same throughout the tombs at Sardis, be they tumuli or rock-cut tombs. This is of particular importance. It demonstrates a koine in artistic style extending across such points as country of origin or ethnic affiliation, uniting the elite in a group linked by status rather than nationality.

It is significant that the gold foil ornaments adorned clothing: they were not necessarily put into a grave because the survivors made a decision that these appliqués belonged with the dead person, but rather because they chose to bury him or her in ornamented clothes. The scenario is probably more complicated than this simple concept of coincidental inclusion, however. Most elite burials include the accoutrements necessary for banqueting, apparently in a formal mortuary context. These gold-ornamented garments may therefore be clothes the individual had for a (ritual?) funerary banquet, designed as specifically funerary attire. Or perhaps such clothes would reflect those the individual had for elaborate state or private functions. If so, the clothes may reflect those that the individual wore while living – in this sense, they would be key indicators of what mattered to that person in life. That a sartorial koine existed amongst the Achaemenid elite is suggested by the statue of the Egyptian Udjahorresnet (see chapter 4), who

**Fig. 55** From Sardis: IAM 4652. Bearded sphinx, winged disk, and crenelations.

wears Persian-style jewelry; the clothing appliqués from Sardis underscore this similarity of dressing style.

This point makes the homogeneity of style and the apparent popularity of the ornaments all the more interesting:[69] their style may be an accurate reflection of what people had been doing and what mattered to them while alive. The appliqués reflect choices a person may have made while alive about the social identity he or she wished to signal to contemporaries. Given their high visibility in use, the homogeneity of style in appliqués found in tombs of different types is important.[70] They demonstrate the elite differentiated

69 Of the seventy-nine tombs listed in this catalogue, fully eleven, or 14 percent, included gold clothing appliqués. This number is probably an under-representation, as the depredations of tomb robbers would tend to remove a disproportionate amount of gold from the graves.

70 For style as a strategy of information exchange, see Wobst (1977:317).

**Fig. 56** From Sardis: IAM 4543. Earring with lion's-head terminals.

themselves from non-elite by status and affiliation with a hegemonic stylistic code, regardless of ethnic background.

The jewelry found in Sardian tombs of the Achaemenid period seems to convey much the same stylistic message as the appliqués. Necklaces and earrings are made of a delicate combination of stylistic traditions to form a new idiom at Sardis and apparently throughout Lydia (fig. 56).[71] And similar earrings are shown being worn by a small ivory head from an Achaemenid-period tomb (fig. 57). As with the clothing appliqués, these objects cannot be attributed to people of one particular ethnic background, but seem rather to convey a message of wealth, status, rank.

The appliqués and jewelry from the Achaemenid-period tombs at Sardis may have figured in reciprocal gift-giving, a key element in cementing power relationships in the Achaemenid empire.[72] How did people come to own gold appliqués for clothing? Perhaps they were the prerogative of the king or at least some upper echelon to give to people as tokens of esteem. In any case, it is quite remarkable that so much gold was removed from circulation in this way within the Achaemenid empire.

71 See, e.g., Özgen and Özturk (1996).
72 See, e.g., Sancisi-Weerdenburg (1989), Cahill (1985), Gunter and Root (1998).

**Fig. 57** From Sardis: IAM 4657. Ivory head with Achaemenid koine earrings.

One particularly significant artifact, from Tomb 213, is a bronze mirror (fig. 58).[73] The face of the mirror has a threefold border, with triangles, a braided guilloche, and projecting knobs and points that slightly resemble the rays customarily shown projecting from the goddess Ishtar. It has a handle terminating in a calf's head, with a double horse protome supporting the face of the mirror. Addorsed animal protomes are, of course, well known from Achaemenid Persia, and this mirror apparently refers directly to the Persian prototype. Protomes on capitals at Pasargadae are apparently

73 First published by Butler (1922:84), discussed in Oliver (1971), illustrated in Turkish Ministry of Culture (1993:186).

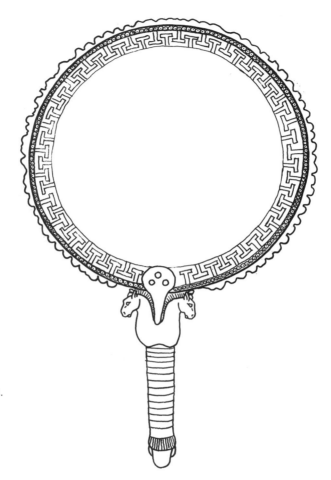

**Fig. 58** From Sardis: IAM 4572. Bronze mirror with calf's-head terminal to handle and horse-protome support.

remnants of horse-protome capitals.[74] Later animal-protome capitals from Persepolis and Susa use other animal types, including lions, griffins, and – importantly in connection with the mirror from Sardis – bulls. This mirror is thus a significant example of Achaemenid Persian ideas and imagery translated into a new context at Sardis.

The sealstones from the Sardian tombs demonstrate the same point as the appliqués and jewelry, pointing to an artistic network uniting a polyethnic elite (see chapter 7). In some of these cases, a given stone may be clearly linked with a particular tradition: so, for instance, IAM 5133 from Tomb 1005 (see fig. 95) is carved in the style and with the iconography traditionally associated with Neo-Babylonian glyptic,[75] while IAM 4518 from Tomb A1 (see

74 Nylander (1970:103).
75 Many such seals are used on the Persepolis Fortification tablets, deep into the reign of Darius,

fig. 99) is carved in a Greek style. But for the most part, the styles of the sealstones reflect the same stylistic koine as do the appliqués and the jewelry. In some cases, these seals provide insights into society at Achaemenid-period Sardis that run counter to traditional expectations. The inhabitant of one of the sarcophagi in Tomb 381, the "Tomb of the Bride," was described by Butler as a young woman of about seventeen years. She was decked out with gold hair fillets, a necklace, earrings, anklets, clothing appliqués, and two seals (of which one, a gold seal ring, survived to be found by the Butler expedition; the other may have been made of glass paste and disintegrated, leaving behind an elaborate suspension device in the form of ducks' heads). The seal ring this young woman used showed a lion advancing to the right, snarling (see fig. 75). Perhaps the use of lions as seal images by women is to be expected in an area famous for its worship of Kybele, where people lived who may have been familiar with worship of Ishtar-Anahita; it certainly acts as a warning against too hasty an assumption about the gender of seal-users based on modern associations with a given image.[76] Such an association of lions with women may also be suggested by the two seals found in Tomb S 16, IAM 4634 and IAM 4637 (see figs. 76, 74), which show, respectively, a snarling lion and a robed woman seated on a chair with curved back and legs, in front of whom are carved two small crescents.

Because of the possibility of multiple interments in graves, it may not be assumed that multiple seals from the same tomb necessarily belonged to a single individual; but they none the less provide interesting pairings. Tomb 1005, for instance, from which came the chalcedony Neo-Babylonian-type pyramidal stamp seal mentioned above (see fig. 95), also produced a chalcedony pyramidal stamp held by silver ducks' heads, showing a winged lion-griffin advancing to the right (see fig. 89). This lion-griffin is carved in the style that apparently signals the Achaemenid-period elite. Whether the two seals belonged to one individual or whether they belonged to two different people interred in the same tomb, their contiguousness in the tomb demonstrates the multicultural associations embraced by the elite at Sardis.

A different scenario of cultural interaction is revealed by Tomb 811. Both of the seals from Tomb 811,[77] IAM 4636 and IAM 4641 (see figs. 73, 83), are carved in the now-familiar unifying style of the western Achaemenid empire.

---

and there is a strong likelihood that many of these "Neo-Babylonian" stamp seals used at Persepolis are *new* products, not holdovers from before 539 BC. The complexity of stylistic deployment among people at Persepolis shows it is oversimplifying to call these seals "Neo-Babylonian." See Root (1998).

76 See also the association of lion-shaped pins with women at Hasanlu: Marcus (1994); she proposes that aggressive (male?) iconography is appropriated by a certain category of women at Hasanlu in their garment pins as a reaction to vulnerability within the Assyrian empire. See also Marcus (1990, 1993).

77 A third stone, IAM 4633, with a silver mounting over its base, may have been carved in intaglio, but the silver is now too corroded to be certain.

They show a lion with an abbreviated sun disk symbol, and a wonderful winged human-headed goat-sphinx with a symbol above it.

In another case, a tomb from which came two seals demonstrates again the phenomenon of Mesopotamian and Achaemenid iconography presented in the apparently local syncretic style. This is Tomb 18, in which a body was found by the Butler expedition and for which there was no evidence recorded of more than one body. On the forehead of the skeleton was a broad strip of gold; with it were a necklace of gold and carnelian, a rock crystal pendant held by a lion's head suspension, two large silver earrings and a small gold one. Also found were two sealstones: one (IAM 4523) is of agate cut into the shape of a sugar loaf with a heavy silver mounting, showing a lion and bull in combat, with a sun disk, a circle of stars, and a crescent moon above their backs (see fig. 93). The other seal (IAM 4524), an oval of dark mottled stone now missing its mounting, shows a bearded crowned figure in a long robe seated facing right on a high-backed throne with his feet on a footstool, holding in one hand something resembling a globe and in his other hand some other uncertain object (see fig. 94). These are both images drawn straight from Achaemenid Persian heartland iconography, both rendered in the new syncretic style of the Achaemenid-period elite of Sardis.

The seals from the tombs of Sardis in the Achaemenid period thus corroborate the social organization suggested by the other grave goods and by the tomb structures. The elite at Sardis apparently comprised a body of people with diverse tastes, who in the living society differentiated themselves from those of lesser status through adaptive referencing to Achaemenid expressions, rather than from each other on the basis of ethnic background.

## Elite unity in Achaemenid Sardis: textual contributions

A similar impression of social organization at Achaemenid Sardis is suggested by the literary sources. Herodotos tells a tale of the wealthy Pythios, son of Atys, entertaining Xerxes and his entire army at Phrygian Kelainai in 480.[78] Pythios even offered Xerxes his entire personal fortune for the support of the army. This man was reputedly the wealthiest in the world (excepting only Xerxes himself), and if Lydian naming patterns were similar to Greek ones may have been descended from the Lydian royal family.[79] In this instance, he may have been granted direct access to the Great King himself, as Herodotos recounts a conversation between the two men

---

78 Hdt. 7.26–29 and 38–39.
79 But cf. evidence from the Sacrilege Inscription, chapter 5.

(7.27–29). Herodotos describes Xerxes' pleasure in Pythios' hospitality and offer of money to support the troops, and his consequent making Pythios a "guest friend" (*xeinos*). Direct access to Xerxes is again suggested in 7.39–40, when Pythios pleads that his eldest son may be exempt from military service. Regardless of its veracity,[80] in the context of understanding elite social organization in Achaemenid-period Sardis, it is important the story could be told at all. To Herodotos, a citizen of the Achaemenid seaport, Halikarnassos, it was possible that an elite Lydian should have been granted access to the Great King himself. This implies easy communication between members of the elite at Sardis in his own time, irrespective of their ancestral ethnicity.[81]

Other stories in Herodotos corroborate this image. When the Persian army retreated from Mykale back to Sardis, angry words were exchanged between Xerxes' brother Masistes and the general Artaÿntes (9.107). A Greek citizen of Halikarnassos not only was standing so close to the Persian nobles that he could intervene, but did so – he threw the general and nobleman Artaÿntes to the ground when he drew his sword. Far from being punished for his assault against a member of the Achaemenid elite, he was rewarded richly by Masistes and his brother Xerxes and was granted the governorship of Kilikia. Apparently loyalty mattered most to the Great King in such circumstances of hegemonic consolidation and security, rather than national origin or "ethnicity."[82]

The access of Alkibiades to Tissaphernes at the close of the fifth century may be another piece of the same puzzle.[83] The presence of non-Persians in Achaemenid courts, and the enthusiastic assumption of Achaemenid trappings and customs by those in such circumstances, are borne out by so many stories as to make their listing tedious: the Spartan general Pausanias is perhaps the most famous example, and the awarding by the Great King to Themistokles the Athenian of a land grant at Magnesia on the Maeander. Kalligeitos the Megarian and Timagoras the Kyzikene, Greeks who were living at the court of Pharnabazos and were used by him to foster contacts with other Greeks, may be more representative of the normal interactions between Greeks and the elite of the Achaemenid courts, however.[84] Perhaps

---

80 The dire consequence of this plea is one of the most famous examples of Xerxes' despotic cruelty (as related by the Greeks). But it is important to remember the malignity of Greek sources towards Xerxes; Near Eastern accounts often give the lie to the Greek version of Xerxes' actions. See Kuhrt and Sherwin-White (1987).

81 The international nature of elite interactions in Lydia is perhaps also demonstrated for the pre-Achaemenid period by the gifts of Croesus to Greek sanctuaries at Delphi and Didyma.

82 See chapter 2 for the king's approaches to "ethnicity" in different situations, however. For satraps and their ethnicities, see, e.g., Petit (1990).

83 Thuc. 8, passim.

84 Thuc. 8.6.

it is indicative that the wording of the King's Treaty (8.57–58) is entirely in terms of the king himself, rather than "the Persians" – the king might choose to grant the land to whomsoever he wished; and the literary sources show he did so without much regard for the nationality of the person, welcoming people of diverse ethnicity into the ranks of the landowning elite.

The marks of favor bestowed by Cyrus the Younger on the Lykian king Syennesis in Xenophon's *Anabasis* conform to this idea and suggest one possible means by which people acquired the paraphernalia that marked them out as members of the elite (1.2): "Syennesis gave Cyrus much money for the army, while Cyrus gave him gifts considered an honor coming from the king: a horse with a golden bridle, a golden necklace and bracelets, a golden akinakes and a Persian robe."[85]

The Greek literary sources are unanimous in confirming the picture suggested so strongly by the mortuary evidence at Sardis: one demonstrated membership in the ranks of the privileged by the prominent display of objects that signaled "Achaemenid elite." Wealth, previous status, or personal favor of the king or his subordinates were all possible avenues for access to this elite. Once accepted into the ranks, individuals had many ways to signal their status to others, including items of apparel and of daily or extraordinary use.

## Conclusion

During the Achaemenid period at Sardis, at least three main forms of funerary structure were used concurrently: built chamber tombs covered by tumuli, rock-cut tombs, and cists. Sarcophagi were sometimes but not always used in the tombs. Energy expenditure does not seem to have been a matter of much concern in symbolizing status: wealthy people were certainly buried in both tumulus tombs and rock-cut tombs, and some wealth is even apparent in cist burials. It seems possible the different tomb types were of differentiated symbolic meaning in and of themselves. Tumulus tombs, for instance, may have been significant for demonstrating either the upwardly mobile status of the people buried within them or the Lydian social identity of their occupants. A straightforward image of ethnic segregation must be

---

85 For gifts of land, see Briant (1985a). Gunter and Root (1998) discuss the removal from circulation of precious metals via gifting in the Achaemenid empire. For gold gifts from the Persian king to favored subjects, see Root (1992). See also the plausible echoes of historical Achaemenid experience in Esther 6.8 and 8.15, recounting royal gifts of golden crowns; for Esther, cf. Berg (1979). For ritual gift-giving in the Achaemenid empire, see Sancisi-Weerdenburg (1989). Herodotos (8.118) also says a story was current in his day that Xerxes rewarded a ship's captain with a golden garland (*chruseos stephanos*) for saving his life. Although Herodotos disbelieves the story (8.119), and although the Book of Esther is suspect, that two such stories should circulate suggests there may be some truth underlying the idea of golden crowns given by the king.

regarded skeptically, however, as tomb inclusions demonstrate the eclectic symbolism of the Sardian elite. And the tumuli, like the rock-cut tombs, show in the Achaemenid period the introduction of funerary couches to support the dead, perhaps a specifically Persian import. Mortuary evidence seems to reflect a society organized not along ethnic lines, but rather along lines of status, where the elite consisted of people of many backgrounds. Although some differences must have remained, mortuary remains demonstrate the mingling and communication that pertained in Sardis in the Achaemenid period.

The syncretic blending of eastern, western and local styles reflects the complex social organization of the elite at Sardis in the Achaemenid period. The culture of the living underwent a major change in this period, with a probably gradual but none the less great shift towards the east in its cultural impetus (see chapter 8). But elite society represented a fusion of cultural traditions, not differentiated on the basis of cultural origin but serving to unite the elite as a more or less cohesive whole with different individuals probably expressing various aspects of themselves and their values to differing degrees.

The plate and furniture, carpets and wall hangings, garments and personal ornaments of the Achaemenid elite were diffused widely.[86] Sardis may perhaps serve as a test case for the exceptionally great territorial area of the Achaemenid empire: it demonstrates that themes and motifs which had developed over centuries in various locales might now be developed by artisans in new areas, providing creative energy and impulse for visible expression of status in a way which, at Sardis, yielded a unifying mode of communication for the elite. Mortuary inclusions at this Achaemenid capital, taken in conjunction with mortuary structures and a rich literary record, provide some clues to better our understanding of this aspect of social organization.

86 See Moorey (1980) for a synthesis of many of these items in Anatolia itself.

# 7 Personal signifiers: sealstones

From Sardis' public space and civic landscape, we now move to artifacts that are in a sense both public and private: sealstones.[1] We have no examples from Sardis of ancient sealings and therefore can say little about Sardian seal use patterns. But as we shall see, the sealstones of Achaemenid-period Sardis can provide particularly valuable insights into Achaemenid ideology and the nature of the elite. This chapter examines the functions and meanings of artistic images and style at Sardis. It begins with a particular stone from Tomb 813, examining it in its immediate context and in relation to excavated material from elsewhere in the empire. It then moves on to consider all of the Achaemenid-period seals excavated at Sardis.

As described in chapter 1, Achaemenid imperial programs for the promotion of ideologies of empire included the manipulation of artistic imagery to bear meaning within a local imperial context. Importantly, seal iconography is shared to a great extent in various locations throughout the empire, so that similar images are carved on seals but in styles that vary quite widely and seem to reflect geographical locale.[2] At Sardis, too, we see official imperial iconography rendered in a local style, with local tastes and preferences reflected in the selection of imperial images.[3] It is impossible to discern the ethnicity of a seal's user – choice of image and artistic style are not indicators of Persian or Lydian or other background. Instead, seal users (the elite) show remarkable conformity of taste in seal imagery, demonstrating an artistic koine that linked the elite across ethnic background. Thus users

---

1 This chapter builds on thoughts about IAM 4581, initially published in Dusinberre (1997a): I hope to contribute to the re-evaluation of sealstones as artifactual category begun by other scholars of Achaemenid glyptic (e.g., Kaptan forthcoming). Achaemenid weights may benefit from a similar analysis; see Trousdale (1968). For problems associated with studying unexcavated Achaemenid art, see Muscarella (1977, 1980). For the importance of style as a semiotic criterion and its use in archaeological inquiry, see, e.g., Conkey and Hastorf (1990).

2 For similar iconography found in Samaria, see Leith (1990, 1997); for Palestine in general, see Uehlinger (1999); for Lebanon, Syria, and Transjordan, see Nunn (1996:126–193); for Mesopotamia, see Invernizzi (1995); for Babylonia, see Bregstein (1993, 1997); for Persepolis, see Garrison and Root (2001), Schmidt (1957); for Susa, see Amiet (1972, 1973); for Ur, see Legrain (1951), Collon (1997); for Egypt, see Flinders Petrie (1910:41); for Daskyleion, see Kaptan (1990).

3 Although imperial coinage may be similarly analyzed (Dusinberre 2002), I do not address coins here because so few have been excavated from Sardis (one silver siglos, well-worn). See Casabonne (1996, 1998). More generally, for coinage in the Achaemenid empire, see esp. Carradice (1987).

**Fig. 59** From Sardis: IAM 4581. Cylinder seal with king controlling lion-griffins, standing on sphinxes.

embedded themselves in an artistic framework that reinforced their own goals or sense of authority and power.[4]

## A cylinder seal from Sardis

The seal that lets us develop the focus of argument in this chapter is now in Istanbul (IAM 4581).[5] It is a straight-sided cylinder of brown agate with four diagonal white bands near the top, engraved in a broad flat style with undisguised use of the drill for detail (fig. 59). It is carved with a group of five figures that cover approximately four-fifths of the cylinder's lateral surface. The remaining one-fifth is left in reserve. In the center of the design, a crowned hero wearing the Persian court robe stands facing right and grasps two rampant lion-griffins by their necks.[6] He stands on the heads of two couchant winged sphinxes which face one another on a groundline, raising a foreleg to touch paws at the center. The vertical spacing of the figures is precise, with the hero's head as far distant from the upper edge of the seal as the groundline is from the lower edge.

The seal was excavated in 1912 by H.C. Butler from a tomb published in 1922 as Tomb 813, called the "stele tomb" because of the two stelae flanking its entrance (see chapter 6).[7] The seal came from a sarcophagus buried in the floor of the tomb, along with four ceramic vessels, a gold ring (now lost),

4 For the importance of "taste" in specific cultural contexts, see Bourdieu ([1979] 1984).
5 A full discussion of this seal, with detailed evidence for the arguments summarized here, is in Dusinberre (1997a).
6 All directions will be described from the viewer's point of view, looking at the seal's impression.
7 Butler (1922:116–117, 159–161).

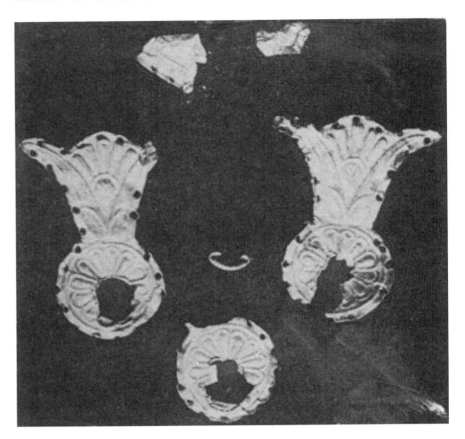

**Fig. 60** From Sardis: rosette and lotus appliqués.

and three gold foil clothing appliqués in the shape of rosettes with lotuses springing from them (fig. 60). The sarcophagus also contained "the bones of a large man, his gold ring and his seal; his head was found pierced in front with some large pointed instrument, making the wound which probably caused his death."[8]

As I have argued in detail elsewhere,[9] the appliqués are an emphatic link to the central imagery of the empire and the art created for the court. Although the gold ornaments from Tomb 813 need not indicate the Persian ethnicity of the man buried with them, they certainly show contact with or taste for central Achaemenid ornament.[10] They seem to demonstrate the high social status of the individual buried in this sarcophagus. His cylinder

8 Butler (1922:116–117).      9 Dusinberre (1997a).

10 See, e.g., Muscarella (1977), Tilia (1978:29–71), Curtis (1925:pls. I, II), Butler (1922:143), Stronach (1978:168–77), Tallon (1992).

    For Babylon and Assyria, see, e.g., Oppenheim (1949). See D. Stronach (1978:93, 97) for Achaemenid reliefs showing evidence of gold attachments to the pleats of garments. Cf. also Roos (1970). For Pazyryk, see Rudenko (1970). See also Metropolitan Museum (1975:110,

seal reiterates his connection to the Achaemenid elite and raises further issues.

The iconography and style of the seal show key connections to central Achaemenid glyptic. The heroic-control motif is common in heartland Achaemenid iconography, one resonant with the traditions of centuries of Mesopotamian artistic imagery. As a careful analysis of sealed tablets demonstrates, the portrayal of pedestal animals in central Achaemenid glyptic art is initially restricted in use to a select group of people, to the upper echelon of the Achaemenid elite. Even the sphinxes and lion-griffins shown on this seal appear in specific contexts in Achaemenid monumental art and glyptic art – contexts fraught with overtones of religion and power.

The hero figure on the Sardis cylinder wears what seems to be a version of the Persian court robe, and a dentate crown. Such a crowned, robed figure plays an important role in Achaemenid glyptic and sculptural art, functioning as a polysemous symbol of king and hero, king and god.[11] On this seal, the hero figure is grouped with mythical composite animals that bear particularly potent meaning in the complex iconographic system of Achaemenid art.

The lion-griffin, the animal with which the hero grapples, appears in Achaemenid art as the adversary of the hero and also on its own, generally pacing forward with open snarling mouth. It is an animal associated in Akkadian and Neo-Assyrian art with malevolent atmospheric demons, the physical manifestation of supernatural evil.[12] In Achaemenid art, the hero is often shown controlling or combating with lion-griffins: this is a thematic nuance of the hero image apparently centered in the Persian heartland, with few examples in provenanced Persian Anatolian glyptic, where the hero figure generally grapples with other animals. Its role as heroic adversary in Persia shows that it retained its traditional meaning of cosmic evil. But the lion-griffin sometimes also plays a role as a helpful, benevolent, protective demon.

The animals on which the hero of the Sardis seal stands are sphinxes: winged beasts with leonine bodies and bearded human heads, in this case wearing flat headdresses. In the Achaemenid empire, the sphinx was a creature with ritual associations, frequently shown with winged disks (with or

---

157–160). For the Persepolitan sculptures, see Schmidt (1953:pls. 143, 198, and for positioning of lions pls. 79, 99, 105, 107, 142), Tilia (1978:29–71). For examples from Lydia, see Özgen and Öztürk (1996). The appliqués from Sardis are published in Curtis (1925:11–14). For the importance of cloth in late Lydian burials at Sardis, see Greenewalt and Majewski (1980); for Lydian cloth in the literary record, see Pedley (1972).

11 See Dusinberre (2002), arguing a nuance of Achaemenid kingship slightly against Wiesehöfer (1996). Images of heroic encounter comprise roughly one-quarter of those preserved as seal impressions on the Persepolis Fortification tablets. See Garrison and Root (2001). The image's potent resonances even spread beyond the imperial borders: see Bivar (1970).

12 Porada (1993:20–21), Black and Green (1992:107–108).

without Ahuramazda figures),[13] ritual objects like incense burners and cult images, and vegetal elements. It is portrayed most often with items that represent the sun or fecundity, usually raising a forepaw to the icon. Alternatively, as on the seal from Sardis, two facing sphinxes may raise a paw towards each other.[14] But the sphinx may also engage in action scenes: on the Persepolis Fortification tablets, sphinxes often take the place of lions in heroic combat scenes; other tablets have the sphinx taking the place of the hero figure. These animals hold a secure place in Achaemenid ritualistic iconographic tradition and use.

The imagery of the Sardis seal thus bears a profound symbolic meaning: the crowned, robed hero masters forces of potent violence and is supported by creatures that symbolize balance and right. This is a powerful image that poises the figure of kingship at the fulcrum of cosmic harmony. It suggests the king may himself be the embodiment of might and justice.

The most important feature of the seal's iconography is the presence of pedestal animals supporting the hero figure. Animals on which a divine figure stands, which represent essential qualities of the divinity, are a well-known tradition in Mesopotamian and eastern Anatolian art.[15] In Egypt, the divine ruler sometimes stands on pedestal animals. These animals stand or crouch beneath a representation of the divinity; they are apparently part of a statue of the divine image but may serve as an extension of the divinity.

Pedestal animals appear in the glyptic art of the Achaemenid empire, but not in other Achaemenid artistic milieux. Although certain of the sculpted reliefs from Persepolis include images of the king lifted on high, borne aloft by the peoples of the realm, this is a different construct and stems from different traditions than the animals.[16] On Achaemenid seals, pedestal animals are resonant with royal imagery and, in the earlier history of the empire, have a very restricted circulation. Those seals in the Achaemenid period inscribed with the name of the king (the so-called royal name seals, generally used not by the king himself but by important imperial administrative offices) are associated with a specific iconography, with a few particular images being favored.[17] Some images are particularly common on royal name seals but only rarely carved on seals that are not inscribed with the name of the king. These images, even when they appear on non-royal name seals, are still resonant with the significance of the royal name seals. Pedestal animals are such an image, quite literally elevating the image to a special rank.

---

13 For the figure in Achaemenid winged disks, see Root (1979:169–176), Kuhrt (1995a:677). See Gunter (1989) for another Anatolian sphinx.
14 Heraldic sphinxes may be found also in monumental art; see Muscarella (1992).
15 For glyptic examples, see, e.g., Collon (1987:75–89), Herbordt (1992:71–78). Porada (1993) discusses parallels in rock-cut reliefs; see also Börker-Klähn (1982), Black and Green (1992:figs. 6, 31, 45, 89, 110, 132).
16 Root (1979).     17 Garrison and Root (forthcoming), Garrison (1998:126).

The images of pedestal animals in the late sixth and early fifth centuries all seem to indicate the high social rank of their owners. They frequently bear royal name inscriptions, and where this is not the case, the earlier examples in particular are none the less resonant with the imagery of royal name seals. Not only do pedestal animals commonly occur in conjunction with such status indicators as inscriptions and palm trees, but in the cases where we can check the background of their owners/users, these are individuals of high social status and administrative responsibility.

## Style

The Sardis cylinder is carved with imagery straight from the center of the Persian empire and charged with meaning in Achaemenid iconography. But it is carved in a flat broad style with undisguised use of the rotating drill, in a manner not represented by the hundreds of seals used on the Persepolis Fortification tablets. Volumes are left precise but unmodeled, and lines are clearly and broadly incised, often to indicate the borders between muscles (as in the haunches of the lion-griffins) or bunched up cloth (as at the borders of the robe's sleeves) that might otherwise have been indicated by more subtle modeling. Indeed, this is a seal carved in one of the styles commonly called "Graeco-Persian."

Scholarly discussion on "Graeco-Persian" seals has by and large focused on the ethnicity of the seal engraver.[18] The name "Graeco-Persian" represents a stylistic grab-bag category that seems to have defied firm definition. Indeed, the most precise stylistic definition is "often sketchy, with frequent use of the round drill."[19] "Graeco-Persian" has been used variously to describe seals of different stylistic qualities – one subset of which strongly resembles the style of our seal from Sardis. Most of the seals studied are not from controlled excavations, but the work done in their compilation and typologizing has none the less drawn primarily upon these unexcavated artifacts.[20] Of those 198 pyramidal stamp seals discussed by John Boardman in 1970, fully 75 percent are unprovenanced; of the remaining seals that do claim some provenance, roughly 40 percent (some twenty seals) come from Sardis.[21] The large majority of "Graeco-Persian" seals are said to have come from or to have been bought in Anatolia, northern Syria, or the area around the Black Sea.[22]

"Graeco-Persian" gems form a different grouping of styles, distinct from the various Greek styles of the Greek mainland and Ionia on the one hand,

---

18  See, e.g., Furtwängler (1903), Moortgat (1926), Maximova (1928), Richter (1946, 1952), Nikoulina (1971), Farkas (1974). Some scholars found other issues more pressing: see, e.g., Seyrig (1952), Boardman (1970a, 1970b, 1976).

19  Richter (1949:296); also Young (1946:33).      20  E.g., Boardman (1970a:303–358, 1970b).

21  Boardman (1970b).      22  Boardman (1970a).

and from the various styles well-documented in the Persian heartland on the other hand. They are almost completely absent from the sealings on the Persepolis Fortification tablets or the Persepolis Treasury tablets.[23] Similarly, they seldom turn up from verifiable contexts in Greece.[24]

Generally, "Graeco-Persian" glyptic is thought to have been created for Persians who preferred stiff, static figures over the imaginative and vibrant beauty of Greek art.[25] Those unusually perceptive eastern patrons who could afford it, the subtext runs, would presumably buy Greek art when possible, commissioning overtly Persian subjects carved in a Greek style. "Graeco-Persian" seals that seem stilted, lacking in volume and naturalism are attributed, instead, to Persian artists. These Persian artists presumably worked within a "Graeco-Persian" milieu of exposure to Greek artists, but without the ability or sensibility to achieve the same results. Such categorization is partly a result of the small number of provenanced seals previously available for study, particularly from the Persian heartland itself – a difficulty now being rectified by the publication of the thousands of seal images preserved as impressions on the Persepolis Fortification tablets.[26] The cylinder from Sardis, viewed in connection with the seals and sealings now available from elsewhere in the empire, suggests that patrons may specifically have opted for one style or another according not only to their tastes but perhaps to the purpose of the seal or the position of the commissioner in the administrative hierarchy. The analytical model used in the study of the enormous corpus of the Persepolis Fortification sealings may productively be brought to bear on the interpretation of the iconography and style of objects from elsewhere in the empire, including our seal from Sardis and its position in the corpus of so-called Graeco-Persian seals.

## Artistic circles at Persepolis

One of the most interesting, and perhaps surprising, features of the Persepolis Fortification corpus is the presence of many different glyptic styles in use concurrently. The simultaneous use of these multiple styles demonstrates several important points about the meanings and uses of artistic style

---

23 PFS 1321s is carved in a style somewhat resembling that of the Sardian seals. Intriguingly, it was used by someone traveling from Sardis to Persepolis, bearing a document from Artaphernes to the king (PFT 1404). See Garrison and Root (1996); *idem* (2001) catalogues the seal. See also Root (1998). For the text of PFT 1404, see Hallock (1969).

24 One of the few examples known to me is BM 89781, significantly said to be from Marathon.

25 Discussion has generally been limited by the assumptions underlying ethnically determinative attributes. Thus Furtwängler (1903:12): "Trotz aller Wandlungen im Einzelnen geht aber ein gemeinsamer Geist durch diese orientalische Kunst. Es ist der Geist der Despotie und Unterwürfigkeit. Wenn wir nun zu den Griechen übergehen, atmen wir auf in der Freiheit, der Freiheit mannigfaltigsten Lebens und freudiger Schönheit."

26 Garrison and Root (2001).

in the Persian heartland. At Persepolis, multiple artistic workshops operated at once. The patrons of these artists had a broad range of styles from which to choose when selecting seals for personal or official use. This situation at Persepolis may shed light on the multiple artistic styles in use through the empire, deriving from local workshops serving a particular clientele, and to some extent being cross-fertilized by distinctively regional artistic traditions.

The various styles represented by the seals preserved on the Fortification tablets were first distinguished and described by M.B. Garrison, who characterized eight significant stylistic categories.[27] The Court Style is that traditionally associated with Achaemenid glyptic art, perhaps best represented in the impressions on the Persepolis Treasury tablets.[28] The Fortification Style, simple and shallow, represents an active local tradition in glyptic art, thriving at Persepolis at the end of the sixth/beginning of the fifth century BC. The Modeled Style is a direct outgrowth and continuation of traditional Neo-Assyrian and Neo-Babylonian modeled styles. Mixed Styles I includes seals with designs sharing stylistic characteristics of the Modeled Style and the Fortification Style. Mixed Styles II comprises seals sharing the characteristics of the Court Style and the Fortification Style. The Broad and Flat Style is self-explanatory; seals in this style are often carved rather coarsely. The Linear Style describes a fairly wide range of linear styles. Two relatively small but ultimately very interesting groups of seals do not fit into any of these stylistic categories. One group, "Anomalous Styles," represents contemporary styles *not* local to the heartland court and region. Lastly, some Fortification tablets were ratified with antique seals. One of the most significant points for the argument here is the numerical dominance of the Fortification Style at Persepolis: of those seals showing scenes of heroic control and combat, fully 50 percent are carved in this local style.[29]

The existence at Persepolis of multiple glyptic styles being produced simultaneously by active workshops operating (it would appear) locally in the Persepolis region creates an exciting impression of a lively and creative artistic environment. The various glyptic styles in concurrent use at Persepolis demonstrate multiple local stylistic phenomena within the context of a court environment. The stylistic categories listed here were permeable in some important ways. Mixed Styles I and II demonstrate the potentially

27 Garrison (1988), Garrison and Root (2001).
28 See Boardman (1970a) who did not analyze the style in detail but used the term to describe a class of Achaemenid seals that he thought showed iconographic connections to architectural relief sculpture at Persepolis. See also Schmidt (1953). For a detailed articulation of the style, see Garrison (1990). Garrison (1996:28) points out that Court Style seals seem at first to be closely connected to the royal Persian court but by the mid-fifth century BC had a very wide distribution.
29 Garrison and Root (2001).

shifting boundaries between categories, the existence of a spectrum of stylistic variation in glyptic art at Persepolis. This has profound implications for our understanding of Achaemenid culture and of the multivalence of artistic style and iconography in the Achaemenid empire. The imperial Court Style is important in this context precisely because it was *not* imposed on the court circle: although people high in the administrative echelon might choose to have seals made in the Court Style, it was not necessary for someone who wanted to impress the king to have a seal carved in the Court Style. Instead, it seems the simultaneity of different styles in use at Persepolis allowed for subtle manipulation of style and iconography to emphasize particular messages conveyed by seals.

The connection between pedestal animals and people of high social status has been made already. The stylistic evidence from Persepolis lets us begin to see further nuances to pedestal animals. The Persepolis Treasury tablets, an archive sealed exclusively by high-ranking officials, includes a high percentage of seals displaying pedestal animals. All of these seals are inscribed (some of them are royal name seals, but others are not), and all of them are carved in the Court Style. The Fortification archive, with its representation of a broad cross-section of society, shows a restriction of pedestal scenes to those seals used by high-ranking people. They are all carved in the local Fortification Style, or in a cross between the Fortification and Court Styles. Such restricted stylistic selection and restricted circulation is highly significant.

## Stylistic spirals in the west

The Sardis cylinder was made by an artist who carved the seal in a style other than that associated with this composition at Persepolis.[30] More than that, it is carved in a style that was not, as far as we can tell, local to Persepolis. Perhaps the seal is a copy of a worn or broken seal originally carved in a heartland style, which its owner needed replaced. But the style of the seal may have been a conscious choice on the part of its commissioner, who could presumably have had a seal made in a more closely imperial style if he had so chosen. Why would someone with the aristocratic credentials to own a pedestal-animal seal commission a work in this schematic style, instead of having it made by artists working in the best central Achaemenid Court Style? The commissioner may have chosen to have it made at Sardis where he could observe its crafting and interact directly with the artist carving it.

---

30 The seal need not necessarily have been carved in Sardis, thanks to the mobility of both item and artist. See Zaccagnini (1983). The large number of "Graeco-Persian" seals with Lydian inscriptions does suggest Lydia as a place of production, however. See Boardman (1970b) and below.

Indeed, he may have been conscious of a purposely created symbolism in the style itself.

The cylinder from Sardis, IAM 4581, shows high-status central Achaemenid imagery on the favored central Achaemenid seal shape, a cylinder, otherwise unusual at Sardis – it is even carved of a stone, banded agate, that was common in central Achaemenid glyptic and very rare at Sardis.[31] But it is carved in a non-central Achaemenid style. It uses the iconographic vocabulary of the Persian heartland, translated into a local Sardian style. It suggests that here, too, patrons may specifically have opted for one style or another according not only to their tastes but perhaps also to the purpose of the artifact or the position of the commissioner in the administrative hierarchy.[32] That the Sardis cylinder was carved in this particular style is highly significant. It stands out instantly from seals with equivalent iconography found in the Persian heartland. It seems to be making a triple claim: its owner had the requisite credentials to own a seal with pedestal animals;[33] he chose an image that was deeply founded in central Achaemenid tradition, rooted in Near Eastern legacy; and he chose to have it carved in a style reflective of his western imperial locus of activity, one of the "Graeco-Persian" styles.

## The seals from Sardis

The thirty-four seals excavated at Sardis by the Butler expedition, like the Persepolis sealings, demonstrate a variety of choices available in shapes and materials.[34] By far the most popular shape is the pyramidal stamp seal, a conical shape with a rounded top, its edges beveled to form a sealing surface with eight faces: fifteen of the thirty-four seals are pyramidal stamp seals. Three are stamps shaped like weights – squat roughly cylindrical forms that are wider at the top than at the bottom, sealing, surface. Only three are cylinder seals. Of the eleven rings, four are simply of gold, with gold bezels, and seven have stones carved in intaglio, generally set on a swivel so the sealing surface could be turned towards or away from the finger. The remaining two stamp seals, both carved in Greek styles, are suspended from a bracelet and a necklace. By far the most common material of which the pyramidal stamp seals are made is blue chalcedony. This is a particularly

---

31 For the importance of the cylinder in signaling status in the Near East, see Gorelick and Gwinnett (1990).
32 See Wallace-Hadrill (1990).
33 High-status Persians in the heartland did not *necessarily* use seals showing pedestal animals, as the seals of Gobryas and Artystone clearly demonstrate (see Garrison and Root 2001).
34 Pyramidal stamp seals: IAM 4521, 4522, 4525, 4580, 4528, 4578, 4579, 4589, 4591, 4641, 4642, 5133, 5134; weight-shaped seals: 4523, 4524, 4590; cylinder seals: 4532, 4581, 4643; rings with gold bezels: 4548 (bezel undecorated), 4585, 4636, 4637; rings with stone bezels: 4519, 4520, 4632, 4633 (sealing surface of scarab undecorated), 4634, 4635, 4639; bracelet: 4518; necklace: 4640.

beautiful and translucent stone in and of itself, but the preponderance of the color blue makes me wonder if it may have had some apotropaic function akin to the evil eye beads of modern Greece and Turkey, to the blue "Hand of Fatma" in modern Egypt, or to the great blue lapis-lazuli eyes of Early Dynastic sculptures from Mesopotamia.[35] The ring bezels, by contrast, are generally made of carnelian, with some bezels of gold.

All of the seals excavated at Sardis have settings that show they were worn on the body in a visible spot, such as on a necklace or a wrist chain, or perhaps pinned to a garment: they were not kept out of sight in a pocket or purse. Many seals have particularly beautiful suspension devices, with elaborate attention paid to the qualities that enhance their value as adornments.[36] IAM 4641, a blue chalcedony pyramidal stamp, has a setting in the shape of two golden ducks' heads rendered with such attention to detail that even individual feathers have been indicated on the backs of their heads (see fig. 83). The highly visible nature of all seals underscores their importance as indicators of individuality: not only the image carved on a seal, but its very form could convey messages about the person using it. And the fact of choice between different shapes and styles is a crucial one.

The seals excavated from tombs at Sardis demonstrate that multiple artistic styles existed concurrently at this satrapal capital, even as they did at Persepolis.[37] Some seals are carved in a style more strongly reminiscent of Greek seals: IAM 4570, a scaraboid that formed part of a necklace, shows a feeding ibis that resembles "East Greek" works (see fig. 96);[38] IAM 4519 is another scaraboid that shows an Eros figure flying to the right, again carved in an archaic Greek style (see fig. 97); IAM 4518 is a large chalcedony seal set in a bracelet, with Hermes and Athena carved in a Greek style probably of the early fourth century (see fig. 99).[39] Conversely, some seals at Sardis strongly resemble Near Eastern seals: IAM 5133, for instance, mentioned already in chapters 3 and 4, is a pyramidal stamp seal showing a Neo-Babylonian worship scene, carved in a Neo-Babylonian style with a winged disk that seems to be a later addition (see fig. 95). This seal may be an import from Mesopotamia, just as the three seals mentioned above may be imports from Ionia or the Greek mainland. Three further seals are carved in a schematic, rounded style: IAM 4640 is a glass paste scarab, much corroded, that may originally have formed a ring bezel and shows a human figure (see fig. 100); 4522 is a pyramidal stamp seal with a winged human figure

---

35 The figures from Tell Asmar are the best known and most frequently illustrated; for color photos, see, e.g., Amiet (1980:pls. 33, 34). See also Guichard (1996:36), Landsberger (1967), Sagona (1995:151–154).

36 For settings, see Collon (1987:108–112).

37 The tombs are described in Butler (1922); the seals are illustrated in Curtis (1925:pls. IX, X, and XI).

38 Boardman (1970a).     39 Curtis (1925:39).

(see fig. 101); and 4524 is a weight-shaped seal with a goat and suckling kid (see fig. 94).

The great majority of the seals excavated from the tombs at Sardis are carved in a style resembling the cylinder IAM 4581 discussed above (see Appendix 4). These seals form a coherent corpus and therefore provide a good starting place for defining the style. It is, of course, one of those so commonly called "Graeco-Persian." As should be clear, this name is a misnomer, assigning ethnic origins to a style that draws little, if at all, on the glyptic precedents of either ethnicity and cannot be said to have been carved by seal carvers of either ethnicity. A current trend to change the nomenclature to "Achaemenid Anatolian" is, to my mind, also misguided, as it locates the style geographically, historically, and culturally in ways that may be far too specific. What is one to do, for instance, with the seals carved in this style that have been found on the Black Sea, in Iraq, in Syria, or in Egypt?[40] Or with seals carved in this style that may be dated to the Hellenistic period? Drop the "Anatolian" part of the name, or the "Achaemenid?" Better, in my opinion, to continue using a name that is clearly erroneous but accepted than to introduce yet another, equally misleading, name to the literature. If a new name must be coined, let it at least be something that allows for the tremendous flexibility and variation of the Achaemenid empire and its artisans, as well as for the aftermath of the style, continuing beyond the empire's demise.

Indicators of this style include numerous aspects of 4581 mentioned already: the undisguised use of the drill, especially in intricate spots like animals' paws or the detailing of furniture, a certain broad quality to the modeling with volumes clearly but often shallowly indicated, and precise edges to figures. The muscles on the haunches of animals are often shown by two parallel grooves running from the knee back in a curve parallel to the animal's buttock. Striations or grooves indicate folds in clothing. Complex surfaces like wings and manes may be more or less intricately carved, often with shallow parallel lines. Although there are exceptions, most of the seals are uncluttered, with a few figures set off by empty space. These empty fields may be filled with inscriptions or linear signs, but the impression remains of figures set off by space. Groundlines are common but not diagnostic.[41]

Seals from Sardis carved in the style outlined here include three of the four rings with gold bezels (see figs. 73–75) (the fourth has an undecorated bezel), four of the seven rings with stone bezels (see figs. 76–79) (one of the

---

40 E.g., from Kertch (now in St. Petersburg, published Furtwängler 1903:117); from Iraq, e.g., Philadelphia CBS.5117; from Syria, e.g., Oxford 1889.382, Oxford 1890.124; from Egypt, e.g., Oxford 1891.324, Munich A 1398.

41 As is clear from the Sardian seals, iconography should not be used to determine stylistic designation (as has so often been the case with "Graeco-Persian" art): winged human figures, for instance, may appear in multiple styles.

remaining three is undecorated, the other two are carved in Greek styles),
one of the three cylinder seals (4581 itself [see fig. 80]; of the remaining two,
one is of glass paste and much corroded, and the other is of bone or shell,
carved in an anomalous linear style), thirteen of the fifteen pyramidal stamp
seals (see figs. 81–92) (the only one certainly carved in a different style is 5133,
mentioned above and in chapter 3, with a Neo-Babylonian worship scene; the
other is 4592, made of blue glass paste and too corroded to see any design),
and two of the three weight-shaped seals (see figs. 93, 94). The tremendous
preponderance of this style at Sardis supports Boardman's suggestion that it
is in some significant way to be associated with the satrapy of Sparda.[42] Until
seal-carving workshops have been found, we cannot be sure, but it seems a
reasonable working hypothesis to suggest the seals were made at Sardis.

Interestingly, seals of multiple styles might be found in the same tomb.
This does not necessarily mean that the same person was using each of them,
as the tombs were used for multiple interments. But some people certainly
had multiple seals carved in different styles, as described in chapter 6. Even
in those tombs where the seals were of the same style, multiple shapes
might be represented.

The iconography of the seals carved in "Graeco-Persian" style forms an
internally consistent set of images. Favored are lions: five seals show single
lions, one shows a lion and bull, one a heroic combat with a lion, one an
archer scene with a lion, and one a heroic control scene with lions. Two
seals show winged lions in heraldic groupings. This predilection for lions is
of course found also in sculpture from Sardis dating to the Achaemenid period. Lion-griffins are also popular: three seals show single lion-griffins, one
shows a heroic combat scene with a lion-griffin, and one shows a heroic control scene with lion-griffins. Other composite animals featured are bearded
winged crowned sphinxes, a goat-sphinx, and a human-headed bird. A bull
and a boar complete the list of animals carved in this stylistic category. As
has been seen, scenes involving the Persian hero figure are present, with
two heroic combats, two scenes of heroic control, and one archer scene. The
remaining seal shows the king enthroned. These images thus include but
are not limited to images favored in Iran, and form a composite group of
figures that is unique to Sardis in the Achaemenid period.

The concurrent existence of multiple styles at Sardis in the Achaemenid
period makes it clear that the inhabitants of Achaemenid-period Sardis had
choice in the style of their seals. This is an important point. Artistic imagery
in the Achaemenid empire operated as an interregional symbolic system,
with great and subtle variation on the local level. At Persepolis, multiple

---

42 Boardman (1970b), on the basis of the Lydian inscriptions common on seals carved in this
   style (which he calls the "Court Style" – this should not be confused with the Court Style
   defined and discussed by Garrison in the context of Persepolitan seals).

glyptic workshops produced seals in different styles concurrently: an atmosphere of stylistic creativity prevailed. Multiple workshops provided choice for patrons according to their desires; the creation of variety for political ends certainly influenced both artists and patrons alike in the choice of styles. It is exciting and significant to find at Sardis what seems to be a similar atmosphere of artistic choice within the confines of imperial symbolism.

The various styles that have traditionally been grouped together under the heading "Graeco-Persian" may be understood differently when integrated with the Persepolis model of local glyptic creation within a lively and complex artistic environment. Analyzed in this manner, the various "Graeco-Persian" styles may be seen as artistic phenomena based probably in western Anatolia, with Sardis perhaps as a main locale of production. Viewed as a conscious choice among many alternatives, the style found on so many of the Sardis seals takes on new meaning. It is not a poor compromise between Greek and Achaemenid glyptic. This style may, rather, be seen as a newly composed and socially symbolic art of empire, demonstrating the network of artistic and sociopolitical connections that united the Persian, and Persianizing, elite. It is a syncretic style, incorporating elements of iconography from the Persian tradition and from the Greek and Anatolian traditions to create a new stylistic mode of expression.[43] It was a style in which one might choose to have artifacts made, thereby claiming adherence to this group of high-status and influential individuals and reinforcing the Achaemenid hierarchy in western Anatolia. The point is not what is Greek (or Lydian) and what is Persian in this art, but something much more complex and interesting than a simple polarization of two distinct ethnically determined styles. It is an issue of stylistic choice and of claiming adherence to an ascribed identity, a citation of power located in the western part of the empire.

---

43 That the style was newly created, without local precedent, distinguishes it from various others found throughout the empire that demonstrate continuity of artistic style and iconography based on pre-Achaemenid art. See, e.g., Amiet (1973), Bollweg (1988); also Potts (1999:340–341). For a much earlier discussion, without the benefit of the Persepolis sealings, see Marvin (1973:13–19).

# 8 Achaemenid bowls: ceramic assemblages and the non-elite

This chapter moves from the public appearance of the city and the public statements of its inhabitants to examine the personal practices of those who were not necessarily in the public eye.[1] It shows Sardian society penetrated as a whole by altered dietary practices, as suggested by changes in vessels used for eating and drinking.[2] The ceramic assemblage demonstrates that the model we have been forming to explain cultural developments among the Sardian elite holds true also for the non-elite: the inhabitants were made part of the empire and linked to other regions by imperial ideology that affected local praxis. These links led to the development of a new culture at Sardis, one that reflects not just acculturation but the creation of something new, growing out of cultural contacts with differing regions of the empire, one that permeated all levels of society.

Until recently, evidence has seemed lacking for understanding the impact of Achaemenid presence on non-elite people at Sardis. In the past sixteen years, however, excavation to the east of the Lydian city wall has revealed a series of deposits that suggest the area was used throughout the Achaemenid period, as discussed in chapter 3. In addition to a few walls of domestic structures, outdoor surfaces and refuse pits attest to human presence and use, although interior spaces are still missing from our archaeological understanding of Achaemenid Sardis. These deposits mean that a sequence of pits and external surfaces may be pieced together: eight secure and datable contexts.[3] This chapter discusses, in the most general terms, the ceramic assemblage of Achaemenid-period Sardis and then moves to concentrate on bowls of an Achaemenid shape, the so-called Achaemenid bowl, that were manufactured at Sardis of local clay.

## The Achaemenid-period ceramic assemblage at Sardis: general remarks

The assemblage as a whole demonstrates a mingling of Lydian and Iranian traditions at Sardis in the Achaemenid period, with some developments of

---

1 This chapter is revised and updated from Dusinberre (1999).
2 For the importance of diet in signifying identity, see Meadows (1994). For ceramics as an indication of consumption patterns, and their use in studying social systems, see, e.g., Östör (1993), Brewer and Porter (1993). Consumption is explored by Campbell (1987, 1993).
3 I follow traditional dates for ceramic chronologies here, rather than those suggested by Francis and Vickers (1981, 1983).

**Fig. 61** Sardis: pre-Achaemenid Lydian pots.

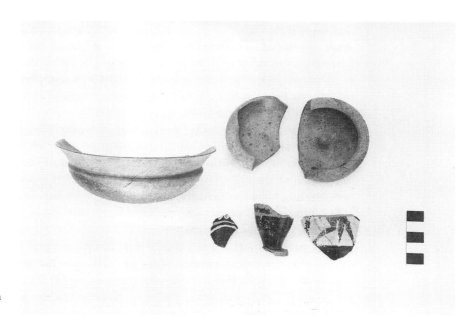

**Fig. 62** Sardis: Achaemenid-period pots from Deposit 1.

uncertain origin. Pre-Achaemenid Lydian vessels are illustrated in (fig. 61); a photograph of the full Achaemenid-period ceramic assemblage is unfortunately not available at this time, but (fig. 62) shows a selection of objects from Deposit 1 described below. Wine-drinking was popular at Sardis in Achaemenid as in pre-Achaemenid times, and the Lydian-era column krater continues to be made through the Achaemenid period. These kraters show a development towards greater angularity of rim and thinner walls as well as a tendency to be fired red, although the decorative scheme and size remain otherwise similar to those of the Lydian period. Trefoil oinochoai and small pitchers suggest one means of serving wine at table; although further work may clarify the question, it is as yet unclear to me if wine drunk from ceramic vessels was flavored, as is suggested by the silver finds from tombs at Sardis, Güre, and elsewhere.[4] The Achaemenid bowls that form the focus of this chapter were the primary vessels used for drinking wine; as will be discussed, the quantity of bowls found demonstrates the importance of wine-drinking in Achaemenid Sardis.[5]

Achaemenid-period vessels for the preparation and consumption of food, on the other hand, show some striking differences from their earlier counterparts. Pre-conquest Lydian cookpots are globular, usually with one vertical strap handle and a round mouth. They are apparently made of local clay, with sand, lime, and mica added. They have been found on hearths, resting on stones, on or near trivets made of a similar fabric, or resting on wave-line hydria necks apparently trimmed for use as trivets. The contents of these pots suggest they were used for cooking various kinds of porridges and stews made of grains and, presumably, vegetables and meat. Bread was apparently baked on large flat trays with thickened edges, again made of local clay with some added grit, of a rather crumbly consistency. Some but not all of these trays show signs of burning on the bottom, leaving open the question of where and how the bread was actually baked.

Food was eaten in the Lydian period from two main vessel shapes, it seems: the "fruitstand" or stemmed dish, and, to a lesser extent, a bowl with ring foot and simple rim. Although the vessels may be quite deep, the norm is a fairly shallow dish. They were often decorated in "black-on-red" technique, with bands of black concentric circles on a bright red surface.

The Achaemenid period sees changes in all of these forms. Cookpots are made of essentially the same materials, but are somewhat thinner walled and are fired harder; often they are fired red rather than grey as had been common in the Lydian period.[6] Many of them have flat bottoms, and there may be the introduction of a variety with a horizontal loop handle as well as those with the familiar vertical strap handle. The flat bottoms mean the pots could stand alone, placed next to a fire rather than over it. Trivets also

---

4  See, e.g., Waldbaum (1983:146–149), Özgen and Öztürk (1996:nos. 11–32).

5  Bowls, rather than rhyta, were generally used for drinking wine in Achaemenid Sardis. Rhyta show a similar process of high-status Achaemenid metalwares copied in local clays in other areas, though; see, e.g., Iranian examples in Kawami (1992:nos. 141–144). An early discussion of the phenomenon in Iran and the northeastern parts of the empire is Cattenat and Gardin (1977). See also discussion of Athenian adoption and adaptation of Iranian ceramics in Miller (1993, 1997:135–153 for rhyta).

6  There is not yet evidence to confirm that all these cooking pots – of the Lydian or Achaemenid periods – were made at Sardis. This point is significant in light of the proof now that cookware was a trade item in the Aegean world: perhaps the residents of Sardis were obtaining their cookpots from a different source in the Achaemenid period?

continue in use, however: these are often rather thinner and harder than their Lydian-era counterparts. The added grit may include somewhat more mica and less lime. Bread trays are markedly thinner in the Achaemenid period and fired substantially harder than in Lydian times. They include not only grit temper but also large flakes of muscovite mica, all aligned flat with the tray. The rims of the trays are more pronounced than in earlier periods, with a curve steeper towards the interior and more gradual at the exterior side, like a poisson curve.

Tablewares also show marked change in the Achaemenid period at Sardis. The stemmed vessels of the Lydian period fall into disuse and are replaced by a thin-walled bowl with a ring foot and an incurved thickened rim formed by folding the top back. The bowls with folded rims for the most part take the place of the simple-rimmed early variety, although some continue to be made. Bowls of both types are slipped on the interior and to below the rim on the exterior, sometimes as far down as half the bowl. Like the Achaemenid drinking bowl, the bowl with thickened incurved rim is an Iranian shape: it is ubiquitous in western Iran and Media from the late seventh century on.[7] Thus we see the Lydian stemmed vessel replaced by a bowl of apparently Iranian origin in the Achaemenid period.

Storage vessels demonstrate a slightly greater continuity: the wave-line storage vessels of the Lydian period continue to be made through the Achaemenid period and into Hellenistic times. These vessels, like so many others, are thinner walled in later times and tend to be fired so the slip fires to red rather than black, although black varieties continue also. I am aware of no definitive wave-line hydriai from the Achaemenid or Hellenistic periods: the examples known to me in which one may be certain of the shape are all amphorai. Deep undecorated thick-walled basins may represent some form of storage basin; if so, they are probably a new addition to the storage-vessel repertoire of Sardis.

These changes in the ceramic assemblage suggest a possible shift in dietary habits in the Achaemenid period at Sardis, although more faunal and botanical evidence must be examined before this question can be settled satisfactorily. Such a shift would be somewhat surprising, as one might expect the inhabitants of the same city to continue eating roughly the same foods: local environmental considerations as well as the force of tradition might suggest similar crops would be planted and harvested over time, to be prepared in similar ways for consumption. But the pottery at Sardis suggests that this may not have been the case.

The flat bottoms of cookpots show they may have stood alone, either next to a fire or perhaps even in an oven, operating as a sort of deep

---

7 T.C. Young, personal communication, 1994. See also Young (1965).

casserole; but the continuation of trivets demonstrates the cookpots were still used over heat sources at least part of the time. No destruction levels from the Achaemenid period have been excavated to offer a parallel to those of the mid-sixth century Lydian period, and we do not know if slow-cooking porridges remained part of the diet. The remains of hot fast-burning fires from Achaemenid-period external surfaces (Deposits 5, 7 below) suggest people may have been boiling water or roasting strips of meat outside, at any rate.[8] The shape of the later bread trays suggests bread was cooked faster than in the Lydian period, with a thinner dough and crispier end result. Perhaps most provocative, however, is the supplanting of the Lydian stemmed dishes by the bowls with inverted rims, bowls of Iranian shape. Bowls are one of the most common vessel shapes in Media and western Iran, with great numbers of vessels and varieties of forms found.[9] To find at Sardis a shift in tablewares towards bowls, and indeed bowls of Iranian origin, is therefore particularly interesting. Whether or not it suggests a shift towards the consumption of more liquid foods that would need to be contained in deeper vessels rather than being heaped up on shallower ones, it certainly suggests an Iranian influence on tableware use at Sardis. With these food bowls and the Achaemenid drinking bowls represented in such number, the place-settings of Achaemenid-period Sardis show a proclivity towards eastern practices and perhaps culinary tastes that is striking. Indeed, the drinking vessel called an Achaemenid bowl is one of the most overtly eastern forms found at Sardis, found in such great numbers that it suggests a shift in drinking practices that reached to all levels of society.

## Achaemenid bowls: history and morphology

Achaemenid bowls are handleless cups apparently used primarily for the drinking of wine, found throughout the Achaemenid empire and beyond. They were made of ceramic, glass (usually clear), and metal (bronze, silver, and gold-plated): the glass and ceramic varieties seem to imitate metal prototypes. They have a shallow body and a small base, sometimes flat and sometimes with an omphalos; the bowl is sometimes decorated with horizontal or vertical fluting or with protruding lobes that are often tear-shaped. An everted rim rises from a carination that may be more or less well defined, sometimes as a sharp ledge and sometimes as a simple line drawn

---

8 These fires may of course have been for non-culinary purposes instead.

9 T.C. Young, personal communication, 1996 and 1997; see also Young (1969). At Pasargadae, 142 of the total 340 vessel shapes from the Achaemenid and Hellenistic periods are bowls (D. Stronach 1978). For Median Baba Jan, see Meade (1969), Goff (1977, 1978). For Nush-i Jan, see Roaf and Stronach (1973), R. Stronach (1978).

with a pointed tool. In some cases, the carination is so subtly suggested as to be defined only by the beginning of the everted rim.

The vessel is the descendent of a long line of bowls with everted rims, found in southeastern Anatolia as well as Iran and Mesopotamia.[10] By the early first millennium BC, the shape is prolific and two varieties may be distinguished: one shallow vessel with an omphalos in its base and an everted rim forming a rather angular shoulder; and one rather deeper bowl, with an everted rim often but not always flaring from a carination, with only a shallow omphalos or none at all.[11] The shallow version is the so-called phiale mesomphalos, often decorated with gadrooned lobes; it was a shape adopted by the Greeks to be used primarily as a libation vessel. The phiale is known in the Near East at least as far back as the ninth century and continued in use through the eighth and seventh centuries into the Achaemenid period.[12] Four large silver phialai with royal inscriptions, apparently found at Persepolis, are known dating to the Achaemenid period.[13]

The other version of the vessel type, with its deeper bowl and higher rim, is the progenitor of the Achaemenid bowl proper.[14] The earliest examples of this version are those represented on the reliefs of the Assyrian king, Tiglath-Pileser III (c. 745–727 BC), but it was a common ceramic vessel shape in the seventh century.[15] In the Achaemenid period its manufacture and use was widespread, with examples found from Palestine to Russia, from western Turkey to southeastern Iran as well as beyond the imperial borders to the west. Perhaps the best-known examples are the metal versions portrayed on the Apadana reliefs at Persepolis, where they are brought as gifts for

10 The earliest examples of the shape known to me were excavated at Tülintepe in eastern Anatolia, found in a context dating to the Halaf period (c. 4500 BC): Esin (1982). The closest parallels from Halaf itself date to the eighth to seventh centuries BC: Hrouda (1962:98–100). The shape turns up again in southeastern Anatolia in contexts dating to the fourteenth century BC: van Loon (1975:45, 66).

11 Luschey (1939) is a magisterial survey of the various bowl shapes. More recent works on the vessels include Pfrommer (1987) and particularly Miller (1993, 1997). Discussions of smaller collections of vessels include Iliffe (1935), Fossing (1937), Matz (1937), Dohen (1941), Gjerstad (1953:405–460), Hamilton (1966), Hestrin and Stern (1973), Moorey (1988), Yağcı (1995).

12 See Luschey (1939). For illustrations of the phiale, discussion and references, see Moorey (1980); for Gordion, Young (1981), van Saldern (1959). For Greece, see esp. the examples from Perachora, Payne (1940). Mesomphalic phialai dating to the Achaemenid period were excavated at Ur; see Woolley (1914–1916, 1962, 1965). Moorey (1980:32) has also collected examples without good context from western Iran.

13 See Gunter and Jett (1992:69–73), Gunter and Root (1998) for the significance of these objects as recognizable royal gifts. In addition, two silver phialai were excavated at Persepolis in 1943 (Tehran 2421 and 2422): Sami (1955:62).

14 "Achaemenid bowl" refers to this type, not the phiale type. For illustrations of the Achaemenid bowl, see Moorey (1980:nos. 103–113). See also Howes Smith (1986). There are, however, two general variations within the Achaemenid bowl vessel shape: one rather deeper, with a smaller diameter; and one with a shallower bowl and wider diameter. D. Stronach (1978:243) calls these "goblets" and "cream bowls," respectively.

15 Moorey (1980:37); also Barnett and Falkner (1962:pl. 47a), Oates (1959:132).

the king by the Lydian delegation as well as other peoples of the empire.[16] Throughout the empire, the ceramic varieties are fired very hard, often to a pinkish or reddish color, with particularly thin walls. Hellenistic versions of the shape spread well beyond the borders of the now-dissolved empire, into Greece, Pelagonia, and beyond.[17] This history is important: the vessels evolved directly from first-millennium bowls used in Iran. Their introduction in the Achaemenid period to Sardis, where there were no precursors to such a shape, demonstrates a profound departure from local tradition, inspired by vessels from the Persian heartland.

The Achaemenid bowl is an extremely common shape at Sardis in deposits dating to the Achaemenid and Hellenistic periods.[18] There is no example of an Achaemenid bowl from the mid-sixth century destruction levels or earlier; all Achaemenid bowl sherds come from contexts overlying those dating to the Persian conquest. How late they continue is yet unclear: they do not turn up in Roman deposits at Sardis, although it seems they are still being used at the end of the third century BC. The introduction of the bowls therefore seems to correspond with Persian presence at Sardis after the defeat of the city in the mid-sixth century, and their use continues for over a century after the city surrendered to Alexander and ended its role as a satrapal capital. The implications of this will be discussed below.

## The deposits

This study of Achaemenid bowls draws on eight deposits to trace the vessels' development over approximately three centuries, from the early fifth to the late third century BC. The deposits are closed contexts and may be dated on the basis of external evidence: in the descriptions below, they are listed in chronological order. In each deposit, drinking vessels (skyphoi and Achaemenid bowls) comprise approximately 25 percent of the vessels found. I wish to emphasize that the questions and ideas raised here are the result of preliminary work and must be re-examined when the complete ceramic assemblage has been fully studied.

16 For the delegations bearing the vessels on the Apadana (V,VI, VIII, XII, XV), see Schmidt (1953); for a more specialized study, see Calmeyer (1993). For Delegation VI as Lydians, see Koch (1993).

17 The Hellenistic Greek adoption of the Achaemenid bowl, the "calyx cup", is widespread in ceramic and metal versions, especially silver. For this shape and its possible significance, see Miller (1993, 1997). Glass versions were also common: see, e.g., Yağcı (1995), Stern and Schlick-Nolte (1994), Grose (1989), Barag (1985), Goldstein (1979).

18 Two silver examples that apparently date to the Achaemenid period, found by H.C. Butler in his excavation of tombs in 1912–1914, are now in Istanbul and New York (IAM 4540? and MMA 26.164.13: Waldbaum 1983:nos. 964, 974). These bowls have not been examined as part of this study, however, which focuses on excavated ceramic examples.

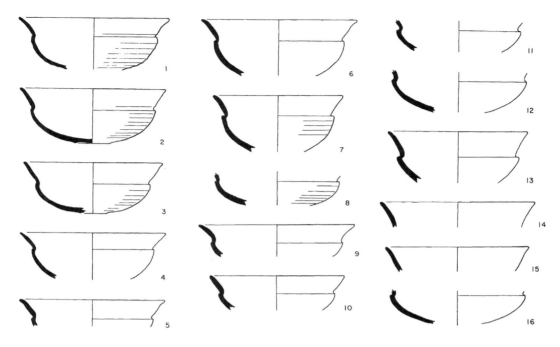

0  1  2  3  4  5 cm.

**Fig. 63** Sardis: Achaemenid bowls from Deposit 1.

## Deposit 1 (fig. 63)[19]

This was a refuse pit filled with bright green soil, interspersed with ashy lenses and containing much bone and a considerable amount of pottery. The pottery consisted largely of domestic ware, especially large closed vessels such as jars, and various open drinking vessels and bowls. Cooking ware was relatively scarce. The most common diagnostic shapes were Achaemenid bowls and circular open lamps of Greek type (Broneer type 1). The most datable objects from the pit included an Attic white ground lekythos fragment with a Dionysiac scene, dating to about 500 BC, and the foot of an Attic mottled black-glaze lekythos, transitional between *Agora* XII #1114 and #1119, and so perhaps of the earlier fifth century BC, as well as various late banded lydion shapes. A fragment of core-formed glass was also found, and a number of bronze trilobate arrowheads. The complex stratigraphy of the pit probably results from a fairly prolonged period of digging and dumping, perhaps extending from the later sixth century into the fifth. A final use

19 MMS-I Lot 17 pit, 1984 to 1986 (E148.1–151/S66.5–70; *101.43–*99.67). Stratigraphic information drawn from N.D. Cahill, MMS-I fieldbooks and reports, 1984, 1985, 1986.

**Fig. 64** Sardis:
Achaemenid
bowl from
Deposit 2.

0  1  2  3  4  5 cm.

date of the earlier fifth century seems probable, the Attic lekythos foot being the latest securely datable object.

## Deposit 2 (fig. 64)[20]

This wall was constructed of untrimmed fieldstones of uniform size set in fine mud mortar. Originally running east–west, it collapsed to the south, probably as a result of the erosion suggested by waterborne deposits. The wall was preserved to eight courses, found toppled on their sides; crushed under the wall were the sherds of a cooking ware vessel, an Achaemenid bowl, and an Attic bolsal most closely resembling *Agora* XII #539 in shape and #551 in decoration. The later of the Athenian bolsals (#551) dates to *c.* 400 BC, suggesting a date of the earlier fourth century for the collapse of the wall.

## Deposit 3 (fig. 65)[21]

This pit opens directly underneath and is associated with a building phase represented by two walls constructed of untrimmed or roughly trimmed fieldstones, well set in fine mud mortar, enclosing a floor made of thin fairly friable white plaster with traces of burning on its surface. There was a notable absence of clearly fourth century material such as closed body lamps from this phase, while shapes like circular open lamps (Broneer type 1), perhaps typical of earlier years, were very common. The latest diagnostic object, from directly underneath the plaster floor, is a foot of an Attic black-glaze bowl, resembling *Agora* XII #806, #832. The complete lack of Hellenistic pottery or other artifacts in any of the deposits associated with this phase argues against a date much later than the date of this bowl, *c.* 350–325 BC.

20 MMS-I 93.1 Lot 9 fallen wall (E153–156/S64–66, *100.62–*100.45). Stratigraphic information drawn from E.R. McIntosh, MMS-I 93.1 fieldbooks and reports, 1993.
21 MMS-I Lot 15 pit, 1984 and 1985 (E148.5–149.8/S69.5–70, *101.43–*100.61). Stratigraphic information drawn from N.D. Cahill, MMS-I fieldbooks and reports, 1984, 1985.

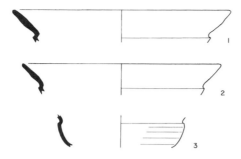

**Fig. 65** Sardis: Achaemenid bowls from Deposit 3.

## Deposit 4 (fig. 66)[22]

This pit, located next to the Lydian city wall just to the north of the city gate, cut through the destruction debris associated with the Persian sack of Sardis and through multiple earlier road metallings. It was filled with disintegrated mudbrick and many small pieces of charcoal as well as ash, burned mudbrick fragments, and chips of limestone. A great deal of local pottery, including fine wares, storage vessels, and cooking wares, was excavated from the pit, representing a wide spectrum of vessels apparently from domestic assemblages. Many bones, predominantly ovicaprid and bovine but also sus, were also recovered. The latest datable object in the pit was an Attic black-glaze "feeder," *Agora* XII #1197, a shape that was made into the fourth century. This pit is therefore probably to be assigned to sometime in the fourth century.

## Deposit 5 (fig. 67)[23]

This almost flat surface comprised fist-sized flat stones, broken rooftiles, and chunks of baked mudbrick forming a rough patchy mixture resembling cobbles that petered out to the north to give way to hard earth. Ashy lenses resting on the surface were the remains of small fires that included a large number of weed seeds but no other botanical remains. The ashes were highly silicaceous, suggesting short hot burning.[24] The cover tiles and the pottery (all local) within and under the surface dated to the fourth century BC.[25]

---

22 MMS/N 96.1 Lot 167 pit (E162.7–165.5/S14–16.8, *97.9–*97.1). Stratigraphic information drawn from A. Prieto, MMS/N 96.1 fieldbooks and reports, 1996, personal communication with the excavator, and personal observation.

23 MMS/S 94.1 Lot 19 surface (E115–118/S150–154, *106.3–*106.0). Stratigraphic information drawn from E.R. McIntosh, MMS/S 94.1 fieldbooks and reports, 1994.

24 M. Nesbitt, personal communication, 1994.     25 Dated by S.I. Rotroff.

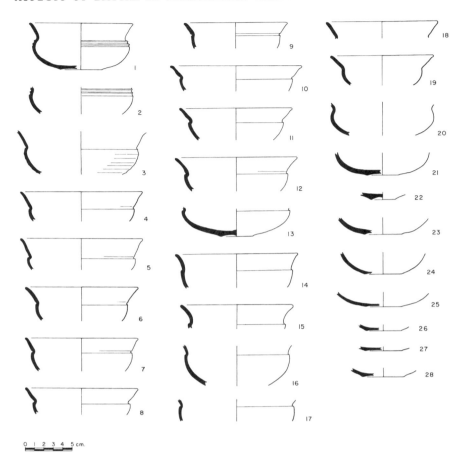

**Fig. 66** Sardis: Achaemenid bowls from Deposit 4.

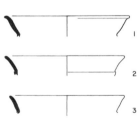

**Fig. 67** Sardis: Achaemenid bowls from Deposit 5.

## Deposit 6 (fig. 68)[26]

This pit was filled with bricky soil, rooftile fragments, limestone chips, and a large amount of pottery. It contained no externally datable chronologically

26  MMS/S 95.2 Lot 71 pit (E116–118.5/S140–143, *105.66–*105.40). Stratigraphic information drawn from E.R. McIntosh, MMS/S 95.2 fieldbooks and reports, 1995.

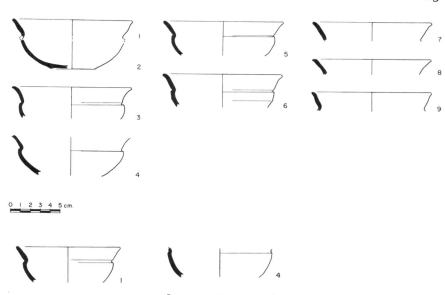

**Fig. 68**  Sardis:
Achaemenid
bowls from
Deposit 6.

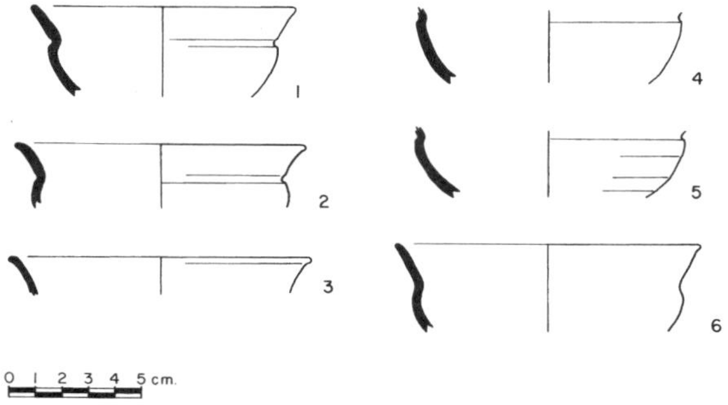

**Fig. 69**  Sardis:
Achaemenid
bowls from
Deposit 7.

diagnostic material and must therefore be dated solely on a stratigraphic basis. The pit underlay the inwash layers beneath the surface described below (Deposit 7) and must have predated it by some uncertain amount; it cut down to and through the levels of Deposit 5 and must postdate it. A date sometime in the third century therefore seems probable.

## Deposit 7 (fig. 69)[27]

Large stones rested on this hard-packed earth surface, piled up against the old Lydian fortification wall which still stood exposed at the time the surface was in use. The surface sloped down to the east away from the fortification wall, and somewhat more gently down to the north, following the natural lay of the land. Twenty-one rooftiles, painted red and white, were exposed lying on the surface in a pattern which suggested that the building from

27 Excavated in four different trenches: as MMS/S-D 1992 bas. 35, as MMS/S 94.1 Lot 48 surface, and as MMS/S 94.3 and MMS/S 95.2 Lot 29 surface. It was located at (E115–120/S137–155, *106.9–*106.1). Stratigraphic information drawn from G. Gürtekin, MMS/S-D 1992 fieldbooks and reports, 1992; E.R. McIntosh, MMS/S 94.1, MMS/S 94.3, and MMS/S 95.2 fieldbooks and reports, 1994 and 1995.

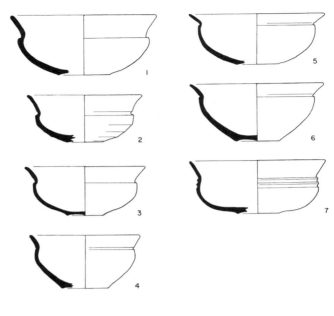

**Fig. 70** Sardis: Achaemenid bowls from Deposit 8.

0  1  2  3  4  5 cm.

which they had slid lay just to the east of the trench and had a roofing structure similar to that used in the archaic period. The pottery from the surface, located in the area between the large stones and rooftiles as well as amongst the stones, suggests a date sometime in the Hellenistic period.[28] Sealed underneath the surface was a lagynos sherd; a pit just above it was filled with moulded bowl sherds dating to c. 224–200 BC.[29] No finds were excavated that dated much, if at all, into the second century. It seems probable, therefore, that the surface dates to the late third/early second century BC.

## Deposit 8 (fig. 70)[30]

A series of destruction deposits scattered about Sardis was at the time of excavation dated to 213 BC, the abortive revolt of Achaios against Antiochos. Various of these deposits included examples of mendable Achaemenid bowls, included in this study. Deposit 8 is not as coherent as one would like. Research in 1994 into these contexts could not confirm the assignation to

28  S.I. Rotroff, personal communication.
29  Dated on the basis of S.I. Rotroff's moulded bowl chronologies. See Rotroff (1982, 1990).
30  Destruction strata found in various places around the site in the 1960s: at PN, located on the east bank of the Paktolos; at HoB, in a shallow depression 100 m to the west of the city wall; at AcT, the top of the Acropolis massif, 410 m above sea level (Hanfmann 1983:2). Stratigraphic information drawn from excavation object cards, fieldbooks, and reports, 1960, 1961, 1964, 1965, 1967; chronological information based on reports by A. Oliver and S.I. Rotroff.

Table 1 *Summary of deposit dates and phases*

| Context | Date | Phase in vessel development |
|---|---|---|
| Deposit 1 | early fifth century | early |
| Deposit 2 | early fourth century | middle |
| Deposit 3 | mid-late fourth century | middle |
| Deposit 4 | fourth century | middle |
| Deposit 5 | fourth century | middle |
| Deposit 6 | third century? | late |
| Deposit 7 | late third century? | late |
| Deposit 8 | late third century? | late |

the destruction of 213.[31] The range of shapes represented in the Achaemenid bowls suggests localized destructions of different dates may have been assigned to the known historical episode. Perhaps the surface treatment of the vessels played a fairly large role in the perceptions of the excavators, leading them to assign vessels to a specific destruction episode in the Hellenistic period that actually dated to a range of times? I include the vessels in this study as they illustrate some versions of the shape not found in other deposits at Sardis.

## Achaemenid bowls at Sardis

### General trends in vessel development

The locally produced Achaemenid bowls contained in these deposits demonstrate some real morphological change over time, outlined here in the most general of terms. Because of the nature of the deposits – mostly refuse pits or exterior surfaces of uncertain function – it may not be assumed that all vessels in each deposit were manufactured or even in active use at the same time. But taking each of these deposits as a group of vessels and comparing general trends over the three centuries they probably represent, we see certain patterns of development.

*Shape*

The earlier Achaemenid bowls (Deposit 1, esp. numbers 1, 2, 3) have a wider diameter[32] than have the later, although the height of the vessel

---

31 S.I. Rotroff comments (progress report, 24 July 1994, pp. 4–5): "I continue to accept it as hypothetically dating to the 213 destruction; if this is so, third-century Sardian potters were still working largely in the Lydian tradition, for the material finds its best parallels in Lydian pottery of an earlier age."

32 Average diameter = 0.14 m, standard deviation 0.025; height of vessel *c.* 0.045–0.05 m.

**Fig. 71** Sardis: horizontal fluting on an Achaemenid bowl (Deposit 1.1).

remains approximately the same through the course of its manufacture.[33] This means the vessels of Deposit 1 seem comparatively broader and shallower than their later counterparts. They are thin walled. The everted lip flares from a carination approximately two-thirds of the way up the height of the bowl. The carination is pronounced, having been leveled with a flat tool; sometimes a mark left by the top of the tool is visible at the bottom of the lip, emphasizing its beginning, but more commonly the lip is smoothed so that it runs in one fluid line from the carination to the rim. Lips are of fairly uniform thickness from base to top, usually flaring out slightly like the bell of a trumpet. The bowl curves rapidly inward from the carination towards the base in a smooth line, creating a broad shallow vessel. Subtle horizontal fluting, trimmed on the wheel with a round-tipped tool, is fairly common on these bowls, with the width so narrow that a bowl may have many flutes (fig. 71). Bases are generally almost flat, carefully but only slightly hollowed out with a round-tipped tool. This is an important deviation from Near Eastern round-bottomed vessels and from metal prototypes with pronounced omphaloi in the base. The Sardian ceramic Achaemenid bowls were string-cut and then trimmed with a tool to form a shallow depression on the bottom of the vessel. The inside of the vessel remained smooth.

---

33 This is not a hard-and-fast rule: two of the three vessels from Deposit 3, in the "middle" phase, are significantly larger than any of the other vessels discussed here, with larger diameter, thicker walls, and more out-flared rims than the norm.

The bowl could thus be rested on a flat surface right way up, removing the need for a stand; no internal protrusion like an omphalos interrupted the interior curve of the bowl.

The vessels from the middle chronological range (Deposits 2 and 4, esp. numbers 1, 4, 14, 16, 24) are of smaller diameter[34] but the same general height as the earlier vessels, leading to a proportionally deeper bowl. Lips are shorter and straighter than in the earlier examples, often slightly thickened at the lower part, drawn up to a thinner section just below the rim and then swelling slightly at the rim. This leads to a straight or slightly out-flared interior surface to the lip, while the exterior exhibits a subtle double curve. The carination from which the lip springs is rather higher up the bowl than on the earlier examples: the lip generally comprises somewhat less than one-third the height of the bowl. The carination is quite deeply drawn with a flat tool, so that a pronounced groove demarcates the beginning of the lip. The upper edge of this groove is left clearly visible. Careful horizontal fluting on the bowl is for the most part replaced by a shorthand version: a pointed tool is held against the bowl as it turns on the wheel, making shallow grooves in horizontal bands. These are generally not regular in their spacing on the bowl, but they are commonly found on the upper part of the bowl near the carination and often near the base as well. Bases show more variation than did the earlier examples: the diameters show a wider range, as does the degree to which the bases are hollowed out. Some examples are quite deeply trimmed, but even these are accompanied by no trace of an omphalos on the interior. The convenience of being able to rest the bowl on a flat surface continued.

The later vessels (Deposit 6, esp. number 4; Deposit 7, esp. number 1; Deposit 8, esp. numbers 5, 6) continue the trends seen in the middle period, towards a slightly smaller and less elaborately decorated shape.[35] The vessels are often thicker walled than their earlier counterparts; the fabric is sometimes rather laminated. The lip is short and often sharply everted, springing from a carination as much as three-quarters of the way up the height of the vessel. Carinations continue to be deeply drawn with a tool. The tall proportions and thick walls of the vessels lead to a different treatment of the exterior line of the bowl: rather than a single smooth curve from carination to base, they often show a subtle S-curve down to the base, providing a proportionally somewhat broader base. These bases remain shallowly hollowed on the bottom, with no trace of an internal omphalos; the

---

34 Average diameter = 0.12 m, standard deviation 0.035; height of vessel *c.* 0.045–0.05 m.
35 All vessels in Deposit 6 have a diameter of 0.12 m; those of Deposit 7 have an average diameter of 0.11 m, standard deviation 0.024. The much wider variation in shape of vessels from the "213 BC destruction" reduces the clarity of the morphological development outlined here, if Deposit 8 is taken as dating to a single destruction episode.

underside seems often to have been gouged out rather quickly and shallowly, with a somewhat uneven result. The visual effect of the S-curve is to make the bowl seem taller and slimmer than it is, although the very sharply everted lip detracts somewhat from this overall impression. Some of these later bowls are very small.

### Surface treatment

Surface treatments also vary over time. The slips of earlier vessels apparently have extra mica added, creating an exceptionally glittery and almost metallic surface, especially when viewed in direct sunlight (or, presumably, lamplight). They are usually fired to mottled red and black patterns, in some cases created simply by stacking the bowls in the kiln when they were fired. This often created flamelike patterns, especially on exteriors. Although some of the later vessels also show these traits, the general trend is towards a simpler surface treatment: the surface is washed with a thin slip to which extra mica has sometimes but not often been added, and the elaborate multicolored surface of the earlier vessels is for the most part supplanted by a simple red. This trend towards an overall red surface treatment is reflected also in other fineware vessels of the ceramic assemblage at Sardis, a trend to be found throughout the eastern Mediterranean that culminates in the Eastern Sigillata wares of the early Roman period.

### Decoration

The decorative schemes on these bowls generally imitate those of the metal and glass versions, particularly those found in Sparda itself, although the ceramic versions discussed in this study are generally simpler in decoration than the more elaborate metalwares.[36] Finds at Persepolis demonstrate the range of decoration current on metal bowls: the single bronze bowl found in the Treasury has no decoration at all, while those illustrated on the Apadana reliefs, presumably of silver, have bowls with horizontal flutes and the zone just below the carination picked out with pendant tongues.[37] Bowls from Achaemenid-period tombs at Güre show the wide variation in decoration on contemporary silver vessels from Sparda.[38] These vessels boast tear-shaped lobes, head-shaped lobes, lobes that function as rattles, relief appliqués with scenes drawn from central Persian iconography, vertical fluting, horizontal fluting, grooves, tongues, lotuses, punched circles, rosettes on bases, and added gold. The two silver bowls excavated from tombs at Sardis are rather simpler, with two horizontal grooves on the bowl just below the carination

36 For a discussion of the metal bowls, see Moorey (1980).
37 Schmidt (1957:pl. 68:1), Calmeyer (1993).     38 Özgen and Öztürk (1996:nos. 33–50, 122–124).

and no further decoration.[39] Core-formed glass versions of the vessel mirror most of these decorative schemes, with the exception of the rattles.[40]

The ceramic Achaemenid bowls from Sardis are necessarily rather simpler in decoration, although the connections to metalwork are clear. The two treatments most commonly found include the groove at the carination and the subtle horizontal fluting on the bowl (fig. 71). As we have seen, both of these find parallels in metal versions of the shape. A caveat seems necessary, however: trimming on the wheel to produce subtle horizontal fluting is a technique of ceramic decoration known also from archaic lydions; it is important to realize both that this is a simple process and that it has a history in Lydia as much connected with ceramic production as with metal. Regardless of its initial influences, however, the surface treatment of the ceramic Achaemenid bowls at Sardis is closely related to the surface treatment of the metal bowls, and the resulting shapes are very similar. The importance of metalwares as prestige items may clearly be seen from the inscribed phialai mentioned above, even aside from the question of the innate value of the metal.[41] The phenomenon of emulation in a ceramic medium, where the potters' craft develops techniques and aesthetics derived from metal vessels, suggests the symbolic significance of the Achaemenid bowl.

## Place of manufacture

These bowls were produced at Sardis. A visual analysis of the fabric demonstrates it is a very fine, highly micaceous clay that fires light red to yellowish red. In its well-levigated form, found uniformly in the Achaemenid bowls, it is so fine as to break conchoidally. In these regards it is precisely similar to the fabrics used for the manufacture of pre-Achaemenid Sardian finewares. And scientific analysis verifies these observations.[42] Neutron Activation Analysis performed on the bowls at the University of Missouri laboratories demonstrates that the chemical "fingerprint" of the fabric of these bowls matches that of the other local Sardian wares, from the Archaic through Roman periods.

---

39  Waldbaum (1983:nos. 964, 974).
40  An extensive bibliography exists on glass bowls of the Achaemenid period. See, e.g., Barag (1968), Fossing (1937), Goldstein (1980), Hogarth (1908), Oliver (1970), Roos (1974), van Saldern (1959, 1975), Vickers (1972), Yağcı (1995).
41  See Vickers and Gill (1994), Vickers et al. (1986).
42  I am indebted to M.L. Rautman for including samples of Achaemenid bowls in his own larger study of Sardian fabrics and ceramic production. Of the Achaemenid bowls tested, only two were imports, both probably from Ionia. The amount of imported wares found in Achaemenid levels at Sardis is very small (see Schaeffer et al. 1997); in this regard it differs from Daskyleion and Gordion. For an early discussion of imported wares in the Achaemenid empire, see DeVries (1977).

Table 2 *Percentages of Achaemenid bowls and skyphoi*

| | Sherd counts | | |
| Context | No. of Skyphoi | No. of Achaemenid bowls | Date |
|---|---|---|---|
| Deposit 1 | 188 (46%) | 219 (54%) | early fifth century |
| Deposit 2[a] | 3 (75%) | 1 (25%) | early fourth century |
| Deposit 3 | 14 (45%) | 17 (55%) | mid–late fourth century |
| Deposit 4 | 142 (47%) | 163 (53%) | fourth century |
| Deposit 5 | 0 (0%) | 6 (100%) | fourth century |
| Deposit 6 | 0 (0%) | 9 (100%) | third century? |
| Deposit 7 | 7 (35%) | 13 (65%) | late third century? |

[a] This apparent discrepancy is misleading: the skyphos sherds are all very small and worn, apparently residue from earlier times, whereas the single Achaemenid bowl sherd preserves almost a complete profile and approximately one-quarter of the circumference of the vessel.

Achaemenid bowls form an important part of the complex development in Sardis' ceramic assemblage during the Achaemenid period.[43] In the Lydian period, the preferred drinking cup was the Lydian skyphos: by vessel count, skyphoi represent approximately one-quarter of the vessels excavated. The skyphos continued to be made and used through the Achaemenid period and late into the Hellenistic period, showing a general trend towards smaller size, thicker walls and handles, and red slip rather than black. But it was to an extent replaced by the Achaemenid bowl.[44] Because skyphoi and Achaemenid bowls are roughly similar in size and thickness of vessel wall, sherd counts are probably more accurate than estimated vessel counts for determining relative frequency of occurrence for the deposits discussed above. The sherds of skyphoi and Achaemenid bowls are always immediately distinguishable in the field because of their differing shapes and surface treatments and because the Achaemenid bowls are fired harder than the skyphoi.[45]

Small numbers may skew the evidence, with only Deposits 1 and 4 being statistically meaningful, but even so these deposits suggest that from the

43 This discussion of Lydian pottery is based on personal observation and communication with A. Ramage, N.D. Cahill, and C.H. Greenewalt, Jr. Greenewalt (1971) published a "trick vase" from Sardis, shaped like a rider with a phallus-shaped spout, that probably dates to the Achaemenid period. For the ways different ethnic influences and presences can affect a ceramic assemblage, see Berlin (1998).

44 While a version of the skyphos continues in use apparently into the Roman period, the Achaemenid bowl is replaced by another vessel modeled on Achaemenid metal prototypes: the moulded bowl.

45 These sherd counts are based on everything found in each deposit; because adequate records were not available for such an assessment of Deposit 8, I have omitted it from this table.

time of their introduction, Achaemenid bowls were consistently more popular than the traditional skyphoi. All together, drinking cups comprise approximately one-quarter of the entire number of vessels in the assemblages in the Achaemenid period as they seem to have in the Lydian period.[46] It is clear, then, that the inhabitants of Achaemenid Sardis continued drinking with their pre-conquest verve – but they drank preferentially out of a cup, made of local clay, that was specifically Iranian in shape.

The dates of these deposits demonstrate the degree to which this change was taken on by Sardians. It was not the result of despotic decree on the part of foreign overlords, obeyed during the Achaemenid period but thankfully thrown off with the liberation from barbarian yoke following the conquest of Alexander. Rather, Achaemenid bowls continued to be a common drinking vessel at Sardis throughout the Hellenistic period. This indicates the vessel was accepted by the populace as part of the cosmopolitan culture of Sardis.

## Indicators of cultural impact

The Achaemenid bowls and shift in the ceramic assemblage demonstrate Sardis was a locus of cultural mingling and development in some very interesting ways. The Achaemenid bowl is a shape that was common in Iran from the first millennium, but it only appears at Sardis after the Persian invasion. It seems to have been primarily a wine-drinking cup.[47] We know from literary sources that wine-drinking played an important role in Persian society; we also can guess from the archaeological record that it played an important role in pre-Achaemenid Lydian society. But in Achaemenid Sardis, the Lydian wine-cup is very largely replaced by this Iranian wine-cup. This indicates some profound shifts in cultural emphasis at Sardis, probably having to do with drinking styles introduced by the elite and emulated by non-elites. One might expect that vessels connected with such public and perhaps political events as banqueting might change to accommodate the tastes and habits of the conquerors. But the uniformity and tremendous numbers of the Achaemenid bowls found in Achaemenid-period deposits at Sardis demonstrate some further points.

---

46 This statement is based on rough sherd counts of Lydian-period deposits. Complete analyses of these deposits will be published by A. Ramage and C.H. Greenewalt, Jr. (PN, HoB) and N.D. Cahill (MMS).

47 Use wear analysis will be an interesting avenue for future research on these vessels; see Skibo (1992). The fact that many beverages drunk by Mesopotamians were signified by written symbols deriving from the drink-specific containers used to hold them may suggest that drinking vessels were of specific form for specific beverages (see Potts 1997:139–163). But one of the Assyrian rites of coronation and kingship seems to have been to drink sour (fermented?) milk from a phiale; see Nylander (1999).

The vessel shows a profound assumption by the Sardians of some important Persian customs. This was probably due initially to new ideas of what
one needed to look sophisticated (an ancient version of the cellular tele-
phone or sport-utility vehicle?): first came the introduction of the metal
shape by Iranians in expensive silver, gold plate, and bronze. The shape
was additionally produced locally or elsewhere in clear glass, a particularly
valuable material. Next the local elite rapidly picked up on the new wine-
drinking customs and began using the vessels themselves, claiming public
adherence to the new polyethnic elite of Achaemenid Sardis. And the scores
of ceramic examples of the vessel indicate another social process in Sardis
at the time.

The vessel shape was highly popular in its ceramic version. This suggests a
marked emulation of the elite by the non-elite,[48] a suggestion perhaps particularly likely when considered in connection with other phenomena like
the great increase in number of tumuli at Bin Tepe (discussed in chapter 6),
an increase notable not only for the number of tumuli but for their diminu-
tive size compared with the vast monuments of the pre-Achaemenid Lydian
era. The seeming contradiction of the two sets of data reflects the cultural developments suggested also by tomb structures and tomb inclusions
(see chapter 6): the Achaemenid bowls represent an assumption of certain
Persian customs, while the increase in tumuli represents an equally avid
assumption of particular Lydian traditions previously limited to kings. Both
may point to the same social phenomenon.

The bowls display a high degree of standardization. No kilns of the pre-
Achaemenid or Achaemenid periods have yet been excavated at Sardis, but
the degree of similarity of fabric, shape, and surface treatment in the
Achaemenid bowls may point to their production by a few limited workshops.[49] The pre-Achaemenid Lydian skyphoi of the sixth century, like the
Achaemenid bowls, are strongly consistent and of very high quality, thrown
with thin walls and fired hard. But they are not as thin as the Achaemenid-
period vessels, nor are they fired as hard and with such attention to the surface decoration that adjusting kiln temperature and oxidation levels may
create. Is it possible the Achaemenid period saw an introduction of new
kiln technologies? Until more kilns have been excavated, at Sardis and in
Iran, this can be only a matter of speculation. The uniformly high quality
of Achaemenid-period ceramics, and in particular the standardization of
the Achaemenid bowls, may attest to a very high degree of specialization
of skilled production and to the restriction of production to a few individuals or workshops.[50] Government regulation can increase the degree of

48 Cf., e.g., Miller (1987).
49 For craft specialization, see Stein and Blackman (1993), Rice (1996a, 1996b).
50 For potters' workshops and their functioning within an imperial system, see Peacock (1982).

standardization of a product, an economically useful development as such wares may be easier to price and often easier to store or transport.[51]

The wares may, however, have been standardized because consumers demanded it for the important information the style communicated about social status and group information.[52] If the bowls were indeed as linked to perceptions of the elite and to signaling social identity as I have suggested, the producers of the vessels may have had little leeway in determining their appearance: consumer demand for a standard product could seriously limit the amount of variation a potter might introduce in his vessels. In this case, the standardization of the bowls would be socially mandated rather than economically. Their lack of stylistic variation may therefore not be a good indicator of the number of producers, but may instead be due to their symbolic significance in signaling the new social customs and social identities of the Achaemenid-period Sardians.[53]

## Sardis in the Achaemenid empire

Developments in the ceramic record at Sardis during the Achaemenid period suggest the degree to which local culture changed. Sardian Achaemenid bowls, based on an imported Iranian vessel shape, were produced locally and adapted to fit local customs. We are lacking stratified, externally datable deposits for the period from the conquest of Sardis in *c.* 547 (?) until *c.* 500 BC. The earliest securely datable deposits excavated so far, however, already include quantities of Achaemenid bowls. These bowls outnumber skyphoi on a sherd count, showing the supplanting of the local Lydian vessel by the imported form even in ceramic tablewares. Those missing five decades between the conquest and our earliest deposit were apparently enough to allow for the shape to be introduced, probably as a metal luxury ware, and to find its way into the common ceramic repertoire of the Sardian potters and drinkers. A particularly interesting point has to do with transmission and symbol: the Achaemenid bowl was unknown in Lydia before the Achaemenid conquest, and yet Lydians are shown on the Apadana bearing this particular vessel as gifts to the Persian king. Perhaps the gold and silver resources of Lydia meant it became a primary center of production for vessels in precious metals during the period of Achaemenid hegemony? In any case, these particular metal vessels of Achaemenid Lydia were tied to the imperial

---

51  See Costin (1991:34), Torrence (1986:197), Clark (1981:8).
52  "The involvement of vessels in the highly ritualized and meaning-laden food systems of a culture contributes both to the conservatism of vessel forms and to the assignment of symbolic significance to vessels and their use." Sinopoli (1991:122). See also Hodder (1983), Costin (1991:33–39).
53  See Costin (1991:34).

centers of the empire in Iran in explicit and symbolic ways. Its presence in
this context on the Apadana reliefs links the vessel to Lydian–Persian interactions and charges it with royal significance.

Non-elite emulation of elite utensils and their associated practices was
not documentable before the recent discoveries provided good evidence to
prove the kind of long-term impact Persian occupation had on Sardis that
one would assume from the recurrence of Persian names in Hellenistic and
Roman Anatolia.[54] Achaemenid bowls demonstrate the assumption of certain aspects of Persian material culture. They suggest an open atmosphere
in Sparda, one open to outside influence, open to acculturation, and also
perhaps open to social mobility.

The ceramic record includes very little in the way of Greek imports, unlike the satrapal headquarters of Hellespontine Phrygia to the north at
Daskyleion.[55] Daskyleion had been a Lydian garrison town without much
in the way of indigenous local tradition built up before the arrival of Cyrus
and the Persians; is this perhaps why it turned so much to the west and
Greece for cultural impetus, rather than to its own culture? The changes
in the ceramic assemblage suggest Sardis looked to the east for impetus
and inspiration in such fundamental matters as the production and consumption of food, rather than to the west. That these changes were real and
not just a temporary attempt to curry favor with new foreign overlords is
demonstrated by the continuation of the use of Achaemenid bowls through
the Hellenistic period.

In Achaemenid-period Sardis, ceramic styles – here represented by
Achaemenid bowls – indicate not ethnicity but the assimilation of new cultural impetus and the development of local social systems. Achaemenid
bowls are linked to new social definitions, new social identities. They
demonstrate a new elite that took on aspects of local and newly introduced culture; they show the assumption of Iranian customs that became
part of the display of non-elite emulation of elite customs. Achaemenid
bowls and the ceramic assemblage suggest striking changes at Sardis even
in such inherently conservative areas as foodways and food consumption.
They make clear the degree to which the city's inhabitants threw themselves into the exciting new syncretic culture and fluid social structure
of the Achaemenid period. This addition to Lydian culture could happen
without Sardians, old and new, needing to abandon many pre-Achaemenid
Lydian customs and habits such as mixing wine in kraters and serving it in
oinochoai.

---

54 See, e.g., Balcer (1984), Sekunda (1988, 1991), Hanfmann (1987).
55 The presence of some Greek imports, however, suggests this discrepancy may be due to the
   continuing lack of good classical strata at Sardis compared with Daskyleion. For Greek pottery
   at Sardis, see Schaeffer et al. (1997).

The local social organization at Sardis combined aspects of local culture with external ideas to create a new system that might thrive independently of the areas of original influence. This development was a complex process of interaction, reaction, reception, adaptation, and creation. At Sardis in the Achaemenid period, acculturation did not mean the simple taking on of external attributes by a pre-existing culture. Rather, it meant the development of a new culture, a new context in which new forms might develop. Importantly, it was not only the elite that responded to Achaemenid presence: the ceramic assemblage demonstrates that the changes in material culture due to Achaemenid ideas and presence extended throughout the social hierarchy. The Achaemenid bowls of Sardis are made of local clay; their bases are somewhat modified so that the vessels rest upright on a flat surface – to which drinkers in this land of footed vessels would have been accustomed. Acculturation in Achaemenid-period Sardis, the complex process of interaction and creation in a new context, affected people from high to humble rank in society. It penetrated deep into consciousness and custom, continuing particular traits and forming the basis for further development long after the fall of the Achaemenid empire.

# 9 Conclusion: imperialism and Achaemenid Sardis

## Sardis in the Achaemenid empire: imperial ideology and praxis

A recent review of the archaeology of ancient empires, describing the multiple definitions of empire that have emerged in historical and anthropological literature, summarizes:[1]

> They share in common a view of empire as a territorially expansive and incorporative kind of state, involving relationships in which one state exercises control over other sociopolitical entities (e.g. states, chiefdoms, non-stratified societies), and of imperialism as the process of creating and maintaining empires. The diverse polities and communities that constitute an empire typically retain some degree of autonomy – in self- and centrally-defined cultural identity, and in some dimensions of political and economic decision making. Most authors also share a conception of various kinds of empires distinguished by differing degrees of political and/or economic control, viewed either as discrete types or as variations along a continuum from weakly integrated to more highly centralized polities.

This broadly conceived working definition of empire suggests a study of Sardis in the Achaemenid empire might fit well within the sorts of questions being explored in other historical settings.

The Achaemenid empire lasted approximately 220 years, from the accession of Cyrus to the conquest by Alexander. Its length thus compares well with other ancient empires: although some lasted only as long as the first ruler (Timurid in Central Asia if not in Iran, Ch'in of China, Perikles of Athens), and others continued for less than a century (Inka, Aztec, Mongol), a number of ancient empires ruled for approximately 200 years (Agade and Neo-Assyrian empires in the Near East, and Mauryan, Gupta, Mughal, and Vijayanagara empires in South Asia).[2] Those that lasted longer, like the Roman empire, were anomalous.[3] In the time-frame of their duration, each

---

1 Sinopoli (1994:160).
2 For Timur, see Manz (1989). For Ch'in, see Bodde (1967). The Inka, Aztec, and Mongol empires are much studied: e.g., Morris (1988), Davies (1987), Allsen (1987). Recent work on Near Eastern empires includes Kuhrt (1995a), Liverani (1993), van der Spek (1993), Postgate (1992). For South Asia, see, e.g., Thapar (1984), Sharma (1989), Richards (1993), Sinopoli and Morrison (1995). See citations in Sinopoli (1994:162).
3 For Roman imperial provinces, see esp. Alcock (1993), Woolf (1998); see also below.

of the empires underwent processes of expansion, of consolidation, and of collapse.

An empire is created, its geographic and demographic composition set, through territorial expansion by means of conquest or other methods of incorporation such as marriage or treaties. Understanding the motivation for initial expansion is highly problematic, not least because the sources available to the modern scholar are often directly or indirectly the result of *ex post facto* legitimation on the part of the conquering power.[4] The ability to expand rests in secure military power.[5] As this is a particularly costly method involving loss of life and maintenance of the military, as well as disruption of local ecology and production activities, however, diplomacy backed by the threat of military power is often used in imperial expansion.[6] In either case, a military must be sufficiently strong to put down rebellions or other forms of resistance that may rise in the wake of imperial incorporation.

In contrast to the traditional views of Achaemenid "non-impact" described in chapter 1, we see both the processes and the effects of imperial expansion at Sardis in the Achaemenid period. The conquest of the city not only is described in literary sources but left a tangible result in the massive destruction levels at Sardis associated with the burning of parts of the city and the partial demolition of the city wall. After the conquest, Greek literary sources describe the rebellion of a Lydian left in charge, followed later on by two Ionian-led revolts. It was thanks to the military power of the Achaemenid regime that these rebellions were put down.

The rebellion of Oroites in Sardis at the beginning of Darius' reign is of a slightly different nature, being a revolt at a time of contested succession to the throne in Persia, apparently in an effort to expand his power base in his own name. Here, too, the military power of the army at Sardis, persuaded to follow Darius rather than Oroites, was effective in removing him from power. The response of the army at Sardis to the letters from Darius is interesting: this dynamic and innovative leader combined military skill with administrative genius, and it may have been a direct result of his personal charisma that the soldiers at Sardis chose to follow him rather than Oroites. Such a bond was important. Indeed, "the creation of personal loyalties and alliances between emperors and newly conquered elites may ameliorate costs of military domination, and the awesome or sacred name and reputation of the emperor may encourage conciliation and submission without the need for military activity or a permanent military presence."[7] Darius was not

---

4 See Sinopoli (1994:162).
5 For the role of the military in the Achaemenid empire, see, e.g., Briant (1999). See also Mann (1986), Hassig (1988), Foster (1993).
6 See, e.g., Schreiber (1992).     7 Sinopoli (1994:163).

the initial founder of the Achaemenid empire, but he was responsible for expanding its territories by war and diplomacy in a series of tactics that united expansion with consolidation of the empire.[8]

The close link between Sardis and the capitals of Persia was an important part of this consolidation. The Royal Road allowed for the rapid transit of messages and armies across vast distances.[9] Darius appointed his brother Artaphernes satrap at Sardis after his expansion into Thrace, Makedon, and northern Greece, an appointment that both forged the link more strongly and placed a man in an influential role at Sardis who was himself full of vision for the consolidation and continuity of the empire. For the empire to abide, personal loyalties to an individual king had to be transcended by a complete system of connections, obligations, and dependencies throughout the empire. Such a process requires "a range of constructive and destructive strategies, including the creation of new institutions, administrative structures, and ideological systems, and the disruption of previously autonomous local institutions, as imperial elite seek to strengthen political and ideological allegiances to the center and regulate the flow or resources to imperial coffers."[10] We see all of these features of consolidation at Sardis during the Achaemenid period.

The creation of a new administrative structure at Sardis is attested in ancient literary sources and left profound marks on the material record of Achaemenid-period Sardis, as we have seen. The new ideology of the Achaemenid empire was signified in artistic objects, particularly those intended for public display such as appliqués on clothes or sealstones.[11] Further manifestations of Achaemenid ideas and culture systems included the introduction of funerary couches and the probable association of eternal banqueting with mortuary ritual, and the use of the Achaemenid bowl for drinking by people of many different social ranks. The possible centralization of ceramic production in the Achaemenid period may be an example of the disruption of local customs. New religious syncretisms and the likely conversion of one cult site to a fire altar also demonstrate the modification of local customs to bring them into accordance with imperial ideology.

The composition of the elite who acted as intermediaries between imperial representatives and the local population points to another interesting feature of imperial consolidation. The imperial elite at Sardis included members of the local population. This co-option of loyalties and incorporation of the local elite into the Achaemenid elite probably strengthened the political and ideological allegiance of the local population – elite and non-elite – to

8 For the political measures taken by Darius and their impact on various regions in the empire, see, e.g., Dandamaev (1999).
9 Briant (1991), Graf (1994).     10 Sinopoli (1994:163). See also Streusand (1989).
11 For ideological signaling at Hasanlu in the Assyrian period, see Marcus (1990).

the imperial administration.[12] Such an allegiance was signaled on the one hand by conspicuous artifacts displayed on the body or used at the table; on the other hand, it might be demonstrated also by high-status gifts from the king or his representatives to loyal followers.[13]

At Sardis we have seen the development of a new artistic style, found in new objects (e.g., pyramidal stamp seals and cylinder seals, gold clothing appliqués), that united the elite regardless of their places of national origin. Although the iconography of this new art to some extent reflects influences from the center of the empire, the ultimate effect of the artifacts is one wholly different from those found in Persia, in other regions of the empire such as Palestine, or indeed in Lydia before imperial hegemony (where no sealstones or clothing appliqués have yet been found certainly dating before the Achaemenid period). This is a clear example of the effect of Achaemenid presence on the satrapal capital; the distinctive style of the Sardian seals demonstrates the specific local response to imperial ideology.

The development of new sacred monuments in the Achaemenid period at Sardis attests to even more complicated manifestations of cultural interaction and imperial consolidation. Emotional investment in cult is great; sacred practices are particularly sensitive indicators of human relationships in their demonstration of authority and status, or their overseeing of social transitions.[14] The symbolic or literal reorganization of sanctuaries and cult may be a particularly potent expression of imperial will:[15] at Sardis, as we have seen, it might take the form of coopting an altar to a local deity, rebuilding it and perhaps converting it to a fire altar, or constructing a new altar to a different local deity in a style that linked the monument with Greek traditions and Persian ones. The symbolically charged displacement of the one cult and the building of a monument for the other both occur under the overarching ideology of the Achaemenid empire, the one instance perhaps reflecting the (conflicting) traditions of the local Lydian population and the Persian, and the other the (confluent) traditions of Lydians, Persians, and Greeks.

12 One of the best examples of the co-option of local elite is Mania, whose allegiance to Pharnabazos was famous. See Xen., *Hell.* 3.1.10 ff. For the cultural assimilation of Persian elites in provincial areas with which they developed familial and cultural links (like Droaphernes; see chapter 5), see Briant (1985b).

13 Multiple examples have been mentioned above. For the role redistribution of symbolic and actual wealth played in the Achaemenid empire, see Sancisi-Weerdenburg (1989). The continuation of this concept into post-Achaemenid periods is discussed in Sherwin-White and Kuhrt (1993). For symbolic and material benefits bestowed on loyal retainers in another empire with a monarch controlling a great administrative web, see Brumfiel (1987).

14 For emotional investment, see Alcock (1993:178); for the importance of sacred practices, see Alcock (1993:172 and discussion), Geertz (1973).

15 Augustus' removal of cultic objects from Tegea to Rome is a strong example (Pausanias 8.46.1–5). See Alcock (1993:175–180) for numerous examples and their significance. For Achaemenid imperial ideology and local religions, see Bedford (1996).

Another aspect of imperial consolidation at Sardis is the revision of taxation instigated by Artaphernes. Facilitating the flow of money through the regional capital was an important part of Sardis' function in the Achaemenid empire. Artaphernes, put in power by his brother as Darius was returning from expansionist forays into Skythia, was responsible for a new survey of land throughout his province in 493 BC.[16] From this survey, he assessed taxes and military obligations. The acquisition of regular revenue by means of tribute or taxes "is both a major goal and a significant outcome of imperial expansion and consolidation."[17] This was one means, then, by which Sardis contributed to imperial consolidation. Another contribution was the labor of its inhabitants. Laborers were coordinated in work groups and moved about the empire: as we have seen, Sardians assisted in the construction of imperial monuments at Pasargadae, Susa, and perhaps Persepolis. Sardian men are also documented working near Persepolis as smiters of iron and specialty craftsmen producing *halapzi*.[18]

The dietary shift that took place in Achaemenid-period Sardis may conceivably reflect another form of economic consolidation: is it possible that the crops planted at Sardis were to some degree mandated from the imperial center, thereby bringing about a change in the diet of its inhabitants?[19] This suggestion receives additional support from the letter of Darius I to Gadatas, in Magnesia on the Maeander, which gives royal commendation for transplanting fruits from Syria to western Turkey.[20] The letter reads:

> The king of kings, Darius, son of Hystaspes, to his servant (*doulos*) Gadatas speaks thus:
>     I hear that you are not carrying out my instructions in all respects: that you are cultivating my land by planting fruits from the other side of the Euphrates in the region of Lower Asia, this decision of yours I praise and for this reason great favor will continue to exist for you in the house of the king...

The direct concern of the king with transplanting fruits from different parts of the empire in this case suggests it may have been the case also at Sardis, and may have been partially responsible for the change in dietary patterns implied by the ceramic record.

Imperial consolidation at Sardis involved both military and diplomatic channels in a manner similar to the expansionist phase. As is clear from the machinations of Cyrus the Younger, standing armies were kept at Sardis: armies that might include mercenary soldiers of other nationalities as well

---

16 Hdt. 6.42.     17 Sinopoli (1994:165).     18 PFT 1409. See chapter 2 above.

19 Such change of local produce in accordance with imperial requirements is well documented in other empires. So, for example, instances in the monarch-controlled Aztec empire are discussed in Berdan (1986, 1987). For the ancient Near East, see Hunt (1987).

20 Lecoq (1997:277), Lochner-Hüttenback (1964), Boffo (1978); but see also Hansen (1986), Wiesehöfer (1987). This translation quoted from Kuhrt (1995a:699).

as those fulfilling their military obligations in accordance with the survey conducted by Artaphernes. So, too, Herodotos tells of "Persian" soldiers, settled with allotments in the Sardis region, all of whom rush to the aid of their commander during the Ionian revolt in 499;[21] a similar story is told of Mysia by Xenophon.[22] Diplomacy was the tactic preferred by such satraps at Sardis as Tissaphernes, intent on re-expanding the empire into areas previously held by the king. The promise of imperial funding to loyal Greeks played a role in this diplomacy, perhaps even more important in the aftermath of the battle of the Eurymedon than the threat of Achaemenid armies. The punning remark of the Spartan king Agesilaos in 394 BC that he had been driven from Asia by the king's thirty thousand archers (read: coins with the royal archer device) demonstrates the efficacy of such modes of consolidation.[23]

The importance of ideology in consolidating the empire can hardly be over-emphasized. I distinguish here between imperial ideology motivating expansion and that legitimating the new empire, including the new power relations that resulted from imperial actions.[24] At Sardis, it is perhaps possible to distinguish two types of ideology: a top-down introduction of imperial ideology, and a bottom-up ideology that may stem from a local reaction against the top-down. Imperial ideology is clearly manifested in the material remains of Achaemenid Sardis. The adaptation of religion is one obvious example. The altar to Artemis was built at this time; the altar to Kybele was reconstructed, perhaps converted into a fire altar. The co-option of local religious beliefs and the creation of new religious systems that build on local traditions are highly significant ideological actions, not only establishing relations of dominance but endowing cults and images with new meaning reflecting new political and cultural circumstances. Such a creation of new belief systems may reposition the empire in traditional interpretive frameworks and may simultaneously reposition the local area in an imperial setting.[25] Such may perhaps also have been the purpose of introducing *paradeisoi* to Sardis in the Achaemenid period. The iconographic and stylistic expression of imperial Achaemenid ideology in art at Sardis has been demonstrated in objects that combine personal and public functions: sealstones and clothing appliqués. The presence of funerary couches in mortuary treatment at Sardis may represent an assumption of

---

21 Hdt. 5.102.     22 Xen., *Anab.* 7.8.     23 Plutarch, *Artaxerxes* 20.

24 Sinopoli (1994:167–168) discusses imperial ideologies. For the role of ideology in the expansionist phases of other monarch-controlled ancient empires, see, e.g., Conrad and Demarest (1984), Liverani (1993). The legitimating role of ideology has been much discussed. Most important in helping inform my thinking have been Kolata (1992), Adams (1992), McEwan and van de Guchte (1992), Price (1987).

25 Liverani (1979) discusses this phenomenon in the Near East just before the Achaemenid period. See also Conrad and Demarest (1984), Kolata (1992), Price (1987).

Achaemenid Persian ideas by the elite at Sardis, a process of acculturation perhaps to be directly linked not to official imperial ideology so much as to elite Achaemenid practices. Such developments would have been important in establishing connections that unified the polyethnic elite, however, just as official ideology was.

Certain changes in material culture at Sardis probably reflect the assimilation of top-down expressions of ideology and Achaemenid ideas by the entire population at Sardis. So the shift from using skyphoi to using Achaemenid bowls for drinking probably resulted from an internalization among the Sardian populace of Persian customs. That tablewares might be explicit bearers of ideological messages is demonstrated by the vessels found in the Treasury at Persepolis inscribed "I am of Xerxes the King," intended as gifts to distribute to worthy followers.[26] Their message was apparently received by the elite at Sardis and passed to the non-elite population through a process of emulation. In this way, imperial ideology might be internalized by the entire population.

It is possible that we also see at Sardis an example of local ideology working as social subversion. Conceivably, the tumulus tombs constructed in the Achaemenid period were used by ethnic Lydians to signify their Lydian heritage during the period of Achaemenid hegemony. If this is the case, it is particularly interesting that so many of them include the funerary couches probably introduced into Sardian mortuary treatment as a result of Achaemenid Persian practices, as well as quantities of gold foil clothing ornaments in the style current among the Achaemenid elite at Sardis: they show a combining of traditions that demonstrates the united culture of the elite far more than any disparateness. Alternatively, of course, some Persians may have appropriated prestige Lydian elements for their associations with, e.g., the legendary wealth of Croesus. In either case, the development of emblems perhaps associated with specifically "Lydian" cultural identity had to do with defining oneself more emphatically within the local society, now differently configured as a result of new power relations: old, epichoric traditions can serve as powerful markers in creating an appropriately dignified social niche, from which position one may "collaborate" even more effectively with the new rulers.

Some aspects of Achaemenid ideas were so fully internalized that they lost their "foreign" or "imperial" status and simply became part of the way one lived.[27] The new styles associated with signaling elite status are an example of this. It is very likely that the same development occurred in the way

26 Cahill (1985).
27 See the discussion of Athenian adoption and adaptation of numerous Persian paraphernalia, especially clothes, in Miller (1997).

people thought of the Achaemenid bowls that became the favored drinking vessel for several hundred years. Significantly, these internalized features of Achaemenid ideology continued long after the collapse of the Achaemenid political structure brought about by the campaigns of Alexander.

## Administering imperial provinces: Roman province and Persian satrapy

Achaemenid Sardis demonstrates some of the ways the Persians might incorporate a city into their new empire. Early students of the Achaemenid empire (and its aftermath in the time of Alexander and his successors) tended to spend much time discussing "hellenization"; this study has concentrated on the impact of imperialism on Sardis, on some of the ways in which the satrapal capital may or may not have been "Persianized." The Roman empire was an anomalous one. But the emphasis of many scholars on "Romanization" in the various provinces and on the impact that imperial presence had on provincial lifeways makes the Roman one a particularly interesting and appropriate comparison for the Achaemenid empire and its impact on Sardis.[28]

Two recent works on Roman Gaul and Roman Greece approach the topic of "Romanization" very differently. G.D. Woolf, in *Becoming Roman: The Origins of Provincial Civilization in Gaul* (1998), addresses the notion of "Romanization" directly: he rejects the concept as a valuable one, instead considering the idea of "civilizing" the province – a translation of the Romans' own ideologically charged description, *humanitas*. S.E. Alcock's *Graecia Capta: The Landscapes of Roman Greece* (1993) examines the various landscapes (rural, civic, provincial, sacred) of the imperial province of Achaea to determine the impact of Roman domination; she debunks the stereotypical images of Roman Greece as either fundamentally untouched by Roman hegemony or a country in decline, offering instead a complex and nuanced picture of the social developments in the province. These two models for considering Roman impact on imperial provinces underscore the common features shared with Achaemenid Sardis as well as its idiosyncracies.

Alcock argues for a pronounced impact of Roman rule on Greece, one that changed over time as taxation and landholding patterns developed. The province of Achaea was formed in 146 BC, after the defeat of the Macedonian king Andriskos. While nothing can obscure the ultimate result of total Roman control of Greece, professed Roman policy was one of

28 Studies of Romanization abound. Two interesting recent works, with bibliography, are Freeman (1993, 1997). A discussion that focuses on the interface between textual sources and material culture is Millett (1990). See also Hingley (1996).

minimal intervention in defeated territory.[29] Textual sources point to growth in the size of rural estates, tied to the growing importance of individual wealth in civic life.[30] This is borne out by the evidence of surface survey, which demonstrates a drop in rural site numbers between the second century BC and the third century AD, when the numbers increase again.[31] The loss of small sites is particularly pronounced, especially those that seem to reflect the presence of small-scale independent landholders; many of those sites that do remain active increase in size in the Roman period. Alcock argues (p. 72) that these factors "represent *either* increasing preference for nucleated settlement *or* the dominant presence of an élite landowning stratum in the countryside." The appearance of remains suggesting wealth – indeed, ostentation – demonstrates the presence of wealthy landholders, possibly with expanded properties; the construction of new monumental structures and villas shows increased rural social stratification. Developments in the land-tenure system of Roman Greece point to demographic decline, an unusual response in newly incorporated imperial provinces.[32] This may be linked to stringent imperial taxation. Roman imperial presence in Greece was thus responsible for altered landholding patterns, with larger estates being concentrated in the hands of fewer people, and for an overall decline in population and, perhaps, in the extent of land brought under cultivation.

So few regional surveys have been done in the provinces of the Achaemenid empire that it is impossible to know if the patterns reflect those of Roman Greece. The impression gained from Achaemenid Sardis, however, suggests that this city – and certain key parts of its hinterland, such as *paradeisoi* – prospered in the Achaemenid period. The relatively large number of statues dating to the Achaemenid period suggest disposable wealth in the hands of private citizens; the same impression is gained by the removal from circulation of gold and precious stones seen in Achaemenid-period grave goods. These are features of elite society alone, however. Do they reflect an amassing of wealth in the hands of a few, similar to that suggested for Roman Greece? Textual sources might confirm such a picture: the fabulously wealthy Pythios, for instance, may have been unusually prosperous,

29 See, e.g., Crawford (1986), Harris (1979), Badian (1968).
30 Alcock (1993:72–73), drawing on Migeotte (1984), de Ste. Croix (1981), Préaux (1978), Will (1975), Tarn and Griffith (1952), Tarn (1925), Ferguson (1911).
31 This trend is widespread and great, being found in Boiotia, eastern Phokis, the Argolid, Nemea valley, the Methana peninsula, Messenia, and the islands of Melos and Keos. The principal publications of these projects on which Alcock drew (1993:35) are: Boiotia: Bintliff and Snodgrass (1985); eastern Phokis: Fossey (1986); southern Argolid: van Andel and Runnels (1987); Nemea valley: Wright et al. (1990); Methana: Mee et al. (1991); Messenia: McDonald and Hope Simpson (1972); Melos: Renfrew and Wagstaff (1982); Keos: Cherry et al. (1991).
32 Alcock (1993:91, with bibliography on demography).

but there is nothing in the sources to suggest he was an exception in being able to collect riches. Indeed, the practice of distributing wealth and
luxury goods seen in gifts from the king to favored subjects – gifts which
would be symbolically as well as economically profitable – tends to support the notion that a few individuals controlled a high percentage of the
available resources. Moreover, the reed and mudbrick houses of Sardis may
reflect a lack of wealth on the part of the non-elite populace. The adoption
in fictile medium of high-prestige metal drinking-vessel shapes may also
underscore this: the signifiers of the wealthy elite were of such symbolic
value in Achaemenid Sardis that others tried to adopt them even in less
valuable materials. Although it would be rash to claim a situation for the
province of Sparda that resembled the province of Achaea without intensive surface survey to support it, the material remains of Sardis suggest that
we may see significant concentration of wealth in the hands of a few. If the
pattern suggested by Roman Greece applies to Sparda as well, this might
reflect altered landholding patterns, perhaps resulting from Artaphernes'
assessments.

The urban landscape of Greece also reflects the changed individual and
collective social identities and relationships resulting from Roman domination.[33] Unlike the uniform appearance of the rural landscape in the Roman
period, the civic landscape presents a mixed picture of urban growth and urban decline, demonstrating that multiple explanations must be sought for
the rural developments visible in different regions of Greece.[34] In general,
increased nucleation of settlement seems to have covaried with increased
concern over the clear demarcation of boundaries between *poleis*; perhaps
this concern reflects an ideologically charged desire to maintain memory
of a past era, when *poleis* were independent (and often at war).[35] This point
raises interesting issues concerning the restructuring of the imperial periph-
eries. Before Roman domination, the Greek peninsula was indeed divided
ideologically and often practically into independent *poleis*, each with its individual history. With incorporation into the empire came imposed unity,
in certain key ways.

Diversity was a hallmark of the Achaemenid empire, as of the Roman.[36]
Indeed, adaptability to differing local landscapes is a crucial feature of any

33 Alcock (1993:93). See also Gauthier (1981).        34 Alcock (1993:96–99).
35 See Alcock (1993:114–120). She quotes Elsner (1995): "The very conflicts of the *hellenika* as
   tirelessly repeated in the myths and histories of internecine war become a cohesive factor,
   a shared myth that brings them together against the Other of non-Greece, which is to say
   Rome. The divisions of Greece themselves become the definition of a unified identity, a past
   when it was possible to be divided before the present of integration within a larger and more
   dominant whole."
36 For provincial diversity in the Roman empire, see Alcock (1993:220–224 and bibliography).

successful empire. Again, the kind of archaeological exploration hitherto undertaken in Lydia precludes a precise comparison with Greece, but certain features of Achaemenid Sardis suggest an imposed unity that linked the city to other regions, not dissimilar to that posited for Roman Greece. One obvious parallel is the incorporation of a new province under a particular capital: as Corinth served as provincial capital for the new province of Achaea, so too Sardis served as satrapal capital for the new satrapy of Sparda. In both cases, the region administered from the capital not only included the land that had previously fallen under its control but also involved drawing new boundaries and subordinating different territories under its rule; for Sardis, the incorporation of the Ionian seaboard into the satrapy of Sparda (at least until the Ionian revolt) is perhaps the most obvious example. Despite differing local histories, the cities were all subsumed under the same administrative umbrella, perhaps with differing results: while Sardis seems to have prospered, many of the Ionian Greek cities seem to have entered an economically depressed period under Achaemenid hegemony, with less superfluous wealth in the hands of patrons to devote to artistic or architectural endeavor.

Roman responses to Greece, with its complex and fragmented political nature, stemmed both from imperial needs and the conditions of the subordinate population.[37] The widely adopted distinction made by Luttwak between force and power is important in considering information flow within Greece.[38] Although the Romans were unwilling to use force as the regular instrument of imperial rule, the success of the empire was predicated upon its ability to spread information of its willingness to act when necessary. The pan-Hellenic sanctuaries provided a local mechanism for such communication. The Romans also relied heavily on the local elite to administer small towns; the movement of provincial elite might help spread information and ideology through the province – or indeed from one province to another – more readily.[39] These local elite were also attuned to local history, traditions, and attitudes: they were easily the most efficient and effective way of implementing new imperial policies and ideologies. And yet it is clear that the local elite operated within a social hierarchy where the upper tiers were occupied by Romans: Plutarch advised a young man thinking of entering public life:[40]

> when entering upon any office whatsoever, you must not only call to mind those considerations of which Perikles reminded himself when he assumed the cloak of a general: "Take care, Perikles, you are ruling free men, you are ruling

37 Alcock (1993:131–170).     38 Luttwak (1976).
39 Alcock (1993:144 for reliance on local elite, 156–157 for movement).
40 (Praecepta gerendae reipublicae 813d–f, 824e–f); quoted in Alcock (1993:150).

Greeks, Athenian citizens," but you must also say to yourself, "You who rule are a subject, ruling a State controlled by proconsuls, the agents of Caesar...You should arrange your cloak more carefully and from the office of the generals keep your eyes upon the orators' platform, and not have great pride and confidence in your crown, since you see the senatorial shoes of the proconsul just above your head..." [The statesman] will instruct his people both individually and collectively and will call attention to the weak condition of Greek affairs, in which it is best for wise men to accept one advantage – a life of harmony and quiet – since fortune has left us no prize open for competition. For what dominion, what glory is there for those who are victorious? What sort of power is it which a small edict of a proconsul may annul or transfer to another man and which, even if it last, has nothing in it seriously worth while?

This notion of power, but limited power, of influence that is subordinated to another, within a landscape that included local elite continuing to retain a certain degree of prestige and wealth, seems to characterize the upper social echelons of Roman Greece.

Achaemenid Sardis bears some similarity to this scenario but does not conform in all respects to the Roman model. Local elite were retained in positions with status and adopted many of the external signifiers of the empire-wide Achaemenid elite: the iconography of their seals, for instance, was shared by seal-users in many other parts of the empire, and their jewelry reflected styles worn not only at Persepolis but in Achaemenid Egypt.[41] Like the Roman elite, the local elite will have been particularly useful disseminators of imperial messages because of their familiarity with local practice and ideology. It is certain that people moved around in the Achaemenid empire: some forcibly, some by choice. That the Sardian elite did so is suggested by Herodotos, who says Pythios entertained Xerxes and his entire army at Kelainai, at the headwaters of the river Maeander in Phrygia.[42] The impression gained from both archaeological exploration and the textual sources, however, is that the local elite at Sardis had greater prestige and wealth than their Roman Greek counterparts. Here it should be re-emphasized that it is impossible to discern the *ethnicity* of the elite at Sardis; certainly the satraps were ethnic Persians, and indeed by and large related to the king, and onomastic evidence suggests there were Lydians as well as Persians among the elite at Sardis, but we cannot tell the ethnic background of the elite in general. Their very sharing of material culture demonstrates that ethnicity was less important to signal than wealth. In any case, the sparring between the satraps of Sparda and Hellespontine Phrygia, and the eventual uprising of certain satraps in revolt against the king, suggests the regional governors,

41 For the seals, see chapter 7; the statue of Udjahorresnet wears Persian jewelry: Baines (1996).
42 Hdt. 7.27.

at any rate, considered themselves of importance and influence in the hierarchy of the empire (if not, perhaps, as much as they wished).

Roman Gaul provides another province for comparison with Sparda – like Sparda, a province rich in agricultural, mineral, and human resources that lay at the northwestern edge of the empire – and Woolf's recent study affords an approach different to that of Alcock. Woolf's analysis is strongly influenced by core–periphery models.[43] He begins by rejecting the notion of "Romanization" as a useful concept: it is too nebulous and is used to describe a multitude of processes.[44] After describing instances of modern scholarship in which "Romanizing" is equated with "civilizing," he replaces the idea with one of acculturation, discussed solely from the perspective of Gaulish assumption of aspects of Roman culture. "I shall define Roman culture as the range of objects, beliefs and practices that were characteristic of people who considered themselves to be, and were widely acknowledged as, Roman," he says,[45] without problematizing the issue further. But his subsequent discussion raises important points about the process of importing culture: he suggests that goods can be imported more easily than information, so that Gauls might build houses in a style reflecting those of Rome but inhabit them in very different ways than did Romans in Italy.[46] He mentions the varying importance of different aspects of a cultural system in cultural self-definition, using religion as an example of a particularly important one; he touches also on the predilection of societies to equate their own cultural systems with Culture and their value systems with Truth. He ends his discussion of these matters by pointing out the Romans' own adherence to this way of thinking:[47] "The notion of Civilization, as opposed to barbarism or savagery, is another example of such a belief, and the Roman version of this ideal, *humanitas*, was a central component of Roman culture under the early empire." Much of the remainder of his discussion is couched in terms related to this Roman notion of *humanitas*.

Woolf makes the important point that imperialism and culture are often linked: in the case of the Roman empire, he argues, the shared culture of the elite – for whom "political assimilation corresponded to a cultural assimilation"[48] – formed a powerful link across the empire that both united the

---

43 Woolf (1998:27 et passim). He first grapples with the idea in Woolf (1990); it informs his discussion in subsequent articles, including Woolf (1993, 1994).

44 Woolf (1998:7). He admits that some have seen this very nebulousness as a useful characteristic of the term; so Goudineau (1979:312), Mócsy (1970:7).

45 Woolf (1998:11).

46 Woolf (1998:16); he seems to imply such difference must be due to Gallic ignorance rather than to local factors such as, e.g., a different environment or different gender relation systems.

47 Woolf (1998:16).

48 Woolf (1998:18–19 and n. 60). Woolf quotes Brunt (1976), who linked the extension of citizenship to the local elite in Italy to their success in acquiring Roman culture through imitation.

elite and set them apart from lower classes. "[E]mpire-formation may have entailed the cultural unification of the ruling strata of formerly independent states, while the subject populations remained as segmented [culturally from other regions of the empire] as before."[49] Alternatively, he argues, resistance to Romanization could be empowering to local cultures.[50] Thus, aspects of local culture that remain unchanged by Roman domination may reflect not inability but unwillingness to change.

Indeed, deciding which aspects of an imperial culture to take on and which to reject, which aspects of local culture to retain and which to change, could be highly symbolically important. Another author has developed three (not mutually exclusive) explanations for reasons one culture may assume attributes of another in cases of imperialism:[51]

1 the psychological: the "need" to incorporate the alien within the society so as to diffuse its threat;
2 the social: the "need" to expand the vocabulary marking social relations in face of increasing social complexity;
3 the national: the "need" to develop new expression for the emergent empire.

How does Achaemenid Sardis fit into this picture? Shared artistic iconography certainly seems to be a feature of the Achaemenid empire, and that some elites at Sardis knew Aramaic is demonstrated by the bilingual inscriptions. The sealstones examined in chapter 7 may well result from both social and national "needs" – are there examples of psychological "need" for incorporation or rejection of Achaemenid culture? As mentioned before, we simply do not have enough evidence from Sardis to make a clear statement about resistance to Achaemenid ideology.[52] Perhaps we see a psychologically driven incorporation of the alien into local culture in the many small burial tumuli with benches, however: the fusion of cultures these tombs represent, especially when combined with the gold clothing appliqués that have been found associated with them, demonstrates an acculturation that may reflect all three "needs" outlined above. The same may be true for the construction of the altar to Artemis, with its Lydian, Greek, and Persian features.

Gaul was a wealthy province.[53] Southern Gaul's economy resembled that of Spain, where Mediterranean crops (olives, wheat, and vines) flourished.[54] Roman imperialism could hope to extract surpluses from this area and transport them to distant markets; new crops and technologies might contribute

---

49 Woolf (1990:49).     50 Woolf (1998:19–20).     51 See Miller (1997:248).
52 This is a pity, for resistance to imperial control can provide particularly illuminating insight into local concerns. For a study of resistance and the forms it may take, see Bowersock (1986).
53 For discussion and bibliography, see Woolf (1998:40–47).
54 Py (1990), Bats (1988).

to added productivity. Continental Gaul was even more fertile and rich. The economic prosperity of all of Gaul was seriously hindered by intertribal warfare, as well as by Republican Roman wars when allies were compelled to provide supplies and enemies were plundered.[55] The transition of Rome from a conquest state to a tributary empire was marked in Gaul by economic measures that happened very quickly, concentrating in the second half of the last century BC, and were more or less disruptive to pre-existing local practices.[56] Land was confiscated, reallocated between tribes, centuriated and given to colonists, or concentrated in the hands of the wealthy for their use or sale. People were captured and sold as slaves. Taxation and political structures were formalized, so that appointed or elected officials oversaw the regular exaction of taxes – a far cry from the previous extraction of large profits at irregular intervals, taxes were probably exacted by the local elite.[57] Taxes were high, however; from the time of Augustus on, taxes were repeatedly adjusted to make the tax burden "the highest sustainable level that would not prompt unrest."[58] Such taxation forced the economic life of Gaul's populace to conform more to Roman economic patterns. The Roman rhetoric that accompanied these changes clearly distinguishes between the civilization and *humanitas* of the Romans and the Romanizing Gauls, and the barbarian nature of other Gauls.[59]

We do not know what taxes were levied on Sardis in the Achaemenid period, nor how – or by whom – they were paid. That taxes were exacted is clear, and it seems likely that some of them were paid in gold, one of Sparda's natural resources. Other raw materials may have included other metals (silver and lead?), stones, crops, and timber; worked goods may have included coined metals, perfumes, and textiles.[60] The reference on Persepolis Fortification tablet 1409 to Lydians working on specialty tasks in Mesopotamia may support the suggestion that some taxes were exacted in the form of labor. The Mnesimachos Inscription suggests taxes were assessed on the basis of wealth held in land, tenants or laborers, metals (gold and silver), and agricultural produce: perhaps one-twelfth of the total value assessed might be demanded in the form of tax. Presumably, it was not up to the satrap (or landowner) to determine what fraction of each year's taxes might be rendered in what form, but there may have been some leeway in shuffling funds to balance the budget, so that a bad agricultural year could see an increased payment in precious metals and labor.

---

55 See Woolf (1998:41–42).     56 Woolf (1998:42–43 with references).     57 Woolf (1998:44).
58 Woolf (1998:44). Tacitus (*Ann.* 3.40), Dio (54.36 and 62.2), and Suetonius (*Vesp.* 1) all link debt and money-lending with subsequent unrest.
59 Woolf (1998:3, 59, 67 et passim).
60 For Sardian textiles at the Persian court, see chapter 2. For the form and degree of taxation in earlier periods in Mesopotamia, see, e.g., Salonen (1972).

**Fig. 72**
Persepolis:
Apadana
staircase. Lower
register: Lydian
delegation.

Other sources give us an idea of the symbolic function of Sparda in the empire, and may suggest the specific kinds of items that the region contributed to the central Achaemenid administration. The Lydians that appear on the Apadana reliefs at Persepolis bear two elaborate metal amphorai with animal finials, two equally elaborate metal Achaemenid bowls, two torques with animal finials, and a chariot drawn by two horses (fig. 72). In the symbolically charged artistic rhetoric of the imperial heartland, then, Lydians were associated with ornate vessels made of precious metals, and with horses and the apparatus of warfare. Interestingly, these are the same symbolic associations the area had for Greeks in the Archaic period:[61] Greek writings about easterners before the wars of 490 and 480 BC, when the Persian kings sought to annex the Greek mainland into the Achaemenid empire, mainly focused on Sardis and the Lydians, the closest neighbors of the Greek colonies in Asia Minor. Greek poets of the seventh and sixth centuries describe both the elegant lifestyles of the Lydians and their prowess in war.[62] The Lydian capital Sardis was portrayed as a vastly wealthy city, full of gold, the source

---

61 See chapter 2 above.

62 Archilochos' famous comment about Gyges (Archilochos 15) is one of the few references to wealth, rather than goods. Alkaios commemorates the gift by the Lydian king (Croesus?) of 2,000 talents to Lesbos (F 116 [69]). Alkman refers only twice to the east (1, 16): once to Lydia, land of his fathers, and once as a comparison between country boors and the denizens of lofty Sardis. A scholiast comments that for Anakreon, *lydopatheis* means the same as *hedopatheis*. Sappho describes as Lydian elaborate headbands, footgear, and textiles (e.g., F 219 [98]). She implies Lydian women were particularly beautiful (F 218 [96]). She also mentions the war

of luxury goods such as worked and painted ivory, a special rich purple-red dye, perfumes, and elaborate textiles. Archaic Greeks attributed to the Lydians a love of pleasure, a worldliness, an expertise in crafts such as textile weaving and music. At the same time, the Greeks also commented on the Lydians' warlike nature, their horses and chariots, and their success on the battlefield. This dual nature of Lydians – pleasure-loving, yet fierce – is found in both Greek poetry and prose.[63]

It is therefore particularly interesting to find the same associations symbolically represented on the Apadana reliefs at the Achaemenid royal capital of Persepolis. Could the stereotype hold a grain of truth? We should not take the Apadana representations as *factual* renderings of tribute brought by Lydians to the king, of course, but the *artistic rhetoric* of the empire, couched in terms of production resources and harnessed expertise, is relevent to this discussion. In imperial Achaemenid rhetoric as well as Greek, Sparda was a land of horses, of warlike citizens, of skilled craftsmen, of expert textile weavers, and of gold and other precious resources. We might expect that all of these assets were taxed.

Roman rhetoric surrounding imperial expansion into Gaul revolved around civilizing the barbarians: this was an ideology that seems to have been fastened upon particularly by local elite.

> If [the Gauls] had been barbaric they were not predestined to remain so, indeed the recognition of their former barbarism provided some sort of explanation for their conquest by Rome . . . [A]cceptance of Roman myths of civilization offered the Gallo-Roman aristocracies a place in the future, a place they were quick to take as the Gallic participation in the conquest, garrisoning and civilizing of Britain and Germany makes clear. *Humanitas* also provided Gallo-Roman aristocrats with a title to rule over their less educated subordinates. No longer barbarians, they acquired a sensitivity to the cultural deficiencies of their subjects, so education provided a means of conceptualizing and expressing the economic and political gulfs that had opened up within Gallic societies as a result of incorporation into the empire. The success of those who did adopt Roman culture will have made the Roman myths learned at school seem all the more persuasive.[64]

chariots of the Lydians, and Lydian warriors (Sappho 16). Mimnermos describes the battle of the Smyrnaians against the armies of Gyges, as well as the Kimmerians (e.g., F 13). Hipponax mentions Lydian public monuments (the tomb of Alyattes and the sema of Gyges) almost in passing, as if they were works of monumental labor that everyone would know (F 42).

63 The few fragments of Hekataios and Hellanikos are not helpful in this regard, consisting primarily of place-names, but Xanthos is more informative (preserved in Nikolaos of Damaskos, *FGrHist* 90). That he should call himself "the Lydian" rather than, say, "Sardian," may suggest Lydia was thought of as a cohesive whole, rather than as a composite of individual cities and their hinterlands. Xanthos' *Lydiaka* is full of scandal and intrigue, but also of tales of war and of military prowess.

64 Woolf (1998:74).

Thus Roman ideology and concern with civilization spread through the elite, with the powerful reinforcer that those who conformed to Roman concepts of *humanitas* were often more successful in the new imperial framework than those who did not: it was in the interests of the new Gallo-Roman aristocracies to adhere to this ideology.

Woolf describes a few ways in which Romanization, or the conformation to Roman ideology and cultural practices, may be traced in the province of Gaul. He finds that the numbers of inscriptions are greatest (clusters being most frequent and largest) in the lower valley of the Rhône and the middle Rhine[65] – concentrations that might be expected, given the importance of rivers as routes of communication and trade and of river valleys as arable land. But concentrations of inscriptions also are larger and more frequent farther east, while there is a real paucity of inscriptions in the northwest, including Atlantic France, the Loire valley, and the Paris basin. Poor soil or low population cannot account for this lack. Woolf suggests the road network may have been largely responsible for the trend, and the establishment of Roman colonies and military garrisons.[66] This study of inscriptions may afford some insight into the practices of the elite in France, without providing insight into the doings of the non-elite.

Sardis' placement on the Royal Road was important for its position in the empire, both literal and metaphorical. It figures in imperial rhetoric as one of the edges of the empire; its status as terminus on the road from Susa is surely linked to this concept. But the road network bound Sardis to other sites in the empire and provided quick and sure means of communication and transportation with other areas. The degree to which Sardis prospered in the Achaemenid period is no doubt in part due to these links – in this way, it represents a response similar to that suggested in Roman Gaul by clustering of inscriptions. Like Gaul, at this point we primarily have information about the elite in this context;[67] the prosperous nature of Sardian elite seems sure, but we cannot yet tell the relative prosperity of the non-elite populace.

The material culture of Roman Gaul was much more complex and differentiated than was its Iron Age predecessor, with new customs such as wine-drinking introduced as well as the artifactual paraphernalia to go with them.[68] Roman ceramic wares were imported into Gaul even before its conquest; over time, Gaulish potters began imitating finewares in local clay that to some extent replaced the imported sigillatas. The consumption of Roman goods must not be equated with the assumption of Roman styles of consumption, of course, but local adaptation of Roman ceramic forms

---

65 Woolf (1998:77–88).     66 Woolf (1998:88–91).

67 Woolf focuses primarily on the elite, apparently for reasons of availability of information. See, e.g., Woolf (1998:68, 100, 125, 162, 169), as well as the examples discussed here.

68 Woolf (1998:181–193).

and experimentation with local variations is an important indication of acculturation in Roman Gaul. Social distinctions based on wealth might have been reiterated and reinforced precisely by the *ways* in which one used one's Romanizing possessions; thus ideology and praxis might combine to cement the privileged position of the wealthy.[69]

We may see similar processes at Achaemenid Sardis. It has been suggested that the ceramic Achaemenid bowls were an adaptation of metal versions first introduced by the Persian elite. Lydia had previously been a land of stemmed dishes and footed cups with handles; the Achaemenid bowl, with its flat base and lack of handles, was a real departure from previous drinking practices and shows a great degree of acculturation on the part of the local Sardian populace. A new way of holding cups, at least, is implied; the elite social connotations of drinking from metal vessels of this particular shape may have continued to resound even in their more humble counterparts.[70] The shift in the ceramic assemblage to include many more bowls may reflect the tremendous use of bowls in the Achaemenid heartland; it may represent acculturation in the form of changing dietary practices at Sardis. Sardis, like Gaul, shows through its ceramic record the degree to which non-elites were affected by imperialism; the sepulchral sculptures discussed in chapter 4, showing the deceased as a banqueter, may support the notion that superior practice of imperial ideology went hand-in-hand with superior social status.

Another avenue Woolf explores is the building of cities: new cities were built along the road network, rather than the roads being built to pass by old cities.[71] This is a clear example of Roman impact on the Gaulish landscape. The organization of urban space also changed in the province of Gaul: cities were laid out on a grid plan, fora were constructed, burials were moved to extramural locations, temples were concentrated at the center of town or in suburban sanctuaries, the large houses of the wealthy were built in particularly choice locations within a city, while manufacturers were pushed to the outskirts.[72] Woolf comments on these last, "If towns mould and reflect cultural practices and habits, zoning is in some ways a more significant expression of the Roman styles of urbanism than is the grid plan."[73] Public cults were reworked, again at the hands of the new elite: Roman-style

---

69 See Woolf (1998:162–174).

70 For the social significance of the cup and its association with elite drinking, see Nylander (1999).

71 Woolf (1998:114–116 with references).

72 Woolf (1998:116–117). For public buildings, see Ward-Perkins (1970). For city plans, see von Hesberg (1991), Pinon (1988). For central Italian models for private houses, see, e.g., Bedon et al. (1988), Goudineau (1979). For grids and the ideology behind them, see Purcell (1990), Rykwert (1976). For the placement of larger houses, see Wallace-Hadrill (1994), Perring (1991).

73 Woolf (1998:117).

temples were built, Roman gods introduced, and provincial cults intervened in to make them conform to ideas of *humanitas*.[74] The "new monumentality of the sacred"[75] was an important part of this process: Gallo-Roman sacred space was a built phenomenon, where structures formed an important part of the re-creation and re-representation of religion.

Even the small percentage of Sardis that has been excavated can give us an idea of ways in which it responded to Persian presence. The city wall was first destroyed and then rebuilt by the Achaemenids; by the beginning of the fifth century BC if not before, the city had multiple rings of walls offering varying degrees of protection to its inhabitants. Although this does not necessarily represent social zoning of the sort Woolf posits for Roman Gaul, it does suggest zoning of a different sort, focusing on safety. And if Sardis followed the common pattern of larger, richer houses at higher elevations on the acropolis, those houses and their occupants would have enjoyed a greater degree of protection than their more humble neighbors down below. In this way, Sardian zoning may well have reflected social status. Burial locations seem to have remained the same in the Achaemenid period: extramural disposal of the dead was the norm, with the Achaemenid-period occupants burying their dead in the same places that the earlier populace had. The major difference was the sudden escalation in burials at Bin Tepe, which may previously have been the burial ground only for kings. As no pre-Achaemenid sanctuaries have been excavated, it is impossible to tell what the impact of Achaemenid hegemony was on monumentality; but certainly at least two cultic spaces were adorned in the Achaemenid period with altars which formed some focus for ritual.

Woolf and Alcock take very different approaches to the study of two Roman provinces. Woolf's is a synthesis of Roman textual sources and modern archaeological exploration, especially excavation, at particular sites in the province of Gaul. He presents his findings through the lens of Roman ideology about civilizing the Gauls. His suggestion that it was in the self-interest of the local elite to adopt aspects of Roman material culture and ideology – to acculturate, to Romanize – is a powerful one and may well provide an explanation for the processes he sees in Gaul during the Roman period. Alcock focuses on surface surveys and regional archaeology in the Roman province of Achaea, again considering the archaeological evidence in tandem with textual sources. Whereas Woolf presents a picture of Gaul that reflects the emphasis on "civilizing" found in Roman imperial rhetoric, Alcock concludes that Achaea did not conform to the morbid picture of decline suggested by Roman rhetoric but rather responded in regionally specific ways to Roman presence that defy such simplistic moral or evaluative description.

74 Woolf (1998:215–237).     75 Woolf (1998:224).

We lack the kind of information about Persian imperial rhetoric directed specifically towards our province that Woolf and Alcock draw on in their analyses. But the forms of acculturation described by Woolf, and the response to domination discussed by Alcock, both correspond in certain key ways to the processes we see at Sardis in the Achaemenid period. Urban and sacred landscapes, social and political systems, ideology and praxis were all transformed because of Achaemenid hegemony at Sardis.

## Overview

As described in chapter 1, discussions of regions within the purview of the Achaemenid empire have on occasion given the impression that Achaemenid hegemony made no impact on the cultures of local populations. At the end of a long and apparently frustrating session of the 1986 Achaemenid history workshop that sought archaeological confirmation of the Persian empire, the exasperated chair exclaimed, "Was there ever a Persian empire?"[76] This ironic exclamation focused on the difficulties of the sources and on the historiographic burdens faced by students of the Achaemenid empire, of course, rather than on the possibility that Persian domination truly produced no significant impact. This study demonstrates the profound effect of Achaemenid hegemony on local culture at the satrapal capital of Sardis.

This study of Sardis in the Achaemenid period has incorporated textual sources and material culture, using approaches stemming from literary, archaeological, art historical, and cultural anthropological perspectives. Combining these methods for examining and interpreting the various complementary forms of evidence has demonstrated that Achaemenid presence and the role of the city in the empire made a readily discernible impact on the life of the city's inhabitants. The multiple sources of evidence consistently suggest the same patterns of social adaptation to Achaemenid hegemony and of developments in lifestyle at Sardis in the Achaemenid period. They demonstrate the presence of a sophisticated polyethnic elite that embraced many aspects of the newly developed local culture of urbane Achaemenid society, often with deliberate reference to central Persian customs and practices. An interesting point is that the elite may also have adapted or revived local traditions at times, perhaps in a conscious and symbolic emphasis on a particular cultural identity. Imperial ideology was represented by a new symbolic language of personal ornamentation and funerary inclusion to symbolize membership in and adherence to the elite of the Achaemenid empire. Certain aspects of ideology were so thoroughly

76 Kuhrt and Sancisi-Weerdenburg (1988).

internalized at Sardis that they became seen as part of local culture and continued long after the collapse of the Achaemenid administration.

This study of Sardis suggests a radical revision of conventional notions of imperial interactions in the Achaemenid empire. The impact of Achaemenid presence in the literary and archaeological records was great. We see here a city that thrived under Achaemenid hegemony, that served as a locus for new creative endeavor within the framework of the empire. It is to be hoped that further work at Sardis and elsewhere will continue to develop and elaborate on this picture, filling out our conception of the operation and impact of the Achaemenid empire throughout its vast range, throughout the tremendous variety of cultures it encompassed.

# Sculpture

## Kybele and Artemis

### S63.51:5677, Manisa 4029 (fig. 45)

Temple-like marble monument decorated in low relief, with a female figure at its front. Upper part and two lower corners broken. Frontal three-quarter columns are lost except one base. Preserved height (PH) 0.62 m; W at back 0.57 m; PW at front 0.41 m; PD at left 0.33 m, at right 0.442 m. Found August 9, 1963 in Syn M where it had been reused, E73.5/N17.2–17.7 *97.26–97.75.

A frontal female figure in high relief (Kybele?) wearing a chiton stands between two vertical wavy lines in the entrance of a temple. Her head and most of her upper half have been broken off. She held an object in one hand, perhaps a lion. The shrine has seven Ionic or Proto-Ionic columns: three-quarter columns at the corners and engaged half columns at sides. Maeanders separate sides and back into three horizontal friezes, subdivided by the central columns into eighteen reliefs. The figures on the side walls move towards the front of the building (maidens, komasts, and dancers on the left side; maidens and lions on the right side). The mythological reliefs on the back wall show two birds attacking animals climbing a tree; a lion and boar approaching a tree in which Peleus has taken refuge; Herakles and the Nemean lion; Pelops in his chariot; a centaur; the murder of Agamemnon (?). Anathyrosis demonstrates the monument was set up on a stone pedestal.

*Date*
c. 540–530 BC.

*Bibliography*
Hanfmann and Ramage (1978:7), Hanfmann (1964), Hanfmann and Waldbaum (1969), Rein (1993).

### S68.6:7678, Manisa 3937 (fig. 46)

Marble stele from Sardis showing two draped females holding animals and approached by two smaller worshipers. A tympanum hangs in the upper right corner. W 0.667 m; H 0.99 m; maximum thickness (at bottom) 0.29 m; height of larger female (left), 0.63 m; height of smaller female (right), 0.61 m; height of male worshiper 0.45 m; height of female worshiper 0.38 m.

The stele's pediment was broken in antiquity but had acroteria, supported on Ionic pilasters on rectangular plinths. Two frontal females, apparently Artemis and Kybele, occupy two-thirds of the niche space. The taller goddess (Artemis?) holds a deer, the smaller (Kybele?) a lion. Two worshipers approach on the right in profile, raising their hands.

*Date*
Perhaps c. 430–420 BC.

*Bibliography*
Hanfmann and Waldbaum (1969, 1970), Hanfmann and Ramage (1978:20).

### NoEx 58.27 (fig. 47)

Marble relief showing Kybele seated on a square throne with a lion in her lap facing right and another at her feet. The upper left and lower right corners are broken, top chipped. H 0.345 m; W 0.285 m; D at bottom 0.075 m, at top 0.07 m. Found reused in a modern wall near the Artemis precinct.

The front is cut to suggest a shallow pitched roof with three acroteria, with un-elaborated sides acting as pilasters. The back is very roughly trimmed; the top and sides have cuttings for clamps and dowels to fasten the relief into a stone frame or wall.

Kybele's head extends over the frame of the relief. She wears a chiton with a cloak over her lower body and legs and holds a tympanon and a small round bowl.

*Date*
Later than 400 BC.

*Bibliography*
Hanfmann and Ramage (1978:21), Hanfmann (1960b:530–531).

## Other female figures in relief

### NoEx 60.13, in Manisa (fig. 48)

Standing frontal draped female figure, of imported limestone, much weathered. H 0.495 m, of figure 0.411 m, of relief 0.04 m; W 0.31 m, of figure 0.13 m; Th 0.215 m; projection of "roof" beyond pilaster 0.015 m. Found *c.* 1.5 km west of Sart, *c.* 0.5 km south of Izmir–Ankara highway.

The limestone block is plain on the sides and back; its front was cut down with a claw chisel and smoothed. The figure faces out, her feet parallel, her arms at her sides. She had long hair; drill-holes above each temple suggest she wore a metal wreath or diadem as well as a necklace of acorns. She wears a belted chiton.

A large semicircular hollow at her feet has in it a hole made by a round metal peg. A naiskos-like frame extends all around the rectangular block, projecting at the top beyond the side pilasters.

*Date*
*c.* 520–500 BC.

*Bibliography*
Hanfmann and Ramage (1978:9), Hanfmann (1961:49).

### S69.11:8032 (fig. 49)

Veiled frontal female, in bluish gray marble. Much trimmed in antiquity for reuse. PH 1.01 m; W 0.49 m (with moulding 0.51 m); D 0.21 m; PH of panel 0.65 m; W of panel 0.34 m.

The back is finished, indicating the stele was meant to be free-standing.

A woman's body is preserved to the upper legs. Her left side touches the edge of the panel. She stands frontally, with hair on either side of her head. Her neck is incised with horizontal creases. A claw chisel was used in smoothing the background; the figure stands out sharply and crisply from the background.

*Date*
Fifth century BC.

*Bibliography*
Hanfmann and Ramage (1978:19).

## Funerary sculptures

### Manisa 1
Inscribed marble stele with a man (Atrastas, son of Sakardas) seated at a table, holding writing implements. The top is broken, and the relief very worn. H 0.97 m, of relief 0.30 m; W at top 0.305 m, at bottom 0.32 m; Th at side top 0.09 m, at bottom including back 0.16 m. Found at Sardis in 1935.

The stele was set into a base. Its sides are finished with a claw chisel; its back is very roughly trimmed. The front has a six-line Lydian inscription (App. 2, No. 28).

A male figure sits in profile on a stool before a table with legs ending in bulls' hooves, holding a long thin object that may be a scroll. The man has no beard; his hair forms a roll at the back of his neck. He wears a cloak and a high shoe with an upturned toe. Behind him is a dog.

*Date*
*c.* 520–500 BC.

*Bibliography*
Hanfmann and Ramage (1978:17), Gusmani (1964:no. 54).

### S69.14 and NoEx 1978.1, Manisa 4427 and 5526 (fig. 35)
Pediment of two triangular halves, with Lesbian cyma and bead-and-reel. The bottom ledge is undecorated. Badly weathered relief shows a reclining male at center, with three seated females at left. A servant brings a vessel to the reclining figure, while another stands by a laden table. Max. L 2.60 m; H 0.58 m; W at top 0.36 m, at bottom 0.36 m. H of figures: 0.44–0.26 m. H. of relief of figures 0.06–0.10 m. Slope of pediment 25 percent.

The left piece of the pediment was found in 1969 near "Pactolus Cliff," 2 m below the present bed of the Paktolos at W360/S588. The right piece was found in 1977, also in the Paktolos river channel near "Pactolus Cliff." The relief of the left block is higher than that of the right, but the two pieces were apparently joined by dowels and almost certainly represent two halves of a single pediment.

A bearded man reclines on a couch at center, his left elbow resting on a folded cushion. He holds a vessel, perhaps a rhyton, in his raised right hand and an indistinct object in his left. His head was apparently turned up and left. Hair falls down his back, and there may be traces of a wreath. In front of the couch is a low table with an object standing on it, possibly a bowl.

A draped female to the left is seated diagonally on the end of the couch. Her head is almost entirely lost but overlapped the pedimental band. Her right arm is bent and rests on her chest. She wears a long cloak and a chiton.

A vertical hollow indicates the beginning of another couch to the left with a smaller woman seated in profile. Her worn head overlaps the pedimental band. Her right arm is bent, her hand resting on her chest; her left hand is placed on a flat cushion.

The smallest female figure, at far left, is seated on the same couch, with her upper body turned to the front. Her right hand rests behind her on the couch, her left hand on her knee. Her head apparently turned right. Her foot is outlined by incision. A double line over her left shoulder may indicate part of a dress.

The right block shows two standing males wearing knee-length belted tunics. The taller figure, at left, walks left, carrying an Achaemenid bowl. His head and right leg are in profile and his left leg frontal. The smaller figure is almost frontal, his right leg relaxed with bent knee. To his left is a long table with a column krater under it. On the table are a large Achaemenid bowl on a low stand and a footless conical cup. Three round objects and six low flat objects probably represent food or vessels containing food.

*Date*
*c.* 430–420 BC.

*Bibliography*
Hanfmann and Erhart (1981), Hanfmann and Ramage (1978:18), Demargne (1976:87), Hanfmann (1974a, 1975).

## NoEx 77.15; IN 77.8 (fig. 36)
Marble stele with a man reclining on a kline, a seated woman and a servant. Found in 1977 in the Paktolos river bed, to the south of the area "Pactolus Cliff." H 0.41 m; W at bottom 0.30 m; W at top 0.26 m. A small ledge protrudes at the bottom of the relief; the back is unfinished.

The man leans on his left elbow on two cushions, or perhaps a single folded one. He raises a round-bottomed vessel in his right hand and holds a round object in his left. He wears a short-sleeved tunic. His face is missing but apparently faced out. The kline is covered with a cloth, so that only the lower parts of the legs show beneath.

The woman sits on the couch, probably in three-quarter view, with her feet on a footstool. She wears a himation and chiton.

A smaller figure standing facing right at the foot of the couch is probably a servant rather than a child. She wears a long robe and mantle and holds a lotus flower.

*Date*
First half of the fourth century BC.

*Bibliography*
Ramage (1979), Gusmani (1979), Greenewalt (1978a, 1977), Mellink (1978).

## Atrastas stele; IAM 4030
A Lydian text above a man reclining on a couch and a woman seated at its foot. The stele is broken at the bottom. Found in 1913, reused in the necropolis. PH 0.61 m; W at top 0.57 m; W at bottom 0.57 m.

At top is an egg-and-dart motif painted yellow on a black background. The Lydian inscription (App. 2 No. 52) has red color preserved in some letters. The relief shows a man reclining on a couch, propped with his left elbow on a cushion, his head turned to face outward. His right arm extends over his bent right knee and holds an indistinct object. At the left, a (veiled?) woman is seated on the foot of the couch, her head in profile.

*Date*
330–329 BC.

*Bibliography*
Buckler (1924:3), Littmann (1916:12), Gusmani (1964), Hanfmann and Ramage (1978:234), McLauchlin (1985:278–279).

## Comparanda from elsewhere in Lydia, now in Manisa

*Manisa 172*
Marble stele, from cemetery at Bagis. H 0.70 m; W 0.65 m. A male figure reclining on a kline, leaning on his right arm and holding a small indistinct object in his right hand. His head is missing. A young male figure with a fly-whisk stands to right. Under the kline is a hound.

*Manisa 6225*
Rectangular marble stele from Alaşehir. H 0.74 m; W 0.65 m; Th 0.11 m. A male figure wearing chiton and mantle reclines on his left arm, his head turned to his right in profile. He extends his right hand, now missing. A woman seated at the foot of the kline faces him in profile, pulling with her left hand at the shoulder of her gown. To the right is a small female holding a flower. At the left, a male figure in a knee-length tunic holds a phiale. The kline is draped with a tasselled cloth.

*Manisa 6226*
Weathered marble relief from Alaşehir, broken at top, lower left corner; back left unfinished. H 0.61 m; W 1.04 m; Th 0.10 m. A naked helmeted male lies to left on uneven ground beneath a horse galloping right; the ground is a lumpy mass. A fallen helmet lies by his side. Two naked men at right, one lunging and one kneeling, battle with the rider of the horse, of whom only the boots remain. He appears to wear trousers.

*Manisa 7759*
Worn marble relief with a male figure in low relief, broken at top and lower right corner. The back is flat but unfinished; a Lydian inscription is at the top of the right side. H 0.85 m; W 0.34 m; Th 0.10 m. A beardless, round-headed male faces right in profile; his eye is probably a modern addition. He wears a knee-length tunic and trousers (?), a cloak and low boots. His right hand holds an indistinct object. A dagger hangs from his belt, and a quiver (?) hangs before him.

## Human figures sculpted in the round

### Manisa 325
Marble statue, the "Mantle-Wearer," missing head, legs, and the fingers of its right hand. PH 0.63 m. Found at Sardis in 1954 at W268/S367.
  The left leg is advanced, arms at sides. The figure wears a chiton and cloak, with a simple bracelet on each wrist. Six long locks of hair extend down the arms and

chest, while a broad rectangle of hair in horizontal rows falls below the shoulders in back. The figure's sex is uncertain.

*Date*
*c.* 530–520 BC.

*Bibliography*
Turkish Ministry of Culture (1993:133), Hanfmann and Ramage (1978:8), Hanfmann and Polatkan (1959).

### S67.37:7593 (fig. 38)
Marble torso, probably of a kore, missing head, back, mid-to upper arms, and much of the chest. H 0.133 m, to chest 0.125 m; W shoulder to shoulder 0.225 m. Found W of B, trench C, in stone pile.

The figure wore a plain upper garment with an overfold on the left shoulder. Its left upper arm is virtually intact, but only the front part of the right arm remains. A curl of hair rests on the right shoulder. The figure holds the tail and body of a bird or animal.

*Date*
*c.* 500 BC?

*Bibliography*
Hanfmann and Ramage (1978:10).

### S59.10:1419 (fig. 39)
Marble upper torso of an Amazon or Artemis. The back of the upper body and part of the left arm are preserved. PH 0.125 m; PW 0.16 m. Found in HoB, area 14, E20/80 *100.68–100, in fill.

The head of the figure was turned to its left, the right arm raised, and the left extended out. A himation was tied over the left shoulder. Three short locks of hair fall on the back of the right shoulder; one lock lies on the left.

*Date*
Probably *c.* 510–460 BC.

*Bibliography*
Hanfmann and Ramage (1978:12).

### NoEx 63.12 (fig. 40)
Marble upper part of a small female torso. PH 0.12 m; PW 0.22 m. Found at Çaltılıköy.

The figure wears a heavy cloak and a chiton with round buttons.

*Date*
Fifth century BC.

*Bibliography*
Hanfmann and Ramage (1978:11).

## Lions

### IAM 4028

Marble lion lying with head turned sideways, roaring. Its eyes are hollowed out. A mane of incised curly triangles runs to the tail. Its ears are nubbins; it has dew-claws.

*Date*
*c.* mid-sixth century BC.

*Bibliography*
Hanfmann and Ramage (1978:236).

### S70.7:8108 (fig. 44)

Right foot of a marble lion, resting on a plinth broken at side and back. PH of plinth in front 0.12 m, in back 0.21 m. PH of paw *c.* 0.09 m; PL 0.36 m; W at back 0.23 m. Found reused in the synagogue.

The plinth was flat and smoothed with a claw chisel. The paw and part of the leg are from a recumbent lion.

*Date*
*c.* 550 BC?

*Bibliography*
Hanfmann and Ramage (1978:33).

### Manisa 303

Marble lioness. H 0.61 m; L 0.95 m; W 0.33 m. Found during highway construction in 1951.

The roaring, recumbent lioness has large frontal eyes and a mane of regular triangular incisions flaring out from her face and down her chest and underbelly, decorated with six floppy teats. The left side is more carefully finished than the right. Her toes and teeth are roughly indicated. She lies on a low rectangular plinth with cuttings for clamps.

*Date*
*c.* 550–530 BC.

*Bibliography*
Hanfmann and Ramage (1978:34).

### Manisa 318

Recumbent weathered marble lion, missing head and forelegs. H 0.45 m; L 0.80 m. Probably from Sardis.

The lion's rear half is fluidly carved, its foreparts more linearly. An incised mane runs down the chest.

*Date*
*c.* 540 BC.

*Bibliography*
Hanfmann and Ramage (1978:35).

## B-10

Small recumbent marble lion, perhaps an acroterion from a sarcophagus lid? Max. H 0.195 m; max. L 0.165 m. Found in Butler's dump.

The lion lies on a base; it has a massive chest and shoulders and short squat hind legs with incised claws.

*Date*
*c.* 500 BC?

*Bibliography*
Hanfmann and Ramage (1978:36).

## NoEx 63.1 (fig. 43)

Marble lion's paw, broken at top. H 0.15 m; L 0.17 m. From Sardis.

High well-modeled toes, with stylized claws, may be part of ornamental furniture.

*Date*
Late sixth or early fifth century BC.

*Bibliography*
Hanfmann and Ramage (1978:37).

## S62.31:4548, S63.37:5394; Manisa 4030, 4031 (fig. 42)

Two pairs of addorsed marble lions that apparently served as supports for a table or couch. Manisa 4031 m: L 1.04 m; W 0.29 m. Manisa 4030 m: L 1.03; W 0.29 m.

The lions sit upright, with haunches touching and tails curled over hindquarters. Their incised manes extend down their chests to the foreleg in a triangle. Small roundish faces and small eyes have pronounced bolsters over the eyes and noses wrinkled in a snarl. They have four claws and a dew-claw on each paw.

*Date*
*c.* 450–350 BC.

*Bibliography*
Hanfmann and Ramage (1978:25), Hanfmann (1964:38).

## S63.35:5356 (fig. 41)

Marble relief fragment with a lion walking right. Battered, broken at sides, head and back of lion missing. L 0.16 m; PW 0.06 m; H 0.078 m. Found reused in the synagogue.

*Date*
*c.* 400 BC.

*Bibliography*
Hanfmann and Ramage (1978:39).

## Manisa 306

Weathered marble lion. H 0.66 m; L 0.98 m. Probably from Sardis.

The lion has powerful muscles in shoulders and haunches; its incised mane extends halfway down its spine.

*Date*
*c.* 350–300 BC.

*Bibliography*
Hanfmann and Ramage (1978:38).

## Other animals

### B-7
Lower part of a marble siren or eagle, broken above legs and at feet. PH 0.26 m; W 0.30 m. Found in Butler's dump in 1971.

Legs feathered with rows of leaf-like feathers, the tail with longer more rectangular feathers.

*Date*
*c.* 530–500 BC.

*Bibliography*
Hanfmann and Ramage (1978:40).

### Manisa 311
Headless recumbent weathered marble sphinx. PH 0.44 m; L 0.90 m. Probably from Sardis, found in 1946.

The tail curves up over the back of the sphinx. The wings are broken at the back but seem about to curve forward; their feathers are indicated by horizontal lines. The volumes of the lion's body are simple and smooth. Large claws are indicated on the left rear paw, which is tucked under the body.

*Date*
Late sixth or fifth century BC?

*Bibliography*
Hanfmann and Ramage (1978:41).

### IAM 4031
Marble statue of a sphinx, its head broken off, finished on one side only. The wing is flat but differential weathering suggests pigment for feathers. Rounded areas on the chest may suggest breasts. Broken at its haunches.

*Date*
Late Archaic, first quarter of the fifth century BC.

*Bibliography*
Hanfmann and Ramage (1978:239).

### IAM 4032
Marble statue of an eagle clutching a rabbit between its talons. Its wings overlap in back. The rabbit is rounded and soft.

*Date*
Late Archaic, fifth century BC.

*Bibliography*
Hanfmann and Ramage (1978:238).

## Manisa 21

Marble sphinx, missing head and forelegs. PH 0.47 m; L 0.73 m.

The sphinx sits in relief on a flat back, probably the support of a throne. Its body is slim and taut, with a long narrow tail and a band around its neck. Only part of the wing is preserved.

*Date*
Fourth or third century BC?

*Bibliography*
Hanfmann and Ramage (1978:42).

# Datable inscriptions[1]

## Pre-Achaemenid period

**1.** ? Gusmani 4b. (Lydian) Limestone slab "carved in imitation of a panelled wooden door," found in the necropolis "in the...wall closing the dromos of a single-chamber tomb." (L.4, B.4, F.4)[2]

> This grave chamber [is that] of Manes,
> the son of Alus; if to it
> anybody does damage,
> then him may Qλdāns
> and Artemis destroy.

**2.** Gusmani 6. (Lydian) Marble stele found in Sardis "in a thick low wall on the northern slope of the Nekropolis hill." (L.11, B.6, F.6)

> This grave chamber [is] that of Sivāms, son of Armāvs.
> If anybody to this grave chamber
> or this grave stele or this
> dromos does damage,
> then may the pious one his impiety
> punish.

**3.** Gusmani 30. (Lydian) Boat-shaped vase found in Sardis "in a square chamber-tomb crushed in and filled with earth on the eastern slope of the Nekropolis hill." (L.13, B.30, F.30)

> Titis : my . contents : prepared
> for Atas . for Kitvas

**4.** Gusmani 32. (Lydian) Small vase found in a grave of the necropolis. (B.32, F.32)

> of [ ]ralus prepared

**5.** Gusmani 48. (Lydian) Marble fragment found in the Artemision at Ephesos. (B.48, F.48)

> [ ]is made it

**6.** Gusmani 52. (Lydian) Inscription on Lydian coins found at Ephesos. (F.52)

> of Valve[s]

**7.** Gusmani 61. (Lydian) Potsherd, found in Sardis in 1962.

> of [ ]vas *ana. q*[ ]

---

1 Dates follow Gusmani (1964); a question mark denotes an inscription with probable but not certain date.
2 L. stands for Littmann (1916), B. for Buckler (1924), F. for Friedrich (1932).

**8.** Gusmani 31. (Lydian) Potsherd found in Sardis "in the earth filling a tomb on the south side of the Nekropolis hill." (B.31, F.31)

> *sasa*

## Achaemenid period

**9.** Gusmani 1. (Lydian–Aramaic bilingual) Marble stele, found in Sardis "in a thick low wall on the northern slope of the Nekropolis hill." (L.1, B.1, F.1)
Lydian text:

> [missing at least one line]
> in the beginning of the month of Bakkhos. This stele and this [grave chamber]
> and this dromos and the property which to this grave chamber
> belongs, now [they are] of Manes, son of Kumli, son of Siluka. And if anybody
> to this stele or this grave chamber or this dromos or this land belonging to
> this grave chamber
> and also if anybody to the land does damage, then may Artemis
> of Ephesos and Artemis of Koloe his holding and his house
> and his soil and water and everything of his destroy.

Aramaic text (after Kahle-Sommer 1927):

> On the 5th of Marheswan [of the] 10th year of King Artaxerxes,
> in the fortress of Sardis. This stele and the cavern [and] the wall (?),
> the piece of land (?) and the fore-court which is the fore-court of this grave
> chamber (?), [are]
> of Mani, son of Kumli, son of Siruka (?). And if anybody against this stele or
> the cavern or the wall (?) or (?) or against the land in front of this cavern,
> that is to say, if anybody destroys or breaks anything, then
> may Artemis of Koloe and of Ephesos his holding, his house,
> his land, soil and water, and everything that is his, destroy him and crush
> him (or destroy him and his heir(s)).

**10.** Gusmani 2. (Lydian) Marble stele, found in Sardis "in a thick low wall on the northern slope of the Nekropolis hill." (L.8, B.2, F.2)

> In the year fifteen in the month of Cuves of Artaxerxes
> the king. This tomb and stele and also the [grave part]
> which were set up and the dromos which establishes it now
> [are] of Karos, the son of Sabλas, the son of Istubeλ-. And if
> anybody does damage to all these [grave] parts,
> whatever I indicated, or this grave chamber or the stele or
> this [grave part] of the dromos or another
> part of the grave, and whoever buries (?) in this grave of Karos,
> son of Sabλas, and appropriates the possessions of Karos, then
> Artemis of Ephesos and Koloe, her Council of Priests
> I call on, and if anybody does damage also here may
> [. . ]ra (god's name) the requiter destroy [negative attribute] him and his
> possessions.

**11.** ? Gusmani 4a. (Lydian) Limestone slab "carved in imitation of a panelled wooden door," found in the Necropolis "in the . . . wall closing the dromos of a single-chamber tomb." (L.4, B.4, F.4)

This is the [grave part (door-stone?)] of Manes, son of Alus. If anybody
damages it
or these grave stelae or
this [grave part], then may Sandas
and Kufada (Kybele?) and Marivda
inflict damage on him.

**12.** Gusmani 41. (Lydian) Marble slab (perhaps a stele), found in the Kaÿstros valley.
Lydian–Aramaic bilingual, Aramaic missing except for illegible traces of the last line.
(B.41, F.41)

In the year sixteen of Artaxerxes
the king in
the month Kanlala on the ... st day
[*trolλ*] on the Feast of Artemis
this votive tablet Bantakasas,
the son of Abrnas, and his [*kănas* – perhaps spouse?]
and [proper name]ret *asav qalem*[   ]

**13.** ? Gusmani 23. (Lydian) Limestone block, found by the Artemis temple at Sardis.
(B.23, F.23)

This temple to Qλdãns (Apollo?) and Artemis is dedicated
as an offering, and if anyone damages this temple,
on account of his godlessness then let Qλdãns the mighty
and Artemis of Ephesos destroy [him]. In the year
five decrees as follows Mitridastas the son of Mitratas,
priest: this document of gift, by this I gave the property.
These documents the officials in the official place keep, where
I declare: if I possess anything then to them I bestow it.
And if then someone does evil [to it]
then may both Qλdãns and Artemis destroy
him and his own property. And moreover
he who is an evil-doer and an ill-doer against these gods never
shall prosper, neither he nor any property of his.
And if I possess anything and
I entrust it to the sanctuary and the association, not to any other
person, and another magistrate maintains the property
then this, however it will be, will be executed
as I, Mitridastas, have decreed it. And if anybody
disregards my decree I have written or also
injures or does any kind of damage, then
that which this decree I have written prescribes [for him], that let Artemis
bring to pass.

**14.** ? Gusmani 24. (Lydian) Marble stele, found by the Artemis temple at Sardis. (B.24,
F.24)

Thus decrees Mitridastas, son of Mitra[tas],
priest: now I make known the order:
if ever to the association of the temple[3] anything

---

3 I cannot see how *serlis srmlis* serves as anything but a dative in this sentence, despite its
nominative form.

I entrust or indeed give
to do or I have given it as a pledge,
and also whatever else I appoint,
if anyone usurps the record of possessions
or indeed destroys it or also if anyone
[effaces?] or indeed injures
in any kind of evil way or
[does something bad] or does any kind of damage,
now therefore may Artemis of Ephesos
destroy him and his own property;
he who is an evil-doer against Artemis
and an ill-doer never shall prosper,
neither he nor any property of his. And the association of the temple
decrees, and also I make known the decree of Mitridastas: if I
possess anything and also house and holding
and my property, then I [these things] of Mitridastas
the priest entrust for safe-keeping. And if
no one else, and somebody, a criminal (?), the property from Mitridastas
[. . . . . . . . . . . . . .] *itad* Mitridastas [   ]

**15.** Gusmani 55. (Lydian) Seal of unknown origin, showing a bull.
    of Manes

**16.** Boardman (1970b) 6; Gusmani 56. (Lydian) Seal of unknown origin, acquired at Latakia, showing a bull. Geneva 20564.
    I am [the sign] of Manes

**17.** Boardman (1970b) 1. (Lydian) Seal from Sardis. London WA 115591.
    This is the sign of Mitratas

**18.** Boardman (1970b) 2; Gusmani 51. (Lydian) Seal from Sardis. Louvre A 1226.
    [this is the sign] of Bakivas [the son] of Sams

**19.** Boardman (1970b) 3. (Lydian) Seal of unknown origin, showing a lion and lioness. Naples 1475.
    I am [the sign] of Sivams, [son] of Ates

**20.** Boardman (1970b) 4. (Lydian) Seal of unknown origin, showing a lion-griffin. Bibl. Nat. 1086.
    of Manes

**21.** Boardman (1970b) 5. (Lydian) Seal from Kertch, showing two sphinxes. Now in St. Petersburg.
    I am [the sign] of Manes

**22.** Boardman (1970b) 7. (Lydian) Seal of unknown origin, showing a human holding two lions.
    *mane.omen* (Manes . . .)

**23.** Boardman (1970b) 8. (Lydian) Seal of unknown origin, acquired in Baghdad, showing a monster. Philadelphia CBS.5117.
    I am [the sign] of Tafus

**24.** Gusmani 57. (Lydian) Potsherd found near the Artemis temple at Sardis.

[ ]rlam[ ]

**25.** Gusmani 60. (Lydian) Potsherd found at Sardis.

es[ ]
fa[ ]
fa[ ]

**26.** Gusmani 61. (Lydian) Potsherd found at Sardis.

[ ]valis ana.q[ ]

## Second half of the sixth century

**27.** Gusmani A III 2. (Lydian) IN64.15/P64.43:6008. Potsherd found at Sardis, *c.* 550–450 BC.

[a dedication; unclear if to man or god]
] kāl : labλ : vr?it [
τakm [

## End of the sixth/beginning of the fifth century

**28.** Gusmani 54. (Lydian) Inscribed and sculpted stele found at Sardis in 1935 (Manisa 1).

This is the grave stele of Atrastas the son of Sakardas. And thus whoever destroys or mishandles it, he shall pay. (And him?) and whatever possession[s of his] thus to Artemis of Ephesos I consign.

**29.** Gusmani A II 10. (Lydian) IN65.20A/P65.82A:6696. Potsherd found at Sardis, sixth or early fifth century BC.

]? kunxxx [

**30.** Gusmani A II 6. (Lydian) IN58.14/P58.110:124. Potsherd found at Sardis, sixth to fifth century BC.

]x(?) l a m [

**31.** Gusmani A II 13. (Lydian) P62.392:4732. Potsherd found at Sardis, sixth to fifth century BC.

]u? l i s? [

**32.** Gusmani A II 19. (Lydian) P63.114:5168. Potsherd found at Sardis, sixth or fifth century BC.

]m a [

**33.** Gusmani A II 12. (Lydian) P61.186:3473. Potsherd found at Sardis, sixth (?) century BC.

]u l i [

**34.** Gusmani A III 3. (Lydian) IN70.12/P70.22:8098. Potsherd found at Sardis, sixth to fifth century BC?

]x a? x s

**35.** IN84.14/P84.47:8896). (Lydian) Graffito on Achaemenid bowl.

eυ

## Fifth century

**36.** Buckler 102. (Greek) Marble stele found in May 1911 at the entrance to Tomb 212 west of the Paktolos. Date probably fifth century, perhaps after 450.

> I am [the stele] of Leomandros

**37.** Gusmani A II 2. (Lydian). IN64.54/P64.315:6423. Potsherd found at Sardis, fifth (?) century BC.

> [apud Gusmani: perhaps a dedication or similar.]
> ]*alis at* [
> ]*u? art* [

## Fifth or fourth century

**38.** Gusmani A II 20. (Lydian) P64.14:5955. Potsherd found at Sardis, fourth (or fifth?) century BC.

> [apud Gusmani: the beginning of a personal name]
> ]        *b a* [

**39.** Gusmani A I 2 (Lydian) IN 67.1. Top part of grave stele, late fifth or fourth century BC.

> This is the inscription and this the grave stele [of . . . ]
> the son of Artimus; now this inscr[iption or]
> [this grave stele, whoever does them damage . . . ]

**40.** Droaphernes inscription. (Greek) 367 or 429 BC.

> In the thirty-ninth year of Arta-
> xerxes' ruling, the statue of a
> man Droaphernes (set up),
> the son of Bar(a)kes, hyparch of Lydia, to
> Zeus of Baradatas. *[leaf ornament]* He orders those
> who have entered into the adyton,
> the neokoroi therapeutes [those who serve the god and temple]
> of him, and who garland the god
> that they not take part in the mysteries of Saba-
> zios, of those who lift up the burnt
> offerings either of Angidistis or Ma. They
> order the neokoros for Dorates
> to abstain from these mysteries.

*Bibliography*
Briant (1998a), Frei (1996), Herrmann (1996), Greenewalt (1978c, 1995b), Chaumont (1990), Gauthier (1989), Baslez (1986), Gschnitzer (1986), Robert (1975).

**41.** Gusmani A I 1. (Lydian) IN 62.107. Marble fragment.

> In the year ten (?), in the mo[nth . . . ]
> [under] the king . . .

**42.** Gusmani A II 1. (Lydian) IN62.259/P62.312:4621. Potsherd found at Sardis, fourth or third century BC.

[this pot belongs to x] son of (Karos or Bakis), now whoever [damages] it . . .

**43.** Gusmani A II 8. (Lydian) IN63.91/P63.465:5620. Potsherd found at Sardis, about 400–350 BC.

]*f a d* [

**44. ?** Gusmani B II 6. (Lydian) P67.132:7567. Potsherd found at Sardis, fifth or fourth century BC.

*m a v?*

## Fourth century

**45.** Gusmani A I 3. (Lydian) IN 67.31. Marble stele fragment found at Sardis.

] *s*[
associa]tion (?) of the temple
]? Artaxerxes
] in the grave chamber [I] gave
] *bisfatx*[ ? ]
]*i* the year (?) [
of Ka(?)ros and no other (?)

**46.** Gusmani A I 4. (Lydian) IN 71.1. Marble stele fragment found at Sardis.

. . .

he himself *fatixs(?)x*[
]ing (?) here [does – *amito*[ ]
now *torso* entrusts it to (?) [
and to him, may he prosper [
and his relative Is the mighty [
but now him does not possess *ifx* [
*aktas avladλ*. Now whom he *nsa* [
the holy oath dedicates *nānsk[ā]ns ka* [
And the wife (?) to him *kimλad nān* [
while him *isfollad borfcv a* [
*qrifrit* he rendered his own *τa* [
the *temnas* and *tutras bsles*, the father [did] [
The *avladis* the moveable goods to *anātli-* [
now whatsoever to him *Saristross* [
[. . ]*tkas* he cares for (?) will be carried out[
[. . .] he ordered so, and him [
[. . . . . . . . .] *baritod dum?* [

## Second half of the fourth century

**47.** Gusmani 16. (Lydian) Marble stele found in Sardis at the bottom of a gully on the west side of the acropolis. (B.16, F.16)

[this is the gr]ave chamber of Tivdas [   ]
[            ]of –λ*ms* in the year *s* [   ]
[            ] under King [        ]

[          ] himself *sidλ* [          ]
[          ] *el* [          ]

**48.** Gusmani 42. (Lydian) Marble slab, probably part of a stele, from Emre (Maeonia). (B.42, F.42)

In the year eleven in the mon[th    ]
under the King *es* [        ]
[Ka]ros, son of Artima[s    ]
and his wife (?), and if [    ]
and to him and his possessions [    ]
and this *labta*, whoever damages [it    ]
[. . . . . ]*vad* and [his] mother [    ]

**49.** Gusmani 20. (Lydian/Greek) Marble statue base, found in situ by the Artemis temple at Sardis. (L.2, B.20, F.20)

Nannas, son of Bakivas (Dionysikles), (dedicated this) to Artemis

**50.** Gusmani 43. (Lydian) Limestone stele from Eğriköy (Aeolis). (B.43, F.43)

In the year two
in the month Kanlela
[on the . . . th day] this votive tablet
Manes the son of Betovs
dedicated, the sacred thing
to [S]alidens *bar* [. . ]

**51.** Gusmani 59. (Lydian) Marble fragment from Sardis.

in the year *du* [    ]
[.....traces......]

## Hellenistic inscriptions

**52.** Gusmani 3. (Lydian) Inscribed and sculpted marble stele found in the necropolis of Sardis "in the . . . wall closing the doorway of a single-chamber tomb." (L.12, B.3, F.3)

In the fifth year of Alexander. This grave chamber and this stele
[are] those of Atrastas, the son of Timles, his heir from his own property
erected [it],
and whosoever looks after or also cares for and does not damage it, then
may Levs be kindly [to him], and if anyone destroys this grave chamber
or this stele, then may Levs destroy him.

**53.** Gusmani 50. (Lydian) Marble slab from the Kaÿster valley. (B.50, F.50)

In the twelfth year in the month Kanlela
on the [. . .]th day under Alexander
the king, this votive tablet
Timles, the son of Brduns, dedicated.
Levs watch over [his] protection and also
be [?] favor and Levs be well-meaning.

**54.** Sacrilege Inscription (Greek). Found at Ephesos (inv. no. 1631). Fifty-seven lines; *c*. 334–281 BC.

The judges for the goddess brought in
the sentence of death on account of the accusation
of the following crime: when sacred messengers
had been sent by the city to
the Chitons for Artemis according to the customs of our ancestors and the sacred objects and
the sacred messengers had arrived at Sardis and the Sanctuary of Artemis
founded by the Ephesians, the
sacred objects they profaned and the sacred messengers they assaulted.
The punishment for the crime is death.
The following were sentenced:
Tuios son of Manes son of Saplous,
Strombos son of Manes son of Saplous,
Mousaios son of Herakleidos, Paktyes
son of Karous son of Herakleidos,...
son of Karous, Miletos son of Karous,
Pytheas son of Karous, Paktyes son of
Atis, Saplous son of Pilos,
Herakleidos son of Artymas son of Manes
the bathman, Herakleidos
son of Artymas son of Manes the bathman
son of his brother Ilos, Maneas son of Atis
son of Ariotes, Moxos son of Atas
the shoe seller,
Moxos son of Atas
the shoe seller his brother,
Moxos son of Oilos son of Saplas the
sandal seller, Moschion and
Hermolaos brothers, Pilos son of Kar-
os son of Boukopos (or "the bull slayer"), Artymas son of S...
mos son of Boukopos (or "the bull slayer"), Strombos son of
Karous son of Kondas, Strombos
son of Pakyos son of Manes, Strombous [son of]
Herakleidos the goldsmith, Saplous
son of Strombos, Tamatis son of Strom-
bos, Zakrores son of Kados son of Manes,
Strombos son of Manes son of Ephesos,
Artymas son of Daos, Tuios son of Pytheas,
Artymas son of Manes son of Kotylos,
Sisines son of Eumanes from Hiera
Kome, Pytheas son of Strombos son of...
stes, Paktyes son of Atis the priest,
Paktyes son of Manes the oil seller [,.....?]
son of Karous, Papes son of Ephesos [son of]
Karous, Mithradates son of Tuios [son of]
Manes the slave of Attis, Strombos

son of Karous son of Kotylos, Strombos
son of Karous, Pytheas son of Strombous
son of Kados son of Babas, Paktyes son of
Manes <Karos>, Moxos son of Strombos son of
Pytheas, Spelmos son of Tuios, Baga[da?]-
tes the sacred herald, Batopates (?) son of
Papas, Karous son of Manes son of Atas
from Ibis Kome, Atas who has [as wife?]
the daughter of Paktyes son of Atis,
Samatikes son of Potas.

*Bibliography*
Hanfmann (1987), Knibbe (1961–1963).

**55. Mnesimachos Inscription (Greek).**

(Column I)

...Chaireas having made inquiry...and afterwards Antigonos awarded the *oikos* to me. Since now the temple-wardens are demanding back from me the gold lent on deposit and belonging to Artemis, but I do not have the funds with which to pay it to them, therefore these are the items of which the *oikos* consists; the *komai* named as follows: Tobalmoura, a *kome* in the Sardian plain on the Hill of Ilos, and connected with this *kome* are other *komai* also: that which is called of Tandos, and Kombdilipia; the dues paid by the *komai* to the chiliarchy of Pytheos...are 50 gold staters a year. There is also a *kleros* at Kinaroa near Tobalmoura; its dues are 3 gold staters a year. There is also another *kome*, Periasasostra, in the Water of Morstas; its dues, paid to the chiliarchy of...-arios, are 57 gold staters a year. There is also in the Water of Morstas a *kleros* at Nagrioa; its dues, paid to the chiliarchy of Sagarios son of Koreis, are 3 gold staters and 4 gold obols. There is also another *kome* in Attoudda which is called The Kome of Ilos; its dues are 3 gold staters and 3 gold obols a year. Therefore from all the *komae*, and from the *kleroi* and the house sites (*oikopeda*) connected to them, and from the people with all their households and belongings, and from the jars of wine and the dues rendered in silver and in labor, and from the revenues of other kinds from the *komai* and in addition to these any surplus, when the division happened, Pytheos and Adrastos received as separate property an *aule* at Tbalmoura; and apart from the *aule* are the *oikiai* of the people and slaves, and two *paradeisoi* requiring 15 artabas of seed, and at Periasasostra house sites requiring 3 artabas of seed, and *paradeisoi* requiring 3 artabas of seed, as well as the slaves who are dwelling at that place: at Tbalmoura, Ephesos son of Adrastos, Kadoas son of Adrastos, Kerakleides son of Beletras, Tuios son of Maneas Kaikos; those dwelling at Periasasostra, Kadoas son of Armanandas, Adtrastos son of Maneas......

(Column II)

...............it shall no longer *be permissible* either for me or for *my descendants, or for*...or for anyone else to redeem anything. And if someone should lay claim to any of the *komai* or of the *kleroi* or to any of the other things written here, I and my descendants will guarantee it and will remove the claimant; but if we should not guarantee it, or if we should transgress the written contract with respect to the *komai* and the *kleroi* and the *choria* and all the slaves, they will pass to the treasury of Artemis, and the temple-wardens on account of them shall initiate legal proceedings and obtain judgment against the claimants however they may wish, and I Mnesimachos and my heirs will pay to the treasury of Artemis 2650 gold staters; and concerning the produce and the fruits, if they do not receive fruits in that year, we will pay into the treasury of Artemis as much gold as these things are worth; and the value of the building and of the planting done by Artemis, or of anything else they may do, we will pay that value whatever it may be worth; and as long as we shall not have paid, the debt shall constitute a deposit-loan to us until we shall have paid the whole. And if the king because of Mnesimachos should take away from Artemis the *komai* or the *kleroi* or any of the other things mortgaged, then the principal in gold of the deposit-loan, the 1325 gold staters, we ourselves, I Mnesimachos and my descendants, will immediately pay to the treasury of Artemis, and the value of the building and of the planting done by Artemis, we will immediately pay that value whatever it may be worth; and concerning the produce and the fruits, if they do not receive fruits in that year, we will pay into the treasury of Artemis as much gold as these things are worth; and as long as we shall not have paid, the debt shall constitute a deposit-loan to me and my descendants until we shall have paid the whole to the treasury of Artemis; and the transaction, so long as it is not yet had from us, is to be enforceable.

*Bibliography*
Buckler and Robinson (1932), Descat (1985), Atkinson (1972).

# Mortuary remains

Adapted from Dusinberre (1997b). For tomb masonry, see Ratté (1989b, forthcoming); for tombs and contents, see McLauchlin (1985), Greenewalt (n.d.). A question mark indicates a tomb that is probably but not certainly of Achaemenid date.

## Tumuli (built chamber tombs)

### Tomb BT 62.4

Tumulus tomb oriented N–S, with entrance at south, approx. 0.75 km from the Tomb of Alyattes, with dromos, antechamber, and chamber. Dromos walls are limestone rubble set in mud; chamber and antechamber are ashlar limestone blocks with anathyrosis, clamped with iron staple clamps in fish- or butterfly-shaped lead settings. The door frame has red lines on it, probably masons' setting marks. The blocks were dressed with a claw chisel.

*Furniture*
Couch set against back wall of chamber.

*Associated finds*
  Original presence of one or more coins is implied by its local name, "para bu-
    lunduğu tepe (trans. the mound where coin[s] was/were found)."
  Round-mouthed oinochoe, bichrome (P62.350:4669)
  Black-glaze skyphos (P62.422:4781)
  Jar with pendant hooks (P62.423:4783)
  Wave-line amphora/hydria (P62.424:4784)
  Iron spearbutt (M62.73 [Waldbaum 1983:32 no. 16])
  Worked ivory fragment (BI62.9)
  Flint blade (flint 62.1)
  Small animal skeleton.

*Date*
Late sixth or early fifth century.

*Bibliography*
Ratté (1989b:169–176), Hanfmann (1963:57–59), McLauchlin (1985:179–182).

### Tomb BT 63.2

Tumulus tomb approx. 300 m SSW from Karnıyarık tepe. Oblong chamber oriented E–W, without doorway or dromos, built of rusticated blocks.

*Furniture*
Four square cuttings in floor probably cut to receive the legs of a wooden sarcophagus, of which fragments are extant.

*Associated finds*
   Iron fittings with pseudomorphs of textiles
   Amphora body (P63.402:5540)
   Three lekythoi (P63.443:5592, P63.445:5594, P63.446:5595).

*Date*
Mid- or later sixth century.

*Bibliography*
Ratté (1989b:176–179), Hanfmann (1964:55), Greenewalt and Majewski (1980), McLauchlin (1985:182–184).

## BT 66.1–66.6 (Duman Tepe)
Located on a low limestone ridge roughly 1300 m NNE of Alyattes.

## Tomb BT 66.1
Tumulus tomb with dromos, antechamber, and chamber, oriented E–W, opening W. Dromos of rough hunks of limestone spanned by limestone beams; antechamber of plastered limestone blocks with limestone flake floor and a door plug. The chamber is a cube with point-dressed stones; a semicircular opening was cut into one of the two ceiling beams at the joint.

*Furniture*
Bench slotted into back and side walls.

*Associated finds*
   Fragment of small cup or bowl (P66.56:7063).

*Date*
Sixth to fourth century.

*Bibliography*
Ratté (1989b:179–181), Hanfmann (1967:47–50), McLauchlin (1985:184–187).

## Tomb BT 66.2
Tumulus tomb with dromos and chamber, oriented roughly N–S, opening S. Dromos slopes down towards the chamber, cut into bedrock. Doorway into chamber plugged. Chamber itself partly carved from bedrock, partly built; the back was left as a couch.

*Associated finds*
   Dish rim (P66.46:7031)
   Jug (P66.47:7032)
   Achaemenid bowl (P66.48:7033)
   Lekythos (P66.49:7034)
   Alabaster alabastron rim (S66.12:7089).

*Date*
Late sixth century.

*Bibliography*
Ratté (1989b:181–183), Hanfmann (1967:50–51), McLauchlin (1985:201–203).

## Tomb BT 66.3 (?)

Oblong chamber oriented NE–SW with dromos at SW. Dromos is unroofed, cut into bedrock, with walls of limestone rubble. Chamber paved with limestone slabs.

*Date*
Sixth to fourth century?

*Bibliography*
Ratté (1989b:184–185), Hanfmann (1967:51–52), McLauchlin (1985:187–189).

## Tomb BT 66.4 (?)

Chamber tomb oriented E–W, dromos at E. Dromos floor carved out of bedrock, steps down before chamber. Chamber floor hollowed out of bedrock; walls partly bedrock, partly built. A slot in the back wall may have held a couch.

*Associated finds*
Lydion fragment (P66.102:7138)
Amphoriskos fragment (P66.107:7141).

*Date*
Late sixth century?

*Bibliography*
Ratté (1989b:185–187), Hanfmann (1967:52), McLauchlin (1985:203–205).

## Tomb BT 66.6 (?)

Chamber tomb oriented N–S, without dromos or entranceway: doorway in N wall approached by chute cut into bedrock. Chamber floor partly hollowed out of bedrock, partly laid with blocks fitted into slots.

*Associated finds*
Lydion fragments (P66.63:7212, P66.95:7173, P66.147A-C:7202, P66.160C-D:7216, P66.160A-B:7216)
Cup (P66.106:7143, P66.153:7209)
Skyphos fragment (P66.148:7203)
Stone alabastron (S66.19)
Bones of individual *c.* 20 years old.

*Date*
Later sixth century?

*Bibliography*
Ratté (1989b:187–189), Hanfmann (1967:52), McLauchlin (1985:189–191).

## Tomb BK 71.1

Tumulus a few kilometers south of Sardis in the village of Keskinler, oriented N–S, with rubble-built dromos leading at north to small porch and chamber. Dromos unpaved and unroofed except at chamber; filled with rubble after construction. Chamber paved with limestone slabs.

*Furniture*
Limestone couch at west wall, legs carved with double volutes.

*Associated finds*
> Achaemenid bowl fragments
> Dish fragments
> Alabaster alabastron rims (S71.1:8125, S71.2:8126).

*Date*
Second half of sixth century.

*Bibliography*
Ratté (1989b:189–95), Ramage (1972:11–15), McLauchlin (1985:197–200).

## Tomb 77.1 (?)

Chamber tomb east of Paktolos, across from Pyramid Tomb, oriented E–W with unroofed dromos at W of irregularly coursed sandstone and conglomerate and a floor of limestone chips. Chamber walls and floor of limestone slabs, with no trace of a ceiling.

*Furniture*
Two couches run the full length of the chamber.

*Associated finds*
> Various clay vessel fragments.

*Date*
Second half of sixth century?

*Bibliography*
Ratté (1989b:195–199), Greenewalt (1979:9–19), McLauchlin (1985:193–199).

## Tomb 82.1 (?)

Chamber tomb oriented N–S with shallow porch at north end, located approx. 350 m south of Artemis temple. Partly dug into bedrock, partly built.

*Furniture*
Two upright blocks at back end of chamber supported couches along side walls.

*Associated finds*
> One lamp
> Various Hellenistic sherds.

*Date*
Third quarter of sixth century?

*Bibliography*
Ratté (1989b:200–204), Greenewalt et al. (1985:81–84), McLauchlin (1985:195–197).

## Tomb BC/T 2 (?)

Chamber with antechamber or dromos opening south, somewhere in Bin Tepe. Dromos and chamber both ashlar blocks, probably limestone, roofed with blocks spanning the width of the tomb.

*Furniture*
Fragments of a carved and painted stone couch.

*Date*
Sixth to fourth century?

*Bibliography*
McLauchlin (1985:174–175).

### Tomb BC/T 5 (?)
Chamber tomb somewhere in Bin Tepe, of ashlar blocks with paved floor and roof beams.

*Furniture*
Stone couch at rear.

*Associated finds*
   A skeleton on the couch
   Pots and glass vessels on the floor.

*Date*
Possibly sixth to fourth century; probably reused in Roman period.

*Bibliography*
McLauchlin (1985:177), Butler (1922:7, 10).

### Tomb 1976–1
Three chambers in cloverleaf arrangement, with dromos and antechamber, approx. 10 km south of Gygaean lake and 3 km north of Kestelli Köyü. Dromos of trimmed plastered blocks; antechamber and chambers of plastered limestone blocks, roofed and paved with limestone. Roofs of rear chamber and antechamber pitched, side chambers flat. Floor slabs of rear chamber clamped with staple clamps in dove-tail settings.

*Furniture*
Two rudimentary marble couches in rear chamber, resting on floor rather than uprights.

*Date*
Fifth century or later.

*Bibliography*
McLauchlin (1985:191–192), Greenewalt (1978c:70).

## Rock-carved chamber tombs

### Tomb 1 (or Tomb I?)
*Associated finds*
   IAM 4532, Curtis 103 Small worn faience ornament in two pieces: standing figure with animal's head.

*Bibliography*
Curtis (1925).

**Tomb 4**
*Associated finds*
>   IAM 4543, Curtis 67 (see fig. 56) Two large heavy gold earrings, molded to look like thirteen contiguous spheres, terminating in lion's heads
>   IAM 4552, Curtis 47 Two long perforated club-shaped gold beads, with granulation.

*Bibliography*
Curtis (1925).

**Tomb 5**
*Associated finds*
>   IAM 4579, Curtis 114 (see fig. 88) Rock crystal pyramidal stamp seal, held by cap (silver?): sphinx and lion-griffin.

*Bibliography*
Curtis (1925).

**Tomb 18**
*Associated finds*
>   IAM 4523, Curtis 121 (see fig. 93) Low cylindrical agate seal with heavy silver mounting (strap and ring): lion and bull combat on groundline
>   IAM 4524, Curtis 123 (see fig. 94) Oval seal of dark mottled stone, mounting missing: man seated right on high-backed chair
>   IAM 4526, Curtis 50 Pendant of rock crystal with cap in shape of lion's head holding suspension ring in its mouth
>   IAM 4546, Curtis 60 Small crescent earring.
>   IAM 4553, Curtis 13 Broad strip of gold, found on forehead of skull
>   IAM 4568, Curtis 42 Chain of gold and carnelian
>   IAM 4573, Curtis 82 Two heavy circular earrings of thick wire (museum label says from tomb 35).

*Bibliography*
Curtis (1925).

**Tomb 22**
*Associated finds*
>   IAM 4527, Curtis 119 (see fig. 92) Small chalcedony pyramidal stamp seal, mounting missing: hero stabs lion
>   IAM 4565, Curtis 56 Two small ribbed carnelian beads
>   IAM 4566, Curtis 29 Five small gold beads.

*Bibliography*
Curtis (1925).

**Tomb 24**
*Associated finds*
>   IAM 4521, Curtis 107 (see fig. 82) Chalcedony pyramidal stamp seal with gold mounting: bearded harpy
>   IAM 4531, Curtis 5 Two gold rosettes of eight petals each
>   IAM 4567, Curtis 41 Nineteen gold beads and two gold pendants.

*Bibliography*
Curtis (1925).

## Tomb 25
*Associated finds*

IAM 4544, Curtis 68 Gold earring of hollow cylinder, molded to look like contiguous spheres, lion's head terminals

IAM 4556, Curtis 38 Circular button-shaped banded agate, cut to look like eye, with gold mounting

IAM 4558, Curtis 34 Gold pendant – holder for glass paste (?) cylinder seal; rosettes top and bottom

IAM 4559, Curtis 35 Gold pendant – holder for stone – very worn

IAM 4560, Curtis 36 Gold pendant – holder for carnelian stamp seal: man bending backward, very worn

IAM 4561, Curtis 37 Gold pendant with flattened blue glass paste bead

IAM 4570, Curtis 33 (see fig. 96) Chain of gold, agate, and carnelian (including carved carnelian scarab).

*Bibliography*
Curtis (1925).

## Tomb 26
*Associated finds*

IAM 4549, Curtis 78 Heavy gold circular earring.

*Bibliography*
Curtis (1925).

## Tomb 27
*Associated finds*

IAM 4528, Curtis 110 (see fig. 84) Chalcedony pyramidal stamp seal, held by silver ducks' heads: lion-griffin

IAM 4529 Pierced carnelian cylinder

IAM 4530, Curtis 54 Perforated agate bead

IAM 4646, Curtis 9 Small hollow gold cylinder

IAM 4650, Curtis 8 Gold ornament, male figure with five wings.

*Bibliography*
Curtis (1925).

## Tomb 50
*Associated finds*

IAM 4547, Curtis 61 Crescent earring, granulated, with pendants

IAM 4555, Curtis 48 Small gold pendant in shape of transport amphora

IAM 4557, Curtis 39 Banded agate, button-shaped.

*Bibliography*
Curtis (1925).

### Tomb 59.2 (?)

Double chamber with passageway between chambers and open dromos leading to first, on south side of a necropolis gully, approx. 1 km west of Artemis temple. Rock above arched doorway trimmed to triangular shape; border around door perhaps meant to hold door plug. First chamber has flat roof, second chamber pitched.

*Furniture*
First chamber has bench to right of entrance, with terracotta sarcophagus.
Second chamber has continuous horseshoe-shaped bench around walls, and terracotta bathtub sarcophagus set into floor.

*Associated finds*
   Alabaster alabastron fragment.

*Date*
Sixth to fourth century.

*Bibliography*
McLauchlin (1985:231–232), Hanfmann (1960a:10–12).

### Tomb 59.3 (?)

Two chambers in irregular L, on south side of a necropolis gully, approx. 1 km west of Artemis temple. Dromos to first chamber, L-shaped corridor from back wall into second chamber.

*Furniture*
No benches in first chamber.
Two benches along side walls of interior chamber, and fragments of terracotta sarcophagus.

*Associated finds*
   Lydian lekythos fragments.

*Date*
Interior chamber dates to sixth to fourth century?

*Bibliography*
McLauchlin (1985:233–234), Hanfmann (1960a:10–12).

### Tomb 75

*Associated finds*
   IAM 5140, Curtis 44 Forty-four gold beads
   IAM 5141, Curtis 69 Gold earrings
   IAM 5142, Curtis 89 Small gold seal ring with unornamented diamond-shaped bezel
   IAM 5143–5145, Curtis 86 Three small gold lions on rectangular perforated bases, perhaps for attachment to clothing or a box.

*Bibliography*
Curtis (1925).

## Tomb 77.1 (?)

*Associated finds*

Fragments of skyphos
Other cups
Jars
Oinochoe.

*Bibliography*

Ratté (1989b:195–199), Greenewalt (1977:9–19), McLauchlin (1985:193–199).

## Tomb 100

*Associated finds*

IAM 4537 Silver spouted dish
IAM 4533 Silver ladle with calf's head finial.

*Bibliography*

McLauchlin (1985:248–249), Butler (1922:83).

## Tomb 201

*Associated finds*

IAM 4545, Curtis 77 Two circular earrings of twisted wire
Two silver bracelets.

*Bibliography*

Curtis (1925).

## Tomb 213

*Associated finds*

IAM 4522, Curtis 108 (see fig. 101) Chalcedony pyramidal stamp seal with gold
    holder: winged man
IAM 4548, Curtis 95 Gold ring with large flat undecorated bezel
IAM 4550, Curtis 88 Gold ring (museum label says from tomb 26)
IAM 4562, Curtis 85 Hollow gold rattle or reel
IAM 4563, Curtis 55 Perforated barrel of banded agate
IAM 4571, Curtis 52 Chain of 165 gold and carnelian beads
IAM 4572 (see fig. 58) Bronze mirror; handle terminates at bottom in calf's head
    and at top in double horse protomes
IAM 9740 Silver Achaemenid bowl.

*Bibliography*

Curtis (1925), Oliver (1971:113–120), Butler (1922:84), Waldbaum (1983:964 [tomb
number erroneously listed as 113]).

## Tomb 220

*Associated finds*

IAM 4520, Curtis 96 (see fig. 77) Gold ring with large carnelian scarab on swivel:
    bull
IAM 4525, Curtis 112 (see fig. 86) Chalcedony pyramidal stamp seal held by silver
    cap: seated winged lions
IAM 4564, Curtis 28 Short chain of gold and carnelian beads.

*Bibliography*
Curtis (1925).

## Tomb 232
*Associated finds*
> IAM 4554, Curtis 32 Ten gold lotus pendants
> IAM 4569, Curtis 31 Chain of thirty-six gold and three carnelian beads.

*Bibliography*
Curtis (1925).

## Tomb 311
*Associated finds*
> IAM 4593, Curtis 14 Long narrow strip of gold, pierced at each end.

*Bibliography*
Curtis (1925).

## Tomb 326
*Associated finds*
> IAM 4577, Curtis 49 Pendant of rock crystal with gold cap terminating in a lion's head holding suspension ring in its mouth
> IAM 4580, Curtis 106 (see fig. 81) Carnelian pyramidal stamp seal; held by gold strip with palmettes at ends: lion
> IAM 4605, Curtis 46 Four gold pendants.

*Bibliography*
Curtis (1925).

## Tomb 327
*Associated finds*
> IAM 4590, Curtis 122 (see fig. 102) Chalcedony stamp seal, nearly cylindrical, perforated but mounting lost: goat.

*Bibliography*
Curtis (1925).

## Tomb 329
*Associated finds*
> IAM 4606, Curtis 18 Three crumpled fragments of gold foil.

*Bibliography*
Curtis (1925).

## Tomb 340
*Associated finds*
> IAM 4607, Curtis 45 Ten flat triangular gold beads.

*Bibliography*
Curtis (1925).

## Tomb 342

*Associated finds*

IAM 4598, Curtis 58 Two crescent earrings
IAM 4598, Curtis 59 Two crescent earrings
IAM 4601, Curtis 57 Fragments of two crescent earrings
IAM 4603, Curtis 62 Two gold wire earrings.

*Bibliography*
Curtis (1925).

## Tomb 343

*Associated finds*

IAM 4602, Curtis 15 Sixteen fragments of a diadem or wreath.

*Bibliography*
Curtis (1925).

## Tomb 348 (?)

Rock-cut tomb.

*Furniture*
Probably more than one bench.

*Associated finds*

Several stone alabastra
Bronze mirror
Assorted ceramic vessels associated with drinking and anointing
IAM 4578, Curtis 111 (see fig. 85) Conical chalcedony seal with rounded top and
bevelled sides (eight faces) and with (very corroded) silver mounting: winged
figure holds two lions.

*Date*
Sixth to fourth century?

*Bibliography*
Curtis (1925), Greenewalt (n.d.).

## Tomb 354

*Associated finds*

IAM 4594, Curtis 16 Long narrow strip of gold foil.

*Bibliography*
Curtis (1925).

## Tomb 364

*Associated finds*

IAM 4591, Curtis 118 (see fig. 91) Carnelian pyramidal stamp seal, mounting missing: archer shoots lion.

*Bibliography*
Curtis (1925).

### Tomb 368
*Associated finds*
> IAM 4608, Curtis 11 (see fig. 53) Two gold "kite-shaped" plaques with palmette designs
> IAM 4609, Curtis 53 Pierced barrel-shaped agate bead
> IAM 4610, Curtis 30 Six gold pendant beads.

*Bibliography*
Curtis (1925).

### Tomb 369
*Associated finds*
> Several glass and bronze beads.
> IAM 4582, Curtis 74 Circular gold wire earring
> IAM 4600, Curtis 73 Circular gold wire earring
> IAM 4604, Curtis 17 Six small fragments of gold wreath.

*Bibliography*
Curtis (1925).

### Tomb 371
*Associated finds*
> Several beads and a silver ring.
> IAM 4589, Curtis 116 (see fig. 90) Chalcedony pyramidal stamp seal, mounting missing: hero attacks lion
> IAM 4592, Curtis 117 Blue glass paste pyramidal stamp seal; very badly corroded
> IAM 4595, Curtis 19 Fragments of gold.

*Bibliography*
Curtis (1925).

### Tomb 381
Chamber tomb with double-width bench at back and one or more benches along side walls, on crest of necropolis directly below main summit.

*Furniture*
Two large terracotta sarcophagi, side by side, on rear couch.

*Associated finds*
> Sarcophagus A contained the bones of a female not older than seventeen, as well as:
>> Rows of stone alabastra
>> Gold fillets above the head of the skeleton
>> IAM 4584, Curtis 71 One simple wire earring
>> IAM 4585, Curtis 92 (see fig. 75) Gold ring with heavy hoop and broad, flat, oval gold bezel: lion
>> IAM 4586, Curtis 70 Two gold earrings at sides of head
>> IAM 4587, Curtis 27 Forty-four small gold barrel-shaped beads with ring at each end, found near ankles

> IAM 4588, Curtis 25 Chain of 150 gold beads, 8 blue glass beads and 1 carnelian cylinder, found on neck
>
> IAM 4596, Curtis 27 Five barrel-shaped beads and one eight-petaled rosette
>
> IAM 4597, Curtis 26 Twenty-four small gold beads and pendants.

Sarcophagus B contained the bones of an old man.

Also in tomb:

> Silver perfume stirrer
>
> Iron strigil
>
> Six ivory cylinders
>
> Ivory fragments.

*Date*
Mid-sixth to fourth century.

*Bibliography*
McLauchlin, (1985:226–227), Greenewalt (n.d.), Butler (1922:144), Curtis (1925).

## Tomb 611
*Associated finds*
> IAM 4642, Curtis 113 (see fig. 87) Blue chalcedony pyramidal stamp seal with silver strap holding: lion-griffin.

*Bibliography*
Curtis (1925).

## Tomb 620
*Associated finds*
> IAM 4644, Curtis 84 Small silver pendant or earring.

*Bibliography*
Curtis (1925).

## Tomb 701
*Associated finds*
> IAM 4639, Curtis 99 (see fig. 79) Very heavy silver ring with oval stone (black with red bands) on swivel: lion.

*Bibliography*
Curtis (1925).

## Tomb 722
Chamber with dromos, on N slope of necropolis ridge directly opposite Artemis temple.

*Furniture*
Sarcophagus.

*Associated finds*
> In sarcophagus were: Bronze box-mirror (Br131)
>
> Iron spear head (M22)
>
> Two stone alabastra (SV53 and 54)

IAM 4632, Curtis 98 (see fig. 78) Heavy gold ring with carnelian scarab on a swivel: boar.

Outside sarcophagus were:

Oinochoe

Five lekythoi

Two lydia

An inscribed alabastron (P1319, P1314, P1315, and P1318, P1316, P1317, P1309, P1313, P1320 [Gusmani no. 33])

One melon-shaped glass bead (G1 18)

Bronze mirror (Br 130)

Thirteen more artifacts.

*Date*

*c.* 500–475 BC.

*Bibliography*

McLauchlin (1985:229–230), Greenewalt (n.d.), Butler (1922), Curtis (1925), Gusmani (1964:263).

## Tomb 805

*Associated finds*

IAM 5135, Curtis 40 Gold pendant – cap with ring, with blue glass bead

IAM 5136, Curtis 43 Long chain of forty-one gold beads, glass beads, many glass paste beads of white, blue, green, and yellow

IAM 5137, Curtis 75 Two fine gold wire earrings

IAM 5138, Curtis 7 Gold "button" with frontal face

IAM 5139, Curtis 76 Circular gold earring.

*Bibliography*

Curtis (1925).

## Tomb 811

Chamber tomb on main necropolis hill.

*Furniture*

At least one sarcophagus, perhaps also wooden coffin.

*Associated finds*

IAM 4633, Curtis 97 Heavy gold ring with carnelian scarab in silver mounting, found on finger in sarcophagus

IAM 4636, Curtis 90 (see fig. 73) Gold seal ring with diamond-shaped bezel: lion

IAM 4641, Curtis 109 (see fig. 83) Chalcedony pyramidal stamp seal, held by gold ducks' heads: human-headed winged goat.

*Date*

Probably early fifth century.

*Bibliography*

Curtis (1925).

## Tomb 812
*Associated finds*
    Bronze bracelet with overlapping ends
    IAM 4648, Curtis 20 Three gold strips with traces of stamped circles
    IAM 4649, Curtis 83 Large circular silver earring or perhaps child's bracelet.

*Bibliography*
Curtis (1925).

## Tomb 813
Chamber tomb with vestibule and dromos in a gully of necropolis opposite Artemis temple, opening E. Floors are even, cut into bedrock; dromos ceiling lower than those of vestibule and chamber. In front of vestibule is an ornamental limestone staircase of four steps, with a limestone stele on either side: bases of staircase and stelae all rest on the bedrock floor, with top of staircase ending 1.2 m above floor surface.

*Furniture*
Rock-cut bench at back of rear chamber, with limestone bathtub sarcophagus.
Bathtub sarcophagus sunk into the floor at back of vestibule.
Two limestone stelae and one staircase.

*Associated finds*
    Bronze bier pole end
    Faience "eye of Horus" amulet
    Part of an orientalizing vessel
    Attic black-figure oinochoe
    Skyphos
    Five zoomorphic terracotta figurines (MMA 26.164.5, MMA 26.164.8, MMA 26.164.9, MMA 26.164.20, and 26.164.21).
    In sarcophagus:
        Three ceramic ovoid jugs
        Ceramic alabastron
        Possibly another stone alabastron
        IAM 4581, Curtis 104 (see fig. 80) Banded agate cylinder seal on suspension ring, with gold disks at either end of cylinder: hero holds lion-griffins on sphinxes
        Curtis 12 (see fig. 60) Three rosette-and-lotus gold foil ornaments for attachment to clothing
        Gold ring.

*Date*
c. 550–475 BC.

*Bibliography*
Ratté (1989b:204–206, 1994a), Greenewalt (n.d.), Butler (1922:118, 159–162), Hanfmann and Ramage (1978:75), Greenewalt et al. (1987:36–44), McLauchlin (1985:216–220), Dusinberre (1997a).

## Tomb 826
*Associated finds*
    IAM 4638, Curtis 72 Two gold wire earrings.

*Bibliography*
Curtis (1925).

## Tomb 836
Chamber tomb with dromos, oriented E–W, on main necropolis hill near top of north face of ridge extending west from first tomb hill.

*Furniture*
Benches at back and probably both sides of chamber.

*Associated finds*
    A few pottery items
    Coins (two sigloi, coins of Alexander and Macedon, three coins of Ephesos)
    Four clay alabastra
    Amphora
    IAM 4601, Curtis 6 Two small circular gold buttons
    IAM 4645, Curtis 51 Gold chain formed of forty elements (nineteen ribbed cylinders, twenty floral pendants or beads, one disk)
    IAM 4652, Curtis 1 (see fig. 55) Six stamped gold plaques in the shape of a rectangle with crenelations at the top, showing bearded winged sphinxes
    IAM 4653, Curtis 2 (see fig. 54) Nine small gold plaques in stamped relief, showing walking beardless winged sphinxes
    IAM 4654, Curtis 3 Forty-three small gold rosettes of eight petals each
    IAM 4655, Curtis 4 Seven very small gold rosettes of eight petals.

*Date*
Perhaps constructed in fifth century, reused in late third.

*Bibliography*
McLauchlin (1985:227–228), Greenewalt (n.d.), Butler (1922:143), Curtis (1925).

## Tomb 837
*Associated finds*
    IAM 4640, Curtis 102 (see fig. 100) Scarab of white paste: male.

*Bibliography*
Curtis (1925).

## Tomb 920
*Associated finds*
    IAM 5132, Curtis 66 Gold crescent-shaped earrings with pendants and granulation.

*Bibliography*
Curtis (1925).

## Tomb 921
*Associated finds*
    IAM 5147, Curtis 22 Short chain of thirty gold and agate beads
    IAM 5148, Curtis 64 Two gold earrings

IAM 5149, Curtis 65 Small gold crescent earring with granulation

IAM 5150, Curtis 22 Three beads: one cylindrical banded agate, one barrel banded agate, one barrel paste.

*Bibliography*
Curtis (1925).

## Tomb 1005
*Associated finds*

IAM 5133, Curtis 120 (see fig. 95) Neo-Babylonian-type blue chalcedony pyramidal stamp seal with several flaws, mounting missing: worship scene

IAM 5134, Curtis 115 (see fig. 89) Chalcedony pyramidal stamp seal with silver ducks' heads mounting: lion-griffin.

*Bibliography*
Curtis (1925).

## Tomb 1100
*Associated finds*

IAM 5151, Curtis 23 Gold chain of fifty-eight beads

IAM 5152, Curtis 24 Small gold chain of twenty-three beads.

*Bibliography*
Curtis (1925).

## Tomb 1104
*Associated finds*

IAM 5146, Curtis 21 Short chain of twenty-five smooth gold biconical beads.

*Bibliography*
Curtis (1925).

## Tomb A1 (?)
*Associated finds*

IAM 4518, Curtis 101 (see fig. 99) Bracelet of gold wire with large chalcedony seal on a swivel: Hermes and Athena

IAM 4542, Curtis 80 Two large circular gold earrings

IAM 4551, Curtis 79 Gold earring of heavy wire with square cross-section.

*Bibliography*
Curtis (1925).

## Tomb B1
*Associated finds*

IAM 4519, Curtis 93 (see fig. 97) Gold ring with carnelian scarab on a swivel: winged male.

*Bibliography*
Curtis (1925).

## Tomb CC 7 (?)

Double chamber on necropolis directly opposite Artemis temple: a flight of steps leads down from first chamber to second.

*Furniture*
Benches in first chamber on side walls.
Second chamber apparently has at least one bench along the side wall and a double-width bench at the back with two shallow rectangular depressions for sarcophagi or bodies.

*Date*
Mid-sixth century or later?

*Bibliography*
McLauchlin (1985:220), Butler (1922:162).

## Tomb CC 18 (?)
Double chamber with dromos on southwest necropolis. Both chambers have pitched ceilings and fine pink plaster on all walls; second chamber stepped down from first.

*Furniture*
First chamber has bench at right and narrow ledge at left.
Second chamber has a bench on each side, with rectangular depressions in the top to hold sarcophagi or bodies.

*Date*
Sixth to fourth century?

*Bibliography*
McLauchlin (1985:234), Butler (1922:163–164).

## Tomb CC 22 (?)
Double chamber with dromos opening E, approx. 3 km south of Artemis temple; one of a group of five (along with CC 23). Dromos door probably plugged, ceiling pitched. First chamber divided into two sections by a projecting ridge of untrimmed rock that separates two benches on either side. An irregular passageway leads into much eroded second chamber.

*Furniture*
Four benches in first chamber.
Two benches in second chamber with a narrow aisle between.

*Date*
Sixth to fourth century?

*Bibliography*
McLauchlin (1985:237–239).

## Tomb CC 23 (?)
Single chamber with dromos opening east, approx. 3 km south of Artemis temple; one of a group of five (along with CC 22). Door to dromos and dromos ceiling pitched; chamber has very irregular ceiling and a deep cleft in the rear wall.

*Furniture*
L-shaped bench at left of entrance to chamber.

*Date*
Sixth to fourth century?

*Bibliography*
McLauchlin (1985:239).

## Tomb G5
*Associated finds*
  IAM 4583, Curtis 81 Circular gold earring.

*Bibliography*
Curtis (1925).

## Tomb G 61.50
*Associated finds*
  Three plainware lekythoi (P61.571, P61.572, P61.573)
  Bone fragments.

*Bibliography*
McLauchlin (1985:247), Hanfmann (1962:28–30).

## Tomb S1
Double tomb opening north in south necropolis, perhaps originally two separate adjacent tombs joined by a hole broken through the connecting wall. Dromos and first chamber have pitched ceilings; at east end of chamber is a broad irregular opening on to large oblong chamber with pitched ceiling. At back is another oblong room extending east at a sharp angle, with a rounded ceiling. Interior walls of all three chambers are highly finished, all angles cut sharply.

*Furniture*
Western chamber has on eastern wall a bench with a step leading to it, and at west a raised bench hollowed out to hold a sarcophagus or body.
Eastern chamber includes a long narrow cist dug on axis with the dromos of the chamber to hold a body or sarcophagus.
Third chamber includes no trace of funerary furniture.

*Associated finds*
  Various bronze items
  Attic red figure
  Stone hone (?)
  IAM 4657, Curtis 87 (see fig. 57) Small head of ivory, perhaps from a female chryselephantine statuette. Each cheek is inscribed with a crescent shape; another crescent is inscribed below the lower lip. The figurine wears large circular earrings with radiating ribs
  Pyxis.

*Date*
Sixth to fourth century.

*Bibliography*
McLauchlin (1985:235–236), Greenewalt (n.d.), Butler (1922:140–141, 162–164), Curtis (1925), personal observation.

### Tomb S4
*Associated finds*
   IAM 4651, Curtis 10 Two gold "kite-shaped" plaques with elaborate palmette designs.

*Bibliography*
Curtis (1925).

### Tomb S10
*Associated finds*
   IAM 4647, Curtis 63 Gold earrings.

*Bibliography*
Curtis (1925).

### Tomb S16
Cross-shaped chamber tomb with unroofed dromos, on the north side of a ravine in the south necropolis opening west towards the Paktolos. Door between dromos and chamber has a curved pediment roughly carved in low relief; slots in the side walls would hold a door stone. The chamber includes a central space having two sarcophagi carved into the rock on either side. The sarcophagi rise in tiers like steps, with outer faces of upper sarcophagi slanting out into chamber. At rear, a step up to a platform into which was set another sarcophagus, covered with stone slabs. Above this platform, a deep niche with a curved ceiling and another rock-cut sarcophagus. All interior surfaces covered with fine plaster.

*Furniture*
At least six sarcophagi.

*Associated finds*
   IAM 4634, Curtis 94 (see fig. 76) Gold ring with carnelian scarab on a swivel: lion
   IAM 4637, Curtis 91 (see fig. 74) Gold seal ring with large convex oval bezel: woman
      seated
   Bronze pitcher
   Other jewelry
   Three stone alabastra.

*Date*
Sixth to fourth century.

*Bibliography*
McLauchlin (1985:236–237), Butler (1922:141, 164–165), Curtis (1925).

## Sarcophagi

### Sarcophagus C 2
Sarcophagus of unknown type, apparently for child burial, covered by a limestone sarcophagus lid. From Bin Tepe, between Ahlatlı Tepecik and Eski Balıkhane.

*Associated finds*
    Small streaky glaze skyphos (P68.88)
    One-handled "feeder" vase (P68.92)
    Limestone "offering table" with lion's paw feet (S68.11).

*Date*
*c.* 500 BC.

*Bibliography*
McLauchlin (1985:207–208).

## Tomb G 61.50

Fragmentary terracotta sarcophagus, covered by schist slabs, approx. 1.5 m west of the Pyramid Tomb, in a niche cut into bedrock.

*Associated finds*
    Three plainware lekythoi (P61.571, P61.572, P61.573)
    Bone fragments.

*Date*
Postdates construction of Pyramid Tomb, perhaps fifth/fourth century BC.

*Bibliography*
McLauchlin (1985:247), Hanfmann (1962:28–30).

## Tomb 100

Limestone sarcophagus with a rectangular depression and a flat limestone lid with beveled edges, on the south edge of the necropolis.

*Associated finds*
    IAM 4537 Silver spouted dish
    IAM 4533 Silver ladle, terminating in calf's head finial.

*Date*
Fifth century BC.

*Bibliography*
McLauchlin (1985:248–249), Butler (1922:83).

## Inhumation/cists

### Tomb 61.1 (?)

Inhumation in the necropolis hill, approx. 1,180 m west of the Artemis temple, with two cover slabs oriented roughly E–W, covering earthy debris in which were three vessels. The original form of the grave is unclear, but it seems to have been a simple cist dug into the earth.

*Associated finds*
    Two lydia, slipped (P61.8:3143, P61.9:3144)
    Lekythos fragment.

*Date*
Probably sixth century?

*Bibliography*
Hanfmann (1962:24), Greenewalt (1972:116–118).

## Tomb 61.2
Inhumation 3–4 m south of Tomb 61.1. A rectangular cist oriented roughly N–S, lined with four schist slabs and probably three cover slabs; floor of tamped earth, covered in a few patches with carbonized material.

*Furnishings*
Fragments of wood and nails suggest the original presence of a wooden couch or sarcophagus.

*Associated finds*
    Skyphoi (P61.1:3130A, P61.1:3130B, P61.3:3132, P61.4:3133, and uninventoried)
    Bowls (P61.6:3136 and P61.5:3135)
    Band cup (P61.2:3131)
    Four undecorated vessels
    Alabaster alabastron (S61.1:3134)
    Barrel-shaped banded agate bead on gold wire (J61.2:3127)
    Gold melon-shaped bead with granulation (J61.1:3126).

*Date*
*c.* 575–540 BC.

*Bibliography*
Hanfmann (1962:27), Greenewalt (1972:118–145).

## Other

## Pyramid Tomb
Located east of the Paktolos, on the north side of a high ridge that runs down from the acropolis. As preserved, a stepped platform of which six limestone steps survive, laid around a core of earth and rubble. The burial chamber has disappeared except for two displaced wall blocks and several floor blocks; the positions of all four walls of the chamber, however, are marked by finely incised lines. The entrance to the chamber was most likely centered in the front (north) wall, perhaps at a higher level than floor. The chamber blocks are only finished on one side.

*Associated finds*
    Achaemenid bowl fragments
    Skyphos fragment (P61.80:3296)
    Jar fragments
    Dish fragments
    Greyware open vessel fragment.

*Date*
Second half of sixth century.

*Bibliography*
Ratté (1992, 1989b:206–215), Butler (1922:167–170), Hanfmann (1961:31, 1962:28–30), Hanfmann and Waldbaum (1970:36–38).

## Mausoleum

Temple-mausoleum implied by marble pediment from probable tomb-temple facade (NoEx 1978.1 and S69.14, see fig. 35). If reconstruction of tomb as temple-like mausoleum is correct, tomb chamber may have been the "cella" of the temple; or it may have been hidden in or under a stepped or podium-like platform. The pediment may also form part of an architectural facade decorating a rock-cut tomb.

*Date*
c. 430–420 BC.

*Bibliography*
Hanfmann (1974a:289–302, 1975:19), Hanfmann and Erhart (1981), Hanfmann and Ramage (1978:18), Demargne (1976:87).

## Tomb number unknown

*Associated finds*
  IAM 4635, Curtis 100 (see fig. 98) Heavy circular ring of gold with carnelian seal: woman holding objects.

*Bibliography*
Curtis (1925).

## Tomb number unknown

*Associated finds*
  IAM 4643, Curtis 105 (see fig. 103) Bone (?) cylinder: two animals.

*Bibliography*
Curtis (1925).

## Miscellaneous other tombs 1

Grave of unknown type at Bin Tepe, near Üç Tepeler, on south edge of ridge between Kocayaşlı and Kendirlik.

*Associated finds*
  Bronze mirror
  Lekythos
  Alabaster alabastron fragments.

*Date*
Fifth century BC.

*Bibliography*
McLauchlin (1985:244).

## Miscellaneous other tombs 2

Grave of unknown type at Bin Tepe, near Üç Tepeler, on south edge of ridge between Kocayaşlı and Kendirlik.

*Associated finds*
Twelve vases, including two large lydia, red and grey ribbed jars with flat bottoms and flaring rims.

*Date*
Fifth century BC.

*Bibliography*
McLauchlin (1985:244–245).

## Miscellaneous other tombs 3
Grave of unknown type at Bin Tepe, in a field just west of Ahlatlı Tepecik.

*Associated finds*
    Two lydia
    Oinochoe
    Plates
    Lekythos
    Achaemenid bowl.

*Date*
Mid-sixth to mid-fourth century.

*Bibliography*
McLauchlin (1985:245).

## Miscellaneous other tombs 4
Confiscated by the Manisa Museum from an inhabitant of Akhisar; these apparently come from the same tomb at Gökçeler Köyü antik devir mezarlığı.

*Associated finds*
    Manisa 5289 One gold sheep couchant
    Manisa 5290 One gold earring of the crescent "boat" type.

## Miscellaneous other tombs 5
Confiscated by the Manisa Museum from an inhabitant of Kendirlik Köyü; all come from a single tumulus at Bin Tepe.

*Associated finds*
    Manisa 6277 Stamped gold foil ornament in the shape of a winged human-headed
        bull with ibex horns
    Manisa 6278 Twenty-nine stamped gold foil ornaments in the shape of eight-petaled
        rosettes
    Manisa 6279 Forty-one stamped gold foil ornaments, crescents formed of eight tiny
        circles
    Manisa 6280 Twenty-nine stamped gold foil ornaments in the shape of eight-petaled
        rosettes
    Manisa 6281 Fifteen stamped gold foil ornaments in the shape of buds
    Manisa 6282 Twenty-six stamped gold foil ornaments in the shape of lotuses
    Manisa 6283 Two tiny pegs with miniscule granulations under the spherical heads

Manisa 6284 Two hollow gold beads in the shape of pomegranates suspended from ribbed cylinders

Manisa 6285 Four ribbed cylinders as 6284, with pegs decorated with six-petaled rosettes

Manisa 6286 Seven six-petaled rosettes on pegs

Manisa 6287 196 stamped gold foil ornaments in the shape of four-petaled rosettes.

*Appendix 4*

# Seals

## Seals carved in imperial koine styles apparently of local Sardian production

### IAM 4636 (fig. 73)

Gold seal ring with diamond-shaped gold bezel, with no separation between bezel and ring. The bezel is carved in intaglio with an open-mouthed lion walking right, its tail curled up over its back. In front of the lion is a circle with two curved lines below; behind it is a bird with hooked beak. Tomb 811. Diam. 2.25 cm; length of bezel 1.6 cm; width of bezel 8.5 mm. "Found in the sarcophagus. In the same tomb were found ring No. 97 [found on the finger of the skeleton in the sarcophagus] and seal No. 109." Curtis No. 90.

### IAM 4637(?) (fig. 74)

Gold seal ring with slightly convex oval bezel, without separation between bezel and ring. The bezel is carved in intaglio with a seated woman facing right and holding out her left arm, sitting on a chair with curved back and legs. Her breasts are accentuated. She wears a long robe; her hair is tied in a knot behind her head. In front of her knees are two small crescents, the upper one horizontal and the lower vertical. The ring is very worn. Tomb S 16. Diam. 1.8 cm; length of bezel 1.5 cm; width of bezel 8.5 mm. "In the sarcophagus with this was also found ring No. 94." Curtis No. 91.

### IAM 4585 (fig. 75)

Gold seal ring with a heavy hoop, much thicker at the ends where it joins the broad, flat, oval gold bezel. The bezel is carved in intaglio with an open-mouthed lion walking right on a groundline, its tail extending behind with the end bent up and forward. Tomb 381. Wt 8 g; diam. ring 2 cm; length of bezel 1.6 cm; width of bezel 1.25 cm. "In the same tomb were found chain No. 25 and beads No. 26." Curtis No. 92.

### IAM 4634 (fig. 76)

Gold seal ring, with carnelian scarab mounted on a swivel. The hoop is of 1.5 mm wire. Thinner wire runs through a hole drilled through the scarab, then passes through perforations in the ends of the hoop wire and wraps six times around the hoop wire on each side. The back of the scarab is shallowly and indistinctly modeled, although its folded wings are indicated by two incised lines. The underside is carved in intaglio with an open-mouthed lion crouching right, its tail curved forward over its back. Tomb S 16. Diam. ring 2.1 cm; length of scarab 1.2 cm; width 8 mm. "In the same sarcophagus was found ring No. 91." Curtis No. 94.

**Fig. 73** From Sardis: IAM 4636. Gold seal ring with lion.

**Fig. 74** From Sardis: IAM 4637. Gold seal ring with seated woman.

**Fig. 75** From Sardis: IAM 4585. Gold seal ring with lion.

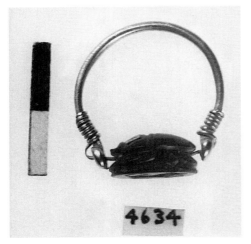

**Fig. 76** From
Sardis: IAM 4634.
Gold and
carnelian scarab
seal ring
with lion.

**Fig. 77** From
Sardis: IAM 4520.
Gold and
carnelian scarab
seal ring with
bull.

## IAM 4520 (fig. 77)

Gold seal ring, with carnelian scarab mounted on a swivel. Thin wire runs through a hole drilled through the scarab, then passes through perforations in the ends of the hoop wire and wraps six times around the hoop wire on each side. The scarab is explicitly modeled, including the head of the beetle and several ridges on the sides to represent its legs. The flat oval undersurface is carved in intaglio with a long-legged bull walking right on a groundline, its tail held in a high loop. Tomb 220. Diam. 2.1 cm; length of scarab 1.6 cm; width 1.25 cm; ht. 1 cm. "In the same tomb were found chain No. 28 and seal No. 112." Curtis No. 96.

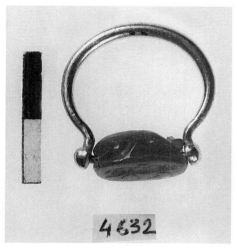

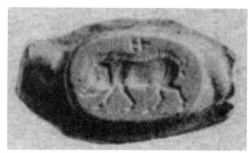

**Fig. 78** From Sardis: IAM 4632. Gold and carnelian scarab seal ring with boar.

**Fig. 79** From Sardis: IAM 4639. Silver and hematite (?) seal ring with lion.

## IAM 4632 (fig. 78)

Gold seal ring, with carnelian scarab mounted on a swivel. The hoop is made of gold wire in the form of a horseshoe that terminates in hemispherical knobs. A pin running through the scarab is riveted to the knobs on either side. The scarab is delicately modeled, with a few incisions to represent the head, wings, and legs. The flat undersurface is carved in intaglio with a bristly boar walking left on a groundline. Above the boar's back is a symbol like the Lydian letter S rotated 90 degrees counter-clockwise. Tomb 722. Diam. 2.2 cm; length of scarab 1.3 cm; width 8.5 mm. Curtis No. 98.

## IAM 4639 (fig. 79)

Very heavy silver ring of horseshoe shape with an oval hematite (?) intaglio mounted on a swivel. A silver wire passes through the stone and the thickened ends of the hoop and is wrapped twice on each side. It has a rounded top and flat oval base

**Fig. 80** From Sardis: IAM 4581. Agate cylinder seal with king figure controlling lion-griffins, standing on sphinx pedestal animals.

**Fig. 81** From Sardis: IAM 4580. Carnelian pyramidal stamp seal with lion.

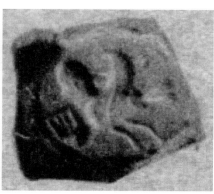

**Fig. 82** From Sardis: IAM 4521. Chalcedony pyramidal stamp seal with human-headed bird.

on which is deeply carved in intaglio a lion crouching right on a groundline, its head small and bent down and its tail curling up and back. Its bristling mane is meticulously shown. In the field above the lion's back is a key-shaped symbol. Tomb 701. Diam. hoop 2.5 cm; diam. wire of hoop 4 mm; length of stone 1.7 cm; ht. 7 mm. Curtis No. 99.

### IAM 4581 (fig. 80)
Agate cylinder seal in a gold mounting consisting of a pin held in place by two gold plates, with a gold loop on top set with granulations. The seal shows a crowned hero-king figure controlling two rampant lion-griffins, with two winged crowned sphinxes as pedestal figures crouching on a groundline. Tomb 813. Total ht. 3 cm; ht. of stone 1.85 cm; diam 7.5 mm. "In the same tomb were found gold ornaments of No. 12." Curtis No. 104.

### IAM 4580 (fig. 81)
Small carnelian pyramidal stamp seal with gold mounting. The setting is a flat gold strip extending down each side of the stone and terminating in a palmette; a pin running through the stone is attached to the strip on either side above the palmettes. A suspension ring is made of three gold wires, the external ones decorated with impressed triangles. The flat sealing face of the stone is carved in intaglio with an open-mouthed lion walking right with its tail raised over its back. Tomb 326. Ht. with mount 1.7 cm; greatest diam. 1 cm; ht. of stone 1.2 cm; base 8 × 7 mm. "In the same tomb were found pendants No. 46 and No. 49." Curtis No. 106.

### IAM 4521 (fig. 82)
Chalcedony pyramidal stamp seal with gold mounting. The setting is a flat gold strip extending roughly halfway down each side of the stone and terminating in

**Fig. 83** From Sardis: IAM 4641. Chalcedony pyramidal stamp seal with goat-sphinx.

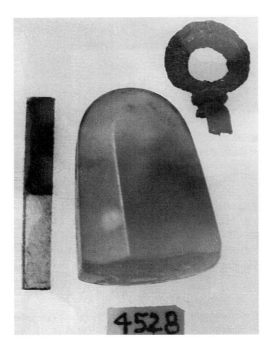

**Fig. 84** From Sardis: IAM 4528. Chalcedony pyramidal stamp seal with lion-griffin.

rounded swellings; a pin runs through the stone halfway down it to attach to the strip. A suspension ring is a gold band with three ribs. The sealing surface is engraved in intaglio with a bearded human-headed bird facing left, holding a lyre before it with one wing. Tomb 24. Total ht. 2.2 cm; greatest diam. of stone 1 cm; width 0.75 cm; ht. of stone 1.5 cm. "In the same tomb were found the two rosettes No. 5 and beads No. 41." Curtis No. 107.

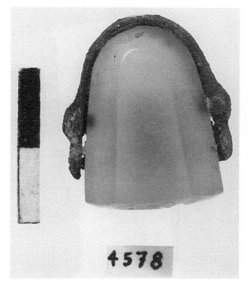 

**Fig. 85** From Sardis: IAM 4578. Chalcedony pyramidal stamp seal with winged figure controlling lions.

### IAM 4641 (fig. 83)

Chalcedony pyramidal stamp seal with gold mounting. The mounting is a gold strip terminating on either side with a carefully executed duck's head with a long broad bill; the ducks' eyes are shown, and the feathers on the backs of their heads are indicated by minute hatching. A pin runs through the stone and connects inside the ducks' heads. A suspension ring is formed of three gold wires, of which the central is the heaviest; the outer wires are beaded. The sealing surface is carved in intaglio with a crouching winged bearded goat-sphinx facing left, with a broad knobbed horn, raising its right forepaw. Above its haunch is a symbol resembling a pointed U with looped ends. Tomb 811. Total ht. 2.95 cm; ht. of stone 2.15 cm; engraved face 1.6 cm broad. "Found in SE corner of a tomb from which came also rings Nos. 90 and 97 [found on the finger of the skeleton in the sarcophagus]." Curtis No. 109.

### IAM 4528 (fig. 84)

Chalcedony pyramidal stamp seal, with silver mounting. The mounting is a flat band extending nearly to the base of the stone and terminating in simplified ducks' bills that hold the pin running through the stone. A suspension ring consists of a larger wire in the center with a smaller beaded wire on either side. The flat sealing surface is carved in intaglio with an open-mouthed winged horned lion-griffin walking right on a groundline. A crescent is in the field before the lion-griffin. Tomb 27. Total ht. 2.9 cm; engraved face of stone 1.3 cm × 0.9 cm. "In the same tomb was found onyx bead No. 54." Curtis No. 110.

### IAM 4578 (fig. 85)

Chalcedony pyramidal stamp seal, with silver mounting consisting of a flat band with simplified ducks' bills holding the pin. A rounded silver band forms the suspension. The flat sealing surface is carved in intaglio with a scene of heroic control: a winged

**Fig. 86** From Sardis: IAM 4525. Chalcedony pyramidal stamp seal with heraldic seated winged lions.

figure in Persian court robe walks left on a ground line, holding by their tails two lions that turn their snarling heads back over their shoulders. Tomb 348. Total ht. 3.1 cm; ht. of stone 2.2 cm; length of engraved face 1.6 cm; width 1.15 cm. Curtis No. 111.

### IAM 4525 (fig. 86)

Chalcedony pyramidal stamp seal, with silver mounting. The mounting consists of a cap that fits over the top two-thirds of the stone, with a raised band around its base; a simple suspension ring is attached to its rounded top. The sealing surface is carved in intaglio with two heraldic seated winged lions, their heads turned back over their wings. Tomb 220. Total ht. 2.3 cm; length of carved face 1.2 cm; width 0.7 cm. "In the same tomb were found chain No. 28 and ring No. 96." Curtis No. 112.

### IAM 4642 (fig. 87)

Blue chalcedony pyramidal stamp seal, with a portion of a silver mounting consisting of a flat silver strip and the pin running through the stone. The flat sealing surface is carved in intaglio with a winged horned lion-griffin walking right on a groundline. In the field before it are three small dots. Tomb 611. Present ht. 2.4 cm; length engraved face 1.5 cm; width 1.05 cm. Curtis No. 113.

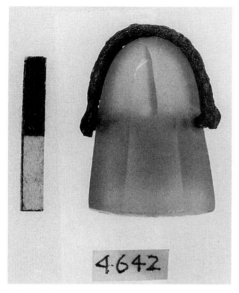

**Fig. 87** From Sardis: IAM 4642. Chalcedony pyramidal stamp seal with lion-griffin.

### IAM 4579 (fig. 88)

Rock crystal pyramidal stamp seal with fragmentary silver mounting in the form of a cap. The sealing surface is carved in intaglio with a seated crowned bearded winged sphinx at left facing a seated winged horned open-mouthed lion at right. They are situated on a double groundline. Tomb 5 (A). Total ht. 2.9 cm; ht. of stone 2.1 cm; length of engraved face 1.65 cm. Curtis No. 114.

### IAM 5134 (fig. 89)

Chalcedony pyramidal stamp seal, with corroded silver mounting consisting of a flat band with simplified ducks' bills holding the pin. The sealing surface is carved in intaglio with an open-mouthed lion-griffin walking right. Tomb 1005. Total ht. 2.6 cm; length of engraved face 1.5 cm. "In the same tomb was found seal No. 120." Curtis No. 115.

### IAM 4589 (fig. 90)

Chalcedony pyramidal stamp seal, missing any mounting. The convex sealing surface is carved in intaglio with a scene of heroic combat: the hero figure wearing Persian military or hunting garb and holding a straight short sword stands at right and grasps by its throat a rampant open-mouthed lion standing on one foot and clawing with the other three. Between the lion and the hero is a symbol resembling a crescent moon with a projection from the inside curve. Tomb 371. Ht. 2.1 cm; length of engraved face 1.6 cm; width 1.2 cm. "In the same tomb were found the gold fragments and beads No. 19 and seal No. 117 [a pyramidal stamp of corroded blue glass paste]." Curtis No. 116.

**Fig. 88** From Sardis: IAM 4579. Rock crystal pyramidal stamp seal with heraldic seated sphinx and lion.

### IAM 4591 (fig. 91)

Carnelian pyramidal stamp seal, missing any mounting. The sealing surface is carved in intaglio with an archer scene: the hero, in Persian military or hunting garb, kneels at right on a groundline and shoots towards a rampant lion with forepaws outstretched and snarling head turned back over its shoulder. Between the hero and the lion is an elaborate symbol. Tomb 364. Ht. 1.9 cm; face 1.3 cm × 1 cm. Curtis No. 118.

### IAM 4527 (fig. 92)

Small chalcedony pyramidal stamp seal, missing any mounting. The sealing surface is carved in intaglio with a heroic combat scene: the hero stands at right on a groundline, wearing Persian court robe and a crenelated crown, holding a short sword in his left hand and grasping a rampant winged horned lion-griffin with his right. Tomb 22. Ht. 1.7 cm; face 1.4 cm × 1.1 cm. "In the same tomb were found beads Nos. 29 and 56." Curtis No. 119.

### IAM 4523 (fig. 93)

Agate (?) weight-shaped seal, with corroded silver mounting of heavy wire forming a large ring (1.1 cm outside diam.) from which extend two wires clasping the sides of the stone and terminating in thickened swellings at the point where a pin runs through the stone. Two short projections protrude laterally from the top of the stone. The bottom surface is carved in intaglio with a lion and bull in combat on a

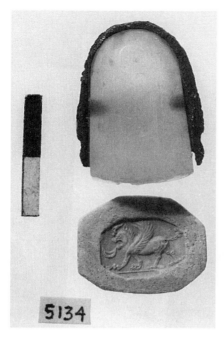

**Fig. 89** From Sardis: IAM 5134. Chalcedony pyramidal stamp seal with lion-griffin.

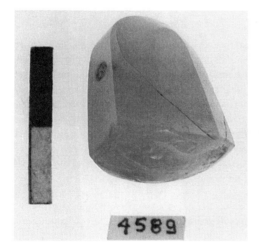

**Fig. 90** From Sardis: IAM 4589. Chalcedony pyramidal stamp seal with hero combating lion.

groundline. The bull faces left and is on its knees with its head thrown back and mouth open; the lion attacks it from the side, clawing with its hind paws at the bull's chest and seizing the bull's back with its teeth as it grips it with its forepaws. An elaborate star and crescent are in the field above the animals' heads; a floral symbol appears above the bull's haunch. Tomb 18. Total ht. 2.4 cm; ht. of stone 1 cm;

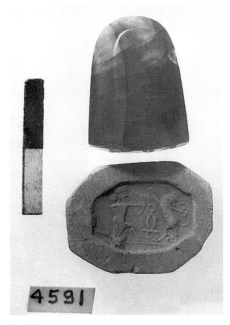

**Fig. 91** From Sardis: IAM 4591. Carnelian pyramidal stamp seal with archer shooting lion.

diam. 1.75 cm. "From the same tomb came gold band No. 13, chain No. 42, pendant No. 50, earrings Nos. 60 and 82 and seal No. 123." Curtis No. 121.

### IAM 4524 (fig. 94)

Agate(?) weight-shaped seal, perforated but missing its mounting. The bottom surface is carved in intaglio with a figure wearing Persian court garb and a crenelated crown sitting on a throne with an elaborate stretcher between the legs and a curved-over back, resting his feet on a footstool. The furniture stands on a groundline. In one hand the figure holds what may be a flower and in the other a round object that may represent the top of a staff. Tomb 18. Ht. 0.85 cm; greatest diam. of engraved face 1.45 cm. "In the same tomb were found gold band No. 13, chain No. 42, pendant No. 50, earrings Nos. 60 and 82 and seal No. 121." Curtis No. 123.

## Seals carved in Neo-Babylonian style

### IAM 5133 (fig. 95)

Large blue flawed chalcedony pyramidal stamp seal, missing any mounting. The sealing surface is carved in intaglio with a Neo-Babylonian worship scene. A bearded figure wearing long fringed belted robe and rounded cap stands at right facing left with one arm raised to a Marduk-dragon crouching on an altar. A winged disk has been carved between their heads; it seems to be carved in shallower depth than the other figures and may be a later addition to the scene. Tomb 1005. Ht. 2.9 cm; intaglio 2.3 cm × 1.5 cm. "In the same tomb was found seal No. 115." Curtis No. 120.

**Fig. 92** From Sardis: IAM 4527. Chalcedony pyramidal stamp seal with hero combating lion-griffin.

## Seals carved in various Greek styles

### IAM 4570 (fig. 96)
Carnelian scarab, one bead from a chain formed of gold and stone beads. Sketchy indication of beetle form on back. On the flat sealing surface is carved in intaglio a heron, or ibis, feeding to the right. Tomb 25. 1.2 cm long. "From the same tomb came pendants Nos. 34–37, mounted button No. 38 and earring No. 68." Curtis No. 33.

### IAM 4519 (fig. 97)
Gold seal ring, with engraved carnelian scarab mounted on a swivel. The hoop is of 2 mm wire. Thinner wire runs through a hole drilled through the scarab, then passes through perforations in the ends of the hoop and wraps five times around the wire on each side. The scarab has very little modeling: two incised lines mark the wings. The flat undersurface is carved in intaglio with a winged Eros figure flying right, holding a wreath in his left hand and a branch in the right. Tomb B (1). Diam. ring 2.2 cm; length of scarab 1 cm; width 6 mm. Curtis No. 93.

### IAM 4635 (fig. 98)
Heavy gold seal ring, thickening from back to front, with a carnelian bezel set in a cavity in the broadest part. It is engraved in intaglio with a skirted figure moving right, holding objects (sistra?) in upraised hands. No tomb number given. Diam. hoop 2.5 cm; length of stone 9 mm. Curtis No. 100.

### IAM 4518 (fig. 99)
Bracelet of gold wire, with a large chalcedony seal mounted on a swivel. The bracelet is of 3 mm thick wire with loops at each end; the seal is secured to the bracelet by a wire that runs through the stone and the loops and is then wrapped back around

**Fig. 93**   From Sardis: IAM 4523. Agate (?) weight-shaped seal with lion and bull.

**Fig. 94**   From Sardis: IAM 4524. Agate (?) weight-shaped seal with seated king figure.

**Fig. 95** From Sardis: IAM 5133. Chalcedony pyramidal stamp seal with worship scene.

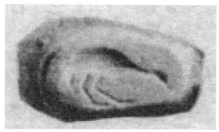

**Fig. 96** From Sardis: IAM 4570. Carnelian scarab with bird.

itself between the stone and the loops. The seal is rounded above; its flat underside is carved in intaglio with Athena and Hermes facing each other on a groundline. Athena, at left, wears a Corinthian helmet with her weight on her left foot and her spear held upright in her left hand, holding her shield with her right hand. Hermes, at right, is naked but has a chlamys draped over his left arm and wears a petasos. He stands on his right foot; with his left hand he holds the caduceus, and his right hand is extended towards Athena's spear. "The bracelet was found in a sarcophagus of different type from the usual variety." Tomb A (1). Diam. 7.1 cm; length of stone 3 cm; ht. 1.3 cm. "In the same tomb were found earrings 79 and 80." Curtis No. 101.

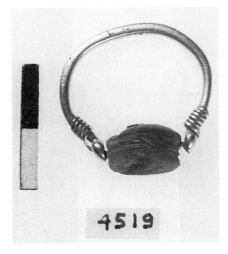

**Fig. 97** From Sardis: IAM 4519. Gold and carnelian scarab seal ring with winged Eros.

**Fig. 98** From Sardis: IAM 4635. Gold and carnelian seal ring with winged figure.

## Seals carved in schematic rounded styles

### IAM 4640 (fig. 100)

White paste scarab (faience?), perforated lengthwise but with no trace of mounting. The scarab preserves little modeling. The flat undersurface is carved in intaglio with a schematic representation of a man running right. Two vertical gouges in the field may be crescents, fish, or other. Tomb 837. Length 1.7 cm; width 6.5 cm; ht. 8 mm. Curtis No. 102.

### IAM 4522 (fig. 101)

Chalcedony pyramidal stamp seal with gold mounting of a flat gold strip and pin, with swellings at the terminations of the strip. A suspension ring is made of two

**Fig. 99** From Sardis: IAM 4518. Bracelet with chalcedony seal with Athena and Hermes.

**Fig. 100** From Sardis: IAM 4640. White paste scarab with figure running right.

parallel gold wires with granulation of different sizes between. The flat sealing surface is engraved in intaglio with a winged human figure moving left, holding uncertain objects in outstretched hands. Tomb 213. Total ht. 2.3 cm; ht. of stone 1.5 cm; greatest diam. of face 1 cm; width 0.7 cm. "In the same tomb were found chain No. 52, rattle No. 85, rings Nos. 88 and 95 and probably bead No. 54." Curtis No. 108.

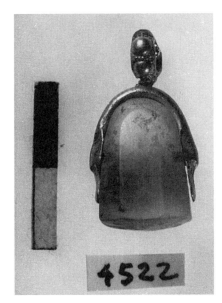

**Fig. 101** From Sardis: IAM 4522. Chalcedony pyramidal stamp seal with winged figure.

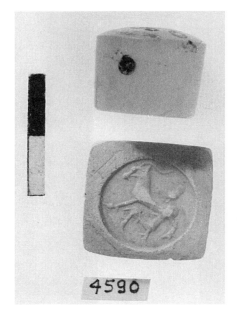

**Fig. 102** From Sardis: IAM 4590. Chalcedony weight-shaped seal with suckling goat.

## IAM 4590 (fig. 102)

Chalcedony weight-shaped seal, perforated but with its mounting missing. The sealing surface is carved in intaglio with a nanny goat facing right with a suckling kid facing left. A bird stands on the goat's back, facing left with its head turned back to

**Fig. 103** From Sardis: IAM 4643. Bone or shell cylinder seal with heraldic animals.

the right; a fish swims downward behind the goat's haunches. Tomb 327. Ht. 1.4 cm; diam. of engraved face 1.5 cm. Curtis No. 122.

## Seals carved in linear styles

### IAM 4643 (fig. 103)

Bone or shell cylinder seal, with a trace of a silver pin at one end. A schematic, linear rendering of two heraldic animals, either horses or stags, standing with a tree between their heads and another between their tails. Uncertain symbols in the field above each animal's back. No tomb number. Ht. 2 cm; diam 1.2 cm. Curtis No. 105.

# Achaemenid bowls

For complete information on these pots, see Dusinberre (1999).

### Deposit 1 (earlier fifth century BC) (fig. 63)

1. P84.46:8895, 2. P84.47:8896, 3. 87.1, 4. 328.1, 5. 138.1, 6. 88.3, 7. 90.2, 8. 82.2, 9. 93.1, 10. 88.2, 11. 88.1, 12. 82.1, 13. 90.1, 14. 94.1, 15. 99.1, 16. 82.3.

### Deposit 2 (earlier fourth century BC) (fig. 64)

1. 76.1.

### Deposit 3 (*c.* 350–325 BC) (fig. 65)

1. 53.1, 2. 53.2, 3. 53.3.

### Deposit 4 (fourth century BC) (fig. 66)

1. 25.1, 2. 11.3, 3. 11.2, 4. 25.3, 5. 13.2, 6. 25.2, 7. 11.1, 8. 12.1, 9. 17.1, 10. 13.3, 11. 13.5, 12. 13.1, 13. 25.6, 14. 13.4, 15. 12.2, 16. 17.3, 17. 25.5, 18. 12.3, 19. 17.2, 20. 25.4, 21. 25.7, 22. 25.8, 23. 17.4, 24. 13.6, 25. 13.7, 26. 25.9, 27. 25.10, 28. 25.11.

### Deposit 5 (fourth century BC) (fig. 67)

1. 63.1, 2. 63.2, 3. 63.3.

### Deposit 6 (third century BC) (fig. 68)

1. 92.1, 2. 92.2, 3. 92.3, 4. 92.5, 5. 92.4, 6. 92.6, 7. 92.7, 8. 92.8, 9. 92.9.

### Deposit 7 (late third/early second century BC) (fig. 69)

1. 35.1, 2. 46.2, 3. 46.3, 4. 46.5, 5. 46.4, 6. 46.1.

### Deposit 8 "Hellenistic Lydian 213 BC Destruction" (fig. 70)

1. P60.392:2844, 2. P61.343:3746, 3. P65.249:6911, 4. P98.198:11022, 5. P64.91:6095, 6. P61.115:3357, 7. P.65.257:6919.

# References

Abdi, K. (forthcoming) "Hamadan," in A. Green ed., *Archaeological Encyclopaedia of Syro-Mesopotamia, Iran and the Arabian Peninsula*

Abraham, K. (1995) "The Egibis in Elam," *Languages and Cultures in Contact: Programme and Abstracts of the 42e Rencontre Assyriologique Internationale* (Leuven) (unpaginated)

Adams, R.McC. (1979) "Late Hispanic Empires of the New World," in M.T. Larsen ed., *Power and Propaganda: A Symposium on Ancient Empires* (Copenhagen):59–73

  (1992) "Ideologies: Unity and Diversity," in A.A. Demarest and G.W. Conrad eds., *Ideology and Pre-Columbian Civilizations* (Santa Fe):205–222

Agricola, E.F.M. (1900) *De Aristidis censu* (Berlin)

Ahn, G. (1992) *Religiöse Herrscherlegitimation im achämenidischen Iran* (ActIr 31) (Leiden)

Akurgal, E. (1956) "Recherches faites à Cyzique et à Ergili," *Anatolia* 1:15–24

  (1966) "Griechisch-Persische Reliefs aus Daskyleion," *IrAnt* 6:147–156

Alcock, S.E. (1989) "Archaeology and Imperialism: Roman Expansion and the Greek City," *JMA* 2:87–135

  (1991) "Tomb Cult and the Post-Classical Polis," *AJA* 95:447–467

  (1993) *Graecia Capta: The Landscapes of Roman Greece* (Cambridge, UK)

Allsen, T.T. (1987) *Mongol Imperialism* (Berkeley)

Al-Masudi ([1863] 1977) *Les prairies d'or*, Vol. II. Trans. by C.B. de Meynard and P. de Courteille (Paris); English translation by G. Herrmann, in *The Iranian Revival* (Oxford)

Altheim-Stiehl, R., D. Metzler, and E. Schwertheim (1983) "Eine neue gräko-persische Grabstele aus Sultaniye Köy und ihre Bedeutung für die Geschichte und Topographie von Daskyleion," *Epigraphica Anatolica* 1:1–23

Amiet, P. (1972) *Glyptique susienne des origines à l'époque des perses achéménides* (Mémoires de la DAFI 43) (Paris)

  (1973) "La glyptique de la fin de l'Elam," *Ars Asiatiques* 28:3–45

  (1974) "Quelques observations sur le palais de Darius à Suse," *Syria* 51:65–73

  (1980) *Art of the Ancient Near East* (New York)

  (1994) "Un étage au palais de Darius à Suse?" in M. Dietrich and O. Loretz eds., *Beschreiben und Deuten in der Archäologie des Alten Orients: Festschrift für Ruth Mayer-Opificius* (Munster):1–5

Anderson, B. (1991) *Imagined Communities: Reflections on the Origin and Spread of Nationalism*, rev. edn. (London)

Appadurai, A. ed. (1986) *The Social Life of Things: Commodities in Cultural Perspective* (Cambridge)

Arcelin, P. (1992) "Société indigène et propositions culturelles massaliotes en basse Provence occidentale," in M. Bats, G. Bertucchi, A. Congès, and H. Treziny eds., *Marseille grecque et la Gaule* (Études Massaliètes 3) (Aix):305–336

Asheri, D. (1996) "L'ideale monarchico di Dario: Erodoto III.80–82 e DNb Kent," *AASA* 3:99–106

Ateşlier, S. (1997) "Daskyleion'da Satraplık Dönemine Ait Erken Klasik Bir Yapı Üzerine Düşünceler," Paper read at the First International Symposium on Anatolia in the Achaemenid Period (Bandırma)

Atkinson, K.T.M. (1972) "A Hellenistic Land-Conveyance: The Estate of Mnesimachos in the Plain of Sardis," *Historia* 22:45–74

Badian, E. (1968) *Publicans and Sinners* (Oxford)

Baines, J. (1996) "On the Composition and Inscriptions of the Vatican Statue of Udjahorresnet," in P. der Manuelian ed., *Studies in Honor of W.K. Simpson*, Vol. I (Boston):83–92

Bakır, T. (1991) "Daskyleion," *Höyük* 1:75–84

(1995) "Archäologische Beobachtungen über die Residenz in Daskyleion," in P. Briant ed., *Dans les pas de Dix-Mille. Peuples et pays du Proche-Orient vus par un grec* (Actes de la Table Ronde Internationale, Toulouse, 3–4 February 1995) (*Pallas, Revue d'études antiques*, 43) (Toulouse):268–285

(1997) "Satrapie in Daskyleion," Paper read at the First International Symposium on Anatolia in the Achaemenid Period (Bandırma)

Balcer, J.M. (1972) "The Date of Herodotus IV. 1. Darius' Scythian Expedition," *HSCIP* 76:99–132

(1977) "The Athenian *Episkopos* and the Achaemenid 'King's Eye,'" *AJPh* 391:252–263

(1984) *Sparda by the Bitter Sea: Imperial Interaction in Western Anatolia* (Chico, Calif.)

(1997) "The Liberation of Ionia: 478 BC," *Historia* 46(3):374–377

Balkan, K. (1959) "Inscribed Bullae from Daskyleion-Ergili," *Anatolia* 4:123–128

Barag, D. (1968) "An Unpublished Achaemenid Cut Glass Bowl from Nippur," *JGS* 10:17–20

(1985) *Catalogue of Western Asiatic Glass in the British Museum*, Vol. I (London)

Bares, L. (1996) "Foundation Deposits in the Tomb of Udjahorresnet at Abusir," *ZÄS* 123:1–9

Barnett, R.D. (1976) *Sculptures from the North Palace of Ashurbanipal* (London)

Barnett, R.D. and M. Falkner (1962) *The Sculptures of Assur-nasir-apli, c. 883–859 BC, Tiglathpileser III, c. 745–727 BC and Esarhaddon, 681–669 BC from the Central and South-West Palaces at Nimrud* (London)

Barth, F. (1969) *Ethnic Groups and Boundaries: The Social Organisation of Cultural Difference* (London)

Baslez, M.F. (1986) "Présence et traditions iraniennes dans les cités de l'Egée," *REA* 87(1–2):137–155

Bats, M. (1988) *Vaisselle et alimentation à Olbia de Provence (v. 350–50 av. JC). Modèles culturels et catégories céramiques* (*RAN* Supplement 18) (Paris)

Beaulieu, P.-A. (1989) *The Reign of Nabonidus, King of Babylon, 556–539 BC* (New Haven and London)

Bedford, P.R. (1996) "Early Achaemenid Monarchs and Indigenous Cults: Towards the Definition of Imperial Policy," in M. Dillon ed., *Religion in the Ancient World: New Themes and Approaches* (Amsterdam):17–39

Bedon, R., R. Chevallier, and P. Pinon (1988) *Architecture et urbanisme en Gaule romaine* (Paris)

Bekker-Nielsen, T. (1989) *The Geography of Power: Studies in the Urbanisation of Roman North-West Europe* (BAR International Series 477) (Oxford)

Benveniste, E. (1965) "Termes de parenté dans les langues indo-européennes," *L'Homme* 5:5–16

Berdan, F.F. (1986) "Enterprise and Empire in Aztec and Early Colonial Mexico," in B.L. Isaac ed., *Research in Economic Anthropology: Economic Aspects of Prehispanic Highland Mesoamerica* (Greenwich, Conn.):281–302

(1987) "The Economics of Aztec Luxury Trade and Tribute," in E.H. Boone ed., *The Aztec Templo Mayor* (Washington, DC):161–183

Berg, S.B. (1979) *The Book of Esther: Motifs, Themes and Structure* (Society of Biblical Literature, Dissertation Series 44) (Missoula).

Berlin, A. (1998) *Tel Anafa, Vol. II: The Persian, Hellenistic and Early Roman Plainwares* (*JRA* Supplement) (Portsmouth, R.I.)

Bernard, P. (1964) "Une pièce d'armure perse sur un monument lycien," *Syria* 41:195–212

Binford, L.R. (1971) "Mortuary Practices: Their Study and Potential," *American Antiquity* 36(3–2):6–29

Bintliff, J.L. and A.M. Snodgrass (1985) "The Cambridge/Bradford Boeotian Expedition: The First Four Years," *JFA* 12:123–161

Birmingham, J.M. (1961) "The Overland Route across Anatolia in the Eighth and Seventh Centuries BC," *Anatolian Studies* 11:185–195

Bittel, K. (1970) *Hattusha: The Capital of the Hittites* (Oxford)

Bivar, A.D.H. (1961) "A 'Satrap' of Cyrus the Younger," *Numismatic Chronicle* (Series 7) 1:119–127

(1970) "A Persian Monument at Athens, and Its Connections with the Achaemenid State Seals," in M. Boyce and I. Gershevitch eds., *W.B. Henning Memorial Volume* (London):43–61

Black, J. and A. Green (1992) *Gods, Demons and Symbols of Ancient Mesopotamia: An Illustrated Dictionary* (London)

Blagg, T.F.C. (1985) "Cult Practice and Its Social Context in the Religious Sanctuaries of Latium and Southern Etruria: The sanctuary of Diana at Nemi," in C. Malone and S. Stoddart eds., *Papers in Italian Archaeology IV. Part iv: Classical and Medieval Archaeology* (BAR International Series 246) (Oxford):33–50

(1986) "Roman Religious Sites in the British Landscape," *Landscape History* 8:15–25

Blázquez, J.M. (1989) "¿Romanización o asimilación?" in J.M. Blázquez ed., *Nuevos Estudios sobre la Romanización* (Madrid):99–145

Blegen, C.W. (1963) *Troy and the Trojans* (London)

Blegen, C.W., J.L. Caskey, M. Rawson, and J. Sperling (1950) *Troy I: The First and Second Settlements* (Princeton)

Blegen, C.W., J.L. Caskey, and M. Rawson (1951) *Troy II: The Third, Fourth, and Fifth Settlements* (Princeton)

(1953) *Troy III: The Sixth Settlement* (Princeton)

Blegen, C.W., C.G. Boulter, J.L. Caskey, and M. Rawson (1958) *Troy IV: The Seventh Settlement* (Princeton)

Boardman, J. (1959) "Chian and Early Ionic Architecture," *The Antiquaries Journal* 39:173–217

(1970a) *Greek Gems and Finger Rings: Early Bronze Age to Late Classical* (London)

(1970b) "Pyramidal Stamp Seals in the Persian Empire," *Iran* 8:19–46

(1976) "Greek and Persian Glyptic in Anatolia and Beyond," *RA*:45–54

(1998) "Seals and Signs. Anatolian Stamp Seals of the Persian Period Revisited," *Iran* 36:1–13

Bodde, D. (1967) *China's First Ruler* (Hong Kong)

Boffo, L. (1978) "La lettera di Dario I a Gadata: i privilegi del tempio di Apollo a Magnesia sul Meandro," *Bollettino dell'Istituto di Diritto Romano "Vittorio Scialoja"* 81:267–303

Bollweg, J. (1988) "Protoachämenidische Siegelbilder," *AMI* 21:53–61

Bookidis, N. (1967) "A Study of the Use and Geographical Distribution of Architectural Sculpture in the Archaic Period." Ph.D. Dissertation, Bryn Mawr College

Borchhardt, J. (1968) "Epichorische, gräko-persische beeinflußte Reliefs in Kilikien," *IstMitt* 18:161–211

(1980) "Zur Deutung lykischer Audienzszenen," in H. Metzger ed., *Actes du Colloque sur la Lycie Antique, Istanbul 1977* (Paris):7–12

Borger, R. (1982) "Die Chronologie des Darius-Denkmals am Behistun Felsen," *Nachrichten der Akademie der Wissenschaften in Göttingen, philosophische-historische Klasse* 3:105–131

Börker-Klähn, J. (1982) *Altvorderasiatische Bildstelen und Vergleichbare Felsreliefs* (Mainz am Rhein)

Boucharlat, R. (1984) "Monuments religieux de la Perse achéménide: État des questions," in G. Roux ed., *Temples et Sanctuaires* (Lyon):119–135

(1990a) "La fin des palais achéménides de Suse: une mort naturelle," in F. Vallat ed., *Contribution à l'histoire de l'Iran: Mélanges offerts à Jean Perrot* (Paris):225–233

(1990b) "Suse et la Susiane à l'époque achéménide: données archéologiques," in H. Sancisi-Weerdenburg and A. Kuhrt eds., *Achaemenid History IV: Centre and Periphery* (Leiden):149–175

(1997) "Susa under Achaemenid Rule," in J. Curtis ed., *Mesopotamia and Iran in the Persian Period: Conquest and Imperialism 539–331 BC* (London):54–67

(1998) "A la recherche d'Ecbatane sur Tepe Hegmataneh," in R. Boucharlat, J.E. Curtis, and E. Haerinck eds., *Neo-Assyrian, Median, Achaemenian and Other Studies in Honor of David Stronach*, Vol. I (*Iranica Antiqua* 33) (Ghent):173–186

Bourdieu, P. (1977) *Outline of a Theory of Practice*. Trans. by R. Nice (Cambridge, UK)

([1979] 1984) *Distinction. A Social Critique of the Judgement of Taste* (London)

Bowersock, G.W. (1986) "The Mechanics of Subversion in the Roman Provinces," in A. Giovannini ed., *Opposition et résistance à l'empire d'Auguste à Trajan* (Entretiens Hardt 33):291–320

Bowman, R.A. (1970) *Aramaic Ritual Texts from Persepolis* (Chicago)

Boyce, M. (1975) *A History of Zoroastrianism*, Vol. I (Leiden)

(1982) *A History of Zoroastrianism*, Vol. II (Cologne)

Bradley, R. (1984) *The Social Foundations of Prehistoric Britain: Themes and Variations in the Archaeology of Power* (London)

(1990) *Monuments and the Monumental* (*WA* 22.2) (London)

Bregstein, L. (1993) "Seal Selection and Seal Usage in Fifth Century BC Nippur, Iraq: A Study of the Murashu Archive." Ph.D. Dissertation, University of Pennsylvania

(1997) "Sealing Practice in the Fifth Century BC Murashu Archive from Nippur, Iraq," in M.-F. Boussac and A. Invernizzi eds., *Archives et sceaux du monde hellénistique. Archivi e sigilli nel mondo ellenistico* (*BCH* Supplement 29) (Paris):53–63

Bresciani, E. (1985) "Ugiahorresnet a Menfi," *Egitto e Vicino Oriente* 8:1–6

Brewer, J. and R. Porter eds. (1993) *Consumption and the World of Goods* (London)

Briant, P. (1973) "Remarques sur *laoi* et esclaves ruraux en Asie Mineure hellénistique," *Actes du colloque 1971 sur l'esclavage. Annales littéraires de l'Université de Besançon* (Paris):93–133

(1982) *Rois, tributs et paysans: études sur les formations tributaires au Moyen Orient ancien* (Paris)

(1984) *L'Asie Centrale et les royaumes proche-orientaux du premier millénnaire* (Paris)

(1985a) "Dons de terres et de villes: l'Asie Mineure dans le contexte achéménide," *REA* 87(1–2):53–71

(1985b) "Les Iraniens d'Asie Mineure après la chute de l'empire achéménide," *DHA* 11:167–195

(1986) "Polythéisme et empire unitaire (Remarques sur la politique religieuse des Achéménides)," *Les grandes figures religieuses: fonctionnement pratique et symbolique dans l'antiquité (Besançon 25–26 avril 1984)* (Centre de Recherches d'Histoire Ancienne, Vol. LXVIII) (Paris):425–443

(1987) "Pouvoir central et polycentrisme culturel dans l'empire achéménide: Quelques réflexions et suggestions," in H. Sancisi-Weerdenburg ed., *Achaemenid History I: Sources, Structures and Synthesis* (Leiden):1–32

(1988a) "Ethno-classe dominante et populations soumises dans l'empire achéménide: le cas d'Egypte," in A. Kuhrt and H. Sancisi-Weerdenburg eds., *Achaemenid History III: Method and Theory* (Leiden):137–174

(1988b) "Le nomadisme du Grand Roi," *IrAnt* 23:252–273

(1989a) "Histoire et idéologie: les grecs et la 'décadence perse,'" in M.M. Mactoux and E. Gery eds., *Mélanges P. Léveque*, Vol. II (Paris and Besançon):33–47

(1989b) "Table du roi, tribut et redistribution chez les Achéménides," in P. Briant and C. Herrenschmidt eds., *Les tributs dans l'empire perse: Actes de la Table Ronde de Paris, 12–13 décembre 1986* (Paris):35–44

(1990) "The Seleucid Kingdom, the Achaemenid Empire and the History of the Near East in the First Millennium BC," in P. Bilde, T. Engberg-Pedersen, L. Hannestand, and J. Zahle eds., *Religion and Religious Practice in the Seleucid Kingdom* (Aarhus): 40–65

(1991) "De Sardes à Suse," in H. Sancisi-Weerdenburg and A. Kuhrt eds., *Achaemenid History VI: Asia Minor and Egypt: Old Cultures in a New Empire* (Leiden): 67–82

(1993) "Alexandre à Sardes," in *Alexander the Great: Myth and Reality* (*ARID* Supplement 21) (Rome):1–15

(1994a) "L'histoire achéménide: sources, méthodes, raisonnements et modèles," *TOPOI* 4:109–130

(1994b) "Sources gréco-hellénistiques, institutions perses et institutions macédoniens: continuités, changements et bricolages," in H. Sancisi-Weerdenburg, A. Kuhrt, and M.C. Root eds., *Achaemenid History VIII: Continuity and Change* (Leiden):283–310

(1996) *Histoire de l'empire perse de Cyrus à Alexandre* (Paris)

(1997a) *Bulletin d'histoire achéménide (I)* (*BHAch* I), *TOPOI* Supplement 1

(1997b) "Greek Epigraphy and Achaemenid Imperial Governing in Western Asia Minor: a View from Xanthos," *Papers Read at the First International Symposium on Anatolia in the Achaemenid Period* (Bandırma)

(1998) "Droaphernès et la statue de Sardes," in M. Brosius and A. Kuhrt eds., *Achaemenid History XI: Studies in Persian History: Essays in Memory of David M. Lewis* (Leiden):205–226

(1999) "War, Persian Society and the Achaemenid Empire," in K. Raaflaub and N. Rosenstein eds., *Soldiers, Society and War in the Ancient and Medieval Worlds* (Cambridge, Mass.):105–128

Brill, R.H. and N.D. Cahill (1988) "A Red Opaque Glass from Sardis and Some Thoughts on Red Opaques in General," *JGS* 30:16–27

Brinkmann, R. (1971) "The Geology of Western Anatolia," in A.S. Campbell ed., *The Geology and History of Turkey* (Tripoli):171–190

British Museum Department of Greek and Roman Antiquities (1900) *The Nereid Monument and Later Lycian Sculpture* (London)

Brosius, M. (1996) *Women in Ancient Persia 559–331 BC* (Oxford)

(1998) "Artemis Persike and Artemis Anaitis," in M. Brosius and A. Kuhrt eds., *Achaemenid History XI: Studies in Persian History: Essays in Memory of David M. Lewis* (Leiden):227–238

Brown, J.A. (1971) "Introduction," in J.A. Brown ed., *Approaches to the Social Dimensions of Mortuary Practices*, SAA Memoir 25:1–5

Brown, S.C. (1986) "Media and Secondary State Formation in the Neo-Assyrian Zagros," *JCS* 38:107–119

(1997) "Ecbatana," *EncIr* 8(1):80a–84a

Brumfiel, E.M. (1983) "Aztec State Making: Ecology, Structure and the Origin of the State," *American Anthropologist* 85:261–284

(1987) "Elite and Utilitarian Crafts in the Aztec State," in E.M. Brumfiel and T.K. Earle eds., *Specialization, Exchange and Complex Societies* (Cambridge, UK): 102–118

(1996) "Figurines and the Aztec State: Testing the Effectiveness of Ideological Domination," in R. Wright ed., *Gender and Archaeology* (Philadelphia):143–166

Brunt, P.A. (1976) "The Romanization of the Local Ruling Classes in the Roman Empire," in D.M. Pippidi ed., *Assimilation et résistance à la culture gréco-romaine dans le monde ancien* (Paris):161–173

Bryce, T.R. (1986) *The Lycians in Literary and Epigraphic Sources* (Copenhagen)

Buckler, W.H. (1924) *Sardis Vol. VI, Part II. Lydian Inscriptions* (Leiden)

Buckler, W.H. and D.M. Robinson (1912) "Greek Inscriptions from Sardis I," *AJA* 16:11–18

(1932) *Sardis Vol. VII: Greek and Latin Inscriptions Part I* (Leiden)

Burkard, G. (1995) "Literarische Tradition und historische Realität. Die persische Eroberung Ägyptens am Beispiel Elephantine," *ZÄS* 122(1):31–37

Buschor, E. (1933) "Altsamische Grabstelen," *AthMitt* 58:22–46

Butler, H.C. (1911) "Second Preliminary Report on the American Excavations at Sardes in Asia Minor," *AJA* 15:445–458

(1922) *Sardis I. The Excavations* (Leiden)

Cahill, N.D. (1985) "The Treasury at Persepolis: Gift-Giving at the City of the Persians," *AJA* 89:373–389

(1988) "Taş Kule: A Persian-Period Tomb near Phokaia," *AJA* 92:481–501.

Calder, W.M. (1925) "The Royal Road in Herodotus," *CR* 39:7–11

Calmeyer, P. (1993) "Die Gefässe auf den Gabenbringer-Reliefs in Persepolis," *AMI* 26:147–160

Campbell, C. (1987) *The Romantic Ethic and the Spirit of Modern Consumerism* (Oxford)

(1993) "Understanding Traditional and Modern Patterns of Consumption in Eighteenth Century England: A Character Action Approach," in J. Brewer and R. Porter eds., *Consumption and the World of Goods* (London):40–57

Cannon, A. (1989) "The Historical Dimension in Mortuary Expressions of Status and Sentiment," *Current Anthropology* 30:437–458

(1991) "Gender, Status, and the Focus of Material Display," in D. Walde and N.D. Willows eds., *The Archaeology of Gender: Proceedings of the 22nd Annual Chacmool Conference* (Calgary):144–149

Cardascia, G. (1951) *Les archives de Murashu: une famille d'hommes d'affaires babyloniens à l'époque perse (455–403 av. JC)* (Paris)

Cargill, J. (1977) "The Nabonidus Chronicle and the Fall of Lydia," *AJAH* 2:97–116

Carradice, I. ed. (1987) *Coinage and Administration in the Athenian and Persian Empires* (BAR International Series 343) (Oxford)

Carter, E. (1996) *Excavations at Anshan (Tal-e Malyan): The Middle Elamite Period* (Philadelphia)

Casabonne, O. (1996) "Présence et influence perses en Cilicie à l'époque achéménide. Iconographie et représentations," *Anatolica Antiqua* 4:121–145

(1998) "Conquête perse et phénomène monétaire: l'exemple cilicien," in O. Casabonne ed., *Mécanismes et innovations monétaires dans l'Anatolie achéménide: numismatique et histoire (Varia Anatolica* 10) (Paris)

Cattenat, A. and J.-C. Gardin (1977) "Diffusion comparée de quelques genres de poterie caractéristiques de l'époque achéménide sur le Plateau Iranien et en Asie Centrale," in J. Deshayes ed., *Le Plateau Iranien et l'Asie Centrale des origines à la conquête islamique* (Colloques internationaux du Centre National de la Recherche Scientifique 567) (Paris):225–248

Chapman, G.A.H. (1972) "Herodotus and Histiaeus' Role in the Ionian Revolt," *Historia* 21:546–68

Chapman, R., I. Kinnes, and K. Randsborg eds. (1981) *The Archaeology of Death* (Cambridge)

Chaumont, M.L. (1990) "Un nouveau gouverneur de Sardes à l'époque achéménide d'après une inscription récemment découverte," *Syria* 57(3):579–608

Cherry, J.F., J.L. Davis, and E. Mantzourani (1991) *Landscape Archaeology as Long-Term History: Northern Keos in the Cycladic Islands* (Los Angeles)

Childs, W.A.P. (1978) *The City-Reliefs of Lycia* (Princeton)

(1981) "Lycian Relations with Persians and Greeks in the Fifth and Fourth Centuries Re-examined," *Anatolian Studies* 31:55–80

(1983) "Lycian Art of the Classical Period," *AJA* 87:229

Claessen, H.J.M. and P. Skalnik eds. (1978) *The Early State* (The Hague)

Clark, J. (1981) "Guatemalan Obsidian Sources and Quarries: Additional Notes," *Journal of New World Archaeology* 4:1–15

Clermont-Ganneau, S. (1921) "Le paradeisos royal achéménide de Sidon," *RBibl* 30:106–109

Clifford, J. and G.E. Marcus eds. (1986) *Writing Culture: The Poetics and Politics of Ethnography* (Berkeley)

Cohen, G.M. (1983) "Colonization and Population Transfer in the Hellenistic World," in E. van Dack, P. van Dessel, and W. van Gucht eds., *Egypt and the Hellenistic World* (Leuven):63–74

Collon, D. (1987) *First Impressions: Cylinder Seals in the Ancient Near East* (London)
   (1992) "Banquets in the Art of the Ancient Near East," *Banquets d'Orient* (*Res Orientales* 4):23–29
   (1997) "A Hoard of Sealings from Ur," in M.-F. Boussac and A. Invernizzi eds., *Archives et sceaux du monde hellénistique. Archivi e sigilli nel mondo ellenistico* (BCH Supplement 29) (Paris):65–84

Conkey, M. and C. Hastorf eds. (1990) *The Uses of Style in Archaeology* (Cambridge, UK)

Conrad, G.W. and A.A. Demarest (1984) *Religion and Empire: The Dynamics of Aztec and Inca Expansionism* (Cambridge, UK)

Cook, J.M. (1982) *The Persian Empire* (New York)

Cook, S.A. (1917) "A Lydian–Aramaic Bilingual," *JHS* 37:77–87, 219–231

Cooney, J.D. (1953) "The Portrait of an Egyptian Collaborator," *Brooklyn Museum Bulletin* 15:1–16

Cosgrove, D.E. (1984) *Social Formation and Symbolic Landscape* (London)

Cosgrove, D.E. and S. Daniels eds. (1988) *The Iconography of Landscape: Essays on the Symbolic Representation, Design and Use of Past Environments* (Cambridge, UK)

Costin, C.L. (1991) "Craft Specialization: Issues in Defining, Documenting, and Explaining the Organization of Production," *Archaeological Method and Theory* 3:1–56

Cowley, A.E. (1921) "L'inscription bilingue araméo-lydienne de Sardes," *Comptes rendus de l'académie des inscriptions et belles-lettres*:7–14

Crawford, M.H. (1986) "Introduction," in M.H. Crawford ed., *L'imperio romano e le strutture economiche e sociali delle province* (Biblioteca di Athenaeum 4) (Como):9–12

Cremer, M. (1984) "Zwei neue gräko-persische Stelen," *Epigraphica Anatolica* 3:89–90

Cuny, A. (1920) "L'inscription lydo-araméenne de Sardes I," *REA* 22:259–272
   (1921) "L'inscription lydo-araméenne de Sardes II," *REA* 23:1–27

Curtis, C.D. (1925) *Sardis XIII. Jewelry and Gold Work* (Rome)

Damerji, M.S.B. (1999) *Gräber Assyrischer Königinnen aus Nimrud* (Mainz)

Dandamaev, M.A. (1963) "Foreign Slaves on the Estates of the Achaemenid Kings and their Nobles, II," *International Congress of Orientalists, XXV, Moscow 1960* (Moscow): 147–154
   (1975) "Forced Labour in the Palace Economy of Achaemenid Iran," *Altorientalische Forschungen* 2:71–78
   (1984) "Royal *Paradeisoi* in Babylonia," in *Orientalia J. Duchesne-Guillemin Emerito Oblata* (Leiden):113–117
   (1989) *A Political History of the Achaemenid Empire* (Leiden)
   (1999) "Achaemenid Imperial Policies and Provincial Governments," in R. Boucharlat, J.E. Curtis, and E. Haerinck eds., *Neo-Assyrian, Median, Achaemenian and Other Studies in Honor of David Stronach*, Vol. II (*Iranica Antiqua* 34) (Ghent):269–282

Dandamaev, M.A. and V.G. Lukonin (1989) *The Culture and Social Institutions of Ancient Iran* (Cambridge, UK)

Danish Archaeological Expedition to Bodrum (1981–1997) *The Maussolleion at Halikarnassos: Reports of the Danish Archaeological Expedition to Bodrum*, Vols. I–III (Copenhagen)

Davesnes, A., A. Lemaire, and H. Lozachmeur (1987) "Le site archéologique de Meydancikkale (Turquie): du royaume Pirindu à la garrison ptolémaïque," *CRAIBL*:365–377

Davies, N. (1987) *The Aztec Empire: The Toltec Resurgence* (Norman, Okla.)

Debord, P. (1972) *Actes du Colloque 1971 sur l'esclavage* (Besançon)

(1982) *Aspects sociaux et économiques de la vie religieuse dans l'Anatolie gréco-romaine* (Leiden)

Demargne, P. (1976) "L'iconographie dynastique au Monument des Néréides de Xanthos," *Recueil Plassart: études sur l'antiquité grecque offertes à André Plassart par ses collègues de la Sorbonne* (Paris)

DeMarrais, E., L.J. Castillo, and T. Earle (1996) "Ideology, Materialization, and Power Strategies," *Current Anthropology* 37:15–31

de Mecquenem, R. (1938) "The Achaemenid and Later Remains at Susa," in A.U. Pope ed., *A Survey of Persian Art*, Vol. I (Oxford):321–329

(1947) "Contribution à l'étude du palais achéménide de Suse," in R. de Mecquenem, L. Le Breton, and M. Rulten eds., *Archéologie Susienne* 30 (Paris):1–119

Dentzer, J.M. (1969) "Reliefs au banquet dans l'Asie Mineure du Ve siècle av. J-C," *RA*:215–258

(1971) "Aux origines de l'iconographie du banquet couché," *RA*:215–258

(1982) *Le motif du banquet couché dans le Proche-Orient et le monde grec du VII au IV siècle avant JC* (Rome)

des Courtils, J. (1995) "Un nouveau bas-relief archaïque de Xanthos," *RA*: 337–364.

Descat, R. (1985) "Mnésimachos, Hérodote et le système tributaire achéménide," *REA* 87(1–2):97–112

(1989) "Notes sur la politique tributaire de Darius Ier," in P. Briant and C. Herrenschmidt eds., *Le tribut dans l'empire achéménide* (Paris):77–93

(1992) "Le paradis de Tissapherne," *Data, note n. 6, Achaemenid History Newsletter*, April (Utrecht)

de Ste. Croix, G.E.M. (1981) *The Class Struggle in the Ancient Greek World from the Archaic Age to the Arab Conquests* (Ithaca)

DeVries, K. (1977) "Attic Pottery in the Achaemenid Empire," *AJA* 81:544–548

Dieulafoy, M. (1893) *L'acropole de Suse, d'après les fouilles exécutées en 1884, 1885, 1886, sous les auspices du Musée du Louvre* (Paris)

Dillemann, L. (1962) *Haute Mésopotamie orientale et pays adjacents, BCH* 72 (Paris)

Dillery, J. (1992) "Darius and the Tomb of Nitocris (Hdt. 1.187)," *CP* 87(1): 30–38

Dodge, H. (1990) "The Architectural Impact of Rome in the East," in M. Henig ed., *Architecture and Architectural Sculpture in the Roman Empire* (Oxford):108–120

Dohen, E.H. (1941) "Review of H. Luschey, *Die Phiale*," *AJA* 45:125–127

Dolunay, N. (1967) "Daskyleion'da bulunan Kabartmalı Steller," *Istanbul Arkeoloji Müzesi Yıllığı*:13–14

Dominian, L. (1912) "History and Geology of Ancient Gold-Fields in Turkey," *Transactions of the American Institute of Mining Engineers* 42:581–584

Douglas, M. and B. Isherwood (1978) *The World of Goods. Towards an Anthropology of Consumption* (London)

Drews, R. (1997) "Review of R. Rollinger, *Herodots babylonischer Logos* (1993)," *JNES* 56:125–126

Driver, G.R. (1957) *Aramaic Documents of the Fifth Century BC* (Oxford)

duBois, P. (1982) *Centaurs and Amazons: Women and the Pre-History of the Great Chain of Being* (Ann Arbor)

Dusinberre, E.R.M. (1997a) "Imperial Style and Constructed Identity: A 'Graeco-Persian' Cylinder Seal from Sardis," *Ars Orientalis* 27:99–129

(1997b) "Satrapal Sardis: Aspects of Empire in an Achaemenid Capital." Ph.D. Dissertation, University of Michigan

(1999) "Satrapal Sardis: Achaemenid Bowls in an Achaemenid Capital," *AJA* 103:73–102

(2002) "King or God? Imperial Iconography and the 'Tiarate Head' Coins of Achaemenid Anatolia," in *Across the Anatolian Plateau: Readings in the Archaeology of Ancient Turkey. AASOR* 57:157–171

(in press) "A New Ivory from Kerkenes Dağ, Turkey: Reconsidering Ethnic Signifiers, Cultural Exchange, and the Problem of Median Art," in M. Cool Root ed., *Medes and Persians. Reflections on Elusive Empires. Ars Orientalis* 32

Eck, W. (1991) "Die Struktur der Städte in den nordwestlichen Provinzen und ihr Beitrag zur Administration des Reiches," in W. Eck and H. Galsterer eds., *Die Stadt in Oberitalien und in dem nordwestlicheen Provinzen der römischen Reiches* (Mainz):73–84

Elderkin, G.W. (1925) "The Lydian Bilingual Inscription," *AJA* 29:87–89

Elsner, J. (1995) *Art and the Roman Viewer* (Cambridge, UK)

Emery, W.B. (1958) *Great Tombs of the First Dynasty*, Vol. III

Erbse, H. (1979) "Über Herodots Kroisoslogos," in *Ausgewählte Schriften zur klassischen Philologie* (Berlin):180–202

Erdmann, K. (1941) *Das iranische Feuerheiligtum* (Leipzig)

Esin, U. (1982) "Tülintepe Excavations, 1974," *Keban Projesi 1974–1975 Çalışmaları* (Ankara)

Farkas, A. (1974) *Achaemenid Sculpture* (Leiden)

Farrington, I.S. (1992) "Ritual Geography, Settlement Patterns and the Characterization of the Provinces of the Inka Heartland," *WA* 23:368–385

Fehling, D. (1989) *Herodotus and his "Sources": Citation, Invention and Narrative Art*, (trans. J.G. Howie (Liverpool)

Ferguson, W.S. (1911) *Hellenistic Athens* (London)

Flinders Petrie, W.M. (1910) *Meydum and Memphis*, Vol. III (London)

Forbes, T.B. (1983) *Urartian Architecture* (BAR International Series 170) (Oxford)

Fossey, J.M. (1986) *The Ancient Topography of Eastern Phokis* (Amsterdam)

Fossing, P. (1937) "Drinking Bowls of Glass and Metal from the Achaemenian Time," *Berytus* 4:121–129

Foster, B.R. (1993) "Management and Administration in the Sargonic Period," in M. Liverani ed., *Akkad: The First World Empire* (Padua):25–39

Francfort, H.-P. (1979) *Les fortifications en Asie Centrale de l'âge du bronze à l'époque kouchane* (Paris)

(1985) "Fortifications et sociétés en Asie Centrale protohistorique," *Indus*:379–388.

Francis, E.D. and M. Vickers (1981) "Leagros kalos," *PCPS* 207:96–136

(1983) "*Signa priscae artis*: Eretria and Siphnos," *JHS* 103:47–67

Frankfort, H. (1950) "Oriental Institute Museum Notes: A Persian Goldsmith's Trial Piece," *JNES* 9:111–112

Frazer, K.J. and G.M.A. Hanfmann (1975) "The Artemis Altars LA1 and LA2," in *A Survey of Sardis and the Major Monuments Outside the City Walls* (Cambridge, Mass.):88–103

Freeman, P.W.M. (1993) " 'Romanisation' and Roman Material Culture," *JRA* 6:438–445

(1997) "Mommsen through to Haverfield: The Origins of Studies of Romanization in Late 19th-c. Britain," in D. Mattingly ed., *Dialogues in Roman Imperialism:*

*Power, Discourse and Discrepant Experience in the Roman Empire* (JRA Supplement 2) (Portsmouth, R.I.):27–50

Frei, P. (1996) "Zentralgewalt und Lokalautonomie im Achämenidenreich," in P. Frei and K. Koch eds., *Reichsidee und Reichsorganisation im Perserreich* (Freiburg):5–131

French, D. (1980) "The Roman Road-System of Asia Minor," in H. Temporini and W. Haase eds., *Aufstieg und Niedergang der römischen Welt*, Vol. II/7.2 (Berlin):698–729

   (1981) *Roman Roads and Milestones of Asia Minor* Part 1 (BAR International Series 105) (Oxford)

   (1998) "Pre- and Early-Roman Roads of Asia Minor. The Persian Road," *Iran* 36:15–44

Friedrich, J. (1932) *Kleinasiatische Sprachdenkmäler* (Berlin)

Furnivall, J.S. (1944) *Netherlands India: A Study of Plural Economy* (Cambridge, UK)

Furtwängler, A. (1903) *Die antiken Gemmen: Geschichte der Steinschneidenkunst im klassischen Altertum* (Berlin)

Gardin, J.-C. and P. Gentelle (1976) "Irrigation et peuplement dans la plaine d'Aï Khanoum de l'époque achéménide à l'époque musulmane," *Bulletin de l'Ecole Française d'Extrême-Orient* 63:59–99

Garnsey, P.D.A. (1984) "Religious Toleration in Classical Antiquity," in W. J. Scheils ed., *Persecution and Toleration* (Oxford):1–27

Garrison, M.B. (1988) "Seal Workshops and Artists at Persepolis: A Study of Seal Impressions Preserving the Theme of Heroic Encounter Preserved on the Persepolis Fortification and Treasury Tablets." Ph.D. dissertation, University of Michigan

   (1990) "Seals and the Elite at Persepolis: Some Observations on Early Achaemenid Persian Art," *Ars Orientalis* 20:1–30

   (1996) "A Persepolis Fortification Seal on the Tablet MDP 11 308 (Louvre Sb 13078)," *JNES* 55:15–35

   (1998) "The Seals of Asbazana (Aspathines)," in M. Brosius and A. Kuhrt eds., *Achaemenid History XI: Studies in Persian History: Essays in Memory of David M. Lewis* (Leiden):115–131

   (2000) "Achaemenid Iconography as Evidenced by Glyptic Art: Subject Matter, Social Functions, Audience and Diffusion," in C. Uehlinger ed., *Images as Media and Sources for the Cultural and Religious History of the Eastern Mediterranean and the Near East (1st Millennium BCE)* (Fribourg):115–163

Garrison, M.B. and M.C. Root (1996/1998) *Achaemenid History IX: Persepolis Seal Studies. An Introduction with Provisional Concordances of Seal Numbers and Associated Documents on Fortification Tablets 1–2087* (Leiden)

   (2001) *Seals on the Persepolis Fortification Tablets, Vol. I: Images of Heroic Encounter* (Chicago)

   (forthcoming) "Royal Name Seals."

Gauthier, P. (1981) "Le citoyenneté en Grèce et à Rome: participation et intégration," *Ktema* 6:166–179

   (1989) *Nouvelles Inscriptions de Sardes II: documents royaux du temps d'Antiochos III* (Geneva)

Gayet, A. (1894) *Le temple de Luxor. Mem. de la Mission Archéol. du Caire*, Vol. XV fasc. 1 (Paris)

Geertz, C. (1973) "Religion as a Cultural System," reprinted in C. Geertz, *The Interpretation of Cultures: Selected Essays* (London):87–125

Gentelle, P. (1978) *Étude géographique de la plaine d'Aï Khanoum et de son irrigation depuis les temps antiques* (Paris)

Ghirshman, R.M. (1963a) "L'Apadana de Suse," *IrAnt* 3:148–154

(1963b) *Perse: proto-iraniens, mèdes, achéménides* (Paris)

Gilliam, J.F. (1965) "Romanization of the Greek East: The Role of the Army," *Bulletin of the American Society of Papyrologists* 2:65–73

Gjerstad, S. (1953) *Swedish Cyprus Expedition*, Vol. IV, Part 2 (Stockholm)

Goff, C. (1977) "Excavations at Baba Jan: The Architecture of the East Mound, Levels II and III," *Iran* 15:103–140

(1978) "Excavations at Baba Jan: The Pottery and Metal from Levels III and II," *Iran* 16:29–66

Goldstein, S.M. (1979) *Pre-Roman and Early Roman Glass in the Corning Museum of Glass* (Corning, N.Y.)

(1980) "Pre-Persian and Persian Glass: Some Observations on Objects in the Corning Museum of Glass," in D. Schmandt-Besserat ed., *Ancient Persia: The Art of an Empire* (Malibu, Calif.)

Gorelick, L. and A.J. Gwinnett (1990) "The Ancient Near Eastern Cylinder Seals as Social Emblem and Status Symbol," *JNES* 49:45–56

Goudineau, C. (1979) *Les fouilles de la Maison au Dauphin. Recherches sur la romanisation de Vaison-la-Romaine* (Paris)

Goudriaan, K. (1988) *Ethnicity in Ptolemaic Egypt* (Amsterdam)

Gousquet, B. (1996) *Tell-Douch et sa région. Géographie d'une limite de milieu à une frontière d'Empire* (Cairo)

Graf, D.F. (1994) "The Persian Royal Road System," in H. Sancisi-Weerdenburg, A. Kuhrt, and M.C. Root eds., *Achaemenid History VIII: Continuity and Change* (Leiden): 167–189

Gray, G.B. (1969) "The Foundation and Extent of the Persian Empire," *CHI* 4:1–25

Grayson, A.K. (1975) *Babylonian Historical-Literary Texts* (Toronto Semitic Texts and Studies 3) (Toronto)

Greenewalt, C.H., Jr. (1971) "An Exhibitionist from Sardis," in D.G. Mitten, J.G. Pedley, and J.A. Scott eds., *Studies Presented to George M.A. Hanfmann* (Mainz):29–46

(1972) "Two Lydian Graves at Sardis," *CSCA* 5:113–145

(1977) "The Twentieth Campaign at Sardis (1977)," *RdA* 1(1–2):105–108

(1978a) "Sardis, 1977," *Türk Arkeoloji Dergisi* 26:57–73

(1978b) "The Sardis Campaign of 1976," *BASOR* 229:57–73

(1978c) "The Seventeenth Campaign at Sardis (1974)," *AASOR* 43:61–71

(1978d) "Lydian Elements in the Material Culture of Sardis," in E. Akurgal ed., *Proceedings of the Tenth International Congress of Classical Archaeology* (Ankara): 37–45

(1979) "The Sardis Campaign of 1977," *BASOR* 233:1–32

(1992) "When a Mighty Empire was Destroyed: The Common Man at the Fall of Sardis, ca. 546 BC," *PAPS* 136:247–271

(1995a) "Croesus of Sardis and the Lydian Kingdom," in J.M. Sasson ed., *Civilizations of the Ancient Near East* (New York):1173–1183

(1995b) "Sardis in the Age of Xenophon," in P. Briant ed., *Dans les pas des Dix-Mille* (Toulouse):125–145

(n.d.) "Publication of Sardian tombs"

Greenewalt, C.H., Jr. and L.J. Majewski (1980) "Lydian Textiles," in K. DeVries and E. Kohler eds., *From Athens to Gordion: The Papers of a Memorial Symposium for Rodney S. Young* (Philadelphia):133–148

Greenewalt, C.H., Jr., D.G. Sullivan, C. Ratté, and T.N. Howe (1985) "The Sardis Campaigns of 1981 and 1982," *BASOR* Supplement 23:53–92

Greenewalt, C.H., Jr., N.D. Cahill, and M.L. Rautman (1987) "The Sardis Campaign of 1984," *BASOR* Supplement 25:13–54

Greenfield, J. and B. Porten (1982) *The Bisitun Inscription of Darius the Great, Aramaic Version* (London)

Grimal, N. (1995) "Travaux de l'IFAO en 1994–1995," *BIFAO* 95:539–645

Grose, D.F. (1989) *The Toledo Museum of Art: Early Ancient Glass* (New York)

Gruben, G. (1961) "Beobachtungen zum Artemis-Tempel von Sardis," *MDAI (A)* 76:155–196

Gruen, E.S. (1984a) *The Hellenistic World and the Coming of Rome* (Berkeley)

(1984b) "Material Rewards and the Drive for Empire," in W.V. Harris ed., *The Imperialism of Mid-Republican Rome* (Rome):59–88

Gschnitzer, F. (1986) "Eine persische Kultstiftung in Sardeis und die 'Sippengötter' Vorderasiens," in W. Reid and H. Trenkwalder eds., *Im Bannkreis des Alten Orients (Festschrift K. Obenhuber)* (Innsbrück):45–54

Guichard, M. (1996) "À la recherche de la pierre bleue," *NABU*:36

Gunter, A.C. (1982) "Representations of Urartian and Western Iranian Fortress Architecture in the Assyrian Reliefs," *Iran* 20:103–112

(1989) "Sculptural Dedications at Labraunda," *Boreas 17: Architecture and Society in Hecatomnid Caria* (Uppsala):91–98

(1990) "Models of the Orient in the Art History of the Orientalizing Period," in H. Sancisi-Weerdenburg and J.W. Drijvers eds., *Achaemenid History V: The Roots of the European Tradition* (Leiden):131–147

Gunter, A.C. and P. Jett (1992) *Ancient Iranian Metalwork in the Arthur M. Sackler Gallery and the Freer Gallery of Art* (Washington, DC)

Gunter, A.C. and M.C. Root (1998) "Replicating, Inscribing, Giving: Ernst Herzfeld and Artaxerxes' Silver Phiale in the Freer Gallery of Art," *Ars Orientalis* 28: 1–38

Gusmani, R. (1964) *Lydisches Wörterbuch: Mit grammatischer Skizze und Inschriftensammlung* (Heidelberg)

(1979) "Lydische Epigraphik," *Kadmos* 18(1):76–79

(1985) "Anthroponymie in den lydischen Inschriften," in Y. Arbeitman ed., *Gedenkschrift B. Schwartz* (New York)

(1986) *Lydisches Wörterbuch. Ergänzungsband I* (Heidelberg)

Haerinck, E. (1973) "Le palais achéménide de Babylone," *IrAnt* 10:108–132

Hall, R.L. (1976) "Ghosts, Water Barriers, Corn and Sacred Enclosures in the Eastern Woodlands," *AAnt* 41:360–364

Hallock, R.T. (1969) *The Persepolis Fortification Tablets* (Chicago)

(1978) "Selected Fortification Texts," *CDAFI* 8:109–136

Hamilton, R.W. (1966) "A Silver Bowl in the Ashmolean Museum," *Iraq* 28:1–17

Hanfmann, G.M.A. (1960a) "Excavations at Sardis, 1959," *BASOR* 157:1–24

(1960b) *Sardis und Lydien. Akademie der Wissenschaften und Literatur Mainz, Abhandlungen der geistes- und sozialwissenschaftlichen Klasse* 6:499–536

(1961) "The Third Campaign at Sardis (1960)," *BASOR* 162:8–49

(1962) "The Fourth Campaign at Sardis (1961)," *BASOR* 166:1–57

(1963) "The Fifth Campaign at Sardis (1962)," *BASOR* 170:1–65

(1964) "The Sixth Campaign at Sardis (1963)," *BASOR* 174:3–58

(1965) "Greece and Lydia: The Impact of Hellenic Culture," in *Le rayonnement des civilisations grecque et romaine sur les cultures périphériques* (Paris)

(1967) "The Ninth Campaign at Sardis (1966)" [continued from No. 186], *BASOR* 187:9–62

(1974a) "A Pediment of the Persian Era from Sardis," in *Mansel'e Armağan'dan ayrıbasım* (Ankara):289–302

(1974b) "The Sixteenth Campaign at Sardis (1973)." *BASOR* 215:31–60

(1975) *From Croesus to Constantine* (Ann Arbor)

(1983) *Sardis: From Prehistoric to Roman Times* (Cambridge, Mass.)

(1987) "The Sacrilege Inscription: The Ethnic, Linguistic, Social and Religious Situation at Sardis at the End of the Persian Era," *BAI*:1–8

Hanfmann, G.M.A. and M.S. Balmuth (1965) "The Image of an Anatolian Goddess at Sardis," *Anadolu Araştırmaları* 2(1–2):261–269

Hanfmann, G.M.A. and K.P. Erhart (1981) "Pedimental Reliefs From a Mausoleum of the Persian Era at Sardis: A Funerary Meal," in W.K. Simpson and W.M. Davis eds., *Studies in Ancient Egypt, the Aegean, and the Sudan: Essays in Honor of Dows Dunham on the Occasion of his 90th Birthday, June 1, 1980* (Boston):87–89

Hanfmann, G.M.A. and K.Z. Polatkan (1959) "Three Sculptures from Sardis in the Manisa Museum," *Anatolia* 4:55–65

(1960) "A Sepulchral Stele from Sardis," *AJA* 64:49–56

Hanfmann, G.M.A. and N.H. Ramage (1978) *Sculpture from Sardis: The Finds through 1975* (Cambridge, Mass.)

Hanfmann, G.M.A. and J.C. Waldbaum (1969) "Kybele and Artemis: Two Anatolian Goddesses at Sardis," *Archaeology* 22(4):264–269

(1970) "The Eleventh and Twelfth Campaigns at Sardis (1968, 1969)," *BASOR* 199:7–58

(1975) *A Survey of Sardis and the Major Monuments Outside the City Walls* (Cambridge, Mass.)

Hansen, O. (1986) "The Purported Letter of Darius to Gadates," *RhM* 129:95–6

Hansman, J. (1972) "Elamites, Achaemenians and Anshan," *Iran* 10:101–125

Harris, J. ed. (1993) *Textiles: 5,000 Years. An International History and Illustrated Survey* (New York)

Harris, W. (1979) *War and Imperialism in Republican Rome* (Oxford)

Hartog, F. (1988) *The Mirror of Herodotus: The Representation of the Other in the Writing of History* (Berkeley)

Haselgrove, C.C. (1995) "Social and Symbolic Order in the Origins and Layout of Roman Villas in Northern Gaul," in J. Metzler, M. Millett, N. Roymans, and J. Slofstra eds., *Integration in the Early Roman West: The Role of Culture and Ideology* (Luxembourg):65–75

Hassig, R. (1988) *Aztec Warfare: Imperial Expansion and Political Control* (Norman, Okla.)

Hays, K. (1993) "When is a Symbol Archaeologically Meaningful? Meaning, Function, and Prehistoric Visual Arts," in N. Yoffee and A. Sherratt eds., *Archaeological Theory: Who Sets the Agenda?* (Cambridge):81–92

Hegyi, D. (1966) "The Historical Background of the Ionian Revolt," *AJAH* 14:285–286

Helms, S.W. (1982) "Excavations at 'the City and the Famous Fortress of Kandahar,'" *Afghan Studies* 3(4):1–24.

Henrickson, R.C. (1993) "Politics, Economics, and Ceramic Continuity at Gordion in the Late Second and First Millennium BC," in W.D. Kingery ed., *Social and Cultural Contexts of New Ceramic Technologies* (Westerville, Ohio): 89–176

(1994) "Continuity and Discontinuity in the Ceramic Tradition at Gordion during the Iron Age," in D. French and A. Çilingiroğlu eds., *Proceedings of the Third International Anatolian Iron Age Symposium (Van 1990)* (Ankara): 95–129

(1998) "The Achaemenid Impact on Anatolia as Seen in Pottery from Yassı Höyük/Gordion," *Orient-Express*

Herbordt, S. (1992) *Neuassyrische Glyptik des 8.–7. Jh. v. Chr. Unter besonderer Berücksichtigung der Siegelungen auf Tafeln und Tonverschlüssen* (Helsinki)

Hermary, A. (1984) "Un nouveau relief 'gréco-perse' en Cilicie," *RA*:289–300

Herrenschmidt, C. (1980) "La religion des Achéménides: état de la question," *Studia Iranica* 9:325–329

Herrmann, P. (1996) "Mystenvereine in Sardeis," *Chiron* 26:315–341

Herzfeld, E.E. (1933) "'The magnificent discovery' at Persepolis," *Illustrated London News* 182(4901):401–406; 182 (4902):453–455

(1941) *Iran in the Ancient East: Archaeological Studies Presented in the Lowell Lectures at Boston* (London)

Hestrin, R. and E. Stern (1973) "Two 'Assyrian' Bowls from Israel," *IEJ* 23:152–155

Heubeck, A. (1960) "Kleinasiatisches: 2. Lyd. Verwandtschaftsbezeichnungen," *Die Sprache* 6:207–210

Hingley, R. (1996) "The 'Legacy' of Rome: The Rise, Decline and Fall of the Theory of Romanization," in J. Webster and N. Cooper eds., *Roman Imperialism: Post-Colonial Perspectives* (Oxford):35–48

Hinz, W. (1974) "Die Behistun-Inschrift des Darius in ihrer ursprünglichen Form," *AMI* 7:121–134

(1975) "Darius und der Suezkanal," *AMI* 8:115–121

Hodder, I. ed. (1982) *Symbolic and Structural Archaeology* (Cambridge, UK)

(1983) *Symbols in Action* (Cambridge, UK)

ed. (1989) *The Meanings of Things: Material Culture and Symbolic Expression* (London)

Hogarth, D.G. (1908) *Excavations at Ephesus: The Archaic Artemisia* (London)

Hornblower, S. (1982) *Mausolus* (Oxford)

Howes Smith, P.H.G. (1986) "A Study of Ninth–Seventh Century Metal Bowls from Western Asia," *IrAnt* 21:1–88

Hrouda, B. (1962) *Tell Halaf IV: Die Kleinfunde aus Historischer Zeit* (Berlin)

Hrozny, F. (1917) *Die Sprache der Hethiter* (Leipzig)

Hunt, R.C. (1987) "The Role of Bureaucracy in the Provisioning of Cities: A Framework for Analysis of the Ancient Near East," in M. Gibson and R.D. Biggs eds., *The Organization of Power: Aspects of Bureaucracy in the Ancient Near East* (Chicago): 161–192

İlhan, E. (1971) "Earthquakes in Turkey," in A.S. Campbell ed., *The Geology and History of Turkey* (Tripoli):431–442

Iliffe, J.H. (1935) "A Tell Fara Tomb Group Reconsidered," *QDAP* 4:182–186

Invernizzi, A. (1995) "Seal Impressions of Achaemenid and Graeco-Persian Style from Seleucia on the Tigris," *Mesopotamia* 30:39–50

(1996) "Seleucia on the Tigris: Centre and Periphery in Seleucid Asia," in P. Bilde, T. Engberg-Pedersen, L. Hannestad, and J. Zahle eds., *Centre and Periphery in the Hellenistic World* (Aarhus):230–250

Jacobs, B. (1987) *Griechische und persische Elemente in der Grabkunst Lykiens zur Zeit der Achämenidenherrshaft* (Jonsered)

(1994) *Die Satrapienverwaltung im Perserreich zur Zeit Darius' III* (Wiesbaden)

Jeppesen, K. (1990) *The Maussolleion at Ancient Halicarnassus* (Ankara)

Kahle, P. and F. Sommer (1927) "Die lydisch-aramäische Bilingue," *KIF* 1(1):18–86

Kamilli, D.C. (1978) "Mineral Analysis of the Clay Bodies," in A. Ramage, *Lydian Houses and Architectural Terracottas* (Cambridge, Mass.):12–15

Kaptan, D. (1990) "A Group of Seal Impressions on the *Bullae* from Ergili/Daskyleion," *EpAnat* 16:15–27

(1996) "The Great King's Audience," in F. Blakolmer, K.R. Krierer, F. Krinzinger, A. Landskron-Dinstl, H.D. Szemethy, and K. Zhuber-Okrog eds., *Fremde Zeiten. Festschrift für Jürgen Borchhardt*, Vol. I (Vienna):259–271

(1997) "The Establishment of the Satrapy in Northwestern Anatolia: Some Evidence from the Seal Impressions of Ergili/Daskyleion," Papers Read at the First International Symposium on Anatolia in the Achaemenid Period (Bandırma)

(forthcoming) *The Daskyleion Bullae: Seal Images from the Western Periphery of the Achaemenid Empire*

Kaspar, S. (1984) "Zur Steinmetztechnik des Parthenon-Unterbaus," in E. Berger ed., *Parthenon-Kongreß Basel* I:45–46

(1988) Πρακτικα 4:95–99

Kawami, T.S. (1992) *Ancient Iranian Ceramics from the Arthur M. Sackler Collections* (New York)

Kellens, J. (1989) "Avesta," *EncIr* 3:35–44

(1991a) "Questions préalables," in J. Kellens ed., *La religion iranienne à l'époque achéménide* (Ghent):81–86

(1991b) *Zoroastre et l'Avesta ancien* (Paris)

Kent, R. (1953) *Old Persian: Grammar, Texts, Lexicon* (New Haven)

Kervran, M., D. Stronach, F. Vallat, and J. Yoyotte (1972) "Une statue de Darius découverte à Suse," *JA* 260:235–266

(1974) "Une statue de Darius découverte à Suse," with contributions by J. Perrot, D. Ladiray, M. Roaf, and J. Trichet, in *CDAFI* 4

King, L.W. and R. Campbell Thompson (1907) *The Sculptures and Inscription of Darius the Great on the Rock of Behistûn in Persia* (London)

Kirk, G.S. (1974) *The Nature of Greek Myths* (Harmondsworth)

Kleemann, I. (1958) *Der Satrapensarkophag aus Sidon* (Berlin)

Knibbe, D. (1961–1963) "Ein religiöser Frevel und seine Sühne: Ein Todesurteil hellenistischer Zeit aus Ephesos," *ÖJh* 46:175–82

Koch, H. (1977) *Die religiösen Verhältnisse der Dareioszeit* (Gottingen)

(1986) "Die achämenidische Poststrasse von Persepolis nach Susa," *AMI* 19:33–47

(1989) "Tribut und Abgaben in Persis und Elymais," in P. Briant and C. Herrenschmidt eds., *Le tribut dans l'empire perse* (Paris):121–128

(1990) *Verwaltung und Wirtschaft im persischen Kernland zur Zeit der Achämeniden* (Wiesbaden)

(1993) *Achaemeniden-Studien* (Wiesbaden)

Kökten, H. (1997) "Two Wheeled Vehicles from Lydia and Mysia," Papers read at the First International Symposium on Anatolia in the Achaemenid Period (Bandırma)

Kolata, A.L. (1992) "Economy, Ideology and Imperialism in the South-Central Andes," in A.A. Demarest and G.W. Conrad eds., *Ideology and Pre-Columbian Civilizations* (Santa Fe):65–86

Koldewey, R. (1918) *Das Ischtar-Tor in Babylon* (Leipzig)

Kornfeld, W. (1973) "Jüdisch-aramäische Grabinschriften aus Edfu," *Anzeiger der phil.-hist. Klasse der Österreichischen Akademie der Wissenschaften* 110:123–137

Krefter, F. (1971) *Persepolis Rekonstruktionen* (Berlin)

Kuhrt, A. (1990) "Achaemenid Babylonia: Sources and Problems," in A. Kuhrt and H. Sancisi-Weerdenburg eds., *Achaemenid History IV: Centre and Periphery* (Leiden):177–194

  (1995a) *The Ancient Near East c. 3000–330 BC* (Cambridge)

  (1995b) "The Assyrian Heartland in the Achaemenid Period," in P. Briant ed., *Dans les pas de Dix-Mille* (Toulouse)

  (1996) "The Seleucid Kings and Babylonia: New Perspectives on the Seleucid Realm in the East," in P. Bilde, T. Engberg-Pedersen, L. Hannestad, and J. Zahle eds., *Aspects of Hellenistic Kingship* (Aarhus):41–54

  (forthcoming) *Herodotus: A Handbook* (Leiden)

Kuhrt, A. and H. Sancisi-Weerdenburg (1988) "Introduction," in A. Kuhrt and H. Sancisi-Weerdenburg eds., *Achaemenid History III: Method and Theory* (Leiden): xi–xv

  (1990) "Introduction," in A. Kuhrt and H. Sancisi-Weerdenburg eds., *Achaemenid History IV: Centre and Periphery* (Leiden):xi–xv

Kuhrt, A. and S.M. Sherwin-White (1987) "Xerxes' Destruction of Babylonian Temples," in H. Sancisi-Weerdenburg and A. Kuhrt eds., *Achaemenid History II: The Greek Sources* (Leiden):69–78

  (1994) "The Transition from Achaemenid to Seleucid Rule in Babylonia: Revolution or Evolution," in H. Sancisi-Weerdenburg, A. Kuhrt, and M.C. Root eds., *Achaemenid History VIII: Continuity and Change* (Leiden):311–327

Kurtz, D.V. (1981) "The Legitimation of Early Inchoate States," in H.J.M. Claessen and P. Skalnik eds., *The Study of the State* (The Hague):177–200

Kus, S.M. (1982) "Matters Material and Ideal," in I. Hodder (ed.), *Symbolic and Structural Archaeology* (Cambridge, UK)

  (1989) "Sensuous Human Activity and the State: Towards an Archaeology of Bread and Circuses," in D. Miller, M. Rowlands, and C. Tilley eds., *Domination and Resistance* (London):140–154

Kyrieleis, H. (1969) *Throne und Klinen: Studien zur Formgeschichte altorientalischer und griechischer Sitz- und Liegemöbel vorhellenistischer Zeit* (Berlin)

Landsberger, B. (1967) "Über Farben im Sumerisch-Akkadischen," *JCS* 21:139–173

Laroche, E. and A. Davesnes (1981) "Les fouilles de Meydandjik, près de Gülnar (Turquie), et le trésor monétaire hellénistique," *CRAI*:356–370

Lateiner, D. (1982) "The Failure of the Ionian Revolt," *Historia* 31:129–60

Lecoq, P. (1997) *Les inscriptions de la perse achéménide: traduit du vieux perse, de l'élamite, du babylonien et de l'araméen, présenté et annoté par Pierre Lecoq* (Paris)

Lefebure, M.G. (1924) *Le tombeau de Petosiris* (Cairo)

Legrain, L. (1951) *Ur Excavations X: Seal Cylinders* (Oxford)

Leith, M.J.W. (1990) "Greek and Persian Images in Pre-Alexandrine Samaria: The Wâdi ed-Dâliyeh Seal Impressions." Ph.D. Dissertation, Harvard University

(1997) *Wadi Daliyeh, Vol. I: The Wadi Daliyeh Seal Impressions* (Discoveries in the Judaean Desert 24) (Oxford)

Lemaire, A. and H. Lozachmeur (1996) "Remarques sur le plurilinguisme en Asie Mineure à l'époque perse," in R. Briquel-Chatonnet ed., *Mosaïque de langues, mosaïque culturelle. Le bilinguisme dans le Proche-Orient ancien* (Paris):91–123

Lethaby, W.R. (1908) *Greek Buildings Represented by Fragments in the British Museum* (London)

Lewis, D.M. (1977) *Sparta and Persia* (Leiden)

(1980) "Datis the Mede," *JHS* 100:194–195

(1987) "The King's Dinner (Poly. IV.3,32)," *AHW* 2:79–87

Lichtheim, M. (1973–1980) *Ancient Egyptian Literature: A Book of Readings* (Berkeley)

Lipinski, E. (1975) "La stèle égypto-araméenne de Tumma', fille de Bokkorinif," *Chronique d'Egypte* 50:93–104

Littmann, E. (1916) *Sardis VI.I: Lydian Inscriptions* (Leiden)

Liverani, M. (1979) "The Ideology of the Assyrian Empire," in M.T. Larsen ed., *Power and Propaganda: A Symposium on Ancient Empires* (Copenhagen):297–318

(1993) "Model and Actualization: The Kings of Akkad in the Historical Tradition," in M. Liverani ed., *Akkad: The First World Empire* (Padua):41–67

Lloyd, A.B. (1975) *Herodotus Bk II: Introduction* (Leiden)

(1982) "The Inscription of Udjahorresnet: A Collaborator's Testament," *JEA* 68:166–180

Lochner-Hüttenbach, F. (1964) "Brief des Königs Darius an den Satrapen Gadatas," in W. Brandenstein and M. Mayrhofer eds., *Handbuch des Altpersischen* (Wiesbaden): 91–98

Lockwood, W.G. ed. (1984) *Beyond Ethnic Boundaries: New Approaches to Ethnicity* (Ann Arbor)

Luckenbill, D.D. (1927) *Ancient Records of Assyria and Babylonia II* (Chicago)

Luschey, H. (1939) *Die Phiale* (Beicherode am Herz)

(1968) "Studien zu dem Darius-Relief von Bisutun," *AMI* 1:63–94

(1974) "Bisutun: Geschichte und Forschungsgeschichte," *AA* 89:114–149

Luttwak, E. (1976) *The Grand Strategy of the Roman Empire from the First Century AD to the Third* (Baltimore)

McDonald, W.A. and R. Hope Simpson (1972) "Archaeological exploration," in W.A. McDonald and G.R. Rapp, Jr., eds., *The Minnesota Messenia Expedition: Reconstructing a Bronze Age Regional Environment* (Minneapolis):117–147

McEwan, C. and M. van de Guchte (1992) "Ancestral Time and Sacred Space in Inca State Ritual," in R.F. Townsend ed., *The Ancient Americas: Art from Sacred Landscapes* (Chicago):359–371

McLauchlin, B.K. (1985) "Lydian Graves and Burial Customs." Ph.D. Dissertation, University of California at Berkeley

Magie, D. (1950) *Roman Rule in Asia Minor* (Princeton)

Mallowan, M. (1972) "Cyrus the Great (558–529 BC)," *Iran* 10:7–12

Mann, M. (1986) *Sources of Social Power* (Cambridge, UK)

Manz, B.F. (1989) *The Rise and Rule of Tamerlane* (Cambridge, UK)

Marconi, C. (1994) *Selinunte: Le metope dell'Heraion* (Modena)

Marcus, J. (1973) "Territorial Organisation of the Lowland Classic Maya," *Science* 180:911–916

Marcus, M.I. (1990) "Centre, Province and Periphery: A New Paradigm from Iron-Age Iran," *Art History* 13(2):129–150

(1993) "Incorporating the Body: Adornment, Gender, and Social Identity in Ancient Iran," *CAJ* 3(12):157–178

(1994) "Dressed to Kill: Women and Pins in Early Iran," *Oxford Art Journal* 17(2):3–15

(1995) "Art and Ideology in Ancient Western Asia," in J. Sasson ed., *Civilizations of the Ancient Near East* (New York):2487–2505

Marvin, M.C. (1973) "Studies in Greco-Persian Gems," Ph.D. Dissertation, Harvard University

Mathiesen, I., E. Betles, S. Davies, and H.S. Smith (1995) "A Stela of the Persian Period from Saqqara," *JEA* 81:23–41

Matz, F. (1937) "Altitalische und vorderasiatische Riefelschalen," *Klio* 30:110–117

Maximova, M. (1928) "Griechisch-persische Kleinkunst in Kleinasien nach den Perserkriegen," *AA* 33:648–677

Mayrhofer, M. (1973) *Onomastica Persepolitana: Das altiranische Namengut der Persepolis-Täfelchen* (Vienna)

(1974) "Zu den Parther-Namen der griechischen Awroman-Dokumente," in P. Gignoux and A. Tafazzoli eds., *Mémorial Jean de Menasce* (Louvain):205–213

(1979) *Fouilles de Xanthos, VI. Le stèle trilingue du Létôon* (Paris)

Meade, C.G. (1969) "Excavations at Baba Jan, 1967," *Iran* 7:115–130

Meadows, K. (1994) "You Are What You Eat. Diet, Identity and Romanization," in S. Cottam, D. Dungworth, S. Scott, and J. Taylor eds., *TRAC 94. Proceedings of the Fourth Annual Theoretical Roman Archaeology Conference Durham 1994* (Oxford): 132–140

Mee, C., D. Gill, H. Forbes, and L. Foxhall (1991) "Rural Settlement Change in the Methana Peninsula, Greece," in G. Barker and J. Lloyd eds., *Roman Landscapes: Archaeological Survey in the Mediterranean Region* (London):223–232

Mellink, M.J. (1974) "Notes on Anatolian Wall Painting," in E. Akurgal and U.B. Alköm eds., *Mélanges Mansel* (Ankara):538–547

(1978) "Archaeology in Asia Minor," *AJA* 82:329–330

Mellink, M.J. et al. (1998) *Kızılbel: An Archaic Painted Tomb Chamber in Northern Lycia*, with chapters by R.A. Bridges, Jr. and F.C. di Vignale (Philadelphia)

Metropolitan Museum of Art (1975) *From the Lands of the Scythians: Ancient Treasures from the Museums of the USSR 3000 BC to 100 BC* (New York)

Metzger, H., E. Laroche, and A. Dupont-Sommer (1974) "La stèle trilingue récemment découverte au Létôon de Xanthos," *AIB*:82–149

Mierse, W.E. (1983) "The Persian Period," in G.M.A. Hanfmann ed., *Sardis from Prehistoric to Roman Times: Results of the Archaeological Exploration of Sardis 1958–1975* (Cambridge, Mass.):100–108

Migeotte, L. (1984) *L'emprunt public dans le cités grecques* (Paris)

Miller, D. (1987) *Material Culture and Mass Consumption* (Oxford)

(1989) "The Limits of Dominance," in D. Miller, M. Rowlands, and C. Tilley eds., *Domination and Resistance* (London):63–79

Miller, M.C. (1992) "The Parasol: An Oriental Status-Symbol in Late Archaic and Classical Athens," *JHS* 112:91–105

(1993) "Adoption and Adaption of Achaemenid Metalware Forms in Attic Black-Gloss Ware of the Fifth Century," *AMI* 26:109–146

(1997) *Athens and Persia: A Study in Cultural Receptivity* (Cambridge, UK)

Millett, M. (1990) "Romanization: Historical Issues and Archaeological Interpretation," in T.F.C. Blagg and M. Millett eds., *The Early Roman Empire in the West* (Oxford):35–41

(1995) "Re-thinking Religion in Romanization," in J. Metzler, M. Millett, N. Roymans, and J. Slofstra eds., *Integration in the Early Roman West: The Role of Culture and Ideology* (Luxembourg):93–100

Mitchell, S. (1993) *Anatolia: Land, Men and Gods in Asia Minor, Vol. I: The Celts and the Impact of Roman rule* (Oxford)

Mitten, D.G. (1964) In G.M.A. Hanfmann, "The Sixth Campaign at Sardis (1963)," *BASOR* 174:39–42

Möbius, H. (1971) "Zu den Stelen von Daskyleion," *AA* 9:454–455

Mócsy, A. (1970) *Gesellschaft und Romanisation in der römischen Provinz Moesia Superior* (Amsterdam)

Moerman, M. (1965) "Who are the Lue?" *American Anthropologist* 67:1215–1230

(1968) "Being Lue: Uses and Abuses of Ethnic Identification," in J. Helm ed., *Essays on the Problem of Tribe* (Seattle)

Momigliano, A. (1975) *Alien Wisdom: The Limits of Hellenization* (Cambridge, UK)

Moorey, P.R.S. (1979) "Aspects of Worship and Ritual on Achaemenid Seals," in *Akten des VII. Kongress für iranische Kunst und Archäologie, München 1976* (*AMI* Supplement 6) (Berlin):218–226

(1980) *Cemeteries of the First Millennium BC at Deve Hüyük, near Carchemish, Salvaged by T.E Lawrence and C.L Woolley in 1913 (with a Catalogue Raisonné of the Objects in Berlin, Cambridge, Liverpool, London and Oxford)* (British Archaeological Reports 87) (Oxford)

(1988) "The Technique of Gold-Figure Decoration on Achaemenid Silver Vessels and Its Antecedents," *IrAnt* 23:231–245

Moortgat, A. (1926) "Hellas und die Kunst der Achaemeniden," *MDOG* 2:3–39

Morris, C. (1988) "Progress and Prospect in the Archaeology of the Inca," in R.W. Keatinge ed., *Peruvian Prehistory* (Cambridge, UK):233–256

Morris, I. (1987) *Burial and Ancient Society: The Rise of the Greek City-State* (Cambridge, UK)

Mousavi, A. (1999) "La ville de Parsa: quelques remarques sur la topographie et le système défensif de Persépolis," in R. Boucharlat, J.E. Curtis, and E. Haerinck eds., *Neo-Assyrian, Median, Achaemenian and Other Studies in Honor of David Stronach, Vol II (Iranica Antiqua 34)* (Ghent):145–156

Murray, O. (1966) "Ο ΑΡΧΑΙΟΣ ΔΑΣΜΟΣ," *Historia* 15:142–56

(1996) "Hellenistic Royal Symposia," in P. Bilde, T. Engberg-Pedersen, L. Hannestad, and J. Zahle eds., *Aspects of Hellenistic Kingship* (Aarhus):15–27

Muscarella, O.W. (1976) "Review of A. Farkas, *Achaemenid Sculpture*," in *BASOR* 223:71–72

(1977) "Unexcavated Objects," in L.D. Levine and T.C. Young, Jr. eds., *Mountains and Lowlands: Essays in the Archaeology of Greater Mesopotamia* (Malibu):153–208

(1980) "Excavated and Unexcavated Achaemenian Art," in D. Schmandt-Besserat ed., *Ancient Persia: The Art of an Empire* (Malibu):23–42

(1992) "Achaemenid Brick Decoration," in P.O. Harper, J. Aruz, and F. Tallon eds., *The Royal City of Susa: Ancient Near Eastern Treasures in the Louvre* (New York):223–241

Muss, U. (1983) *Studien zur Bauplastik des Archaischen Artemisions von Ephesos* (Bonn)

Nauille, E. and H. Carter (1906) *The Tomb of Hatshopsitu* (London)

Newton, C.T. (1862–1863) *A History of Discoveries at Halicarnassus, Cnidus and Branchidae* (London)

Nikoulina, N.M. (1971) "La glyptique 'grecque-orientale' et 'gréco-perse,'" *AK* 14(2):90–106

Nollé, M. (1992) *Denkmäler vom Satrapensitz Daskyleion (Die Daskyleionstele): Studien zur graeco-persischen Kunst* (Berlin)

Nunn, A. (1996) *Kontinuität und Wandel im Motivschatz Phöniziens, Syriens und Transjordaniens vom 6. bis zum 4. Jahrhundert v. Chr.: Vorderasiatische, ägyptische und griechische Bilder im Widerstreit* (Munich)

Nylander, C. (1970) *Ionians in Pasargadae: Studies in Old Persian Architecture* (Uppsala)
    (1974) "Anatolians in Susa – and Persepolis (?)" *Acta Iranica* 6:317–323
    (1983) "The Standard of the Great King – A Problem in the Alexander Mosaic," *OpRom* 14:19–37
    (1999) "Breaking the Cup of Kingship. An Elamite Coup in Nineveh?" in R. Boucharlat, J.E. Curtis, and E. Haerinck eds., *Neo-Assyrian, Median, Achaemenian and Other Studies in Honor of David Stronach*, vol. I (*IrAnt* 34) (Ghent):71–84

Oates, J. (1959) "Late Assyrian Pottery from Fort Shalmaneser," *Iraq* 21:130–146

Oliver, A. (1970) "Persian Export Glass," *JGS* 12:9–16
    (1971) "A Bronze Mirror from Sardis," in D.G. Mitten, J.G. Pedley, and J.A. Scott eds., *Studies Presented to George M.A. Hanfmann* (Mainz):113–120

Olmstead, A.L. (1948) *History of the Persian Empire* (Chicago)

Olson, G.W. (1970) "Field Report on Soils of Sardis, Turkey: A Description of Fieldwork and Research Orientation in a Study of Soils Environment around the Ancient Lydian, Greek, Roman and Byzantine Ruins," *Agronomy Mimeo* 70:8
    (1971) "Descriptions, Notes, Maps, and Data on Soils of Sardis, Turkey," *Agronomy Mimeo* 71:1
    (1977) "Landslides at Sardis in Western Turkey," *Geological Society of America, Reviews in Engineering Geology* 3:255–272

Oppenheim, A.L. (1949) "The Golden Garments of the Gods," *JNES* 8:172–193
    (1965) "On Royal Gardens in Mesopotamia," *JNES* 24:328–333

Orlin, L.L. (1976) "Athens and Persia ca. 507 BC: A Neglected Perspective," in L.L. Orlin ed., *Michigan Oriental Studies in Honor of George G. Cameron* (Ann Arbor):255–266

Ortner, S. (1978) *Sherpas Through Their Rituals* (Cambridge, UK)

O'Shea, J. (1984) *Mortuary Variability: An Archaeological Investigation* (Cambridge, UK)

Östör, Á. (1993) *Vessels of Time: An Essay on Temporal Change and Social Transformation* (Oxford)

Özgen, İ. and J. Öztürk (1996) *Heritage Recovered: The Lydian Treasure* (Ankara)

Özkan, T. (1991) "Lydia'da Ele Geçen Bir Greko-Pers Bulutu Grubu," in H. Malay ed., *Erol Atalay Memorial* (Izmir):131–135

Parker Pearson, M. (2000) *The Archaeology of Death and Burial* (College Station, Texas)

Parker Pearson, M. and C. Richards (1994) "Architecture and Order: Spatial Representation and Archaeology," in M. Parker Pearson and C. Richards eds., *Architecture and Order: Approaches to Social Space* (London):38–72

Parrot, A. (1967) "Tête royale achéménide (?)," *Syria* 44:247–251

Pasztory, E. (1989) "Identity and Difference: The Uses and Meanings of Ethnic Styles," in S.J. Barnes and W.S. Melion eds., *Cultural Differentiation and Cultural Identity in the Visual Arts* (Washington, DC):15–39

Payne, H. (1940) *Perachora I* (Oxford)

Peacock, D.P.S. (1982) *Pottery in the Roman World: An Ethnoarchaeological Approach* (London)

Pedley, J.G. (1972) *Ancient Literary Sources on Sardis* (Cambridge, Mass.)

(1976) *Greek Sculpture of the Archaic Period: The Island Workshops* (Mainz)

(1994) "Review of D. Viviers, *Recherches sur les ateliers de sculpteurs et la cité d'Athènes à l'époque archaique: Endoios, Philergos, Aristokles* (Brussels 1992)," *Echos du monde classique* 38:264–268

(1996) "Review of C. Marconi, *Selinunte*," in *AJA* 100:624–625

Peebles, C.S. and S.M. Kus (1977) "Some Archaeological Correlates of Ranked Societies," *American Antiquity* 42(3):421–448

Perring, D. (1991) "Spatial Organisation and Social Change in Roman Towns," in J. Rich and A. Wallace-Hadrill eds., *City and Country in the Ancient World* (London):273–293

Perrot, J. (1974) "Le palais de Darius le Grand à Suse," in *Proceedings of the Second Annual Symposium on Archaeological Research in Iran* (Tehran):94–107

(1981) "L'architecture militaire et palatiale des achéménides à Suse," in *150 Jahre Deutsches Archäologisches Institut 1829–1979* (Mainz):79–94

Petit, T. (1990) *Satrapes et satrapies dans l'empire achéménide de Cyrus le Grand à Xerxès Ier* (Paris)

(1993) "Synchronie et diachronie chez les historiens de l'empire achéménide. A propos de deux ouvrages de M.A. Dandamaev," *TOPOI* 3:39–71

Pfrommer, M. (1987) *Studien zu alexandrinischer und grossgriechischer Toreutik frühhellenistischer Zeit* (Berlin)

Pfühl, E. and H. Möbius (1977) *Die ostgriechischen Grabreliefs* (Mainz)

Piepkorn, A.C. (1933) *Historical Prism Inscriptions of Assurbanipal* (Chicago)

Pillet, M.L. (1914) *Le palais de Darius Ier à Suse* (Paris)

Pinon, P. (1988) "L'urbanisme gallo-romain," in R. Bedon, R. Chevalier, and P. Pinon eds., *Architecture et urbanisme en Gaule romaine*, Vol. II (Paris):4–42

Polat, G. (1994) "Eine Neuerwerbung des Uşak Museums: Eine anatolisch-persische Grabstele," *Arkeoloji Dergisi* 2:61–66

Polish State Enterprise for the Conservation of Cultural Property (1972, 1973, 1979) *The Temple of Queen Hatshepsut*, vols. I–III (Warsaw)

Pollock, S. (1983) "The Symbolism of Prestige: An Archaeological Example from the Royal Cemetery of Ur." Ph.D. Dissertation, University of Michigan

Porada, E. (1993) "Why Cylinder Seals?" *Art Bulletin* 75(4):13–29

Posener, G. (1936) *Première domination perse en Égypte* (Cairo)

Postgate, J.N. (1992) "The Land of Assur and the Yoke of Assur," *World Archaeology* 23:247–263

Potts, D.T. (1997) *Mesopotamian Civilization: The Material Foundations* (Ithaca)

(1999) *The Archaeology of Elam: Formation and Transformation of an Ancient Iranian State* (Cambridge, UK)

Prakash, G. (1990) "Writing Post-Orientalist Histories of the Third World: Perspectives from Indian Historiography," *CSSH* 32:383–408

Préaux, C. (1978) *Le monde hellénistique* (Paris)

Price, S.R.F. (1984) *Rituals and Power. The Roman Imperial Cult in Asia Minor* (Cambridge, UK)

(1987) "From Noble Funerals to Divine Cult: The Consecration of Roman Emperors," in D. Cannadine and S.R.F. Price eds., *Rituals of Royalty: Power and Ceremonial in Traditional Societies* (Cambridge, UK):56–105

Purcell, N. (1990) "The Creation of Provincial Landscape: The Roman Impact on Cisalpine Gaul," in T. Blagg and M. Millett eds., *The Early Roman Empire in the West* (Oxford):7–29

Py, M. (1990) "Chronologie des habitats de la Gaule méditerranéene des IIe et Ier siècles avant J-C," in A. Duval, J-P Morel, and Y. Roman eds., *Gaule Interne et Gaule Méditerranéene aux IIe et Ier siècles avant JC. Confrontations Chronologiques* (Paris):227–242

Radt, W. (1983) "Eine gräko-persische Grabstele im Museum Bergama," *IstMitt* 33:53–68

Ramage, A. (1972) "The Fourteenth Campaign at Sardis (1971)," *BASOR* 206:9–39

(1978) *Lydian Houses and Architectural Terracottas* (Cambridge, Mass.)

(1987) "Lydian Sardis," in E. Guralnick ed., *Sardis: Twenty-Seven Years of Discovery* (Chicago):6–16

Ramage, A. and P. Craddock (2000) *King Croesus' Gold: Excavations at Sardis and the History of Gold Refining* (Cambridge, Mass.)

Ramage, A., S.M. Goldstein, and W.E. Mierse (1983) "Lydian Excavation Sectors," in G.M.A. Hanfmann ed., *Sardis: From Prehistoric to Roman Times* (Cambridge, Mass.):34–41

Ramage, A. and N.H. Ramage (1971) "The Siting of Lydian Burial Mounds," in D.G. Mitten, J.G. Pedley, and J.A. Scott eds., *Studies Presented to George M.A. Hanfmann* (Mainz):143–160

Ramage, N.H. (1979) "A Lydian Funerary Banquet," *AnatSt* 29:91–95

(1986) "Two New Attic Cups and the Siege of Sardis," *AJA* 90:419–24

Ramsay, W.M. (1920) "Military Operations on the North Front of Mount Tarsus," *JHS* 40:89–112

Ratté, C.J. (1989a) "Five Lydian Felines," *AJA* 93:379–393

(1989b) "Lydian Masonry and Monumental Architecture at Sardis". Ph.D. Dissertation, University of California at Berkeley

(1992) "The 'Pyramid Tomb' at Sardis," *IstMitt* 42:135–161

(1994a) "Anthemion Stelae from Sardis," *AJA* 98:593–609

(1994b) "Not the Tomb of Gyges," *JHS* 114:157–161

(forthcoming) *Lydian Architecture: Ashlar Masonry Structures at Sardis* (Cambridge, Mass.)

Reade, J.E. (1983) *Assyrian Sculpture* (London)

(1995) "The Symposion in Ancient Mesopotamia: Archaeological Evidence," in O. Murray and M. Tecusan eds., *In Vino Veritas* (Rome)

Rein, M.J. (1993) "The Cult and Iconography of Lydian Kybele." Ph.D. Dissertation, Harvard University

Renfrew, C. and M. Wagstaff, eds. (1982) *An Island Polity: The Archaeology of Exploitation in Melos* (Cambridge, UK)

Rice, P.M. (1996a) "Recent Ceramic Analysis: 1. Function, Style and Origins," *Journal of Archaeological Research* 4(2):133–163

(1996b) "Recent Ceramic Analysis: 2. Composition, Production and Theory," *Journal of Archaeological Research* 4(3):165–202

Richards, J.F. (1993) *The Mughal Empire* (Cambridge, UK)

Richter, G.M.A. (1946) "Greeks in Persia," *AJA* 50(1):14–30

(1949) "The Late 'Achaemenian' or 'Graeco-Persian' Gems," *Hesperia* Supplement 8:291–298

(1952) "Greek Subjects on 'Graeco-Persian' Seal Stones," in G.C. Miles ed., *Archaeologica Orientalia in Memoriam Ernst Herzfeld* (Locust Valley):189–194

(1968) *Korai: Archaic Greek Maidens* (London)

Ridgway, B.S. (1977) *The Archaic Style in Greek Sculpture* (Princeton)

Roaf, M. (1983) *Sculptures and Sculptors at Persepolis, Iran* 21

(1991) *Cultural Atlas of Mesopotamia and the Ancient Near East* (Amsterdam)

(1995) "Media and Mesopotamia: History and Architecture," in J. Curtis ed., *Later Mesopotamia and Iran* (London):54–66

Roaf, M. and D. Stronach (1973) "Excavations at Tepe Nush-i Jan: Second Interim Report," *Iran* 11:129–140

Robert, L. (1964) *Nouvelles inscriptions de Sardes* (Paris)

(1967) "Sur des inscriptions d'Éphèse," *RevPhil* 41:32–36

(1975) "Une nouvelle inscription de Sardes. Règlement de l'autorité perse relatif à un culte de Zeus," *CRAI*:306–330

Roebuck, C. (1959) *Ionian Trade and Colonization* (New York)

Rogers, R.W. (1929) *A History of Ancient Persia* (New York)

Roos, P. (1970) "An Achaemenian Sketch Slab and the Ornaments of the Royal Dress at Persepolis," *EW* 20:51–59

(1974) "The Rock-Tombs of Caunus. 2. The Finds," *Studies in Mediterranean Archaeology* 34(2)

Root, M.C. (1979) *The King and Kingship in Achaemenid Art: Essays on the Creation of an Iconography of Empire* (Leiden)

(1988) "Evidence from Persepolis for the Dating of Persian and Archaic Greek Coinage," *NC* 148:1–12

(1989) "The Persian Archer at Persepolis: Aspects of Chronology, Style, and Symbolism," *REA* 91:33–50

(1990) "Circles of Artistic Programming: Strategies for Studying Creative Process at Persepolis," in A.C. Gunter ed., *Investigating Artistic Environments in the Ancient Near East* (Washington, DC):115–142

(1991) "From the Heart: Powerful Persianisms in the Art of the Western Empire," in H. Sancisi-Weerdenburg and A. Kuhrt eds., *Achaemenid History VI: Asia Minor and Egypt: Old Cultures in a New Empire* (Leiden):1–29

(1992) "Persian Art" in D.N. Freedman, G.A. Herion, D.F. Graf, J.D. Pleins, and A.B. Bech eds., *Anchor Bible Dictionary*, Vol. I (New York):440–447

(1997a) "Cultural Pluralisms on the Persepolis Fortification Tablets," in J.-F. Salles and M.-F. Boussac, eds., Supplement to *TOPOI* 7:229–252

(1997b) "The Persepolis Fortification Tablets. Archival Issues and the Problem of Stamps Versus Cylinder Seals," in M.-F. Boussac and A. Invernizzi eds., *Archives et sceaux du monde hellénistique. Archivi e sigilli nel mondo ellenistico* (*BCH* Supplement 29) (Paris):3–27

(1998) "Pyramidal Stamp Seals – The Persepolis Connection," in M. Brosius and A. Kuhrt *Achaemenid History XI: Studies in Persian History. Essays in Memory of David M. Lewis* (Leiden):257–289

Rotroff, S.I. (1982) *Hellenistic Pottery: Athenian and Imported Moldmade Bowls. Agora XXII* (Princeton)

  (1990) "Athenian Hellenistic Pottery: Toward a Firmer Chronology," *Akten des XIII internationalen Kongresses für klassische Archäologie: Berlin 1988* (Mainz):174–178

Rudenko, S.I. (1970) *Frozen Tombs of Siberia; The Pazyryk Burials of Iron-Age Horsemen* (Berkeley)

Rugler, A (1988). *Die Columnae Caelatae des jüngeren Artemisions von Ephesos* (IstMitt Beiheft 34)

Rumpf, A. (1920) "Lydische Salbgefässe," *AM* 45:163–170

Rykwert, J. (1976) *The Idea of a Town: The Anthropology of Urban Form in Rome, Italy and the Ancient World* (London)

Sagona, C. (1995) "Red to Blue: Colour Symbolism and Human Societies," *Abr Nahrain* Supplement 5:145–54

Said, E. (1978) *Orientalism* (New York)

Saleh, M. (1998) *Luxor Temple* (Guizeh)

Salonen, E. (1972) *Über den Zehnten im alten Mesopotamien: Ein Beitrag zur Geschichte der Besteuerung* (Helsinki)

Sami, A. (1955) *Persepolis (Takht-i Jamshid)*, trans. R.N. Sharp (Shiraz)

  (1956) *Pasargadae* (Shiraz)

Sancisi-Weerdenburg, H. (1989) "Gifts in the Persian Empire," in P. Briant and C. Herrenschmidt eds., *Le tribut dans l'empire perse* (Paris):129–146

  (1990) "The Quest for an Elusive Empire," in A. Kuhrt and H. Sancisi-Weerdenburg eds., *Achaemenid History IV: Centre and Periphery* (Leiden):263–274

  (1998) "Baji," in M. Brosius and A. Kuhrt eds., *Achaemenid History XI: Studies in Persian History: Essays in Memory of David M. Lewis* (Leiden):23–34

  (1999) "The Persian Kings and History," in C.S. Kraus ed., *The Limits of Historiography* (Leiden):91–111

Sarraf, M.R. (1997) "Ecbatane, capitale des Mèdes, capitale achéménide," *Archéologia* 339:40–41

Saxe, A. (1970) "Social Dimensions of Mortuary Practices." Ph.D. Dissertation, University of Michigan

Sayce, A.H. (1906) *Aramaic Papyri Discovered at Assuan* (London)

  (1925) "The Decipherment of the Lydian Language," *AJP* 46:29–51

Schaeffer, J.S., N.H. Ramage, and C.H. Greenewalt, Jr. (1997) *The Corinthian, Attic, and Lakonian Pottery from Sardis* (Cambridge, Mass.)

Scheil, V. (1929) *Inscriptions des Achéménides à Suse* (Paris)

Schippmann, K. (1971) *Die iranischen Feuerheiligtümer* (Berlin)

Schmidt, E. (1953) *Persepolis I: Structures, Reliefs, Inscriptions* (Chicago)

  (1957) *Persepolis II: Contents of the Treasury and Other Discoveries* (Chicago)

  (1970) *Persepolis III: The Royal Tombs and Other Monuments* (Chicago)

Schmitt, R. (1967) "Medisches und persisches Sprachgut bei Herodot," *ZDMG* 117:119–145

  (1976) "Der Titel 'Satrap,'" in A. Morpurgo-Davies and W. Meid eds., *Studies in Greek, Italian and Indo-European Linguistics Offered to L. R. Palmer* (Innsbruck):373–390

  (1983) "Achaimenidisches bei Thukydides," in H. Koch and D.N. Mackenzie eds., *Kunst und Kultur der Achämenidenzeit und ihr Fortleben* (Berlin):69–86

  (1990a) "Bisotun III. Darius's Inscriptions," *Encycl. Iranica* 4:299–305

(1990b) "Epigraphisch-exegetische Notizen zu Dareios' Bisutun-Inschriften," *ÖAW*, phil.-hist. Kl. Sitzungsberichte 286:3–88

(1991a) *The Bisutun Inscriptions of Darius the Great. Old Persian Text* (London)

(1991b) "Name und Religion," in J. Kellens ed., *La religion iranienne à l'époque achéménide* (Ghent):111–128

Schreiber, K.M. (1987) "Conquest and Consolidation: A Comparison of the Wari and Inka Occupations of a Highland Peruvian Valley," *AAnt* 52:266–284

(1992) *Wari Imperialism in Middle Horizon Peru* (Ann Arbor)

Schüller-Gotzburg, T. (1990) *Zur Semantik der Königsikonographie: eine Analyse des Bildprogrammes der südlichen Räume des Tempels von Luxor* (Vienna)

Segal, C. (1971) "Croesus on the Pyre: Herodotus and Bacchylides," *Wiener Studien* 84:39–51

Seidl, U. (1976) "Ein Relief Dareios' I. in Babylon," *AMI* 9:125–130

Sekunda, N. (1985) "Achaemenid Colonization in Lydia," *REA* 87:1–30

(1988) "Persian Settlement in Hellespontine Phrygia," in A. Kuhrt and H. Sancisi-Weerdenburg eds., *Achaemenid History III: Method and Theory* (Leiden):175–196

(1991) "Achaemenid Settlement in Caria, Lycia and Greater Phrygia," in A. Kuhrt and H. Sancisi-Weerdenburg eds., *Achaemenid History VI: Asia Minor and Egypt: Old Cultures in a New Empire* (Leiden):83–143

Selz, G. (1983) *Die Bankettszene: Entwicklung eines 'überzeitlichen' Bildmotives in Mesopotamien von der frühdynastischen bis zur Akkad-Zeit* (Wiesbaden)

Seyrig, H. (1952) "Cachets Achéménides," in G.C. Miles ed., *Archaeologica Orientalia in Memoriam Ernst Herzfeld* (Locust Valley):195–202

Sharma, T.J. (1989) *A Political History of the Imperial Guptas* (New Delhi)

Sherwin-White, S. and A. Kuhrt (1993) *From Samarkhand to Sardis: A New Approach to the Seleucid Empire* (London)

Sinopoli, C.M. (1991) *Approaches to Archaeological Ceramics* (New York)

(1994) "The Archaeology of Empires," *Annual Review of Anthropology* 23:159–180

Sinopoli, C.M. and K.D. Morrison (1995) "Dimensions of Imperial Control," *American Anthropologist* 97(1):83–96

Skibo, J. (1992) *Pottery Function* (London)

Smith, S. (1924) *Babylonian Historical Texts* (London)

Starr, C.G. (1975) "Greeks and Persians in the Fourth Century BC: A Study in Cultural Contacts before Alexander, Part I," *IrAnt* 11:39–99

Starr, S.F. (1963) "Mapping Ancient Roads in Anatolia," *Archaeology* 16(3):162–169

Stein, G.J. and M.J. Blackman (1993) "The Organizational Context of Specialized Craft Production in Early Mesopotamian States," *Research in Economic Anthropology* 14:29–59

Stern, E.M. and B. Schlick-Nolte (1994) *Early Glass of the Ancient World 1600 BC–AD 50: Ernesto Wolf Collection* (Ostfildern)

Stevenson Smith, W. (1990) *The Art and Architecture of Ancient Egypt* (London)

Stewart, A. (1997) *Art, Desire, and the Body in Ancient Greece* (Cambridge, UK)

Stolper, M.W. (1983) "The Death of Artaxerxes I," *AMI* 16:223–236

(1985) *Entrepreneurs and Empire: The Murasu Archive, the Murasu Firm, and Persian Rule in Babylonia* (Leiden)

(1992) "The Murashu Texts from Susa," *RA* 86:69–77

Streusand, D.E. (1989) *The Formation of the Mughal Empire* (Delhi)

Stronach, D. (1963, 1964, 1965) "Excavations at Pasargadae," *Iran* 1, 2, 3

(1978) *Pasargadae: A Report on the Excavations Conducted by the British Institute of Persian Studies from 1961 to 1963* (Oxford)

(1985) "On the Evolution of the Early Iranian Fire Temple," in J. Duchesne-Guillemin ed., *Papers in Honour of Professor Mary Boyce* (Acta Iranica 25, 2nd ser. [11]) (Leiden):605–627

(1989a) "Early Achaemenid Coinage: Perspectives from the Homeland," *IrAnt* 24:255–279

(1989b) "The Royal Garden at Pasargadae: Evolution and Legacy," in L. Meyer and E. Haerinck eds., *Archaeologia Iranica et Orientalis, Miscellanea in Honorem Louis van den Berghe* (Ghent/Leuven):475–502

(1990) "The Garden as a Political Statement: Some Case Studies from the Near East in the First Millennium BC," *BAI* 4:171–180

(1994a) "Parterres and Stone Watercourses at Pasargadae: Notes on the Achaemenid Contribution to Garden Design," *Journal of Garden Studies* 14(11):3–12

(1994b) "Patterns of Prestige in the Pazyryk Carpet: Notes on the Representational Role of Textiles in the First Millennium BC," *OCTS* 4:19–34

Stronach, R. (1978) "Excavations at Tepe Nush-i Jan: Part 2, Median Pottery from the Fallen Floor in the Fort," *Iran* 16:11–24

Strudwick, N. (1999) *Thebes in Egypt* (Ithaca)

Summers, G.D. (1993) "Archaeological Evidence for the Achaemenid Period in Eastern Turkey," *AnatSt* 43:85–108

Sumner, W.M. (1994) "Archaeological Measures of Cultural Continuity and the Arrival of the Persians in Fars," *AH* 8:97–105

Tainter, J.R. (1977) "Modeling Change in Prehistoric Social Systems," in L. Binford ed., *Theory Building in Archaeology* (Orlando):327–351

(1978) "Mortuary Practices and the Study of Prehistoric Social Systems," *Archaeological Method and Theory* 1:105–141

Tallon, F. (1992) "The Achaemenid Tomb on the Acropole," in P.O. Harper, J. Aruz, and F. Tallon eds., *The Royal City of Susa: Ancient Near Eastern Treasures in the Louvre* (New York):242–252

Tarn, W.W. (1925) "The Social Question in the Third Century," in J.B. Bury and E.A. Barber *The Hellenistic Age: Aspects of Hellenistic Civilization* (Cambridge, UK): 108–140

Tarn, W.W. and G.T. Griffith (1952) *Hellenistic Civilization* (London)

Thapar, R. (1984) *From Lineage to State* (Bombay)

Tilia, A.B. (1978) *Studies and Restorations at Persepolis and Other Sites of Fars* (Rome)

Torrence, R. (1986) *Production and Exchange of Stone Tools: Prehistoric Obsidian in the Aegean* (Cambridge, UK)

Torrey, C.C. (1917–1918) "The Bilingual Inscription from Sardis," *The American Journal of Semitic Languages and Literatures* 34:185–198

Tozzi, P. (1978) *La rivolta ionica* (Pisa)

Tritsch, F.J. (1943) "False Doors on Tombs," *JHS* 63:113–115

Trousdale, W. (1968) "An Achaemenian Stone Weight from Afghanistan," *EW* 18 (3–4):277–280

Tuplin, C. (1987a) "The Administration of the Achaemenid Empire," in I. Carradice ed., *Coinage and Administration in the Athenian and Persian Empires* (BAR 343) (Oxford):109–166

(1987b) "Xenophon and the Garrisons of the Achaemenid Empire", *AMI* 20:167–245.

(1991) "Darius' Suez Canal and Persian Imperialism," in H. Sancisi-Weerdenburg and A. Kuhrt eds., *Achaemenid History VI: Asia Minor and Egypt: Old Cultures in a New Empire* (Leiden):237–283

(1996) *Achaemenid Studies* (Stuttgart)

(1997) "Achaemenid Arithmetic: Numerical Problems in Persian History," *TOPOI*:365–421

(1998) "The Seasonal Migration of Achaemenid Kings. A Report on Old and New Evidence," in M. Brosius and A. Kuhrt eds., *Achaemenid History XI: Studies in Persian History: Essays in Memory of David M. Lewis* (Leiden):63–114

Turkish Ministry of Culture (1993) *Woman in Anatolia: 9000 Years of the Anatolian Woman* (Istanbul)

Turner, V. (1967) *The Forest of Symbols* (Ithaca)

(1974) *Dramas, Fields, and Metaphors: Symbolic Action in Human Society* (Ithaca)

Uchitel, A. (1988) "Organization of Manpower in Achaemenid Persia," *Acta Sumerologica* 11:225–238

(1991) "Foreign Workers in the Fortification Archive," in L. de Meyer and H. Gasche eds., *Mesopotamie et Elam: Actes de la XXXVIème Rencontre Assyriologique Internationale: Gand, 10–14 juillet 1989* (Ghent):127–135

Ucko, P.J. (1969) "Ethnography and the Archaeological Interpretation of Funerary Remains," *World Archaeology* 1:262–290

Uehlinger, C. (1999) "'Powerful Persianisms' in Glyptic Iconography of Persian Period Palestine," in B. Becking and M.C.A. Korpel eds., *The Crisis of Israelite Religion: Transformation of Religious Tradition in Exilic and Post-Exilic Times* (Leiden):134–182

van Andel, T.H. and C.N. Runnels (1987) *Beyond the Acropolis: A Rural Greek Past* (Stanford)

van der Kaaden, G. (1971) "Basement Rocks," in A.S. Campbell ed., *The Geology and History of Turkey* (Tripoli):191–210

van der Spek, R.J. (1993) "Assyriology and History: A Comparative Study of War and Empire in Assyria, Athens and Rome," in M.E. Cohen, D.C. Snell, and D.B. Weisberg eds., *The Tablet and the Scroll: Near Eastern Studies in Honor of William W. Hallo* (Bethesda):262–270

van Loon, M.N. (1975) *Korucutepe: Final Report on the Excavations of the Universities of Chicago, California (Los Angeles) and Amsterdam in the Keban Reservoir, Eastern Anatolia 1968–1970, Vol. I* (Amsterdam)

van Saldern, A. (1959) "Glass Finds at Gordion," *JGS* 1:22–49

(1975) "Two Achaemenid Glass Bowls and a Hoard of Hellenistic Glass Vessels," *JGS* 17:37–46

Verger, A. (1964) "L'amministrazione della giustizia nei papiri aramaici di Elefantina," *Rendiconti dell'Accademia Nazionale dei Lincei. Classe di scienze morali* 8(19):75–94

Vickers, M. (1972) "An Achaemenid Glass Bowl in a Dated Context," *JGS* 14:15–16

Vickers, M. and D. Gill (1994) *Artful Crafts: Ancient Greek Silverware and Pottery* (Oxford)

Vickers, M., O. Impey, and J. Allan (1986) *From Silver to Ceramic. The Potter's Debt to Metalwork in the Graeco-Roman, Oriental and Islamic Worlds* (Oxford)

Viviers, D. (1992) *Recherches sur les ateliers de sculpteurs et la cité d'Athènes à l'époque archaique: Endoios, Philergos, Aristokles* (Brussels)

Vogelsang, W.J. (1987) "Some Remarks on Eastern Iran in the Late-Achaemenid Period," *Achaemenid History I: Sources, Structures and Synthesis* (Leiden):183–189

 (1992) *The Rise and Organisation of the Achaemenid Empire: The Eastern Iranian Evidence* (Leiden)

von Hesberg, H. (1991) "Die Monumentalisierung der Städte in den nord-westlichen Provinzen zu Beginn der Kaiserzeit," in W. Eck and H. Galsterer eds., *Die Stadt in Oberitalien und in dem nordwestlichen Provinzen der römischen reiches* (Mainz):179–199

von Olfers, J.F.M. (1858) "Über die lydischen Königsgräber bei Sardes und den Grabhügel des Alyattes," *AbhBerl*:539–556

von Voigtlander, E. (1978) *The Bisitun Inscription of Darius the Great, Babylonian Version* (London)

Waelkens, M. (1986) *Die kleinasiatischen Türsteine* (Mainz)

Waldbaum, J.C. (1983) *Metalwork from Sardis: The Finds through 1974* (Cambridge, Mass.)

Wallace-Hadrill, A. ed. (1990) *Patronage in Ancient Society* (London)

 (1994) "Elites and Trade in the Roman Town," in A. Wallace-Hadrill, *Houses and Society in Pompeii and Herculaneum* (Princeton):65–174

Wardman, A.E. (1961) "Herodotus on the Cause of the Greco-Persian Wars," *AJP* 82:133–150

Ward-Perkins, J.B. (1970) "From Republic to Empire: Reflections on the Early Imperial Provincial Architecture of the Roman West," *JRS* 60:1–19

Warner, M. (1985) *Monuments and Maidens: The Allegory of the Female Form* (New York)

Weinberg, G.D. and S.S. Weinberg (1956) "Arachne of Lydia at Corinth," in S.S. Weinberg ed., *The Aegean and the Near East*:262–267

Weiskopf, M.N. (1982) "Achaemenid Systems of Governing in Anatolia." Ph.D. Dissertation, University of California at Berkeley

 (1989) *The So-Called "Great Satraps' Revolt," 366–360 BC; Concerning Local Instability in the Achaemenid Far West* (Stuttgart)

Wetzel, F. (1930) *Die Stadtmauer von Babylon* (Leipzig)

Wiesehöfer, J.W. (1982) "Beobachtungen zum Handel des achämeniden Reiches," *MBAH* 1:5–16

 (1987) "Zur Frage der Echtheit des Dareios-Briefes an Gadatas," *RhM* 130:396–398

 (1994) "Zum Nachleben von Achämeniden und Alexander in Iran," in H. Sancisi-Weerdenburg, A. Kuhrt, and M.C. Root eds., *Achaemenid History VIII: Continuity and Change* (Leiden):389–397

 (1996) " 'King of Kings' and 'Philhellên:' Kingship in Arsacid Iran," in P. Bilde, T. Engberg-Pedersen, L. Hannestad, and J. Zahle eds., *Aspects of Hellenistic Kingship* (Aarhus):55–66

Will, E. (1975) "Le monde hellénistique," in E. Will, C. Mossé, and P. Goukowsky eds., *Le monde grec et l'orient* (Paris):337–645

Winfield, D. (1977) "The Northern Routes across Anatolia," *AnatSt* 27:151–166

Winter, F. (1894) "Die Sarkophage von Sidon," *AA*:1–23

Wobst, M. (1977) "Stylistic Behavior and Information Exchange," in C. Cleland ed., *For the Director: Research Essays in Honor of James B. Griffin* (UMMA Anthr. Papers 61):317–342

Woolf, G. (1990) "World Systems Analysis and the Roman Empire," *JRA* 3:44–58

(1993) "European Social Evolution and Roman Imperialism," in P. Brun, S. van der Leeuw, and C.R. Whittaker eds., *Frontières d'Empire. Nature et signification des frontières romaines* (Nemours):13–20

(1994) "Becoming Roman, Staying Greek: Culture, Identity and the Civilizing Process in the Roman East," *PCPhS* 40:116–143

(1998) *Becoming Roman: The Origins of Provincial Civilization in Gaul* (Cambridge, UK)

Woolley, C.L. (1914–1916) "A North Syrian Cemetery of the Persian Period," *LAAA* 7

(1934) *Ur Excavations 2: The Royal Cemetery* (London)

(1962) *Ur Excavations 9: The Neo-Babylonian and Persian Periods* (London)

(1965) *Ur Excavations 8: The Kassite Period and the Period of the Assyrian Kings* (London)

Wright, J., J.F. Cherry, J.L. Davis, E. Mantzourani, S.B. Sutton, and R.F. Sutton, Jr., eds. (1990) "The Nemea Valley Archaeological Project: A Preliminary Report," *Hesperia* 59:579–659

Yağcı, E.E. (1995) "Akhaemenid Cam Kaseleri ve Milas Müzesinden Yayınlanmamış Iki Örnek," *Anadolu Medeniyetleri Müzesi (1995 Yıllığı)*:312–326

Young, G.M. (1946) "A New Hoard from Taxila (Bhir Mound)," *Ancient India* 1

Young, R.S. (1955, 1956, 1957, 1958, 1960) "Excavations at Gordion," *AJA* 59:1–18; 60:249–266; 61:319–331; 62:139–154; 64:227–243

(1963) "Gordion on the Royal Road," *PAPS* 107:348–364

(1981) *Three Great Early Tumuli* (Philadelphia)

Young, T.C. (1965) "A Comparative Ceramic Chronology for Western Iran 1500–500 BC," *Iran* 3:53–87

(1969) *Excavations at Godin Tepe: First Progress Report* (Toronto)

(1988) "The Consolidation of Empire and Its Limits of Growth under Darius and Xerxes," *CAH2*, Vol. IV (Cambridge, UK):99–103

Yoyotte, J. (1974) "Les inscriptions hiéroglyphiques de la statue de Darius à Suse," *Cah.D.A.F.I.* 4:181–3

Zaccagnini, C. (1983) "Patterns of Mobility among Ancient Near Eastern Craftsmen," *JNES* 42(4):245–264

Zettler, R.L. and L. Horne eds. (1998) *Treasures from the Royal Tombs of Ur* (Philadelphia)

# Index